D1551445

Catholic
Theological Union
LIBRARY
Chicago, Ill.

The Edge of Contingency

The Edge of Contingency

French Catholic Reaction to Scientific Change
from Darwin to Duhem

Harry W. Paul

The Catholic
Theological Union
LIBRARY
Chicago, Ill.

A University of Florida Book
University Presses of Florida
Gainesville • 1979

Library of Congress Cataloging in Publication Data

Paul, Harry W.
   The edge of contingency.

   "A University of Florida book."
   Bibliography: p.
   Includes index.
   1. Religion and science—History of controversy—
France.   2. Catholic Church in France. I. Title.
BL245.P38   215'.0944   78-11168
ISBN 0-8130-0582-5

University Presses of Florida is the scholarly publishing
agency for the State University System of Florida.

COPYRIGHT © 1979 BY THE BOARD OF REGENTS OF
THE STATE OF FLORIDA

PRINTED IN FLORIDA

Acknowledgments

My greatest debts are to the National Endowment for the Humanities for a fellowship in 1971–72, to the University of Florida, especially the Humanities Council, for research funds, and to the College of Arts and Sciences and the Department of History for various types of aid. I thank the geologist Albert F. de Lapparent for letting me read the *autobiographie manuscrite* of Albert de Lapparent. I am especially grateful to François Russo for criticizing and correcting the manuscript; I hope that he will not be too irritated by my persistence in using the Kuhnian gospel and by my failure to follow up some of his suggestions. Craig Zwerling also read and criticized an early draft; perhaps he will forgive me for not being so Kuhnian as he wanted. I am grateful to Blandine Malé for her editorial vigilance. Finally, I thank Lil McDowell, Debra Lancaster, and Peggy Lee for typing the manuscript.

I thank the following publishers for granting permission to quote from copyrighted works.

Daedalus, Journal of the American Academy of Arts and Sciences, Boston: "Fiction in Several Languages" (Fall 1966).

Penguin Books Ltd., London: F. C. Copleston, *Aquinas* (Pelican Original, 1955), pp. 32, 33, 34, 35, 70, 71, 85, 86, 87, 88, 89, 90, 239–42, 252, 253 © F. C. Copleston, 1955. Reprinted by permission of Penguin Books Ltd.

Princeton University Press, Princeton, N.J.: Charles Coulston Gillispie, *The Edge of Objectivity: An Essay in the History of Scientific Ideas* (copyright © 1960 by Princeton University Press); Pierre Duhem, *The Aim and Structure of Physical Theory*, translated by Philip P. Wiener (copyright © 1954 by Princeton University Press).

Charles Scribner's Sons, New York: Jacques Maritain, *The Degrees of Knowledge* (translated under the supervision of Gerald B. Phelan).

The University of Texas Press, Austin: Thomas F. Glick, editor, *The Comparative Reception of Darwinism*.

Contents

Abbreviations

AHR	*American Historical Review*
AN	Archives nationales
APC	*Annales de philosophie chrétienne*
E	*Etudes*
RCF	*Revue du clergé français*
RL	*Revue de Lille*
RM	*Revue du mois*
RMM	*Revue de métaphysique et de morale*
RP	*Revue de philosophie*
RQS	*Revue des questions scientifiques*
RS	*Revue scientifique*
RT	*Revue thomiste*

My Dear Wormwood. . . .

Keep pressing home on him the *ordinariness* of things. Above all, do not attempt to use science (I mean, the real sciences) as a defense against Christianity. They will positively encourage him to think about realities he can't touch and see. There have been sad cases among the modern physicists. If he must dabble in science, keep him on economics and sociology; don't let him get away from that invaluable "real life." But the best of all is to let him read no science but to give him a grand general idea that he knows it all and that everything he happens to have picked up in casual talk and reading is "the results of modern investigation."

Your affectionate Uncle Screwtape.

C. S. Lewis, *The Screwtape Letters. Letters from a Senior to a Junior Devil* (London, 1942; 16th impression, Oct. 1970), p. 14.

Introduction

> The God of science is the Spirit of rational order, and of orderly development. Atheism as I understand it is the denial of the existence of the spirit. Nothing could therefore be more antagonistic to the whole spirit of science.
>
> Robert Andrews Millikan, *Evolution in Science and Religion* (New Haven, 1927), p. 88.

In a discussion of Pierre Chaunu's startling thesis that the scientific revolution of the seventeenth century was stimulated by the Protestant and Catholic reform movements, the Jesuit polytechnician Francois Russo noted, with some exaggeration, that the relationships between scientific and religious thought have never been studied profoundly.[1] We have been deluged with studies of the opposition and the conflicts between the two, usually by intellectual imperialists on one side or the other. Thus the issues have been distorted. What is true of the seventeenth century—part of Chaunu's originality was to leave the Galileo problem aside—is a fortiori true of the nineteenth century with its burden of *Darwinismus*. And even the opposition to Darwin has been frequently misunderstood because it has been viewed solely as a religiously based opposition. But it would be absurd to go to another extreme in ignoring the reality of the clash of ideas in the nineteenth century, however feeble the intellectual justification for such an encounter may now seem. Such a clash is a part of this study of the interaction of science and religion in late-nineteenth- and early-twentieth-century France. We must not, however, ignore the more positive aspects of the interaction. This is not a tale of Dover Beach revisited, "where ignorant armies clash by night."

1. Russo, in *Science et théologie. Méthode et langage* (Paris, 1969), p. 245. This volume contains papers given at a meeting in Rome organized by the International Secretariat for Scientific Questions of the International Movement of Catholic Intellectuals (*Pax Romana*) in 1968. See Chaunu, ibid., pp. 221–32, and *La civilisation de l'Europe classique* (Paris, 1966).

1

The reader who wishes to revisit the museum of hopes, disappointments, ambiguities, and fears arising out of nineteenth-century science could do worse than read Gustave Flaubert's *Bouvard et Pécuchet*. Whatever the activity or fantasy of the century, from Celtic archaeology to phrenology, from animal magnetism to Buddhism, Flaubert expertly analyzed it in the human context through a version of the overpowering encyclopedic method of Rabelais and Joyce, though with the saving grace of a clarifying Cartesianism. Flaubert had considered giving his novel the subtitle "Du défaut de méthode dans les sciences." Raymond Queneau argues that this indicates the real subject of the novel: the downfall of the clerks resulted from their lack of method.[2] The encounters of the two heroes with the good Abbé Jeufroy provide a paradigm of the clash of nineteenth-century science and religion. But Flaubert's observation that the middle classes preached the dogma of materialism and the people seemed satisfied is hardly enlightening for the last quarter of the nineteenth century.

Msgr. d'Hulst, rector of the Catholic Institute in Paris, argued in 1885 that one great fact dominated the times and threatened the future: the weakening of religious ideas. With an excessive belief in the influence of the intellectuals over the masses, d'Hulst explained popular irreligion as the result of the irreligion of the intellectual elite. He viewed the people as incapable of thinking by itself; it was the victim of anti-religious propaganda spread by the intellectuals, especially the scientific community. Thinking like a philosophe, d'Hulst advanced a simple solution for the reconversion of the masses: convert the scientific community and the people would follow. What alienated the intellectual community from Christianity was a double tendency in science and in history. Science had an atheistic tendency and history a fatalistic one. Science had no need of a Creator; history, applying the idea of evolution to human facts, had deduced the impossibility of miracle and the equivalence of all religions, which were reduced to successive phases of the natural form of thought and feeling. The good fight for the faith had therefore to be fought on the grounds of science and history. Most modern scientists had, in d'Hulst's opinion, jettisoned the theistic idea because of their lack of a philosophy. Religious philosophy, too literary and too close to art and poetry, was not scientific enough; d'Hulst was not satisfied that it had a place in the Académie Française; it should be present also in the Académie des Sciences. A non-Cartesian, experimental philosophy of religion should be created by the Catholic philosophers.[3] The return to Aquinas solved many problems, although like most cures this one also produced its own diseases.

The Catholic attempt to recapture the intellectual community, especially

2. Flaubert, *Bouvard et Pécuchet* (Paris, 1881; Le Livre de Poche, 1959), preface by Raymond Queneau in 1959 edition. There is an English translation, not without some curiosities, by T. W. Earp and G. W. Stonier, with an introduction by Lionel Trilling. On science and religion, see ibid., pp. 97–98, 107–12, and Paul Bourget, *Essais de psychologie contemporaine*, 2 vols. (Paris, 1926), 1:157.

3. Msgr. d'Hulst, "La science de la nature et la philosophie chrétienne," *APC*, n.s. 13 (1885–86): 1–18, 113–30. On the church and the masses, see the superb chapters (19 and 20) in Eugen Web ., *Peasants into Frenchmen. The Modernization of Rural France, 1870–1914* (Stanford, 1976).

the scientists, transformed French Catholicism intellectually and institution-
ally. It is the transformation of French Catholicism as a result of its trying to
accommodate itself to science that is the essential theme of this work. After
a brief analysis of the view that generally prevailed among the nineteenth-
century clergy and quite a few intellectuals concerning the interaction of science and religion, we turn to evolution, one of the most serious intellectual
problems for religion in the nineteenth century, and its gradual acceptance
by most of the Catholic intellectual community. The Catholic shock at seeing the scientific community change its position on the evolution of species
contributed to the development of a new view of the scientific enterprise.
The implications of an abandonment of absolutes and objectivity were feared
by many Catholic intellectuals and led to sophisticated attempts, like that of
Albert de Lapparent, to save as much of the classical world view as possible.
As this became increasingly difficult, the attractions of the radical separation
of the religious and scientific spheres, especially as put forward with relentless and seductive logic by Pierre Duhem, became irresistible for many in the
Catholic intellectual community. Although Duhem is usually classified as a
Thomist, his views were savagely contested by the hard-line Thomists. A way
out of most intellectual difficulties was offered by the revival of Thomism,
which offered solutions to many of the metaphysical problems of the late
nineteenth century, but it hardly provided the philosophical panacea hoped
for by the guardians of orthodoxy.

The growth of science and its exploitation by the Third Republic produced a French version of the hoary debate over the validity of scientism, a
debate most serious in the 1890s but not without earlier and later manifestations. Anti-clericalism had serious consequences for some Catholic scientists
in the republican university and, at least temporarily, for science itself; the
significance of ideology for science does not disappear with the Counter-
Reformation or begin with the 1930s. One of the most important of the
positive results of anti-clericalism was the growth of a Catholic structure of
science and technology, which has survived today in some dynamic specialized schools, chiefly in Paris and Lille.[4] As Bernard Reardon points out, "the
advance of the sciences, both natural and historical, was bound sooner or
later to re-open the question of the credibility of the faith."[5] Although there
has been a great deal of work on the impact of research into the origins and
growth of religions on French Catholicism, there has been comparatively

4. On Catholics and scientism, on Catholic scientists in the universities, and on Catholic faculties of science, see Paul, "The Debate over the Bankruptcy of Science in 1895,"
French Historical Studies 5 (1968): 299–327; "The Crucifix and the Crucible: Catholic
Scientists in the Third Republic," *The Catholic Historical Review* 58 (1972): 195–219;
and "Science and the Catholic Institutes in Nineteenth-Century France," *Societas—A Re-
view of Social History* 1 (1971): 271–85. See also D. M. Eastwood, *The Revival of Pascal.
A Study of His Relation to Modern French Thought* (Oxford, 1936), esp. chap. 2, "The
Reaction against the 'Reign of Science,'" and J.W. Langdon, "Social Implications of Jesuit
Education in France: The Schools of Vaugirard and Sainte-Geneviève" (Ph.D. diss., Syra-
cuse University, 1973).

5. Reardon, *Liberalism and Tradition. Aspects of Catholic Thought in Nineteenth-
Century France* (Cambridge, England, 1975); see my comments in *Reviews in European
History* (June 1977).

little work on the impact of scientific developments. This volume attempts to analyze the intellectual response of the Catholic community to scientific developments, especially their implications for traditional religion.

Most intellectuals today would probably agree with the opinion of the philosopher Emile Boutroux that "radical dualism" is the phrase best characterizing the relation established between religion and science in the second half of the nineteenth century.[6] Even later serious attempts to achieve unity, such as that by Teilhard de Chardin, have not been widely recognized as successful in overcoming that basic dualism.

The dualistic position was argued in late-nineteenth- and early-twentieth-century France not only by those who, like Pierre Duhem and Maurice Blondel, saw its advantages for the autonomy of religion but also by ideologues of secular republicanism like Emile Durkheim. In his work *Les formes élémentaires de la vie religieuse* (1912), Durkheim's imperialistic scientism seems to take the form of a radically modified Comtean view on the historical development of thought about man, nature, and society. Religious thought does not differ in its nature from scientific thought, but science perfects its method and becomes "a more perfect form of religious thought." Durkheim argued that such a regression of religious thought took place historically. "Having left religion, science tends to substitute itself for [religion] in all that which concerns the cognitive and intellectual functions." Science contests the right of religion to dogmatize on the nature of things and its competence to know man and the world. But science cannot deny religion in principle, for religion is a reality—a system of given facts—as well as a creed men live by; science cannot replace it as a guide to action. Conflict results only from science's usurpation of the cognitive function of religion. Religion speculates on the same subjects as science and provides us with a guide for living; science is incapable of doing this while it is slowly expanding its knowledge. Eventually, even in areas like psychology and sociology, scientific knowledge will be so certain and complete as to drive religion to an epistemological and perhaps practical periphery of human affairs.

Durkheim's futuristic scientism was denied by Catholic thinkers, who simply established religion as an area in which science could have no relevance because of its inherent epistemological limitations rather than because of the particular stage of scientific development. Hence the Blondelian position that religious thought could ignore science. Blondel extended the same privilege to philosophy. The position of religion in Durkheim's scheme bore some resemblance to that of metaphysics in Duhem's, but Durkheim differed ba-

6. "Concerning methods, most writers today see science and religion as *strongly contrasting enterprises* which have essentially nothing to do with each other. We will find that the reasons for this sharp separation of spheres lie partly in the history of recent centuries. For example, when church leaders attacked Galileo's theory of the solar system or Darwin's theory of evolution, they made pronouncements on scientific issues which they were incompetent to judge": Ian G. Barbour, *Issues in Science and Religion* (New York, 1971), p. 1. For a contrasting point of view, see Earl R. MacCormac, *Metaphor and Myth in Science and Religion* (Durham, N.C., 1976), who argues "that scientific language employed metaphors in a manner similar to the religious uses of metaphor." Both science and religion "employ language in similar ways and use conceptual patterns that . . . have some basic similarities."

sically in believing scientific knowledge to be more certain than religious knowledge. A sophisticated philosopher of science, Duhem did not accept this epistemological naïveté. A half-century of wrestling with the nature of biological knowledge and a quarter-century of quarreling over the foundations of scientific theory had led Catholic thinkers to complex views differing radically from Durkheimian dogmas on science and religion.

1

Scientific Revolutions and Religious Knowledge: French Connections

> If one be clear about the nature of science as a description of the world, declarative but never normative, may not the choice between science and religion be refused? Is it not simply a false problem, arising from a confusion—an ancient confusion going back to the beginning of science—between objects and persons? Science is about nature, after all, not about duties. It is about objects. Christianity is about persons, the relation of the persons of men to the person of God.
>
> Gillispie, *The Edge of Objectivity*, pp. 350–51.

The religious-scientific *Weltanschauung* of the nineteenth-century clergy and of most Christians assumed the necessity of the hypothesis of God in order to explain the creation, order, and harmony of the universe, the existence of life, and especially the unique development of man. Although their views were expressed in the language of the science of their time, they dealt with a set of ideas, as old as the thought of man, which had taken on since the seventeenth century a specific set of characteristics consonant with modern science. The Christian virtuosi of seventeenth-century England perceived that science could promote "intellectual arrogance which led a man to prefer his own notions to the inspired word of God."[1] In the end the difference in attitudes of the virtuoso and of the eighteenth-century philosophe boiled down to a difference between uncertainty and open doubt. The piety of the virtuosi kept a rein on their doubts about Christianity.[2] In spite of the impact of the Kantian critical philosophy and the influence of the Enlightenment, scientific—or scientistic—religious rationalism was still alive and flourishing in the nineteenth century; indeed, there seems to be a positive correlation

1. Richard S. Westfall, *Science and Religion in Seventeenth Century England* (New Haven, 1958), p. 24.
2. Ibid., pp. 218–20.

between the scientific takeoff and a resurgence of interest in creating a rational theodicy.

The continuation of belief in an organizing principle of Creation, sometimes called an "anti-chance" by skeptics, is evident well into the twentieth century, and it shows no sign of dying. Pierre Lecomte du Noüy marveled that "The agnostic and the atheist do not seem to be in the least disturbed by the fact that our entire organized, living universe becomes incomprehensible without the hypothesis of God."[3] The need of joining the two realms of science and religion, of embracing the whole universe in a single thought structure, has been emphasized by Planck as well as by Teilhard de Chardin: "Our impulse to gain knowledge demands a unified view of the world and therefore requires the identification with one another of the two powers which are everywhere effective and yet still mysterious, namely the world order of natural science and the God of religion. This would mean that the Diety, which the religious person endeavors to conceive with the aid of his outward and visible symbols, is essentially the same as the power which is present in the laws of nature, the power which the enquirer's sense impressions to some extent make known to him."[4] The scientific-religious problems of nineteenth-century clerical intellectuals fit into the ancient general problem of accommodating religious thought to scientific developments or, perhaps the more frequent procedure, of interpreting the new science as being in accord with the old religion. Because of the unique nature of the scientific developments of the nineteenth century, the discussion and solutions of these problems have certain characteristics necessarily determined by the period. The rapidly changing nature of science, especially in the second half of the nineteenth century, faced the apologist with new problems.

Whitehead has argued that "normally an advance in science will show that statements of various religious beliefs require some sort of modification." This may mean expansion, explanation, or entire restatement. Although physical facts are modified as scientific knowledge advances, their relevance "for religious thought will grow more and more clear. The progress of science may result in the unceasing codification of religious thought, to the great advantage of religion." In Whitehead's opinion, religion would only regain its power when it learned to "face change in the same spirit as does science. Its principles may be eternal, but the expression of these principles requires continual development. This evolution of religion is in the main a disengagement of its own proper ideas from the adventitious notions which have crept into it by reason of the expression of its own ideas in terms of the imaginative picture of the world entertained in previous ages. Such a release of religion from the bonds of imperfect science is all to the good. It stresses its own genuine message."[5] But this is a difficult and dangerous procedure, as became especially evident in the nineteenth century. The danger has been pointed

3. Lecomte du Noüy, *Human Destiny* (New York, 1947), p. 189.
4. Max Planck, *Religion und Naturwissenschaft*, cited in Karl Heim, *Christian Faith and Natural Science* (New York, 1953), p. 169.
5. Alfred North Whitehead, *Science and the Modern World* (Cambridge, England, 1926), pp. 234–35.

out by Karl Heim. Admitting that he was thankful "that at this very time, according to the testimony of such leading scientists as Max Planck, natural science has entered a phase which Bavink was able to describe under the heading 'Science on the Road to Religion,' we still have from the outset, in dealing with this method of apologetic, the feeling that it brings us into a position of complete dependence on the momentary phase in which scientific research happens to be. We are playing the market." The danger is that leading scientists may also interpret the progress of science as inimical to religion. This was the great problem of the nineteenth-century apologists, although its origins lie in the two preceding centuries. Apologetics need a solid foundation to free it from the "momentary currents of scientific opinion."[6] How to maintain that foundation, while keeping the historical dynamic relationship with science, was one of the chief problems of nineteenth-century apologetics.

In commenting on the development of science in the nineteenth century, Whitehead made the curious remark that "in its last twenty years the century closed with one of the dullest stages of thought since the time of the First Crusade." Although this "period was efficient, dull, and halfhearted," "an age of successful scientific orthodoxy, undisturbed by much thought beyond the conventions," one can with hindsight "now discern signs of change."[7] Looking back, we can now see that Catholic scientists, like others, were at this time caught up in the movement that culminated in "the revolution in modern science."[8] It was in December 1900 that Planck sufficiently overcame his conservatism to publish his quantum hypothesis, which could not be accommodated within the framework of classical physics and whose formula "touched the foundations of our description of nature."[9] In 1905 Einstein published his three papers in the *Annalen der Physik*: "One reduced the confusion of the mechanism of Brownian movement to order and, incidentally, established beyond all reasonable doubt the real existence of molecules. Another applied the new quantum theory to the photoelectric effect in a way that revolutionized the study of physical optics. . . . The third dealt with the subject of the electrodynamics of moving bodies [Special Theory of Relativity], that field which Poincaré suggested might reveal important new laws."[10] These "signs of change" developed into a fundamental questioning of classical mechanics and classical physics. What were the implications of these changes for religion? They could be considerable, especially if, as Whitehead argued, "the adequacy of scientific materialism as a scheme of thought for the use of science was endangered"; the "relegation of matter to the background" was already evident in the theories of energy and of electromagnetism.[11]

Although texts generally associate the discoveries of Planck, Einstein,

6. Heim, *Christian Faith and Natural Science*, p. 32. Heim founds his faith on the twin realities of one's own ego and the existence of a personal God.
7. Whitehead, *Science and the Modern World*, p. 127.
8. Subtitle of Heisenberg, *Physics and Philosophy* (New York, 1962).
9. Ibid., p. 31.
10. L. Pearce Williams, ed., *Relativity Theory: Its Origins and Impact on Modern Thought* (New York, 1968), p. 49.
11. Whitehead, *Science and the Modern World*, pp. 127-28.

Poincaré, Heisenberg, Schrödinger, and de Broglie with revolutionary episte-mological implications such as the collapse of absolute determinism, the breakdown of the old notion of objectivity, and the breakdown of the idea of mechanical causality, they frequently forget to point out that the roots of this revolution in the philosophy of science go back to at least the 1870s. What Charlton calls "philosophical positivism," the theory that a sound epis-temology can be built only by accepting science as the model for the only kind of attainable knowledge, implying the illusory nature of religious and metaphysical knowledge, had little real strength in the French philosophical communities of the nineteenth century.[12] If one accepts the existence of Ser-tillanges' "scientistic era," it is reasonable to argue that it was ended through the convergence of two philosophical movements: one originating with Maine de Biran, including Ravaisson, and culminating with Bergson, another origi-nating with Gratry and Ollé-Laprune and culminating with Victor Delbos and Maurice Blondel.[13] The second movement is clearly Catholic as well as philo-sophical. But a key element is missing in this interpretation—the searching neo-Kantian critique of the nature of determinism and of scientific thought carried out by the philosophers Lachelier and Boutroux and carried forward by philosophically minded scientists like Le Roy, Poincaré, and Duhem. In his brilliant work *Du fondement de l'induction* (1871), Lachelier redefined existence in terms of universal contingency rather than universal necessity. "Contrary to what we believed, then, it is not universal necessity but rather universal contingency that is the true definition of existence, the spirit of nature, and the greatest prize of thought. Reduced to itself necessity is noth-ing, since it is not even necessary; what we call contingency, in opposition to a crude and blind mechanism, is, on the contrary, a necessity of convenience and of choice, the only one justifying everything, because the good alone is its own justification. Whatever is must be and yet it could, strictly speaking, not be: according to Leibniz, other possibilities had a claim to existence and did not achieve it because of a lack of the sufficient degree of perfection; things come into existence because they will it and deserve it."[14]

In the quarrel over the bankruptcy of science in the 1890s, Brunetière popularized the idea that the certainty of science is a mirage; the absolute necessity of the laws of nature can at most be defended as only a postulate needed to establish the foundations of science—later commentators would say classical science; it is a law relative to human intelligence. This position was derived from the arguments of the philosophical enemies of determin-ism.[15]

12. D. C. Charlton, *Positivist Thought in France during the Second Empire, 1852-1870* (Oxford, 1959).

13. A. D. Sertillanges, "Science et scientisme," in Louis de Broglie et al., *L'avenir de la science* (Paris, 1941), pp. 64-65.

14. J. Lachelier, *Du fondement de l'induction* (Paris, 1871; 8th ed., 1924), p. 86.

15. Ferdinand Brunetière, *La science et la religion. Réponse à quelques objections* (Paris, 1895). Claude Bernard's *Introduction à l'étude de la médecine expérimentale* (Par-is, 1865) was interpreted by Léon de Rosny as based on the axiom that "le seul critérium du vrai est le critérium intérieur": *La méthode conscientielle, essai de philosophie exacti-viste* (Paris, 1887). On Bernard, see Reino Virtanen, *Claude Bernard and His Place in the*

The distinction between an objective domain subject to the laws of the universe and an internal subjective world of conscience could not be philosophically justified. Marcel Hébert pointed out that there is nothing purely objective or purely subjective: "It is not only in the internal world of conscience that things 'exist for us only if they are known'; this must be true in an absolutely universal and necessary way: there is no *external fact* that is not at the same time an *internal fact*, no *thing* that is not a phenomenon of conscience." Significantly, Hébert could point out a neo-Kantian awareness of this in the scientific community. Charles Richet recognized the relative and limited character of scientific knowledge: "We only know phenomena; the essential nature of things escapes us."[16]

Philosophers within the republican educational establishment also destroyed the idea of an ethics based on science. Catholics were not slow to exploit the advantage of an intellectual alliance with the forces of sedition within the university. Hébert, writing in the *Annales de philosophie chrétienne*, hailed the appearance of Sorbonnard philosopher Émile Boutroux's *Questions de morale et d'éducation*, given as a series of lectures at Fontenay-aux-Roses, for its Huxley-like conclusion that no ethics can be derived from science. Hébert welcomed Boutroux's call for an attempt to reconcile Hellenic ethics and non-dogmatic Christian ethics. Boutroux did not see any way to overcome the antinomy between science, which studies what is, and ethics, which studies what should be. The significance of Boutroux's famous thesis on the contingency of the laws of nature now became clear. "Science cannot know nature in its creative activity or moral being in its power of perfection. The philosophy of nature and moral philosophy demand, therefore, a new knowledge that takes into account the universal contingency of beings and human liberty. Having as its object a reality beyond experience, this knowledge can be given only by metaphysics." Small wonder that anti-clerical republicans looked to Berthelot's scientism and to philosophical biology for salvation from the new philosophy, which sapped the basis of the scientism of the builders of the new republic.[17]

History of Ideas (Lincoln, Neb., 1960). Bergson made similar use of Bernard in his *Evolution créatrice* (Paris, 1907); see Jacques Chevalier, *Bergson* (Paris, 1926), p. 11.

16. Marcel Hébert, "Science et religion," *APC*, n.s. 31 (1895): 570–76.

17. See Emile Boutroux, *Questions de morale et d'éducation. Conférences faites à l'école de Fontenay-aux-Roses de 1888 à 1895* (Paris, 1895; 7th ed., 1914), reviewed by Hébert in *APC*, n.s. 33 (1895–96): 661–62; and Mathieu Schyns, *La philosophie d'Emile Boutroux* (Paris, 1924), p. 108, for quote summarizing relevant ideas of *De la contingence des lois de la nature* (Paris, 1874; 9th ed., 1921). Emile Picard, *La vie et l'œuvre de Joseph Boussinesq* (Paris, 1934), pp. 47–50, notes that the philosophical conclusions derived from the work of Planck, de Broglie, and Heisenberg were anticipated by Boutroux in the 1870s: "Boutroux . . . parlant de fluctuations se servait déjà des vocables de cette théorie des probabilités qui a pris depuis lors en Physique une si grande importance." Boutroux had been influenced by Lachelier at the Normale and by the mathematician Jules Tannery while Boutroux and Tannery taught at the lycée in Caen; he in turn influenced Bergson and Henri Poincaré. Tannery wrote a sonnet for Boutroux in which he versified the contingency thesis:

Il faut en revenir aux doctrines antiques
que le divin Lucrèce a dites dans ses vers,

The importance of Berthelot's *Weltanschauung* for republicans is clear from the perceptive remarks made after Berthelot's death by the mathematician Paul Painlevé, who entered the chamber as an independent socialist from Paris in 1906.[18] The popularity of Berthelot as the republican École scientific guru, the "representative of scientific reason," cannot be fully explained without taking into account the republic's need for a counterweight to Pasteur and especially to the exploitation of Pasteur by anti-republicans. Painlevé deplored Pasteur's attachment to traditional beliefs, which denied science any competence in the great problems of life and death, and praised Berthelot's extension of the authority of reason and the "scientific method" to all phenomena. One of the great figures of the nineteenth century, Berthelot exercised considerable influence both as a scientist and as a historian and philosopher. His general thought and his scientific work were in perfect agreement. "It is the philosopher who . . . inspired and guided the chemist, and all the discoveries of the chemist strikingly confirmed the predictions of the philosopher."[19]

Berthelot's belief in the unity of the universe, in its laws and its phenomena, with no gulf between the organic and the inorganic, was part of a philosophy that was the opposite of that inspiring Pasteur, who clearly separated the determinism of the inorganic world from the liberty associated with the phenomena of life.[20] Painlevé thought that there was no serious connection between Pasteur's view of the universe and his scientific work; a materialistic scientist like Raspail, if he had Pasteur's experimental genius, could have done the same work. But it was different for Berthelot: life has no spe-

---

> lui qui chassa les dieux, qui vida les enfers
> et qui nous délivra de nos peurs fantastiques.
>
> Non! tout n'obéit pas aux lois mathématiques
> et le nombre n'est pas le roi de l'Univers.
> Un jour la liberté saura briser ses fers;
> un jour elle vaincra les forces mécaniques.
>
> Elle réside au sein de l'atome vivant,
> elle est indestructible, elle anime tout être.
> Obscure dans la plante où nous la voyons naître,
> dans l'échelle animale elle va grandissant.
>
> Nous la sentons en nous: O mornes destinées,
> par son progrès sacré vous serez détrônées.

Cited in Emile Picard, *La vie et l'œuvre de Jules Tannery* (Paris, 1925), p. 31. See chap. 1n37.

18. "Professeur illustre, universitaire du premier rang, gloire de l'École Normale, grand savant, membre de l'Institut, philosophe du Nombre et de l'Infini mathématique, Painlevé s'abaissa, pour devenir député, au niveau de la masse électorale et au niveau des luttes de partis": Hubert Bourgin, *De Jaurès à Blum. L'École Normale et la politique* (Paris, 1938; new ed., 1970), p. 300.

19. Painlevé, "La philosophie de Marcellin [*sic*] Berthelot," *RM* 3 (May 19, 1907): 514. Painlevé also wrote Berthelot's obituary in *Le Temps*.

20. See ibid., pp. 515–16, for a cruel exposé of Pasteur's delusions concerning tartaric acid and of the philosophical conclusions which crumbled when Jungfleish showed that all forms of tartaric acid could be reproduced without a vital intervention. See also Reino Virtanen, *Marcelin Berthelot. A Study of a Scientist's Public Role* (Lincoln, Neb., 1965).

cial laws; there is one chemistry, just as there is one mechanics and physics. Painlevé was delighted at the philosophical significance of bold syntheses achieved by Berthelot after 1854. "The ancient division between inorganic and organic substances and the specious fiction of a vital force were finished. A philosophical conquest of inestimable value! From a chemical viewpoint living beings had to be regarded as only types of laboratories in which material elements are unceasingly taken in, eliminated, and transformed according to the invariable laws of inorganic nature."[21] But even Painlevé realized that the best that one could say for Berthelot in the age of Poincaré, Duhem, and Le Roy was that he was the ideal type of scientist fulfilling the scientific ideal of the nineteenth century. Even that was generous.

The implications of the revolutionary developments in the way intellectuals thought about science and its relations with metaphysics were soon evident in religious thought. In contrast to the dangerous flirting of the Thomists with science in order to use it in apologetics and ultimately to subject it to the general science of metaphysics, the thrust of Blondelism was to separate apologetics and philosophy completely from science. Obsessed with the "problem of faith," the philosopher Maurice Blondel protested against the intellectualism of scholastic philosophy, and, following the path indicated by his master, Ollé-Laprune, emphasized the moral character of certainty. Certainty is just as much the result of the free consent of the will as it is an imposed intellectual necessity. Intelligence is realist and can arrive at truth through abstract knowledge and through real or intuitive knowledge. Abstract knowledge is that of the deductive sciences and has truth value as a useful and necessary substitute for arriving at real knowledge. It tends toward intuition, which is achieved by the total activity of the mind or by action. Intuition adapts itself to concrete reality because of a connaturalness between subject and object.[22] In his famous letter of 1896 on the exigencies of contemporary thought in apologetics, in which he clarified his "méthode

21. Painlevé, "La philosophie de Marcellin Berthelot," p. 517. For an analysis of the illogicality of Berthelot's middle position between pure positivism and metaphysical dogmatism, see Paul Albert, "La philosophie de Berthelot," *E* 111 (1907): 721–48. Berthelot's thermochemical system and its philosophical implications were demolished with great glee by Pierre Duhem in a review of the new edition of Berthelot's *Essai de mécanique chimique, fondée sur la thermochimie* (1879; revised under title of *Thermochimie*, 2 vols., 1897); Duhem, "Thermochimie à propos d'un livre récent de M. Marcelin Berthelot," *RQS*, 2ᵉ sér. 12 (1897): 361–92.

22. Georges Van Riet, *L'épistémologie thomiste. Recherches sur le problème de la connaissance dans l'école thomiste contemporaine* (Louvain, 1946), pp. 212, 313; Blondel, *L'action. Essai d'une critique de la vie et d'une science de la pratique* (Paris, 1893). Although Blondel protested against "faux intellectualisme," he also opposed the "anti-intellectualisme" of Bergson and Le Roy: Blondel, *Le procès de l'intelligence* (Paris, 1922). For a complete separation of himself from Le Roy, see Blondel's letter in *RCF* 50 (May 15, 1907): 545–46. Lecanuet, *La vie de l'Église sous Léon XIII* (Paris, 1930), p. 506, notes the traditional Christian meaning Blondel gave to action: "l'*action* c'est ce par quoi l'homme, à travers les circonstances multiples et variées de la vie, prend position relativement à sa fin suprême . . . ce par quoi il est ce qu'il est, moralement et religieusement, au fond de lui-même et devant Dieu. L'*action* ainsi entendue implique à la fois intention et exécution." This action has no connection with pragmatism: "pour qui l'action est un élan vital indéterminé, une poussée intérieure amorphe à laquelle aucune vérité stable ne sert dogmatiquement de guide. . . ."

d'immanence" and made clear the importance of his action thesis for religion, Blondel also dealt with the relationships between science and philosophy and between science and religion.

By 1895 the *Annales de philosophie chrétienne* had subscribed to the view that "scientific apologetics" was on its way out, that "metaphysical apologetics" would not make a comeback, and that the only type of apologetics remaining was "moral, psychological, and social apologetics, which seize the soul through its intimate needs and higher desires." Blondel's *Action* was interpreted as putting Christian apologetics on psychological grounds. Blondel, always careful to emphasize the value of traditional apologetics, did not agree with this exclusive interpretation of his work. In addition to condemning the use of a false philosophy in apologetics, Blondel opposed the abuse of extending science into philosophy and apologetics, although he recognized that some well-meaning people were engaged in that very widespread process. Regretfully, Blondel also admitted that many were working to re-establish harmony between science and metaphysics and religion. Many poor souls accepted the data of the sciences as an expression of absolute reality and tried to reconcile them with their philosophical opinions or their intimate beliefs. How many believe that the ideas of the Scholastics and of modern scientists relating to matter, to force, and to physical agents must be in agreement, enter into the ontological explanation of things, and bear witness in favor of dogma! All labor in vain! Blondel thought that the time had passed when it seemed that mathematics, physics, and biology had a properly philosophical scope. Physical hypotheses and metaphysical explanations have entirely different origins. The sciences do not have to worry about an ontological basis for their activities; starting from different and partly arbitrary conventions, they have only to build a system of increasingly coherent relations, to the extent that each of their different hypotheses is controlled or applicable in reality. It is a waste of time to try to get philosophical lessons out of such ideas of mass, atom, and species. No agreement or disagreement is possible between science and metaphysics. In this sense "scientific apologetics" was on its way out. Blondel's proclamation of this arbitrary and somewhat simple dogma of the separation of science and philosophy and, a fortiori, of science and religion did not mean that he thought that the sciences have no basic relation to vital questions and no role in the solution of the big problems of life. The sciences are not always arbitrarily based or detached from the rest of human life, which forms, as a whole, a single and unique problem to solve. The vague feeling of this deep connection does not justify confusing science and religion, but it does explain why so many people insist on keeping a false position.[23] It is understandable why the collaboration of the Thomists with the *Annales* diminished considerably after 1896 and stopped after the founding of the Thomist *Revue de philosophie* in 1900.

The separation of religion and science was also upheld by Duhem in his reply to Abel Rey's designation of Duhem's philosophy of science as that of

23. Blondel, "Lettre sur les exigences de la pensée contemporaine en matière d'apologétique et sur la méthode de la philosophie dans l'étude du problème religieux," *APC* 33, 34 (1895-96), published as a separate book in 1896.

a believer. The reply was published in the *Annales*, after 1905 under the editorship of the R. P. Lucien Laberthonnière, friend and correspondent of Blondel, who was publicly Catholic but in the Université (Aix-en-Provence). On May 16, 1913, a decree of the Holy Office put two books by Laberthonnière and the *Annales* from 1905 to 1913 on the Index. (The file that was the basis of the condemnation was compiled by Action Française, which thus achieved considerable success in its violent campaign against the *Annales* for the brilliant exposé of the anti-Christian bias of Maurras by Maurice Blondel and Laberthonnière in the pages of the same *Annales*.) It was in the first number of the new series of this venerable seventy-year-old journal, which Bonnetty had founded and run for forty-odd years as a battering-ram for traditional but not always for Roman-oriented orthodox Catholicism,[24] that Duhem's reply appeared. The article took on the aspect of part of a new program of Catholicism. This presents a bit of a paradox, in view of Duhem's cogent case for the absolute separation of physical theory from metaphysics and religion. It contrasted strangely with the decision of Blondel and Laberthonnière to consider religion from a philosophical viewpoint, the result of which would be that philosophy would take on a religious character and religion would take on a philosophical character.[25] But the idea of a separation of science and philosophy, and especially religion, was a favorite Blondelian idea. In this sense, Duhem's article indicated the end of one intellectual approach and the beginning of another for the *Annales*. Duhem argued that "When the theorist [of physics] enters the domain of metaphysics or of dogma, whether he intends to attack them or wishes to defend them, the weapon he used so successfully in his own area remains useless and ineffective in his hands; the logic of positive science, which forged this weapon, has marked out with precision the boundaries beyond which the temper given to it by that logic would soften and its cutting edge be dulled."

The Duhemian and Blondelian position is similar to the one expressed in the novel *Jean Barois*, which Daniel Mornet called "the Summa of the philosophical and social systems of the generation which was young when [the first world] war broke out."[26] Maurice Tillet, whose father was a science teacher in a provincial town, had been "brought up in an aggressively free-thinking atmosphere" and had converted to Catholicism while studying science at the Ecole normale. When Jean Barois expressed the old-fashioned

24. Claude Tresmontant, *Maurice Blondel–Lucien Laberthonnière. Correspondance philosophique* (Paris, 1922). On the *Annales* under Bonnetty, see Paul, "In Quest of Kerygma: Catholic Intellectual Life in Nineteenth Century France," *AHR* 75 (December 1969): 397 ff.

25. "Nous sommes convaincus de la necessité d'aborder philosophiquement tous les problèmes dont on peut dire qu'ils sont des questions d'âme, de scruter philosophiquement même et surtout les fondements de la religion. . . . Et ce qui en résulte, c'est que la philosophie doit prendre un caractère religieux, tandis que la religion prend un caractère philosophique, c'est-à-dire ce caractère de conviction réfléchie et personnelle qui engage l'être tout entier jusqu'en ses dernières profondeurs." Cited in Tresmontant, *Correspondance*, p. 188.

26. Roger Martin du Gard, *Jean Barois* (Gallimard, 1913; Bobbs-Merrill, 1969), trans. Stuart Gilbert, introduction by Eugen Weber. See also Réjean Robidoux, *Roger Martin du Gard et la religion* (Paris, 1954).

idea that "certain discoveries of modern science, the oriflamme of Barois' generation ... strike at the heart of ... dogmatic religion," the science student Tillet destroyed the argument of this obsolescent nineteenth-century philosophe by interrupting him to point out that "there's no question of reconciling anything with anything! Religion moves on one plane; science on another. Scientists can never touch religion; its truths lie far outside their reach." So much for poor old Barois' "cloudy lucubrations whose only effect is to turn men into pessimists and sceptics." Nor should the political significance of the intellectual evolution, presented by the novelist through the existial agonies of the protagonists, be ignored. It is not without a large dose of historical irony that Catholicism became associated with avant-garde intellectual positions, even though some of these positions may be classified by the liberal academic and by Jean Barois as "reactionary." Tillet brutally assigned to the rubbish heap philosophical systems which Barois had deluded himself into seeing as substitutes for the experience of "the practical efficacy of faith." Systems "from your [Jean Barois'] fetish-worship of evolution to the romantic mysticism of your atheist philosophers" could not "answer to the spirit that is stirring in France today." The death of intellectualism, not of the intellect, was a prerequisite for the regeneration of the soul of France, which would be the contribution of the new generation's "zest for action."[27] It was in this intellectual-cultural-social-political matrix so brilliantly presented by *Jean Barois*, so superb a mirror that the narcissistic public made it immediately into a best seller, far outstripping Proust's *Du côté de chez Swann*, that Duhem also conceived his fundamental attack on the horrible misinterpretation of the nature of physical theory that made it possible for a substantial segment of the intelligentsia to delude themselves into believing scientism was scientific and, more serious, that a new social and political order could be built on such intellectual foundations.

If the reactions of Duhem and Blondel to the disintegration of the image of the universe as a great machine were greeted with suspicion and even hostility in the Catholic intellectual community, the radical scientific views of Edouard Le Roy were generally welcomed with overt alarm. It was bad enough to classify scientific theories as recipes—to be thrown away perhaps after the relevant piece of scientific cooking was done—but it was extremely dangerous to connect religion to scientific change by arguing that rethinking the laws of nature implied a rethinking of such basic religious tenets as that on the nature of miracle.

The scientific theories of the seventeenth century had posed the problem of "the reconciliation of providence and miracles with the mechanistic natural order." Boyle's evolution, "from the simple assertion that God can overrule the laws of His creation to the recognition that the Father contradicts

27. *Jean Barois*, pp. 309-23. See Weber's introduction for an excellent evocation of the French *Zeitgeist*. As Reardon points out, Duhem's approval of Action Française "must be balanced by Le Roy's, Laberthonnière's, and Blondel's definite hostility to it": Reardon, "Science and Religious Modernism: The New Apologetic in France, 1890-1913," *The Journal of Religion* 57 (January 1977): 62. Tillet cannot represent the political position of Catholics.

himself in doing so, reflected the changing opinion among the virtuosi as a whole. . . ." But this "compromise with biblical miracles was ended" by Halley, who eliminated the need for particular providence in the material realm by assuming that God generally uses "natural means to bring about His will."[28] Natural religion, developed as a defense of Christianity, eventually eliminated the distinctive supernatural features of Christianity. If Newton the Christian accepted miracles, Newton the scientist made no use of them. Having no intellectual commitment to Christianity, the eighteenth-century philosophes behaved logically in rejecting providence and miracle while retaining the hypothesis of a mechanistic universe.

To meet this challenge, eighteenth-century French Catholic apologists adopted a set of ideas that were, as R. R. Palmer has noted, notoriously close to Hume's. (The orthodox establishment and the apologists, as guardians of the value of rationality, have always been skeptical of the popular religious tendency to resort unduly to miracles and supernatural acts. To offset possible dangers of acceptance and even greater dangers of rejection, an institutional machinery has been devised for a rigorous testing of such phenomena and their eventual cooptation to the institution and its norms.) The eighteenth-century apologists "denied the absolute validity of human reason, the invariable uniformity of nature, the necessary sequence of physical cause and effect. Hume also doubted these things; it was only because he doubted in addition the trustworthiness of testimony that he differed with the apologists on the probability of miracles."[29] In the late nineteenth century, the philosophy of science returned to a much more sophisticated version of the Humean critique of science, which made it possible to employ this dangerous weapon once again in apologetics. In addition, the nineteenth century was one of a resurgence of religious beliefs, in a real sense the century of the Sacred Heart and the century of Mary, and with the appearances at Lourdes, the best known, the century of the greatest miracle since apostolic times.[30] Both rational and historical developments made it imperative to rethink the problems posed by miracle as idea and as fact.

Ironically, the eighteenth-century type of defense was suspect in many orthodox quarters in the late nineteenth century because the clerical community had worked out its own mechanistic model of the universe, accommodating both Newtonian science and providential action. Elements of both views can be seen in a letter written by Lacordaire in 1853 on the possibility of miracle. Lacordaire recognized that a false idea of the immutability of physical laws and of immutability itself could prevent a person from accepting the miracles of Christ. But nothing is absolutely unchangeable except God, the laws of logic and mathematics, and the moral law. Material nature, the work of God, is both immutable and variable: immutable through the mathematical

28. Westfall, *Science and Religion in Seventeenth Century England*, pp. 92, 101.

29. Robert R. Palmer, *Catholics and Unbelievers in Eighteenth Century France* (Princeton, 1939), p. 132.

30. See chaps. 10 ("Le règne de Jésus-Christ—Sacré Cœur, Eucharistie") and 11 ("Marie Immaculée") of Msgr. Baunard, *Un siècle de l'Église de France, 1800-1900* (Paris, 1900). A fifth edition in 1901 brought sales up to 14,000 copies. Baunard was rector of the Catholic Institute in Lille.

law to which all quantity is subject; variable because quantity itself can always be more or less. The action of nature results from the permanent combination of these two elements of immutability and variability. Miracle does not affect the immutable part of nature. "A miracle is the application of an infinite force to finite forces." Following the mathematical law that a smaller force cedes to a greater, a miracle is a mathematical effect that does not derogate any natural law. Man himself uses this law in acting in nature and in making nature do what she would not do without him. "Every action of man in nature is a miracle; the miracles of God are greater. Voilà tout." God's miracles are greater because He has at his disposal a force greater than all the forces of nature. To some extent, Lacordaire anticipated at least the first part of the paradox of Blondel: "No doubt, if one goes to the bottom of things, there is no more in a miracle than in the least of ordinary facts. But there is also nothing less in the most ordinary fact than in a miracle."[31] But this mathematical style of religious argument, which was associated chiefly with the Polytechnique Catholicism of Gratry, soon passed into oblivion. The problem of miracle remained.

More conventional apologetic arguments assumed the "great axiom of reason; there is order and harmony in nature; there exist fixed and regular laws. . . . This implies that nature is governed by a supreme Wisdom."[32] After all, there is a contradiction in the idea of order without an orderer, laws without a legislator, and an effect without a cause. These arguments were founded more on common sense than on logic or science. In this standard nineteenth-century Jesuit definition given by Toulemont, physical laws are simply the constant, regular, and uniform order that providence follows in the conserving and governing of its creatures. In performing a miracle, providence does not disturb this order or suspend the operation of physical laws; rather it uses the laws, neutralizing their effect in a particular case, as "a hand neutralizes the effect of weight in stopping a falling stone." Perhaps aware that an unfriendly reader might interpret this neutralization as Jesuitical casuistry to hide a belief in suspension of natural laws, Toulemont reiterated that there could be no possible contradiction of physical laws. But above the physical order is the providential and supernatural order, as well as the rational and moral order.[33] In such a set of priorities, perhaps the probability of miracle is increased. In any case, this type of argument put the problem back squarely where it had been in the seventeenth and eighteenth centuries.

But after Lourdes, the problem could never be the same again. For believers, Lourdes was God's reply to the Humean objection concerning testimony, which was put bluntly by Littré and subscribed to by Renan as an insuperable obstacle to accepting the possibility of miracle: "Whatever research has been done, a miracle has never happened where it could be observed and verified." Lourdes was regarded as an arena in which the Virgin kept winning a

31. Lacordaire's letter is in *RCF* 87 (1916): 507–9. Blondel is quoted by Louis Maisonneuve, "La notion du miracle," ibid. 50 (1907): 501.

32. P. Toulemont, "La providence et la science. A propos des récentes attaques du journalisme," *E*, n.s. 11 (1866): 343.

33. Ibid., p. 346.

perpetual victory over the "great heresy of the century, naturalism."[34] As Teilhard de Chardin noted, much more than scientific medicine was at stake in the quarrel over the cures at Lourdes. To recognize divine action was to attack the favorite and basic contemporary idea of science. The orientation of medicine was toward physics and chemistry, which gave knowledge of the body as a mechanism, thus permitting the scientist to deduce from a given state the series of successive states of the organism. A miracle cure queered the picture. Doctors were more interested in observation than in health. Teilhard further insisted that from a philosophical viewpoint, determinism was at stake—and a theory is implacable. The partisans of determinism did not hesitate in choosing between the determinist principle of the sciences and the simplest explanation of Lourdes. Facts were ignored in order to save the principle. Taking a pragmatic view, he admitted that the only useful thing to do was to go to Lourdes to see for oneself. For Teilhard a miracle is like the reality of the external world; both are concrete facts whose evidence accompanies their perception. Too close an analysis usually makes one see nothing.[35] For Teilhard, as for Bergson and Le Roy, "one does not demonstrate a concrete reality; one perceives it."[36] Hardly a position with which those Thomists hungering after the certainties of medieval rationalism could agree!

It was Edouard Le Roy, the Catholic mathematician and philosopher who succeeded Bergson at the Collège de France in 1921, who reinterpreted miracle in the light of the new critique of the sciences. Because of his battle against the rationality of Thomism, especially the inadequate and sterile metaphysical proofs of the existence of God, and because of his dependence on the "méthode d'immanence" and the philosophy of Bergson, many Catholics regarded Le Roy as the primary enemy within the church. In order to make miracle intelligible, Le Roy integrated it into a metaphysics based on the contingency of natural laws and the negation of a rigorous and mathematical determinism in phenomena. Boutroux had shown that "the ideal of a universal mathematics no longer inspires modern science," and experience had shown determinism and necessity to vary inversely with one another. ("The most profound laws touching and regulating reality are those also having the highest degree of contingency from a critical viewpoint.")[37] The clas-

34. Cited in H. Martin, "Le miracle au dix-neuvième siècle. Lourdes devant la science," *E* 51 (1890): 355. This article is also good for its consideration of the explanations of Richet, Charcot, Bernheim, etc.

35. Teilhard de Chardin, "Les miracles de Lourdes et les enquêtes canoniques," *E* 118 (1909): 161–83. Determinism is the real enemy of the possibility of miracle, according to the article "Miracle" in the *Dictionnaire de Théologie catholique* (Paris, 1929), vol. 10, cols. 1798–1859.

36. I. Benrubi, *Les sources et les courants de la philosophie contemporaine en France*, 2 vols. (Paris, 1933), 2:1006.

37. Le Roy, "Essai sur la notion du miracle," *APC*, 4th sér. 3 (1906-7): 5–33, 166–91, 225–59, esp. p. 8. See Emile Boutroux, *De l'idée de loi naturelle dans la science et la philosophie contemporaines* (Paris, 1895), course given at the Sorbonne in 1892-93. This work deals with the laws of logic, mathematics, mechanics, physics, chemistry, biology, psychology, and sociology. Boutroux's famous thesis, *De la contingence des lois de la nature* (Paris, 1874), is chiefly a criticism of the idea of necessity in reality and a re-establishment of the role of contingency. For a friendly reception of Boutroux's *De l'idée de loi naturelle*, see Marcel Hébert, *APC*, n.s. 32 (1895): 442–44. A more critical analysis is

sic definition of miracle, which Le Roy interpreted as essentially a derogation or violation of natural law, was indissolubly linked to the classic concept of natural law itself.[38] Contemporary modification of the idea of natural law had to entail a modification of the idea of miracle.

Le Roy argued that both the supporters and opponents of the possibility of a miracle assumed that natural law is an expression of a necessity really inherent in the nature of things. Certain modern apologists, mixing Descartes and Aquinas in a strange corruption of science and tradition, thus accepted the positivist realist position, which gave victory to the opponents of miracle in advance! For according to this definition of law it is not possible to conceive of a miracle "as a sort of *ex nihilo* creation occurring in the midst of phenomenal series." It is a contradiction in thought, "for the reality of a phenomenon is defined and constituted by its insertion in the total series, by the ties which attach it to the whole. . . ." The conflict between the opponents and the supporters is founded on the same mistake and appears insoluble: one group has logic on its side and the other group has truth. The only possible conciliation could come from the modern philosophy of science, which modified the original assumption of both groups concerning natural law.[39]

What were the teachings of the modern *Kritik* of the sciences that promised a solution to an eternal problem? First, "Science has an objective scope but not absolute value. It begins with postulates relative to conveniences of practical action and language. It maintains only a distant relation to reality, of which it gives us symbols to interpret. It lets us *act* on things and *talk* about them rather than let us *see* them." Second, "The free activity of the mind intervenes in the genesis of laws. There is a conventional part inherent in all scientific results. Science reveals to us then only a diffuse necessity penetrated by a great deal of contingency. It conveys a part of necessity rather than exact necessities. It shows us *determinable* rather than *determined* na-

given by Georges Lechalas, "Les lois naturelles d'après M. Boutroux," *APC*, n.s. 33 (1895-96): 483-96; 34 (1896): 58-74, 388-402, 601-13. Boutroux's dream of a reconciliation between religion and modern philosophy ended, like Hébert's, with the condemnation of modernism. See the interesting preface by Boutroux in Maurice Pernot, *La politique de Pie X* (Paris, 1910). Curiously, in spite of his defense of God, of the relationship between man and God, and of immortality, as well as his destruction of scientism, Boutroux was too dangerous for total acceptance in the orthodox Catholic community. He was not sufficiently materialistic. As a Jesuit critic complained, Boutroux lacked a "healthy and robust realism." The first sentence of *De la contingence* identified a leitmotif of Boutroux's philosophy: "L'homme, à l'origine, tout entier à ses sensations de plaisirs ou de souffrances, ne songe pas au monde extérieur; il en ignore même l'existence." It also explains why Catholics, especially Thomists, feared this Catholic neo-Kantian. See Lucien Roure, "Une figure de philosophe: Emile Boutroux (1845-1921)," *E* 170 (1922): 420-30.

38. This definition is denied by Maisonneuve, "La notion du miracle," p. 677. *The Maryknoll Catholic Dictionary* (New York, 1965) defines a miracle in the way specified as conventional by Le Roy: "An observable effect in the moral or physical order which is in contravention to natural laws and which cannot be explained by any natural power but only by the power of God." *The New Catholic Encyclopedia* (New York, 1967), 9: 890, says that "In theological usage, a miracle is an extraordinary event, perceptible to the senses, produced by God in a religious context as a sign of the supernatural." See the various related articles in the *Encyclopedia* for a typology of miracles—moral, physical, intellectual.

39. Le Roy, "Essai sur la notion du miracle," pp. 8-9.

ture."[40] The Cartesian rigor of determinism and the basis of realist ontology were seriously weakened by this critique. Miracle cannot be defined in terms of a defunct mechanical determinism. Purely physical laws have restricted, particular application. *"Miracle agrees with the principle of laws generally understood, if there is a law of miracle or if miracle is itself a law."* What kind of a law? The universe has a unity, in which everything depends on everything else, as in an organism. If physical reality influences moral reality, the reverse is also true. "In this correlation, mechanical determinism represents one side, while miracle and liberty represent the complementary side." Physical laws have no ontological primacy. Following Boutroux, Le Roy asked how physical laws, not independent in reality of other laws hidden in nature, could be immutable and inflexible. "Miracle would thus express the subordination of the material to the spiritual order, or at least the influence of the latter on the former; it would be to mechanism what liberty is to habit."[41] Le Roy emphasized that he was suggesting a way to make miracle intelligible, not putting forth a definitive explanation. All that could be stated definitively was that believer and non-believer could no longer fight over the issue of miracle, at least on the grounds of science. Miracle remained as a question of fact for exegesis, history, and criticism, but not as a question of principle. With a general intelligible idea of miracle, the question of fact could be treated usefully. He had given a preliminary theory to make possible fruitful observation, not a theory to coordinate results.[42] For Le Roy, faith in miracle, like faith in God, is a matter of internal experience, and even the external fact of miracle has the role of turning the mind inward. Miracle too was subjected to apologetics based on the immanent method: no faith, no miracle. Although Le Roy accepted some specific teachings of Aquinas on miracle, his general philos-

40. Ibid., p. 9. The objection that miracle is contrary to the law of causality also disappears in this critique. See ibid., pp. 27–28. For consideration of the historical testimony problem, see ibid., pp. 29 ff.

41. Ibid., pp. 28–29.

42. Ibid., pp. 258–59. For a criticism of Le Roy from an "orthodox" viewpoint and an attribution of the source of his mistakes to his idealism, see Maisonneuve, "La notion du miracle." For a good Thomist criticism of the "new philosophy," see J. de Tonquédec, *La notion de vérité dans la "philosophie nouvelle"* (Paris, 1908), which appeared first in articles in *Etudes*. Even nonbelievers thought that Le Roy had explained miracles away. "Je me rappelle une séance de la Société de philosophie où l'on a discuté sur la notion du miracle. Le Roy a dit des choses extraordinairement subtiles, mais à la sortie quelqu'un (un non-croyant du reste) m'a dit: 'Cela a été très beau, mais après tant de sublimation, qu'est-ce qui reste du miracle?'" *Correspondance entre Harald Høffding et Emile Meyerson* (Copenhagen, 1939), p. 148. The Dominican theologian Schwalm had a similar reaction to Blondel on miracle: "Le fantôme d'une dérogation au fantôme d'une loi." Le Roy tried to avoid becoming embroiled in theological quarrels by emphasizing that he did not deal with the "reality" of such issues as dogma. Cf. "J'avertis une fois pour toutes que par 'dogme' j'entends surtout la 'proposition dogmatique,' la 'formule dogmatique,' non point la réalité sous-jacente": *Dogme et critique* (Paris, 1905), p. 3nl. Poincaré shrewdly noted of Le Roy that "Nominalist in doctrine but realist at heart, he appears to escape absolute nominalism only by an act of desperate faith": cited in Mary Jo Nye, "The Moral Freedom of Man and the Determinism of Nature: The Catholic Synthesis of Science and History in the *Revue des questions scientifiques,*" *The British Journal for the History of Science* 9 (November 1976): 274–92. For further discussion of the miracle dispute, see François Rodé, *Le miracle dans la controverse moderniste* (Paris, 1965), and Reardon, "Science and Religious Modernism," pp. 48–63.

ophy of science was hardly consonant with Thomism or neo-Thomism. Few Catholic intellectuals were willing to take the risks of following him. The alternative Thomist philosophy was also an honest effort to come to grips with the same problems; it possessed in addition the siren charm of orthodoxy.

By the end of the nineteenth century, the sophistication and complexity of Catholic positions on the significance or non-significance of scientific developments and new currents in the philosophy of science are undeniable. It is certain that this awareness of science owed a great deal to Catholic participation in the debate over the Darwinian revolution in the biological sciences. Whether an evolutionist position was accepted or rejected, intelligent commentators necessarily found themselves involved in learning a great deal about the sciences related to the Darwinian debates and eventually found themselves wondering about the nature of science, especially in the light of its ability to reverse itself on fundamental points and make greater advances than ever before. Catholic interest and participation in science increased toward the end of the century, when the mechanistic model in biology came under serious attack and the comparison with developments in other fields was obvious. The disintegration of the mechanistic and deterministic paradigms—"the world view of modern science: the legacy of Galileo and Newton, reinforced . . . by Darwin"—was nowhere more warmly welcomed by Catholics than in natural science. If we accept only part of the exaggerated view that by the end of the century problems associated with "life" had replaced those associated with "science,"[43] the struggle with evolutionary thought still assumes great importance in the development of Catholic thought, especially in forming general attitudes toward science. In no area was the complex interaction of scientific, religious, and political factors more evident than in the debate over evolution.

In France, there was a clear attempt to base anti-clerical republican politics on a scientistic ideology. Darwinism was most susceptible to exploitation by anti-clericals. The intellectual problem of reconciling religious beliefs with new scientific developments was thus connected with republican anti-clericalism. This meant that republicans were encouraged to accept Darwinism and that Catholics had a good political reason to be suspicious of it as an ideological weapon against Catholicism. Only the finest minds were capable of separating the purely scientific aspects of Darwinism from the wider social and political implications.

In the next two chapters we shall examine this encounter of Catholics with Darwinism and evolution, for in many ways it was preparatory to the responses of Duhem and Lapparent to scientific change and its implication for religious thought. It was also related to the revival of Thomism, especially its Aristotelian component. This way of proceeding also corresponds to the chronological development of French Catholic thought itself.

43. Cf. "La pensée d'aujourd'hui a pour pôle toutes les idées représentées par ce mot: la Vie,—comme la pensée de 1860 avait pour pôle toutes les idées représentées par ce mot: la Science." Paul Bourget, "Réponse au discours de réception de Boutroux à l'Académie française," le 23 janvier 1914, cited in Chevalier, *Bergson*, p. 12.

2

Evolution: The Basis of Opposition

> I am an evolutionist. I believe my great backyard Sphexes
> have evolved like other creatures. But watching them in the
> October light as one circles my head in curiosity, I can only
> repeat my dictum softly: in the world there is nothing to
> explain the world. Nothing to explain the necessity of life,
> nothing to explain why the stolid realm of rock and soil and
> mineral should diversify itself into beauty, terror, and uncer-
> tainty. To bring organic novelty into existence, to create
> pain, injustice, joy, demands more than we can discern in the
> nature that we analyze so completely. Worship, then, like the
> Maya, the unknown zero, the procession of the time-bearing
> gods. The equation that can explain why a mere Sphex wasp
> contains in his minute head the ganglionic centers of his prey
> has still to be written. In the world there is nothing below
> a certain depth that is truly explanatory. It is as if matter
> dreamed and muttered in its sleep. But why, and for what
> reason it dreams, there is no evidence.
>
> Loren Eiseley, *All the Strange Hours. The Excavation of a Life*
> (New York, 1975), p. 249.

Yvette Conry has recently argued that Darwinism was not introduced into France at all in the nineteenth century. She has written an indispensable book about the non-introduction of Darwinism; the analysis of disagreements of French scientists with key Darwinian ideas is excellent, but the thesis is absurd. In applying her definition of Darwinism to other countries, we would conclude that Darwinism was not introduced anywhere in the nineteenth century. No doubt a good many French criticisms of Darwinism were based on such French ideas as Bernardian physiology and Lamarckism, but sup-porters of Darwin elsewhere were not paragons of orthodoxy if judged according to Conry's criteria. As Winsor points out, "Neither Huxley nor Ernst Haeckel, for all their enthusiasm for evolution as the explanation for the subject matter of classical zoology, showed much real understanding of Darwin's special contribution." The final paradox is that Darwinism was not truly Darwinist until after the emergence of a genetics of population. At least, even accepting Conry, we may assume that the debate over Darwinism was introduced; otherwise Conry would have had to find another topic for her *grande thèse*. Conry begins her book with the naïve if challenging sentence "We now know that Darwin was right." She could derive considerable enlightenment from Norman Macbeth's *Darwin Retried*; the subtitle—*An Appeal to Reason* —should seduce Conry. Actually, Macbeth's problem is the same as Conry's: the legalistic and logical assumption that science should be a narrowly defined and totally *rational* enterprise. But Macbeth's rationality leads him to the conclusion, based on an analysis of "verbatim statements of eminent biologists," that classical Darwinism is dead. A more reasonable general argument is that of John Farley: "the basic structure of French biology . . . was theoscientific in nature"—its basic hangups being devotion to teleology, belief in the role of God in nature, and worship of Cuvierist empiricism.[1]

Darwinism had a strong English flavor but the idea of evolution also had solid roots in French biological thought. The idea was not killed by the attack of Cuvier on Geoffroy Saint-Hilaire in 1830, although variants of the dogma of the immutability of species remained the critical variable in the biological models of the natural world. French work in prehistory from the 1840s on inevitably raised questions on the origin and development of man, while the origin of life itself, generally discussed under the rubric of "spontaneous generation," was a subject of general scientific concern, even after Pasteur's theatrical experiments of the early 1860s. As Conry, Farley, and Stebbins have shown, there was no immediate conversion of the biological community to the Darwinian paradigm after the publication of the *Origin* in 1859. Since scientific groups do not convert to new paradigms quickly and it is usually the new generation that embraces the new paradigm, a time lag of twenty years or more for the general acceptance of Darwinism was normal for the French situation. It is even less surprising to find nonscientific intellectual groups clinging even longer to "outmoded" scientific paradigms, especially when a component of their *Weltanschauung* had been carefully based on the "certainties of modern science." The agonies of the clergy over the idea of the evolution of organic species, symbolizing "the transition from a static taxonomy-oriented natural history to a dynamic and causal evolutionary biology,"[2] provides a classic case of this type of idea lag. Once the seventeenth

1. Yvette Conry, *L'introduction du darwinisme en France au XIXᵉ siècle* (Paris, 1974), reviewed by Richard W. Burkhardt, Jr., in *Isis* 67 (1976): 494–96, and by J. R. Moore, in *The British Journal for the History of Science* 10 (1977): 246–51. See also Robert E. Stebbins, "France," in *The Comparative Reception of Darwinism*, ed. Thomas F. Glick (Austin and London, 1974), pp. 117–67; Mary P. Winsor, *Starfish, Jellyfish, and the Order of Life. Issues in Nineteenth-Century Science* (New Haven, 1976), p. 168; Farley, "The Initial Reactions of French Biologists to Darwin's *Origin of Species*," *Journal of the History of Biology* 7 (1974): 275–300, and Macbeth, *Darwin Retried* (New York, 1973).
2. John C. Greene, "The Kuhnian Paradigm and the Darwinian Revolution in Natural

and eighteenth centuries had given the concept of species a static clarity it had never possessed before, the theologians found it possible to solidify the idea of a special creation in a way that lack of form and of preciseness had previously prevented. The fight over Darwinism showed more clearly than anything since Copernicus the damage that could be done to religion by mixing theology and science.

The initial rejection of Darwinism by the clerical intellectuals was not simply a matter of opting for the "Mosaic hypothesis" because of the authority of scripture. Refutation was solidly based on current scientific objections to Darwinism. A typical example of the score or so of treatises on the topic was that by Msgr. Guillaume-René Meignan, bishop of Châlons-sur-Marne and later cardinal-archbishop of Tours. In the 1840s Meignan had studied in Germany and had lectured in the Faculty of Theology at the Sorbonne. In 1869 he published *Le monde et l'homme primitif selon la Bible,* a revised version of his lectures for 1861–62.[3] As adviser on the part of his work dealing with geological matters, Meignan used Abbé Edmond Lambert, author of several well-known manuals and of a book upholding orthodox variants of interpretation on the flood in the light of contemporary developments in geology.[4] After dealing with the historical character of the account of the creation given in Genesis, emphasizing how the Mosaic account did not clash with current scientific theories because of the great latitude with which one could interpret Mosaic science, whose glories included not only Divine authority but convenient imprecision, Meignan turned to the burning question of the day— the origin of man.

Meignan did not fail to restate the Judaic-Christian view of the origin and development of man and the world. And his statement of "biblical anthropology" was distinguished by the literary polish common to a small group of the nineteenth-century clergy who were educated in the seminaries that em-

History," in *Perspectives in the History of Science and Technology,* ed. Duane H. D. Roller (Norman, Okla., 1971). Greene doubts the adequacy of Kuhn's thesis as a conceptual model for the development of natural history from Ray to Darwin, but admits that "an inadequate hypothesis is better than none at all." See the conclusion of David L. Hull, *Darwin and His Critics. The Reception of Darwin's Theory of Evolution by the Scientific Community* (Cambridge, Mass., 1973), pp. 450–55. Hull accepts part of Kuhn's argument—"the role of scientific communities in the reception of scientific theories." For a definition of paradigm, see p. 143, infra, especially note 15. Donna Jeanne Haraway, *Crystals, Fabrics, and Fields. Metaphors of Organicism in Twentieth-Century Developmental Biology* (New Haven, 1976), finds Kuhn's idea especially useful in considering the organismic paradigm of Joseph Needham and Paul Weiss. The myth of Pasteurian objectivity is exposed in John Farley and Gerald L. Geison, "Science, Politics and Spontaneous Generation in Nineteenth-Century France: The Pasteur-Pouchet Debate," *Bulletin of the History of Medicine* 48 (1974): 161–98.

3. 3d ed., 1879. Published by the *Société générale de librairie catholique* (Paris: Victor Palmé, directeur général; Brussels: J. Albanel, directeur de la succursale).

4. Among his numerous works were *Accord de la science et de la religion. Le déluge mosaïque, l'histoire et la géologie* (Paris, 1870), which puts forward the clever idea that the flood was universal for the inhabited part of the globe, and his three-volume *Nouveaux éléments d'histoire naturelle à l'usage des séminaires, des pensionnats de demoiselles, des établissements d'instruction publique et des aspirants au Baccalauréat ès sciences* (Paris, 1864–65). Lambert was in charge of the geological and archeological collection at the Grand séminaire of Châlons-sur-Marne and a member of the Société géologique de France.

phasized the classics and literary style. Meignan advanced into battle against the Darwinists under the banner of the concept of "the unity of the human species," a rallying point for Catholics that preserved the possibility of Eden while they engaged in the scientific battle against the counter-idea of the plurality of the human species.[5] Meignan's biblical anthropology gave the Christian view: man, the last form of life created by God, is an intelligent and free creature, the crown of creation, the work of the love of the All-Powerful. Even after the Fall, God loved this privileged creature so much that he let him reconquer part of the lost heritage. Man's rehabilitation would be achieved by slow, laborious progress in the natural sphere and only with considerable assistance from God in the moral sphere. The critical point had been passed in the Incarnation, when God elevated human nature by taking on human form.

But the nineteenth century was particularly distinguished by the birth of a false philosophy and a false science, which, caring little about human dignity, denied humanity its glorious titles; materialism and positivism were systems opposed to biblical truth. Like many Catholics, Meignan blamed the Enlightenment for a revival of Epicurean materialism: Voltaire, Helvétius, and a great number of Encyclopedists viewed man as an organized portion of eternal matter; some denied the existence of the soul; and they did not think it repugnant to consider man congeneric with the orangutang or the gorilla. The nineteenth century rejected these crude theories, only, to substitute an insidious pantheism, beginning with the apotheosis of nature by Goethe, Schelling, and Hegel, which lowered man to an equal footing with the most humble creatures of the universe. A number of French clerical intellectuals, like Henri Maret and Alphonse Gratry, fought long and hard against the dragon of pantheism. But no sooner was the pantheistic dragon slain, or dead from natural causes, than its horrendous relative, the spectre of materialism, returned to haunt the century.

Although the resurrected doctrine of spontaneous generation had been "annihilated" by the work of Schwann, Heule, and Pasteur, a new great threat came from England, the home of several ardently sustained anti-Christian doctrines in the second half of the nineteenth century. No less opposed to biblical anthropology than the other theories was that of *transformisme*. Since Darwin was one of the most distinguished naturalists of England and his *Origin* clearly contradicted biblical anthropology, it deserved much more careful consideration than other theories. Meignan claimed that the doctrine of the *Origin* bore some resemblance to the application of the German pantheist system to the physical world, the difference being that Goethe, Schelling, and Hegel, proceeding as philosophers, began with an abstract principle, the supposition that a powerful God had manifested Himself in matter and in man, whereas Darwin put forward no metaphysical claim. As a naturalist, he accepted life without asking its origin, limiting himself to discovering its different manifestations, including man as one of the higher animals. In his

5. See John C. Greene, *The Death of Adam* (New York, 1961), chap. 8, p. 221, and the Marquis de Nadaillac, "Unité de l'espèce humaine prouvée par la similarité des conceptions et des créations de l'homme," *RQS* 41 (1897): 415–48.

brief summary of Darwinism, Meignan stated that the principles of evolution were, first, the struggle for life and, second, natural selection, which required millions rather than thousands of years for the variations to produce evolution.[6] Meignan's interpretation of the religious and philosophical significance of Darwinism was not fundamentally different from that of a host of foreign intellectuals, of whom Frederick A. P. Barnard and William Graham were typical. Graham thought "that Darwin has at last enabled the extreme materialist to attempt and carry the design argument, the last and hitherto impregnable fortress behind which natural theology has entrenched herself." Christians feared that the materialist could now fall back on the latest rage in science to "prove" that man has originated from "an arboreal primate who in the long course of Tertiary time had descended to the ground and achieved some dexterity in the manipulation of stones. . . . The fallen Adam had stared into the mirror of nature and perceived there only the mocking visage of an ape."[7] Man could be defined perfectly within the Darwinian system in terms that Meignan took from one of the contemporary organs of materialism: "Man, mammal, order of primates, family of bimana, projecting nose, naked ear, etc."[8] The consequences for Christian humanism were frightening.

This stark opposition between Catholicism and Darwinism was developed by Abbé Lecomte in his study of Darwinism and the origin of man.[9] Insisting that the *Origin* applied to man, Lecomte declared that the bestial origin of man found therein was contrary to Catholic doctrine on the state of physical, intellectual, and moral perfection of the human race's first parents. The Fall and original sin were part of an absurd fable, which science replaced by the fact of continuous progress. Not all Catholic scholars followed Lecomte in arguing that the *Origin* applied to man. It was not an unusual response of the Catholic intellectual to declare that even if Darwinism were true, it had no significance for religion.[10] Franz-Heinrich Reusch had argued in the second edition of his book *Bibel und Natur* (1867) that even if Darwin's theory

6. "The major tenet of Darwinian evolution, the struggle for existence, is . . . an old principle. Charles Darwin's later contribution lay, not in the application of the struggle for existence to the entire animal creation, but rather in his discovery that biological variation combined with the pruning hook of selective struggle might be the key to endless organic divergence": Loren Eiseley, *Darwin's Century. Evolution and the Men Who Discovered It* (New York, 1961), pp. 53, 119.

7. William Graham, *The Creed of Science* (London, 1881), p. 319, cited ibid., pp. 194–95.

8. Cited in Meignan, *Le monde et l'homme primitif*, p. 178.

9. Abbé Alphonse-Joseph Lecomte (docteur en sciences naturelles), *Le darwinisme et l'origine de l'homme* ("deuxième édition, considérablement augmentée," Bruxelles and Paris, 1873). Lecomte was professor at the Ecole Normale de l'Etat at Mons, Belgium. The first edition of this work was a reprint of seven articles published in the *Revue catholique* of Louvain in August, November, and December 1871 and in February–May 1872. He used the fifth edition of the *Origin*. There is an appendix on Darwin's *The Expression of the Emotions in Man and Animals* (London, 1872). The work is dedicated to His Highness, Monseigneur le Prince E. de Croy.

10. See, e.g., R. P. E. Pesnelle ("des prêtres de la miséricorde, docteur en théologie, professeur honoraire de la faculté de théologie de Bordeaux"), *Le dogme de la création et la science contemporaine*, 2d ed. (Arras, 1891), and John A. O'Brien, *Evolution and Religion. A Study of the Bearing of Evolution upon the Philosophy of Religion* (New York, 1932).

were shown to be true, there would be no contradiction between the Bible and the natural sciences.[11] He found little in the *Origin* to criticize, although he fought a battle against the disciples of Darwin who argued that man descended from the monkey. Lecomte wrote that when he informed Reusch of his error, the latter suppressed all favorable references to Darwin in the third edition of *Bibel und Natur* (1870), admitting the impossibility of reconciling Christian doctrines with the animal origin of man proclaimed by Darwin. Reusch's mistake was, in Lecomte's opinion, one also made by those rare Catholic writers who saw Darwin as orthodox.

Widespread dissension among scientists over the origin of man led Lecomte to observe that Darwinism had already entered a phase of decline. Had not the co-founder of the theory, Wallace, in his *Contributions to the Theory of Natural Selection: A Series of Essays* (1870), declared and proven that natural selection, this fundamental principle of Darwinism, is absolutely insufficient to account for the appearance of man on the earth? In order to make possible the passage from animal to man, Wallace thought it necessary to introduce the action of a superior and controlling intelligence. This concession to "spiritualism," as pure Darwinists condescendingly called it, was eagerly seized upon by those who, like Lecomte, believed that Darwinism struck a serious blow against traditional Christian teachings on man. Lecomte was also able to draw upon a report by Buckle in *The Popular Science Review* (January 1871) arguing that the intervention of superior intelligences was not limited to the production of man but must be generalized as a law of nature in the formation of species. Buckle interpreted Wallace's higher intelligences as intermediaries between God and man, a point also made by a note in the second edition of Wallace's work. This new gospel elicited Lecomte's scorn: it was a sort of domestication of our ancestors under the rule of special intelligent beings, essentially an arbitrary and gratuitous hypothesis, at least on the origin of man, showing the weakness of Darwinism. Wallace's argument for intermediaries between God and man was quite foreign to the logical consequences of his argument on human characteristics that cannot be attributed to natural selection. For Lecomte the argument led to a single result: man considered as a whole cannot be explained without the intervention of a superior intelligent cause. Since we know God and do not know Wallace's hypothetical beings, is it not scientifically simpler and more rational to admit that man is the immediate work of God?[12]

Man had lost the place of honor that he had been assigned in the creation as recorded in the Bible. This seems to be a minor version of the crisis that developed when acceptance of the Copernican universe was interpreted as a deadly blow against the homocentric universe permitted by the Ptolemaic system and enshrined by Dante. Until the symbiosis of religion and science

11. Reusch (1823–1900), friend and pupil of Döllinger, was on the Catholic theological faculty at Bonn and editor of the *Bonner theologisches Literaturblatt* from 1866 to 1877. Following Döllinger in the controversy over Infallibility, he was excommunicated in 1872 and became rector of Bonn University in 1873.

12. Lecomte, *Le darwinisme*, pp. 2–3n1, 303–4. See Malcolm Jay Kottler, "Alfred Russel Wallace, the Origin of Man, and Spiritualism," *Isis* 65 (1974): 145–92.

characteristic of the West was, for all practical purposes at least, ended in the late nineteenth century, any shift in science inevitably involved a crisis in religion. Meignan's lament about Darwinism was that in this system, man was no longer king of nature by divine right but only *primus inter pares,* and not really that, since he had arrived first at a perfection not yet reached by the other animals. No radical difference in nature existed between monkey and man; the difference was a question of degree. Both were from the same bimanous family; only man's hands were a little more perfect. Similar observations could be made about other organs. They had the same origin and were the products of continuous evolution. Until now man had happily kept his first rank. But now the materialists could pontificate, as Haeckel did later: "In sum, a comprehensive survey of everything that physiology, anatomy, paleontology, anthropology, psychology and cosmology can contribute to the subject, forces one to the conclusion that the belief in the immortality of the soul is simply a baseless and futile superstition," which, along with belief in God, could be relegated to the rubbish heap of "outworn articles of the Christian faith."[13]

The commentary of Eiseley shows why the fears of Meignan were reasonable for the time: "Philosophically Darwin had achieved several things. . . . His work had destroyed the man-centered romantic evolutionism of the progressionists. It had, in fact, left man only one of innumerable creatures evolving through the play of secondary forces and it had divested him of his mythological and supernatural trappings."[14] But Meignan did not attempt to refute Darwin in the name of revelation, an impossible task because the naturalist had limited himself to proving his case with solely scientific arguments. Meignan chose to combat Darwinism on the only intellectually feasible grounds— those of science. The necessity of fighting against certain scientific doctrines that were ostensibly inimical to Christianity but which could be fought only by scientific counter-arguments led an increasing number of the clergy to attempt to involve the church in science by the development of an apparatus of higher education, by the organization of Catholic scientists on an international scale, as in the Société scientifique de Bruxelles, and by international Catholic scientific congresses. A significant increase in the amount of Catholic periodical and newspaper coverage of scientific issues is evident in the second half of the nineteenth century. If the clergy wanted to fight science with science, these developments were inevitable. As Meignan noted, if God had permitted some scientists to ignore and attack His work of the creation, He had also willed that this work be defended by other scientists of unquestionable credentials.

Part of Meignan's model of nature was built upon the science of the great eighteenth-century systematizer Carolus Linnaeus. Although his work seemed

13. Ernst Haeckel, *The Riddle of the Universe* (New York, 1926; originally published in 1901), chaps. 4–6. Haeckel argued that man had descended from the same protype as the old world or Catarrhine monkeys. Haeckel's monism was not, however, "an extension of Büchner's materialism." See Niles R. Holt, "Ernst Haeckel's Monistic Religion," *Journal of the History of Ideas* 32 (1971): 265–80. See p. 56n96, infra.

14. Eiseley, *Darwin's Century*, pp. 195–96.

eminently safe to Meignan, it is amusing to remember that the botanical works of Linnaeus had briefly been taboo in the papal states on the grounds that they were incompatible with the botany of the Bible. He had also "been sharply criticized for including man among the *anthropomorphi* in his *System of Nature.*"[15] But the heretics of one century sometimes become paragons of orthodoxy for another. Does the work of transformation operate incessantly in nature as Darwin and the materialists supposed? To answer his own question Meignan made a conventional division of nature into two orders: unorganized beings, lifeless, having only the properties common to inert matter; organized beings, which are living or have lived, divided into two kingdoms, vegetable and animal. Acting on the old dictum that "God created; Linnaeus arranged," Meignan went on to give the theoretical organization of the orders from branches to species and their varieties, emphasizing that although varieties developed in the process of generation and could easily evolve as they differed from or resembled the "first form," the kingdoms could never interact, and genera and species could not give rise to other genera and species. Here Meignan followed Linnaeus in the assumption that there is in the "underlying pattern of nature an absolute stability appropriate to its divine origin." God had created organized beings according to certain laws establishing the distance between life and death: a mineral would never become a living plant—"Lapides (mineralia) crescunt; vegetalia crescunt et vivunt." Feeling established an equal gulf between plant and animal—"Crescunt, vivunt et sentiunt." A plant would never become an animal. The same was true for classes of animals—an ox would never become a horse. So species were "primordial types created by divine wisdom and perpetuated by generation from the beginning to the end of the world."[16]

It is fitting that one of the last-ditch defenses of theology against the evolutionary hypothesis should have been based upon the work of "a patient and accurate Swede with the soul of a fundamentalist librarian."[17] Although "the notion of the fixed Scale of Being and the Christian conception of time, as well as the Biblical account of Creation, all tended to discount the evolutionary hypothesis . . . it was Linnaeus with his proclamation that species were absolutely fixed since the beginning who intensified the theological trend.... Henceforth the church would take the fixity of species for granted. Science, in its desire for classification and order, had found itself satisfactorily allied with a Christian dogma whose refinements it had contributed to produce." Meignan could stick to the idea of the fixity of species only by following Linnaeus in his honest sophistry of distinguishing "between the true species of the Creator and the varietal confusion of the moment." But so intent was Meignan on maintaining the virginity of the original thesis that he was unaware that through Linnaeus' "multitudinous writings and the ever mounting editions of the *Systema Naturae* one can trace a growing uncertainty and doubt." Linnaeus finally retreated from his old scientific dogma "Nullae spe-

---

15. Greene, *The Death of Adam,* p. 141.
16. Ibid., p. 138.
17. Gillispie, *The Edge of Objectivity*, p. 170.

cies novae."[18] Nor did Meignan note that Linnaeus had put man and monkey among the primates because he was unable to find "a generic character . . . by which to distinguish between Man and Ape."[19] But Meignan, like Linnaeus, would have been able to offset the unpalatable facts of natural history by "an affirmation of human dignity based on man's unique mental and moral life. Man knows himself to be the ultimate end of creation, a rational being introduced onto earth to contemplate and admire the Creator in his works. 'What else has been revealed must be explained by the theologians.'"[20] This was a world view that rapidly disintegrated in the nineteenth century. It was increasingly abandoned by both science and religion. But many scientists and religious thinkers continued to cling to variants of the old view until late in the century. It was not scientifically absurd to hold the scientific views of Meignan in the last quarter of the nineteenth century.

As Abbé Lecomte showed, a quite convincing lawyer's brief type of scientific case could be made against Darwinism. The eminent Munich professor Theodor Bischoff argued that Darwinism was demonstrated only for some plants and animals. James Hunt, the president of the Anthropological Society of London, viewed Darwinism as applying only to geology and botany, without a single fact in it for anthropology. The geologist d'Omalius d'Halloy declared that his version of evolution contained nothing contrary to the fact of the special creation of man or to the dogma of the immortality of his soul. Nor did the well-known Jesuit zoologist at Louvain, J. van Beneden, find any change in bats from the period of the mammoth to the nineteenth century. Fernand Papillon's study of "Les régénérations et les greffes animales" showed Darwinism a hypothesis with no historical examples of the evolution of a species to support it. The evolutionist Trémaux denied that the struggle for life operates in favor of the strong and in effect rejected the whole idea of a struggle. Barrande's study showed little support from paleontology for Darwin's system. Agassiz' work also provided ample ammunition against Darwin.[21] Within the context of nineteenth-century science and the prevailing absolutist conception of scientific theories, it was quite reasonable to use as a weapon in polemic the fact that "the most famous naturalists, such as the great Cuvier, de Candolle, de Blainville, Johannes Müller, Flourens, Agassiz, Adolphe Brongniart, were so far from the ideas of Darwin."[22]

18. Eiseley, *Darwin's Century*, pp. 24–25.
19. Quoted in Greene, *The Death of Adam*, p. 184.
20. Ibid., p. 189.
21. Theodor-Ludwig-Wilhelm von Bischoff, *Über die Verschiedenheit in der Schädelbildung des Gorilla, Chimpansé und Orang-Outan, vorzüglich nach Geschlecht und Alter, nebst einer Bemerkung über die Darwinsche Theorie* (Munich, 1867). D'Omalius d'Halloy, *Bulletin de l'Académie de Bruxelles*, 1st ser. 13 (1866): 581, and other references, cited in Lecomte, *Le darwinisme*, pp. 38–39; J. van Beneden, "Les chauves-souris de l'époque du mammouth et de l'époque actuelle," *Revue générale* (Bruxelles) (November 1871), pp. 556–60; Fernand Papillon, *RDM* 102 (December 1872) (but Papillon thought evolution a future possibility through some type of "genetic engineering"); Trémaux, *Origine et transformation de l'homme et des autres êtres* (Paris, 1865); Lecomte cited J. Barrande, *Trilobites* (Prague, 1871), and de la Vallée-Poussin, "Recherches géologiques," *Revue catholique* (Louvain) 33 (June 15, 1872); Agassiz' *De l'espèce et de la classification en zoologie* (Paris, 1869) was translated by Félix Vogeli.
22. Lecomte, *Le darwinisme*, p. 125.

It was just as easy to find a substantial number of scientists who disagreed with the application of Darwinism to man by Huxley, Vogt, Büchner, Rolle, Haeckel, Canestrini, and Pouchet. In attempting a refutation of Darwinism in relation to the comparative body structure of man and animal, Lecomte quoted an old supporter of Darwinism, *The Popular Science Review* (July 1871), which pronounced that the *Descent of Man* volumes "are in no respect to be compared with either of Mr. Darwin's previous books." Indeed, "the author's case seems to us but little stronger, if anything, than before."[23] Lecomte agreed with Bianconi on the levity and superficiality of the Darwinists in their argument that man alone does not have an upright position, since the penguin also does. Along with Bischoff, Lecomte was able to enlist the support of Christoph Aeby, the learned Berne anatomist who had established even more fully the impossibility of any transition between monkey and man. And Bischoff's comparative study of man and monkey established that at no stage of its development did the brain of the orangutang agree perfectly with that of man.[24] It was also easy for Lecomte to draw upon a series of studies relevant to Quaternary man and Darwinism to show that the discoveries of Neanderthal, Cro-Magnon, Stångenäs, and the Baoussé-Roussé fossils did not support Darwin's thesis on the origin of man.[25] At least Lecomte was able to agree with Wallace that the scientific objections to the Darwinian account of the origin of man were fatal to this aspect of the theory.

Opponents of evolution could also draw on serious scientific work done by Catholic scientists, although this had the obvious disadvantage of being open to the charge that the basis of the opposition was religious rather than scientific. A clear separation of the religious beliefs and the technically scientific works of the group that can be vaguely identified as the Catholic scientific community is a development of the latter part of the nineteenth century.

Joachim Barrande (1799–1883) provides an interesting case of the religious-scientific interaction usually impossible to detect with any certainty.

23. Quoted ibid., pp. 222–23n1. The connection between monkey and man was rejected by Lecomte on three grounds: an enormous distance separating the human type from the simian type; a frequently opposite development of the two types; and the special characteristics of the body structure of man that contradict the principles of Darwinism (ibid., p. 224).

24. Giovanni-Guiseppe Bianconi, *La teoria dell'uomo-scimmia* (Bologna, 1864); see also his *La théorie darwinienne et la création dite indépendante: lettre à M. Ch. Darwin* (Bologna, 1874); Christoph Aeby, *Die Schädelformen des Menschen und der Affen* (Leipzig, 1867). Cf. the contemporary view of Bjorn Kurtén, *Not from the Apes* (New York, 1972): "The ancestry of man . . . and the apes and monkeys . . . has been separate for more than thirty-five million years. . . . Man did not descend from the apes." See Macbeth, *Darwin Retried*, pp. 141–42, on the "A-to-M transition" fantasy, and Paul Overhage and Karl Rahner, *Das Problem der Hominisation* (Freiburg i. B., 1963); Th. L. Bischoff, *Die Grosshirnwindungen des Menschen mit Berücksichtigung ihrer Entwicklung bei dem Fötus und ihrer Anordnung bei den Affen* (Munich, 1868).

25. Among the works cited by Lecomte were P. Gervais, *Recherches sur l'ancienneté de l'homme et la période quaternaire* (Paris, 1867); Prüner-Bey's paper at the International Congress of Anthropology in Paris in 1867; P. Broca, "Les troglodytes de la Verzère," *RS* (November 16, 1872); and E. Rivière's studies on the fossil remains of the caves of Baoussé-Roussé (*Comptes rendus de l'Académie des sciences* of March 26, April 29, June 24, 1872).

After the Polytechnique and the Ponts et Chaussées, Barrande, an *ingénieur de l'Etat*, was called to the Tuileries in 1826 as science tutor to the Comte de Chambord. Like Cauchy, he remained faithful to the Bourbons after 1830, but, unlike Cauchy, he stayed in Prague with the exiled royal family and refused to accept any honors from governments succeeding Charles X. He therefore never took his place at the institute. A practicing Catholic, Barrande loved to evoke God in his scientific works. With the intention of placing the completion of his works under the aegis of the Immaculate Conception, he dated his last volume December 8, 1881. But his rejection of Darwinism was solidly based on his extensive and famous scientific work. Out of the 350 forms of Bohemian trilobites he had studied, only 10 carried any trace of modification; during the great extent of Silurian time, none of the 350 species had produced a new distinct and permanent form through variation. It was the same for the Cephalopoda, Acephala, and Brachiopoda of his collection. As the Catholic Charles de la Vallée Poussin, a Louvain geologist, also anti-evolutionist, pointed out, Barrande rejected all evolutionary combinations advanced to clear up the mystery hovering over fauna fossils but put forward no substitute theory. The harmony of the old organic worlds and their evident irregularities and complications revealed to him a transcendent order of things. "Coming from a divine source and embracing infinite combinations in time and space, this order cannot very well be grasped by human intelligence as long as it is enclosed in its terrestial envelope."[26]

De la Vallée Poussin agreed substantially with Barrande in a study in 1877 on paleontology and Darwinism.[27] He began by recalling a conversation he had with M. d'Omalius a few years after Darwin's *Origin* had appeared: the "vénérable savant" categorized Darwin's theory as an exaggeration of uniformitarianism, the theory that explained past geological phenomena in terms of actions similar to those operating today. De la Vallée Poussin agreed. But he had to point out that the very Catholic M. d'Omalius himself subscribed to the idea of an unlimited evolution of species as a plausible hypothesis to explain the successive changes of fossil flora and fauna. Fortunately, de la Vallée Poussin could argue that d'Omalius' interpretation as a catastrophist was quite different from that of Darwin as a uniformitarian! Certainly, the Louvain geologist was correct to argue that d'Omalius' ideas on evolution were not worked out in detail or developed scientifically. This curious attempt by de la Vallée Poussin to attenuate d'Omalius' evolutionary views was necessary because most Catholics flirting with evolutionary ideas established the orthodoxy of their position by referring to the evolutionary views of the Belgian Catholic scientist. De la Vallée Poussin argued that the paleontological data furnished by contemporary science showed that Darwinian evolution could not explain or justify what was known of fossil creatures. Especially in

26. Cited in Charles-Louis-Joseph-Xavier de la Vallée Poussin, "Joachim Barrande et sa carrière scientifique," *RQS* 16 (1884): 71. In paleobotany the critical anti-Darwinian role of trilobites was played by dicotyledons. Paleontological advances found predecessors for the trilobites and linked them with intermediaries. See Conry, *Darwinisme*, p. 199n20.

27. "Paléontologie et Darwinisme," *RQS* 1 (1877): 274–318. See the important recent study of R. Hooykaas, *Natural Law and Divine Miracle. The Principle of Uniformity in Geology, Biology and Theology* (Leiden, 1963).

the early years of the Société scientifique de Bruxelles, it was common to find in its journal the type of article which, by showing how a certain body of scientific data could not be accommodated by Darwinian theory, incidentally safeguarded the parts of religion putatively threatened by Darwinism. Abbé Boulay of the Catholic Institute in Lille, who took an anti-evolutionary position in botany, stated boldly as late as 1894, showed the continued strength of this line of thinking.[28]

Both Lecomte and Meignan were in the midst of the critical period of paradigm change and simply chose their science from those scientists whose views best substantiated the scientific-religious *Weltanschauung* that had been agonizingly elaborated in a definitive form since the seventeenth century. Meignan was especially insensitive to the ambiguities of his scientific authorities and showed no profound knowledge of them. Buffon, like Cuvier, had become a culture hero and symbol of scientific authority convenient to use as a bludgeon against the evolutionists. Like his choice of Linnaeus, Meignan's choice of Buffon was not entirely without blemish. In 1753 Buffon had been forced to declare in the fourth volume of his *Histoire naturelle* that the "hypothesis concerning the formation of planets," given in the first volume (1749), was "only a pure supposition of philosophy" and that he repudiated "whatever concerns the formation of the earth in my book, and in general everything which could be contrary to the narration of Moses." But the publication of Buffon's *Époques de la nature* in 1779 showed the heretic still trumpeting his version of "Eppur si muove."[29] And although Buffon rejected the idea of the mutability of species as contrary to Genesis, reason, and experience—the intellectual demons to which eighteenth-century science had to burn incense—he continued to suspect its possibility. The facts he had accumulated supported evolution more than they denied it. Eiseley notes the astounding fact that in his own unsystematic way, Buffon succeeded in mentioning *"every significant ingredient which was to be incorporated into Darwin's great synthesis of 1859,"* although the mechanism of change continued to elude him.[30] In falling back on Buffon for anti-evolutionary support, the bishop was leaning on a weak reed.

Superficially at least, choosing "the magician of the charnel house" as a source of anti-evolutionary support was scientifically sounder than leaning on the ambiguous author of the famous *Discours sur le style.*[31] Cuvier, ever conservative in anthropology, as in geology and biology, died in 1832 content that man's origins as revealed by the latest science dated back less than 6,000 years. Like most French intellectuals of the time, and like Velikovsky recently, Cuvier noted the agreement of the Pentateuch with the traditions and sacred writings of the Near East and the Orient in favor of the Mosaic hypothesis. Unlike Linnaeus, Cuvier in his *Tableau élémentaire de l'histoire*

28. Abbé Boulay, "La théorie de l'évolution en botanique," *RQS* 36 (1894): 480–96.
29. See Greene, *The Death of Adam*, pp. 63–67.
30. Eiseley, *Darwin's Century*, pp. 39–45; Greene, *The Death of Adam*, pp. 142–60. On the differences between Buffon and Linnaeus, see Phillip R. Sloan, "The Buffon-Linnaeus Controversy," *Isis* 67 (1976): 356–75.
31. Buffon's inaugural address to the Académie Française (1753).

naturelle des animaux (1798) confirmed the Christian thesis on man by giving him a separate order (*Bimanes*) from the other primates (*Quadrumanes*).[32]
At last man's claim to be lord of the creation was established on an ostensibly scientific basis and, a fact of equal importance, by the overlord of French
science. Cuvier thought that the origin of the lower monkeys was possibly
only a little earlier than that of man, but in 1836 this theory was "breached
in so far as man's simian relatives were concerned" when Edouard Lartet un-
covered the first fossil anthropoid in the Miocene deposits near Sausan.[33]
But neither this nor the human fossil discoveries in the succeeding decades
induced the defenders of the Mosaic hypothesis to cease their adoration of
Cuvier. Nor did his theological epigoni detect in Cuvier what later commentators have made plain. Eiseley has argued that Cuvier cleared the way for
Darwin by his break with the venerable Scale of Being (or Nature) and its
clumsy morphology. Classifying the four great animal groups, whose divergent anatomical organization made it impossible to fit them into a single uni-
linear ascending system, into vertebrates, mollusca, articulata, and radiata,
Cuvier unwittingly opened the way to the idea of divergent evolution. Eiseley
further argues that Cuvier was the first to note what Depéret called a fundamental idea, that "the rocks revealed a gradual advance in the complexity of
life through the several 'revolutions' of the planets." So Cuvier concluded
that there had been "a very remarkable succession in the appearance of the
different species." "It was Cuvier's discoveries that gave the impetus to biological progressionism ... the clear prelude to nineteenth-century evolution."
Eiseley ingeniously argues that even in the famous debate in which Cuvier rejected Geoffroy Saint-Hilaire's attempt to make cephalopods the transitional
form spanning the gap between vertebrates and invertebrates, Cuvier emerges
as ultimately contributing to the triumph of the evolutionary doctrine. Although the debate "had some potential evolutionary overtones, it revolved
about Geoffroy's transcendental unity of plan," which did not necessarily
have our contemporary meaning, i.e., "actual physical descent of related
forms from a common ancestor." Cuvier's "rejection of a universal plan for
all organisms, and his insistence upon unrelated structural types no longer arranged in a unilineal series with man at the head, was a necessary preliminary
to the kind of branching evolutionary phylogeny which is now everywhere
accepted. The attempts to fill in all the gaps represented in the old Scale of
Being were bound to fail and to stand as an impediment to evolutionary
thinking."[34] It would be quite unsporting to criticize Meignan, a nineteenth-
century bishop, and his fellow clerical intellectuals for not perceiving the evolutionary implications of Buffon and Cuvier in the same way that a contemporary anthropologist can. We operate with the immense advantages of the
historical tool of retrodiction, i.e., predicting the past. Nor is it reasonable to

32. See Greene, *The Death of Adam*, pp. 195–98.
33. Eiseley, *Darwin's Century*, p. 271.
34. Ibid., pp. 87–88; Cuvier put the results of his researches on the structure of living
and fossil animals in his *Règne animal distribué d'après son organisation*, 4 vols. (1817;
2d ed., 5 vols. 1829–30). But see William Coleman, *Georges Cuvier. Zoologist* (Cambridge,
Mass., 1964), p. 150, for the limitations of Cuvier's progressionism.

expect the clergy to have perceived what the scientists were glimpsing only through a glass darkly. Buffon and Cuvier were, like many scientists in a period of paradigm change, sleepwalkers in many of the same ways depicted by Koestler in his portraits of Copernicus and Kepler. And certainly few saw initially, as Darwin did, the grandeur of the view of life as a tangled bank.

One of the contemporary authorities on whom Meignan depended most heavily for ammunition against the Darwinists was Jean-Louis-Armand de Quatrefages de Bréau (1810–92), a French naturalist belonging to an old Cévenole Protestant family. In depending on Cuvier and de Quatrefages, the anti-Darwinian Catholics were in the curious position of falling back on Protestants for their science, and in the case of de Quatrefages, a descendent of the *camisards*, those who revolted against the revocation of the Edict of Nantes. De Quatrefages was a tremendously versatile nineteenth-century French scientist. After getting his *doctorat ès sciences mathématiques* at Strasbourg in 1829 with a thesis on a *Théorie d'un coup de canon*, he went on to medical studies and got his *diplôme de docteur* in 1832. In Toulouse, where he took up medical practice, he founded the *Journal de médecine et de chirurgie de Toulouse*. When he moved to Paris in 1840 he made his debut with some remarkable articles in the *Revue des Deux Mondes*, became the friend of H. Milne-Edwards, forged connections with such fellow laborers in the same vineyard as Agassiz and Vogt, and got his *doctorat ès sciences naturelles* (1840). In 1850 he became a professor of natural history at the Lycée Napoléon and in 1852 was elected to the Academy of Sciences. When Pierre Flourens became professor of natural history at the Collège de France in 1855, de Quatrefages accepted the new chair of anthropology at the Muséum d'histoire naturelle. Very religious in his convictions, he rallied to the defense of the theory of the unity of the human species. Indefatigable in exploiting all the sciences dealing with man, he drew upon studies of prehistoric man, studies in anthropology, and studies on the anatomy of the brain and other organs of the body in order to refute the Darwinian hypothesis. He died while finishing a manuscript on Darwin.[35] But he was an important figure in conciliating the different schools of thought. Although he gave an important role to environmental influences, his emphasis on the separate order of nature for man made him beloved in the religious camp; at the same time his technical work ensured respect in the anti-religious camp and, with his official position, gave him the entrée to the Société d'anthropologie and the journal of the society. After the death of conciliators like de Quatrefages, the cold war turned hot.

35. *La grande encyclopédie*, 27:1122. This article gives 1855 as the date of Flourens' death; he died in 1867. Among the works of Quatrefages relevant to the Darwinist quarrel are *Unité de l'espèce humaine*, 1861; *Histoire de l'homme*, 1867; *Rapports sur les progrès de l'anthropologie*, 1867; *Charles Darwin et ses précurseurs français*, 1870; *L'espèce humaine*, 1877; *Hommes fossiles et hommes sauvages*, 1884; *Théories transformistes: Romanes, Carl Vogt, Haeckel, Owen, etc.*, 1892; all published in Paris. See Conry, *Darwinisme*, passim, on Quatrefages, nearly the only French advocate of monogeny; Conry also notes that in *L'espèce humaine*, Quatrefages fell back on Wallace's refusal to apply natural selection to the human order. *Darwin et ses précurseurs français* had considerable impact through publication in article form in the *Revue des Deux Mondes*.

Another of the nineteenth-century naturalists frequently cited by anti-Darwinists was Henri-Marie Ducrotay de Blainville (1777–1850), professor in the Faculty of Sciences (Paris) and at the museum. Brought up by the Benedictines, Blainville went to Paris at the age of nineteen to study painting and for a while indulged in pleasures unavailable with the Benedictines. He then threw himself passionately into science, becoming assistant to Cuvier in his courses at the Collège de France and the Athénée. Although he quarreled with Cuvier, he succeeded him when Cuvier died in 1832. Most of his work was in comparative anatomy. His general conception of the creation was close to that of Geoffroy Saint-Hilaire. An enthusiast of the idea of unity, he upheld the idea that beings are part of a continuous series against Cuvier's idea of the animal kingdom's being made up of clearly delineated, distinct groups.[36] Any extant gaps were filled by species which had by then disappeared, an argument Darwin put to a quite different use. Rejecting successive creations, he argued that there had been only one creation, in which all animals, living or fossil remains, had come from the same act of the Creator. Blainville went on to generalize, as Agassiz would do later in a different way, that all human knowledge forms a complete circle limited by God or the creative intelligent power.[37] The spirit of Marsilio Ficino still flickered in the souls of some nineteenth-century scientists. Abbé F.-L.-M. Maupied organized and published Blainville's lectures at the Sorbonne in the years 1839–41.[38] This labor of love by the abbé, who had his *doctorat ès sciences*, left a monument from another age which could be used for direction by those clergy unwilling to change their scientific ideas for fear of undermining the faith. Many of the secular pillars of the faith so assiduously preserved by the clergy were the monuments erected by a pious science.

To Meignan's delight, de Quatrefages had formally pronounced against the hypothesis of the evolution of the species and supported a variety of the venerable concession admitting a limited variation of the species.[39] By species,

36. See Meignan, *Le monde et l'homme primitif*, p. 185: "Pour Blainville, l'espèce est l'individu répété dans le temps et l'espace."

37. *La grande encyclopédie*, 6: 989–90.

38. *Histoire des sciences, de l'organisation et de leurs progrès, comme base de la philosophie*, 3 vols. (Paris, 1845). "Rédigée d'après ses notes et ses leçons faites à la Sorbonne de 1839 à 1841, avec les développements nécessaires et plusieurs additions par l'abbé Maupied." The Abbé Maupied left several monuments of pious science to posterity: *Du déluge au point de vue scientifique et théologique* (Paris, 1846), and *Dieu, l'homme et le monde connus par les trois premiers chapitres de la Genèse, ou nouvelle esquisse d'une philosophie positive au point de vue des sciences dans leurs rapports avec la théologie. Cours de physique sacrée et de cosmogonie mosaïque, professé à la Sorbonne, 1845–1848*, 3 vols. (Paris, 1851).

39. "Pour moi [Quatrefages] , l'espèce est quelque chose de primitif et de fondamental. Des actions, des milieux ont modifié et modifient sans cesse les types premiers de l'herédité, tantôt pour maintenir, tantôt pour multiplier ou accroître ces modifications. Ainsi prennent naissance les variétés et les races. Les limites des variations résultant de ces actions diverses sont encore indéterminées; mais, en y regardant avec soin, il est facile de constater qu'elles sont parfois remarquablement étendues. Toutefois, il ne se forme pas pour cela des espèces nouvelles, et la parenté spécifique des dérivés d'un même type spécifique peut toujours être reconnue par voie d'expérience, quelles que soient les différences très-réelles qui les séparent," cited in Meignan, *Le monde et l'homme primitif*, p. 186.

de Quatrefages meant the group of individuals, more or less resembling each other, who have descended from a single primitive couple through an uninterrupted succession of families.[40] The idea of a separate human kingdom was put forward by a fairly large number of religiously inspired intellectuals, including some scientists, among whom were Nees von Esenbeck, Jan, Serres, James, and de Quatrefages. In his *Rapport sur les progrès de l'anthropologie* (1867), de Quatrefages attempted to show that in reasoning logically according to the principles of Darwinism, there is a contradiction in the idea that man descended from the monkey. The monkey-origin-theory of man is in clear disagreement with the ideas of Darwin, which were, according to de Quatrefages, also erroneous.[41] "So God created man in His *own* image, in the image of God He created him; male and female created He them." De Quatrefages avoided all the awkward questions about Genesis that arose out of Darwin's view.

Meignan also drew upon some of the work of Agassiz for arguments against Darwinism. Agassiz' basic point, similar to Barrande's argument, was that the zoological fossil record showed a lack of progressive change which was fatal to Darwinism. Meignan, unlike William Barton Rogers, did not see that Agassiz really "recognized the progressive character of the fossil record," and later editions of Meignan's work did not show any knowledge of Agassiz' defeat by Rogers and Gray in the Darwinian debates in the United States. The authority of Agassiz resembled that of Quatrefages in many ways, including a historical connection with French Protestantism. Agassiz' father was the last of a line of clergy stretching back to a first clerical ancestor driven from France by the revocation of the Edict of Nantes. As Jordan observed, although Agassiz was "one of the ablest, wisest and best informed of the biologists of his day," his "attitude toward Darwinism was . . . cold and unsympathetic." Jordan attempted to explain or possibly excuse Agassiz' persistence in an obsolescent paradigm: "It seems possible that his position was determined in part by a misunderstanding but more particularly by his philosophy of biology. He seemed to regard Darwinism as a theory of continued progress instead of one of divergence, tempered by the weeding out of unadapted individuals. He failed to recognize the importance of separation and segregation in the development of specific forms." Ironically, his study of fossils nearly led Agassiz to join the ranks of those history hails as the John the Baptists of Darwinism, but he made no announcement because he discovered that "we had the higher fishes first." But as Jordan remarked, "More important to Agassiz was the fact that in his philosophy each species of animal or plant was in itself 'a thought of God.' Their homologies or fundamen-

---

40. Cf. Buffon: "L'espèce n'est autre chose qu'une succession constante d'individus semblables et qui se reproduisent. L'empreinte de chaque espèce est un type dont les principaux traits sont gravés en caractères ineffaçables et permanents à jamais quoique toutes les touches accessoires varient ou puissent varier," cited ibid., p. 184.

41. Lecomte, *Le darwinisme*, pp. 18–19n1, agrees with the logical impossibility of the descent of man from the monkey but argues that the Darwinian system demands it. He cites two Darwinian disciples: Haeckel, *Natürliche Schöpfungsgeschichte* (Berlin, 1870), and Canestrini, *Origine dell'uomo* (Milan, 1866).

tal unities were 'associations of ideas in the Divine Mind.'"[42] His "intensely religious mind," although not enslaved to any one creed, led him to build a superstructure of Christianized Platonism over his science. This made him a great source of comfort to the opponents of Darwinism, who had to get their technical data from experts interpreting their findings according to anti-Darwinist paradigms.

Further contemporary relevant evidence was interpreted by Meignan as unfavorable to any evolutionary ideas. The Napoleonic Egyptian expedition had shown no change in plants and stock since antiquity. The study of the animals in Egyptian paintings led to the same conclusion. In the words of Lacépède's famous report, "It follows from the collection of citizen Geoffroy that all these animals are identical with those of today."[43] Excavations of bones in various areas in the nineteenth century showed Meignan the same facts: some species have disappeared, but among those remaining we find our species again. Realizing he was open to the criticism that his science was a trifle old, especially with this historically oriented argument, Meignan hastened to point out that more recent expeditions had not changed the conclusions arrived at by Lacépède. The good bishop had no inkling of the immensity of the time required by Darwin's historical view of the natural world.

Meignan explicitly rejected Darwin's idea that all animal species, although descended from a primitive archetype, had been transformed in a thousand ways by external action and the conditions of existence, especially geological phenomena. Darwin had pushed the doctrine found in his French precursors to an outlandish extreme! But Meignan's rejection of this particular argument was based on the not necessarily concordant views of past and contemporary scientists. He noted that Buffon and Cuvier had opposed this supposed change to the fact that the crossbreeding of species nearly always produces sterile offspring. De Quatrefages had also noted that hybridity tends to disappear because of the law of return to type. Meignan could conclude, with the condescension characteristic of those who appeal to the "facts," that gradual evolution from species to species, genus to genus, or class to class was a hypothesis contradicted by the best verified facts. Had not Buffon proclaimed certain inalterable characteristics of species? "La transformation des espèces est impossible; mais il faut reconnaître en elles une variabilité illimitée."[44] Further definitions of species by scientific authorities—Cuvier, Linnaeus, de Candolle, de Blainville, and the chemist Michel-Eugène Chevreul—were invoked to sanction the argument. And Godron, dean of the faculty of

42. David Starr Jordan, "Agassiz," *Encyclopaedia Britannica*, 1:339–41. Agassiz' scientific arguments against Darwinism were nearly completely destroyed by William Barton Rogers in the famous debates of the Boston Society of Natural History. See Edward J. Pfeifer, "United States," in Glick, ed., *Comparative Reception*, pp. 175 ff.; Edward Lurie, *Louis Agassiz. A Life in Science* (Chicago, 1960), chap. 7; A. Hunter Dupree, *Asa Gray* (Cambridge, Mass., 1959), esp. chap. 15.

43. Cited in Meignan, *Le monde et l'homme primitif*, p. 188. Bernard-Germain-Etienne de la Ville Lacépède (1756–1825) was a French naturalist, musician, holder of bizarre theories in physics, whose classifications in natural history were used and purged by Cuvier. He also had a long political career in the Napoleonic empire and in the Restoration.

44. Cited ibid., p. 184.

sciences at Nancy, had declared against the evolution of species: "The earth's revolutions could not have changed the types originally created: the species kept their stability until new conditions made their existence impossible; then they died, but they were not modified."[45] Meignan was following some of the best scientific minds of the day in rejecting or ignoring the Darwinian hypothesis because of a lack of clarity in the direction in which the evidence was pointing. Little did he—or any contemporary—realize that a change of scientific paradigms may possibly be a "conversion experience" for nonscientific reasons. The new paradigm can easily "create" the necessary facts for proof of its "truth" after acceptance.

It is curious that Meignan did not capitalize on Darwin's recognition of the need for a Creator of life who had also let it radiate into divergent forms under the aegis of secondary laws. Darwin had argued that "It is derogatory that the Creator of countless systems of worlds should have created each of the myriads of creeping parasites and slimy worms ... on this one globe." Instead of supervising the birth of each species, God oversees the emergence of species "through the working out of the natural forces implanted in that highly complicated chemical compound known as protoplasm, and the response of this same protoplasm to the environmental world about it."[46] Man himself was not to be exempted from the process, and here, no doubt, was the chief stumbling block for Meignan. Basing his opinion on quite respectable science, Meignan rejected the idea that all living beings descended from an "être type," one original living being, capable of evolving into the most complex organisms. There was no scientific evidence in favor of this primordial cell. De Quatrefages found its "existence unexplained and unexplainable, in disagreement with the little that we know." Meignan argued then that Darwin's hypothesis did not explain the variety of organisms and instincts of living beings. Nor would Meignan allow Darwin his supposition that the passage from one species to another is explicable by intermediary extinct species.[47] As relentlessly empirical as ever, the bishop asked if fossils would not show numerous remains of these intermediary species. Although de Quatrefages acquiesced in the millions of centuries required by Darwin's hypothesis of a slow evolution, he was just as pessimistic as Darwin about the probability of

45. Ibid., p. 185. See D. A. Godron, *De l'espèce et des races dans les êtres organisés et spécialement de l'unité de l'espèce humaine*, 2 vols. (Paris, 1859). In spite of his emphasis on the distinction between man and the other higher animals, Godron recognized resemblances: "Si aidé du microscope, l'histologiste cherche à découvrir la structure intime des différents tissus spéciaux, dont sont formés les organes de l'homme et des animaux supérieurs, la ressemblance est bien plus évidente encore. Les tissus musculaires, fibreux, nerveux, etc., le tissu du cerveau lui-même offrent une si grande conformité, pour ne pas dire une identité telle, que la démonstration devient complète" (2:113).

46. *Foundations of the Origin of Species* ("the first essay of 1842"), cited in Eiseley, *Darwin's Century*, p. 193.

47. Lecomte, *Le darwinisme*, p. 9, attacked Darwin's speculations on this point. He noted that Darwin, basing his position on natural selection with divergence of characteristics, says that it does not seem unbelievable that animals and vegetables are the products of some intermediary form, and, "If we admit this, we must likewise admit that *all the organic beings which have ever lived on this earth*, may be descended from some one primordial form." Quoted by Lecomte from the fifth edition of the *Origin*, p. 573.

finding fossil remains of a graduated series of intermediaries between species. Meignan echoed Pictet's question: "But why . . . does it happen that the species which we find most frequently and most abundantly in all the newly discovered beds are in the immense majority of the cases species which we already have in our collections?" Darwin had built his system on an imaginary basis; too often he substituted for missing facts such dangerous formulas as "I imagine" and "is it not possible." "Are all these hypotheses without a basis of observed fact proper for a science that calls itself positive?"[48] This is not far from the type of "Gallic indifference" to Darwinism personified in Claude Bernard, who did not make any distinction between Darwin's work and *Naturphilosophie*. It did not matter if one was a Darwinist or a Cuvierist! "In the critical tradition of French learning, Darwin's mind and language seemed simply slack."[49] This tradition, which put religion in a defensive position in so many other areas in the nineteenth century, proved a convenient ally in the religious attack on Darwinism.

Catholic journals opposed nearly all forms of evolution from the appearance of the *Origin* until well into the first decade of the twentieth century. Much of the initial reaction in the Jesuit *Etudes* was concerned with the notion of species, especially their fixity or immutability. Following closely the scientific community whose biological paradigms it accepted, especially Cuvier, Flourens, Godron, and de Quatrefages, Matignon rejected Darwin's new system. "Darwin does not know species, for he confuses it with form and then with a totally complete order. Neither does he know varieties, since he calls them emerging species. Should one be surprised that he takes one for the other, variability—the elastic character of accessory attributes in a species—for mutability—which would be the transformation of a species itself." The death of Gratiolet resulted in a eulogy by Larcher in 1865 which emphasized the conclusion of the anatomist on the gulf between man and the other primates. Interest was always keen in prehistoric findings related to man. A review article by Jean in 1868 followed de Quatrefages in relegating all discussion of Tertiary man outside the framework of the discussion of the age of man.[50] In 1869 Carbonnelle coldly dissected Darwinism, finding it of no con-

48. Meignan, *Le monde et l'homme primitif*, p. 190. See review of the *Origin* by François-Jules Pictet, translated in Hull, *Darwin and His Critics*, pp. 142–54.

49. Gillispie, *The Edge of Objectivity*, pp. 320–21. This was not true after the 1870s. Most modern French biologists would probably agree with Michael T. Ghiselin, *The Triumph of the Darwinian Method* (Berkeley, 1969), who argues that the work of Darwin has been chief source of working hypotheses for biological research, in contrast to the sterility of Lamarck's work. See Jean Rostand, *Charles Darwin*, 6th ed. (Paris, 1947). But Lamarck is still a patron saint of research for some scientists: see P. Wintrebert, *Le vivant, créateur de son évolution* (Paris, 1962). We finally have an excellent modern study of Lamarck: by Richard W. Burkhardt, Jr., *The Spirit of System. Lamarck and Evolutionary Biology* (Cambridge, Mass., 1977). On the basic incompatibility of Darwinism and Bernardism, see Conry, *Darwinisme*, especially pt. 2, sec. 4.

50. A. Matignon, "L'unité de l'espèce humaine d'après les travaux récents des physiologistes," *E*, n.s. 3 (1864): 70–88; N. Larcher, "Nécrologie [Louis-Pierre Gratiolet]," *E*, n.s. 6 (1865): 385–96; A. Jean, "Les monuments de l'âge de pierre et les théories sur l'ancienneté de l'homme," *E*, 4th ser. 1 (1868): 31–53, 507–32. Later in the year he dealt with Lyell's reaction to these new theories on man. See A. Haté, "Les résultats des re-

cern to religion as well as completely hypothetical and incapable of stimulating the same works and research that the fixity theory had inspired. Carbonnelle's rejection of Darwinism on scientific grounds fitted into the pattern followed by most Catholic intellectuals who rejected Darwinism, although after the appearance of the *Descent* many also thought there was a clash with religious teachings on man.[51] But as late as 1877 *Etudes* could fall back on de Quatrefages in arguing that the psychological characteristics of man separated him from other species and made him an order apart. Man has three classes of higher properties: that of intelligence (articulated language, social state, and industry); that of ethics (distinction between good and evil); and that of religion (the feelings and convictions making man a religious being—his belief in a future life and in higher beings).[52]

In reviewing Milne-Edwards' *Rapport sur les progrès récents des sciences zoologiques en France* (1868), Bellynck emphasized that the issue of definition of species was still a fundamental one. In spite of his rejection of Darwinism, Bellynck defended Darwin against the liberties that had been taken by his translator and, following de Quatrefages, especially emphasized that Darwin did not argue for the simian origin of man. He had no objection to having man treated in a treatise on zoology, provided he was not confused with the brutes and the distinction between an animal and a human order was maintained.[53]

Although only a few clerical intellectuals supported variants of the evolutionary hypothesis, a substantial number argued that evolution was not contrary to Catholic religious and dogmatic teaching but was unacceptable because of scientific deficiencies. The position of this group, dependent generally on the anti-Darwinian arguments of an important segment of the non-Catholic French scientific community, also provided the foundation of the arguments of the Catholic pro-Darwinist group. If there were no religious objections to evolution and if freedom of discussion prevailed in scientific matters, as even the most obdurate anti-Darwinists allowed, then adoption of a modified pro-Darwinist position could not be rejected except on scientific

---

cherches préhistoriques d'après les congrès et réunions des sociétés," a series of ten articles in *Etudes* beginning in 1875 and ending in 1876; R. P. H. de Valroger, *L'âge du monde et de l'homme, d'après la Bible et l'Eglise* (Paris, 1869), who points out the chronological imprecision of the Bible and argues for a reasonable liberty of opinion in assigning dates to the appearance of man and to other controversial events; and Fabre d'Envieu, *Les origines de la terre et de l'homme* (Toulouse, 1873).

51. I. Carbonnelle, "Bulletin scientifique," *E*, 4th ser. 4 (1869): 472–82.

52. See Joseph de Bonniot, review of A. de Quatrefages, *L'espèce humaine* (Paris, 1877), *E*, 5th ser. 11 (1877): 611–14, and Bonniot, *La bête, question actuelle* (Tours, 1874).

53. Le P. A. Bellynck, "Les progrès récents de la zoologie," *E*, 4th ser. 5 (1870): 838–57. Bellynck was professor of natural history at the Collège Notre Dame de la Paix at Namur, Belgium. The testimony of the chemist Chevreul before the Academy of Sciences was also enlisted in favor of the perpetuity of species in space and in time; see *E*, 5th ser. 6 (1874): 790–93, for this "profession de foi d'un savant." Conry, *Darwinisme*, pp. 37–39, identifies the Milne-Edwards report as the end of radical opposition to Darwinism. In a decade the debate is reoriented toward the legitimation of natural selection as a factor in evolution.

grounds, which became increasingly difficult to do after the 1870s, when a new generation of French scientists did their work within the confines of Darwinism.

Evolution had a strong attraction for some Catholic intellectuals. The Jesuit Joseph Delsaulx confessed the irresistible attraction the doctrine had for him: "If true, the theory of evolution would conform better than the more facile doctrine of successive creations to my ideas of divine wisdom and power." After all, he noted, the evolution of the universe in astronomy and the evolution or at least the transformation of forces in physics were already recognized.[54] Father Carbonnelle was explicit in separating materialism from evolution, while emphasizing that Catholics could accept the latter without harm to their faith. Although many evolutionists were irreligious, their materialism did not belong to the essence of evolution. Trained as a mathematician, he himself rejected evolution for scientific reasons. To believe in the spontaneous organization of matter, leading to the appearance of vegetable and animal life, was a scientific error in Carbonnelle's opinion, but it could not contradict revealed doctrine, which taught absolutely nothing on the subject. Christians were free to choose according to the enlightenment they received from science.[55] As Dierckx emphasized, there were, of course, certain fundamental dogmatic truths sanctioned by reason, such as belief in original matter, the government of the world by providence, and the special intervention of God in the origin of man, which could not be denied by a Catholic and which determined Catholic rejection of such ideas as the eternity of the world and the exclusive role of chance in nature. But issues such as the degree of intervention by God in the creation, whether God had created each specific type individually or whether life was given a single primitive form or a small number of forms at the beginning, all allowed for considerable difference of opinion. "Science alone can answer the question, and Christian dogma is not concerned with it at all."[56]

Suspicions of Catholics concerning the anti-religious nature of Darwinism were confirmed by the radical anti-clerical and anti-religious nature of the appearance of the French translation of the *Origin*. Clémence Royer's translation of the *Origin of Species* appeared in 1862, bristling with provocative notes and armed with a shocking preface. This remarkable disciple of La-

54. Le P. Joseph Delsaulx, *Les derniers écrits philosophiques de Tyndell* (Paris, 1877), p. 61, cited in le R. P. Fr. Dierckx, "L'homme singe et les précurseurs d'Adam en face de la théologie," *RQS* 36 (1894): 84. Delsaulx's work had originally been a series of articles in the *Revue catholique* of Louvain.

55. Dierckx, *RQS* 36 (1894): 84–85. See Carbonnelle, "Bulletin scientifique," *E*, 4th ser. 4 (1869): 472–82. Carbonnelle may have shared the type of skepticism not unusual among physicists—e.g., Kelvin and Duhem—concerning evolution; cf. Karl Popper's rejection of the evolutionary hypothesis as a universal law, in *The Poverty of Historicism* (New York, 1964), pp. 106–9.

56. Dierckx, *RQS* 36 (1894): 85. Jean d'Estienne, "Le transformisme et la discussion libre," *RQS* 25 (1889): 76–141, 373–420, had come to the same conclusion. D'Estienne cited Lavaud de Lestrade, Vigouroux, Ducrost, Hamard, Arduin, and Duilhé de Saint-Projet as contemporary clerical writers, mostly opposed to or reserved toward evolution, who adopted similar positions on the absence of any clash between faith and evolution as a scientific doctrine. Jean d'Estienne is the pseudonym of Charles de Kirwan.

marck, as she styled herself, a former royalist Catholic Bretonne, flaunted her secular and scientistic humanism in the preface to the first edition: "Yes, I believe in revelation, but in a rational revelation, which is only the result of the progress of science and contemporary consciousness."[57] Darwin provided a new religion of progress.

Catholics were not the only ones alarmed by this exploitation of Darwinism. Although Charles Lévêque accused Royer of not making a faithful translation of Darwin, who had allegedly disavowed it, he had to retract this accusation. The faults were not so serious as he thought; Darwin had complained to the publishers when they republished the translation based on the third edition, for it did not take into account his revisions. Royer described the language of the 1873 translation as a sort of "patois roman." Ignoring Darwin's explanation of the need to take his cherished revisions into account, she explained that perhaps many people had at last convinced Darwin that her preface had compromised him in the eyes of the "gens de bien" by presenting him as a revolutionary, even if an unintentional one, and, in spite of himself, a destroyer of the sound doctrines still held as official and as the only respectable ones. Her preface could not be used in seminaries and collèges. There was a need for an edition *ad usum Delphini*, without her "logical commentaries." Darwin wanted to satisfy the need of those who like "to behold contemporary truths through the twilight of old cathedrals" (lettre à M. le président de l'Académie des sciences morales et politiques). He could hardly have been introduced into France by anyone more likely to alarm the defenders of a faith living in a state of intellectual siege since the Enlightenment.

One of the most prolific sources of anti-religious thought and anti-clericalism in France was the Ecole d'anthropologie de Paris, which the Protestant Paul Broca (1824–80) succeeded in founding in 1875, in spite of obstacles such as the opposition of the "clerical party." After the senatorial elections of 1878 the school was given permanent authorization for its courses and its teaching, supported by an annual government subsidy of 20,000 francs. In 1859 Broca founded the pioneering Société d'anthropologie, which grew to over six hundred members in twenty years. He also established a museum and, with the aid of the state, the city of Paris, and private funds, a series of chairs for the teaching of anthropology. When the Ecole pratique des hautes études was established in 1868, Broca's laboratory was among those funded. In 1872 he started the *Revue d'anthropologie*. The society, the laboratory,

57. "La doctrine de M. Darwin, c'est la révélation rationnelle du progrès, se posant dans son antagonisme logique avec la révélation irrationnelle de la chute. Ce sont deux principes, deux religions en lutte, une thèse dont je défie l'Allemand le plus expert en évolution logique de trouver la synthèse. C'est un oui et un non bien catégoriques entre lesquels il faut choisir, et quiconque se déclare pour l'un est contre l'autre. Pour moi, mon choix est fait: je crois au progrès": *De l'origine des espèces, ou des lois du progrès chez les êtres organisés*, trans. from 3d ed. with preface and notes by Clémence-Auguste Royer (Paris, 1862; 2d ed., 1866). In 1873, J.-J. Moulinié made a translation based on the 5th and 6th editions and Ed. Barbier a translation in 1876 based on the 6th edition. See the *Compte rendu, Journal officiel, Académie des sciences morales et politiques*, July 19, 27, August 2, 1873, for the quarrel over Royer's translation. See Conry, *Darwinisme*, pt. 2, sec. 1.

and the school were grouped into the Institut anthropologique.[58] Anthropology, or "the science of man," was frequently regarded by "orthodoxy" as one of the more dangerous sciences of the nineteenth century. The Spanish government under Isabella II prevented the establishment of an anthropological society in Madrid. Anthropologists were frequently dangerous critics of traditional Christian beliefs. Many of those associated with the École d'anthropologie de Paris—Mortillet, Lefèvre, Soury, etc.—were among the bêtes noires of nineteenth-century clergy.[59] This group was ardently evolutionist, sometimes ferociously Darwinian, although, as in the case of Broca, sometimes not uncritically.[60]

The extremes reached by some of those associated with the school are revealed by the career of Gabriel de Mortillet (1821–98) and his work on the prehistory of man. "Prehistoric archeology," as founded by men like Boucher de Perthes, Edouard Lartet, and Mortillet, was really a very important branch of anthropology in France, with close relations on all levels. Mortillet had started as a pupil of the Jesuits in Chambéry from 1830 to 1835. After a radical career involving prison and exile, he returned to Paris in 1864 and after 1868 became head of the Musée de Saint-Germain. A notoriously anticlerical mayor of Saint-Germain, extreme leftist deputy for the Seine-et-Oise, militant freethinker, Mortillet was also famous for his studies in prehistory and became president of the Société d'anthropologie and one of the founders of the Broca school. Like Lefèvre and Soury, he was brutally frank in his attacks on religion and the clergy.[61] The ideological nature of the divisions between clerical groups and those enlightened men inspired by science was pro-

58. *La grande encyclopédie*, 8:82–83, 3:175–82, articles on "Broca" and "Anthropologie" and "Note relative à l'Ecole d'anthropologie" in AN, F^{17} 13396. See L. Manouvrier (secretary general of the society), "La société d'anthropologie de Paris depuis sa fondation," *Revue internationale de l'enseignement* 60 (1910): 234–51. For a Catholic attack, see J. Burnichon, "La dépopulation de la France et la société d'anthropologie de Paris," *E* 51 (December 1890).

59. The versatile Soury shocked the religious world in 1878 with his *Jésus et les Evangiles*, a work in which he, an authority on the nervous system, maintained that Jesus was a victim of meningitis. Soury, along with Charles Letourneau, G. Vacher de Lapouge, Camille Bos, and L. Laloy, was a translator of Haeckel: *Les preuves du transformisme* (1879), *Le règne des protistes* (1879), and *Essais de psychologie cellulaire* (1880). Some of André Lefèvre's works were hardly less outrageous to the faithful. See P. Huard et M.-J. Imbault-Huart, "Jules Soury (1842–1915)," *Revue d'histoire des sciences* 23 (avril-juin 1970): 155–64.

60. See, e.g., Paul Broca, *Sur le transformisme* (1870) in *Mémoires d'anthropologie*, 3:145–204; Mathias Duval, *Le darwinisme. Leçons professées à l'Ecole d'anthropologie* (Paris, 1886); Paul Topinard, *L'anthropologie* (Paris, 1876; 5th ed., 1895). See the remarkably unpolemical review of Duval by Marcel Hébert in *APC* 3 (February 1886): 487–94. Broca rejected natural selection; see Conry, *Darwinisme*, pp. 51–65. For Conry, then, Broca is not a Darwinist. But see David L. Hull, "Darwinism and Historiography," in Glick, ed., *Comparative Reception*, p. 398: "a scientist could be a Darwinist without accepting natural selection as the major evolutionary mechanism."

61. Cf. Soury, in his preface to Haeckel, *Les preuves du transformisme. Réponse à Virchow* (Paris, 1879; 2d ed., 1882), who lists among casualties of Lamarckism-Darwinism "des vieux dogmes sacrosaints, des causes finales, de l'univers, de l'immutabilité des espèces ... des créations successives ... et de la jeunesse de l'homme sur la terre." Also, "La morphologie moderne est inconciliable, je ne dis pas seulement avec le dogme de la création, mais avec celui d'une providence."

vocatively stated by Mortillet in the preface to a work on the antiquity of man. The true friends of education and progress were enthusiastic about "la science préhistorique," which was indissolubly connected with evolutionary theories. Religious opposition continued, of course, with Abbé Hamard and other Oratorians, Moigno and other "canons," as well as with Father Jean and other Jesuits. But this did not disturb Mortillet much because the clergy, too weak in natural science and insufficient in paleo-ethnology, had been left behind by the advance of science. They had also a worse defect: "a mind warped by the hollow study of theology." There was little to fear from the fact that some clericals, drawn by the general trend of the period, had "secularized their attacks" by infiltrating scientific societies, by the editing of specialized journals, and by inducing certain active elements of these journals to cross-fertilize with religious journals. Mortillet referred only to "an important Belgian Catholic journal" *(Revue des questions scientifiques)* and "a no less important Protestant paper of Montauban."[62] Nothing good could come out of Nazareth.

Mortillet showed proof of having learned his religious lessons well by neatly inverting in favor of science the idea that it is impossible for two truths to contradict each other. "A fact that has always surprised me is that orthodoxies everywhere totally oppose the progress of science. If, as they claim, they possess absolute truth, why do they fear the development of human knowledge? This development can only enlighten us and increasingly confirm one another. So in showing so much hostility to scientific truth the orthodoxies should certainly assume that their absolute truth is less absolute than they claim."[63]

As Duilhé de Saint-Projet clearly saw, a vast effort was under way in areas like physiology and experimental and comparative psychology, all harnessed to a general anthropological movement, to explain the origin of thought, of reason, and of moral liberty, i.e., the genesis of the human mind, in terms of purely materialist causes, without any reference to an external and higher cause. All could be explained by environment, selection, experience, heredity, and time. The "anthropological problem" was by far the most hotly debated issue between unbelievers and Christians in the last two decades of the nineteenth century. The weight of the scientific community was preponderantly against the defenders of the idea of the uniqueness of the human species, an idea of increasing scientific obsolescence in spite of its respectable lineage from Buffon and Cuvier to de Quatrefages. "A vast school of very qualified scientists, followed by numerous and ardent disciples, seems to have only one goal: to eliminate the irreducible characteristics that make the hu-

62. Gabriel de Mortillet, preface to 2d ed. of *Le préhistorique. Antiquité de l'homme* (Paris, 1883; 2d ed., 1885), cited in Jean d'Estienne, "Le transformisme et la discussion libre," *RQS* 25 (1889): 79. See also Mortillet's attack on F. Chabas, one of whose sins was to be a member of the Society of Biblical Archaeology of London: Mortillet, *Les études préhistoriques devant l'orthodoxie* (Paris, 1875), and F. Chabas, *Les études préhistoriques et la libre-pensée devant la science. Réponse à M. G. de Mortillet* (Paris, 1875).

63. G. de Mortillet, *Les études préhistoriques devant l'orthodoxie* (extrait de la *Revue d'anthropologie*), p. 3, an attack on H. de Valroger's article in the *Revue des questions historiques* (1874) on the antiquity of man.

man soul a special creation of God in nature, to show man as the last expression of a continuous evolution."[64] Against such an army only the most urgent defensive measures could be taken. There could be no hope of victory while the army remained united on the grounds of eternal hostility to biblical anthropology. This war would, like so many intellectual and scientific quarrels, eventually end with a whimper. As Catholics came to see that the triumph of a biblical anthropology would be a highly undesirable and unscientific victory, their opposition to anthropology per se faded away. Without this opposition to unite them, the anthropologists relegated the anti-religious component of their *Weltanschauung* to the background; from their viewpoint the enemy had been vanquished by science. Each group believed in its own victory; so both could afford to be more tolerant of the other's *idées fixes* and to concentrate on more profitable activities. But this rapprochement was impossible in the days when the sworn enemies of religion joyously proclaimed à la Strauss the banishment of miracle and the rout of all religious doctrines as a result of the scientific advances of the nineteenth century. It was also impossible before the Third Republic effectively curbed the political power of the clergy to influence the diffusion of ideas.

Broca and the few others who started the Société d'anthropologie were all medical doctors and zoologists. Although 16 of the 19 founders were doctors and 73 of the 91 members in 1861 were also doctors, the situation changed; over a 50-year period less than 52 per cent of the French membership was medical—496 civilian and 113 military doctors out of 1,102 members. The early preponderance of anatomists and physiologists in French anthropology gave it a distinctly medical flavor and, when added to the mathematical knowledge of Broca, a decidedly quantitative approach. It is probable that the strength of materialism in French medicine also contributed to the anti-religious slant of the typical French anthropologist.[65] Conversely, French Catholic doctors played a considerable role in Catholic opposition to evolution. Pierre Jousset busied himself with the protection of Catholic teaching from the ravages of an anti-Christian science, which he roundly denounced: "Anti-Christian science has perhaps never been more dangerous than at this moment. Rich in positive knowledge, it has become proud and authoritarian. The intolerance it blames on the Catholic church has become its supreme

64. F. Duilhé de Saint-Projet, "Le problème anthropologique et les théories évolutionnistes," *RQS* 25 (1889): 354. His theme was furnished by the series of annual evolutionary lectures of the Société d'anthropologie de Paris and some recent publications. Evolution seemed the scientific key in all areas: anatomy and physiology (Duval, Beaunis, Testus, Bordier); linguistics (Hovelacque); ethics, the family, and marriage (Letourneau); belief (Van Ende); general psychology (Richet); the mind (Royer, Perrier); and animal intelligence (Romanes). See Périer, *Le transformisme*, pt. 2, "L'origine de l'homme," for an extended treatment of the topic.

65. The university had little love of the new science treating man as an animal any more than did the general public. *Revue d'anthropologie*, 3d ser. 4 (1889): 376 ("Trentenaire de la Société d'anthropologie de Paris"). But work like Gratiolet's on the comparative anatomy of primates and man makes it clear that important related scientific work was done in the faculties of science. See P. Trémaux, *Origine et transformations de l'homme et des autres êtres* (Paris, 1865), for criticism of Gratiolet's comparisons. Trémaux also points out the powerful hostility of Flourens in the Académie des sciences to evolutionary ideas.

law. It imposes its theories as dogmas, its hypotheses as incontestable truths; the dreams of imagination become articles of faith—science is infallible! "[66] Jousset admitted that the Darwinian system was not entirely false, but he did not find that it sufficiently took into account fact controlled by scientific experiment. His chief complaints were against the extension of the doctrine of evolution to the entire universe, including man. As Monsabré noted, Jousset's little volume served to convince readers of good faith of their noble and divine origin. In the same vein, Jousset attacked Topinard's "new demonstration of modern materialism," a confused mixture of the new positivism of Paul Carus and the doctrines of Spencer.[67] Given the propensity of French anthropologists to follow Broca in proclaiming the highest generalities of the science of man ("general anthropology"), Catholic scientists like Jousset were kept busy counter-attacking with the highest generalities of their own science.

Not all segments of the scientific community were as passionately antireligious as the doctor-anthropologist group. Sometimes an attempt was made to calm the anxieties of Catholics about the implications of evolutionary doctrine. A review of Paul Maisonneuve's *Zoologie* by the *Revue scientifique* in 1886 provides a good example of this type of approach.[68] Although a work of popularization for students at the secondary level, it was given the privilege of a review in this journal because it was so competently done that it could also be used by those preparing for the license examinations. It is probable that the reserves of Maisonneuve concerning evolution, although he was well known for his work in the natural sciences, inspired the journal to seize an occasion to criticize this opposition. The reviewer assumed that a professor of the Catholic faculty of sciences in Angers would have certain philosophical ideas in order to be permitted to teach there and that these ideas would predetermine his position on evolution. Since Maisonneuve sincerely expressed his opinion, there was no point in discussing it. But the reviewer argued that evolution was not incompatible with Christian dogmas, or at least this was the opinion of some solid minds who were also firmly Christian. Many persons who misunderstood Darwinism drew illogical and exaggerated conclusions from it. Darwinism did not exclude the existence of God: "Darwinism does not exclude a first cause, whatever name one wants to call it; quite the contrary, it demands it in an imperious way. Darwin refrained from studying this first cause, but its necessity is no less evident for whoever studies the theory of evolution carefully and conscientiously."[69] Maison-

66. Le Dr. P. Jousset, *Evolution et Transformisme. Etat de l'homme primitif des origines de l'état sauvage* (Paris, 1889; 2d ed., 1910), p. vi. The work carries a letter of T. R. P. Monsabré, who also wrote a letter for the pro-evolutionary book of Leroy! See also Jousset, *Essai d'une doctrine spiritualiste en médecine* (Paris, 1897).

67. Jousset, *La doctrine de l'espèce et l'origine du langage. Réfutation du transformisme et de la théorie cellulaire à propos du livre de M. Topinard "Science et foi"* (Paris, 1902; extrait des *Annales de philosophie chrétienne*). Paul Topinard's book, *Science et foi. L'anthropologie et la science sociale* (Paris, 1900), is a revised and expanded version of *Science and Faith; or Man as an Animal and Man as a Member of Society, with a discussion of Animal Societies* (Chicago, 1899). Topinard spent over a decade in the United States.

68. 23ᵉ année (May 22, 1886): 663–64.

69. The reviewer cited only the review of Duval's *Le darwinisme* by Marcel Hébert in

neuve's "opposition" to evolution had to be explained, the reviewer concluded, on the basis of very dogmatic personal opinions. Anti-evolutionary
Catholics would conclude, of course, that Maisonneuve's position was based
on his scientific work. Pro-evolutionary Catholics, on the other hand, now
had an authoritative non-Catholic scientific source to cite in arguing that evolution was quite compatible with Catholicism.

It should be emphasized that the specifically anti-evolutionary message
took up only a small portion of science manuals written for the Catholic educational system. J. Guibert's zoological manual for elementary classes took
one page out of 269 to explain the dual nature of man as the highest of the
mammalia, considered from the physical viewpoint, and man as part of a separate order of nature, outside the animal series because of his unique spiritual
faculties. Only man has intelligence and free will, faculties which are evidence
of a spiritual substance that will survive the death of the body.[70] The rest of
the work was much the same as any other textbook on such a subject. By
adopting the doctrine of the dual nature of man, Guibert also left the way
open for use of the evolutionary hypothesis for the physical past of man belonging to the animal world. This was not the first or the last occasion on
which the elasticity of Catholic theology would allow the Catholic mind to
absorb the latest scientific novelty.

By the end of the nineteenth century some intelligent Catholics like
Charles de Kirwan realized that whatever the scientific validity of Darwinism,
Catholics had made a serious tactical error when evolutionist theories had
begun to spread. Instead of reacting on a priori grounds against the very principle of evolutionary theories, they should have first determined whether the
principle logically and necessarily contained the consequences that the materialist school deduced from it. Catholics had fallen into a trap. Their enemies
had secured an easy victory in cleverly exploiting Darwinism against religion.
Group opposition by Catholics gave their enemies a powerful weapon in the
form of another proof of a favorite anti-Catholic argument that reason and
faith as well as science and theology were in opposition to each other. It was
bad enough that such doctrines existed in higher education; it was intolerable
when the state promoted them in secondary education. But this was precisely
the policy of the anti-clericals of the Third Republic. A decree of August 6,
1898, for example, stipulated that summary ideas of paleontology would be
taught from the evolutionary viewpoint. "The teacher will especially strive to
show the bonds uniting ancient forms to present forms and to demonstrate

---

APC (February 1886), in *RS*, 23ᵉ année (May 22, 1886): 663–64. In Roger Martin du
Gard's novel *Jean Barois*, Jean resigns as professor of natural science at Wenceslas (Stanislas?), a Catholic college, over restrictions on the teaching of evolution.
    70. J. Guibert (prêtre de S.-Sulpice; professeur des sciences naturelles au Séminaire
d'Issy), *Histoire naturelle pour les classes élémentaires. Zoologie* (Paris, 1896). See also
his *L'âme de l'homme*, 2d ed. (Paris, 1899), "Science et religion, Nouvelles études." Edmond Alix, in his zoology course at the Institut catholique de Paris, also rejected the type
of evolution that destroys the idea of species and leads to the monstrous consequence of
the derivation of the human species from an animal species. See *De la classification en général* (Bar-le-Duc, 1880) for "the eminently Christian theory of serial order."

the phenomena of adaptation."[71] Kirwan feared the exploitation of this decree by sectarian teachers. But before long Catholics began to turn out their
own texts for use in the great propaganda battle that was developing. As we
have seen, French Catholic hostility towards Darwinism did not derive solely
from religious or dogmatic factors. Catholic attitudes must be viewed within
the general framework of the French scientific response, which was initially
hostile. Two of the giants of the life sciences, Pasteur and Bernard, set the
tone by their silence or disdain. Henri Milne-Edwards was also publicly silent.
Lacaze-Duthiers did nothing to promote the cause. Other leading scientists,
like de Quatrefages and Barrande, spoke and wrote against Darwinism. But
between 1870 and 1880 the younger men in the laboratories openly showed
their Darwinian leanings. As a result of the efforts of Paul Bert, Alfred Giard,
Edmond Perrier (after 1879), and others, a Darwinian mentality began to
prevail in the French scientific community.[72]

The situation at the Sorbonne was well illustrated by the commentary in
the *Revue scientifique* when Paul Hallez, Giard's student at Lille, defended
his thesis (*Contributions à l'histoire des Turbellariés*, 1879) before the faculty of sciences in Paris. The journal congratulated the faculty for giving
Hallez' work the highest accolade possible ("en le recevant avec unanimité de
boules blanches"), for no one had ever suspected the Paris faculty of any sympathy for evolutionary doctrines or for the modern embryogenetic school.
Instead of trying to hide his Darwinian colors, Hallez had boldly displayed
them at the beginning of his work. He dedicated the thesis to his mentor,
Giard, "the first zoologist who courageously taught Darwinian doctrines in a
French faculty without worrying about clerical attacks." Up to 1879 Giard
did not have many followers in France.[73] But the clerical attacks on members of the university were less important than the opposition of the scientific establishment to Darwinism. Not all of the important academic opponents of Darwinism were in the Catholic camp. Some of the leaders, like
Milne-Edwards and de Quatrefages, were Protestant. The opposition to Darwinism was scientific and based on prevailing "ideologies" in various branches
of the natural sciences.

But the growing scientific fertility of Darwinism, used by Catholic as well
as unbelieving scientists, led to detectable if subtle changes in the outlook of

71. See Jean d'Estienne, "Le transformisme et le programme officiel de paléontologie,"
RT 5 (September 1899): 462–80. D'Estienne reviewed the *Notions sommaires de paléontologie répondant aux programmes des classes de philosophie et de premières* (sciences)
(Paris, 1899) of Paul Maisonneuve, professor of natural sciences at the Catholic Institute
in Angers. All evidence for evolution was presented solely within the framework of hypothesis and completely ignored in the section on man. It was published by the Alliance
des maisons d'éducation chrétienne, which specialized in publishing such works for the
large Catholic educational system.

72. Le R. P. Robert de Sinéty, "Un demi-siècle de Darwinisme," *RQS* 67 (1910): 5–
38, 480–513, esp. pp. 24–25. For further comment on French reaction, see Robert E.
Stebbins, "French Reactions to Darwin, 1859–1882" (Ph.D. diss., University of Minneso-
ta, 1965), and "France," in Glick, ed., *Comparative Reception*, pp. 117–67.

73. *La revue scientifique de la France et de l'étranger*, no. 19 (November 8, 1879), pp.
436–40.

even inveterate anti-evolutionists like the prehistorian the Marquis de Nadaillac. All informed Catholics recognized the great works that had been inspired by the evolutionary hypothesis, especially by Darwinism. But few had
reached the level of sophisticated pragmatism concerning scientific theory
characteristic of Charles de Kirwan's reply to the crude attacks of *Etudes* in
1889. De Nadaillac's agonizing change of position came through clearly in a
long review of the Reverend J. A. Zahm's work *Evolution and Dogma* (1896),
which was put on the Index in 1898 during the frenzy of the Americanist
controversy.[74] Zahm's inclination to accept much of evolution was criticized
by de Nadaillac as an example of the author's habit of taking unproven hypotheses as acquired truths. But de Nadaillac then confessed that if he was
hardly ready to accept the conclusions of the evolutionist school, he could
no longer reject them absolutely. De Nadaillac therefore put forward a compromise idea, which did not really differ essentially from the views of other
Catholic evolutionists or, except on the Creator hypothesis, from the many
other evolutionary views. De Nadaillac found the idea that a Creator had
endowed certain beings with the potential for change, which had actually
occurred over eons of time, more satisfying for the human mind than Darwinism and more religious than the doctrine of successive creations in space
and time by which God modified his works.[75]

In 1898 de Nadaillac emphasized his agreement with d'Omalius d'Halloy
on the difficulty of imagining the continued intervention of the Creator in
His creation over the immensity of time. But it was the works of the paleontologist Albert Gaudry that deeply disturbed de Nadaillac and made him
agree with Gaudry's conclusion: "the living world is a great unity whose development one can follow as that of an individual."[76] The impact of Gaudry

74. Marquis de Nadaillac, "L'évolution et le dogme," *RQS* 40 (1896): 229–40. John
Augustine Zahm, C.S.C. (1851–1921) had started his career at Notre Dame as a physics
professor and was important in building up the university's science program. "American-
ism" was the so-called phantom heresy, condemned in *Testem Benevolentiae* (1899), Leo
XIII's letter to Cardinal Gibbons. Opposing ecumenical cooperation, the letter denounced
such ideas as adapting church discipline and even doctrine to the age and extolling the active external life over the passive inner life.

75. "Ne peut-on pas supposer que le Créateur, au début de son œuvre, a doué tous les
êtres sortis de sa main, créés par sa volonté, ou seulement quelques-uns d'entre eux, d'une
puissance de modification, d'une plasticité—ainsi que l'appelle M. Gaudry—se développant
dans l'immensité des temps, sous l'empire des lois que nous ignorons, de circonstances que
nous ne pouvons dire, par des changements lents et imperceptibles, atteignant parfois des
limites extrêmes et se continuant de génération en génération, jusqu'à l'accomplissement
d'immuables desseins qu'il n'est pas donné à l'homme de pénétrer?" (ibid., pp. 238–39).

76. D'Omalius d'Halloy, "Le transformisme," *Bulletin académique de Belgique*, cited
in de Nadaillac, *RQS* 44 (1898): 442; Gaudry, *Les enchaînements du monde animal dans
les temps géologiques. Fossiles primaires* (Paris, 1883): *Fossiles secondaires* (Paris, 1890);
and especially *Essai de paléontologie philosophique, ouvrage faisant suite aux Enchaînements* (Paris, 1896), which made its debut in the *RDM* in 1896. On paleontology and Darwinism in France, see Conry, *Darwinisme*, pt. 1, sec. 3. Conry sees a latent Leibnizianism
in Gaudry's non-Darwinian evolutionary philosophy on the plan of the creation. She does
not classify French paleontology as Darwinian because it did not use the mechanism of
selection and did not accept Darwin on species extinction. Gaston de Saporta is also non-
Darwinian in Conry's view, for Saporta ignored Darwinian ecology—the idea of selection,
in particular. See Conry, *Correspondance entre Charles Darwin et Gaston de Saporta, pré-
cédée d'une Histoire de la Paléobotanique en France au XIXᵉ siècle* (Paris, 1972).

on Catholic attitudes toward evolution was probably considerable. Apart from the authority of his solid science, done within the parameters of evolutionary theory, it was hard for Catholics to resist the conclusions of a fellow Catholic who found that nature is a mirror reflecting divine beauty.[77] De Nadaillac could easily agree with Gaudry that "the theory of evolution shows, better than the theory of independent multiple creations, the unity and the harmony of the divine plan." Yet de Nadaillac could not completely surrender to evolution, for his old-fashioned view of the nature of scientific theory forbade him to accept a theory based mostly on "isolated facts" about which there were still serious unanswered questions. Whether one accepted Gaudry's version of evolution, in which the causes regarded by the Darwinians as the sole agents of modification in the orders of nature were designated as very secondary causes, whether one rejected evolution, or whether one simply expressed some reserves because of ignorance of the process allowing the strange transformations, one had to recognize the existence of certain lacunae that could not be removed by science. The "mystery of life," i.e., the process of fertilization, the transmission of characteristics of parents, and cell growth and differentiation, contained areas of vast ignorance. "The more science progresses, the more we feel that the foundation of things escapes our investigations."[78] The marquis ridiculed the idea of understanding life through the dissection of a corpse or understanding thought through describing the associations of ideas. The haughty dogmatism of works like Renan's *Avenir de la science* had little foundation in science itself. Evolution, if it exists, is not a general law for all times and all species; but de Nadaillac did not exclude the possibility of its becoming so in the future. For the present, the fearful unknown surrounds man; his only refuge is in the idea of a supreme intelligence from which ours derives.[79] "In the midst of our doubts and our uncertainties a single point remains like a brilliant beacon that no discovery or advance can reach." Who could say it better than Spinoza? "*Quidquid est, in Deo est, et nihil sine Deo esse neque concipi potest.*"[80]

The change that occurred in the Catholic intellectual world in just three decades was well illustrated on the occasion of the appearance in 1898 of the Abbé L. de Casamajor's anti-evolutionary *Hétérogénie, transformisme et darwinisme.* A devastating review by de Kirwan revealed the shortcomings of the work.[81] The type of work acceptable a generation ago in Catholic circles now

77. See Jean d'Estienne, "Le transformisme et la discussion libre," *RQS* 25 (1889): 87–88. Curiously, E. Bourgeat, professor in the natural sciences at the Catholic University of Lille, in "Les travaux de M. Gaudry sur l'évolution," *RL* 1 (April 1890): 689–91, emphasizes Gaudry's recognition of the weak foundation of Darwinian exaggerations.

78. De Nadaillac, *RQS* 44 (1898): 442, 458. Paul Broca, *Sur le transformisme* (1870), in *Mémoires d'Anthropologie* (3:145–204), makes the same point (p. 179).

79. De Nadaillac, p. 459. The marquis cited the astronomer Hervé Faye, *Sur l'origine du monde: théories cosmogoniques des anciens et des modernes* (Paris, 1884) who accepted the traditional formula: "Dieu, père tout-puissant, Créateur du ciel et de la terre."

80. De Nadaillac, *RQS* 40 (1896): 246.

81. *Hétérogénie, transformisme et darwinisme. Problème de l'espèce* (Bar-le-Duc, 1898). "Les deux premières parties (la troisième n'étant pas rédigée encore) ont été couronnées par la Société scientifique des Pyrénées-Orientales": De Kirwan, *RQS* 44 (1898): 296–99.

found powerful opposition from Catholic intellectuals most influenced by scientific developments. It was bad enough that the abbé had spent so many pages arguing against spontaneous generation, which was, in de Kirwan's opinion, to force an open door. But the abbé's chief crime was to condemn en bloc all evolutionary theories, without distinguishing between Haeckelian or monist theory and the spiritual evolution upheld by distinguished scientists like Gaudry as well as by other good Catholics, including some of the clergy. Such confusion in the first two-thirds of the book necessarily destroyed much of the value that the author's arguments might otherwise have had. Not all evolutionists accepted heterogenesis. Casamajor had also misinterpreted the botanical works of Charles Naudin. The abbé seemed unaware that searching in Genesis for arguments for or against evolution had been long abandoned. "The aim of the writers of Holy Writ is not to teach men scientific theories, whatever they may be." A note of scornful despair at the abbé's reasoning ended the review: Casamajor argued that the entire creation had been achieved in six times twenty-four hours; "this time being sufficient for God, He did not need centuries." "With such powerful reasoning, could not one prove anything?" No stronger warning could have been given that works defending ostensibly religious causes would not automatically receive favorable notices in Catholic scientific publications. Unless a work was solidly based on contemporary scientific disputes, it was certain that the reception would be at best an embarrassed note or, as in the case of the unfortunate abbé, a probing exposé of weaknesses.[82]

When the *Revue des questions scientifiques* published Zahm's paper at the International Scientific Congress of Catholics in 1897, it carefully drew attention to different opinions prevailing in other segments of the Catholic world. The editorial note recognized that the *Revue* had usually published essentially anti-evolutionary articles; Zahm's article was the first overtly pro-evolutionary article to appear.[83] Indicative of the editorial *crise de conscience* provoked by the opinions of this bold American, who was the United States Provincial of the Congregation of the Holy Cross from 1898 to 1906, was the editorial note's emphasis on other views. In contrast to Zahm's views, a series of articles in the Jesuit *La Civiltà cattolica* attempted to show that the teachings of Augustine, Aquinas, and Suarez on the origins of life were not favorable to evolution.[84] Somewhat uneasy over Zahm's tampering with stan-

82. It may be that the abbé's quite elementary, even naïve efforts, destined chiefly for adolescents, would not have received such attention had he not made a nuisance of himself at the meeting of the International Scientific Congress of Catholics in 1897, including an exchange with de Kirwan. The book is dedicated to Msgr. de Roverie de Cabrières, Bishop of Montpellier.

83. R. P. Zahm, C.S.P., "Evolution et théologie," *RQS* 43 (1897): 403-19, esp. p. 403.

84. *La Civiltà cattolica*, ser. 16, t. 11 (1897): 421-38, 676-91; t. 12 (1897): 168-76. These articles were published with revisions and additions by Fr. Salis Seewis, S.J., *La vera dottrina di S. Agostino, di S. Tommaso e del P. Suarez contro la generazione spontanea primitiva* (Rome, 1897). See Paul, "Religion and Darwinism: Varieties of Catholic Reaction," in Glick, ed., *Comparative Reception*, pp. 408-13. Father Davis, O.S.F., review of Zahm, *Evolution and Dogma*, in *Dublin Review* 119 (1896): 245-55; and articles of Father Clarke in the *Tablet* of November 1896. At the request of Cardinal Vaughan, Clarke was made a doctor in theology by Leo XIII. See *RQS* 43 (1898): 403.

dard Catholic teleological views, the editors recalled that according to Paul Janet's well-known work on final causes, the facts show, independently of any hypothesis, the finality present in nature.[85] This worry was quite unnecessary. Zahm concluded that teleology had not been banished from modern science and theology by contemporary research or by the theory of evolution. It had been modified but not destroyed: God was now seen as acting through secondary causes rather than directly.

If certain features of the world view of the parson-naturalists had ostensibly been dealt a death blow by Darwinism,[86] and if it seemed no longer intellectually respectable, because of new theodicy problems, to believe in the existence of God on the basis of special design, it soon became clear to acute observers that "Darwin did not destroy the argument from design. He destroyed only the watchmaker and the watch." As Asa Gray noted, Darwin, although rejecting the design argument, was always "bringing out the neatest illustrations of it." Only the finalistic type of design argument—"the creation of an animal or plant for a special purpose and for all time"—was eliminated by "the discovery that organisms change their bodies and the function of their organs. . . . The evolutionists discovered that nature 'makes things make themselves' and thus succeeded in apparently removing the need of a Master Craftsman." Only later was a more profound question asked: "Why *does* nature let things make themselves?" It was "still possible to argue for directivity in the process of life even though that directivity may be without finality in a human sense."[87]

The persistence of a strong anti-Darwinist element in French Catholic circles cannot be explained completely without recognizing the existence of strong anti-teleological and anti-religious elements in the outlook of many of the leading Darwinists. Catholic writers who tried to explain the attraction of Darwinism to most scientists usually referred to these elements, as well as to the obvious scientific advantages of Darwinism. Proost explained this attraction through the example of the German physiologist Du Bois-Reymond, who accepted natural selection as a means of getting rid of the idea of finality in nature. Since finality is irreconcilable with the intelligibility of nature, and the aim of the naturalist is to understand nature, which is assumed to be intelligible, natural selection was accepted by Du Bois-Reymond as a temporary convenience until the revelation of a new substitute order. Proost concluded, with some perversity and with a certain abandonment of logic, that materialists were drawn to Darwinism not by scientific demonstration but by their desire to jettison the God hypothesis. This ignored the fact that materialist scientists found Darwinism as useful *scientifically* as did non-materialist scientists and that Darwinism could be interpreted in an ultimately nonmaterialist as well as in a materialist fashion.[88]

85. Janet, *Les causes finales*, 2d ed. (Paris, 1882).
86. For the debt of Darwin to the natural theologians, see Walter F. Cannon, "The Bases of Darwin's Achievement: A Revaluation," *Victorian Studies* 5 (December 1961): 109–34.
87. Quotes from Eiseley, *Darwin's Century*, pp. 195–99.
88. A. Proost, "Les naturalistes philosophes," *RQS* 3 (1878): 157. Proost's remarks are based on a distinction between *Darwinisme* ("qui a la prétention d'expliquer le pour-

In a critical survey of half a century of Darwinism, the Jesuit biologist Robert Sinéty remarked in 1910 that the philosophical poverty of Darwinism about which his contemporaries complained was nearly a guarantee of its success twenty or thirty years before.[89] According to Sinéty, the claim of Darwinism to explain evolution without recourse to final causes accounted for much of its success. Before Darwin the preoccupation was with the final causes of biological phenomena; after Darwin the only interest was in the efficient determinism connecting phenomena. The enthusiastic endorsements of scientists like Alfred Giard claimed that this was the distinctive characteristic of Darwinian theory. Natural selection and adaptation, its immediate corollary, ended all interest in the question of the purpose of an organ; it had become anti-scientific to define an organ by its function; the scientist no longer had the right to admire the marvelous order and harmony of an animal body abstracted from the physico-chemical conditions that produced it. All teleological commentary had been made tautological. Such an intimate union existed between Darwinism and anti-finalism that Sinéty regretfully recognized that teleophobia, a quasi-universal disease that had raged in the community of biologists for two decades, was one of the most important reasons for the favor shown Darwinism.

Sinéty might have strengthened his case by reference to the frank arguments of another French biologist, Yves Delage. Noting that evolution, in its broadest sense, was closely allied with the idea of causality—"nothing can happen without a cause"—Delage argued, in a general survey of evolutionary theories (1909), that the "theory of causality" eliminated from human speculation all supernatural elements, thus compelling man to make explanations solely on the basis of natural factors. "It obliges him to create conceptions of the world which presuppose no miraculous act of creation, of creation from nothing." This theory had "led man to abandon... the geocentric conception of the planetary system and ... the anthropocentric viewpoint in the study of animal nature." It had also "compelled him to reject the too facile explanations offered by teleological systems and to consider causal explanations as the only satisfactory ones."[90] No philosophy could be accepted, then, except that of an a priori rejection of any role for metaphysics in biology. When Delage's *La structure du protoplasma* appeared in 1895, the reviewer for the *Revue des questions scientifiques* was very critical of the arrogant scientistic imperialism of certain biologists concerning philosophy and theology.[91] Delage considered descent "as certain as if it were objectively demon-

quoi, de formuler la loi de l'évolution organique") and *transformisme* ("qui suppose le fait sans prétendre l'expliquer"); ibid., p. 155. For further comment on the teleological issue, see Paul, "Religion and Darwinism: Varieties of Catholic Reaction," pp. 403-36, and Hull, *Darwin and His Critics*, pp. 55-66.

89. Sinéty, "Un demi-siècle de darwinisme," *RQS* 67 (1910): 5-38, 480-513.

90. Yves Delage and Marie Goldsmith, *The Theories of Evolution*, trans. André Tridon, 2d printing (New York, 1913), p. 6. Curiously if cleverly, Sinéty, *RQS* 67 (1910): 506-17, uses this work to show "le piteux échec des théories antifinalistes"; see esp. p. 511.

91. A.D., "Un mot de biologie générale. A propos d'un livre de M. Yves Delage" [*La structure du protoplasma et les théories sur l'hérédité et les grands problèmes de la biologie générale* (Paris, 1895)], *RQS* 44 (1898): 586-605.

strated," for the only other possible hypotheses were the spontaneous generation of all the higher species or their creation by some divine power. Both were nonscientific hypotheses, as unworthy of discussion by a biologist as discussion by a physicist of a theory based on the nonconservation of energy.[92] The reviewer noted that Delage, like many theoreticians, instead of expressing his reserve on questions concerning the origins and the essence of life, questions outside his competence, had simply introduced a postulate which he believed to be a negative answer effectively dismissing the questions as useless. This foolhardy procedure of ignoring neighboring disciplines did not go unpunished. Delage had joined biology to a philosophical hypothesis of scientists who, quite careful and competent in their own area, had carelessly entered the philosophical arena and had given themselves the task of clarifying the presuppositions of their hypotheses, such as those on the origin of matter and the law of finality in matter. But these are all higher metaphysical issues, not to be tackled without proper preparation, although they had to be tackled and resolved if the word evolution and others directly related were to have any meaning.[93] All the anti-clerical and usually materialistic biologists were committing the fatal error Duhem had warned about in his reply to Rey's accusation that his physics was influenced by his religious beliefs: they had not made a sharp distinction between the positivistic results of their science, which were widely regarded as free from any metaphysical assumptions, and the philosophical conclusions they interpolated because of nonscientific preconceptions and predilections.

Sinéty's survey placed great emphasis on the enormous role of anti-religious factors in the success of Darwinism. An alliance developed between Darwinism and the anti-clerical "party." This alliance was not expected as late as 1869, at least by intelligent apologists like Carbonnelle, because of the absence of any anti-religious tendency in Darwin's theory.[94] Two years later, Sinéty argued, Carbonnelle could not have taken this position, for *The Descent of Man* (1871) made it necessary to choose between the contradictory positions of the catechism and Darwin, between the idea of the immediate creation of man by God and the evolution of the whole man. "One cannot, without making an error in faith, maintain that the whole of man is the product of evolution."[95] Thus Darwin had put science and revealed religion in opposition and had given, unconsciously perhaps, the anti-religious and anti-Christian group a powerful weapon, which they were not slow to use in

92. A favorite analogy; cf. "The law of conservation of energy merely expresses the same truth in different words" as the idea of causality, which is closely allied to the idea of evolution: Delage, *The Theories of Evolution*, pp. 5–6.

93. A.D., *RQS* 44 (1898): 604–5.

94. I. Carbonnelle, "Bulletin scientifique," *E*, 4th ser. 4 (1869): 472–82. Sinéty scorns the "fâcheuse méthode apologétique" of Lavaud de Lestrade's *Transformisme et darwinisme* because of its naïve literal interpretation of Genesis and weak exegesis in general: *RQS* 67 (1910): 31n2.

95. As evident from the quarrels over Leroy's work, Sinéty grossly oversimplified the issue, a position rather typical of *Etudes* and even some Jesuits writing in the *RQS*. Although noting that Darwin was impressed by the order of the universe, presumably not the work of chance, Sinéty emphasized Darwin's agnostic prejudices and his lack of firm confidence in metaphysical reasoning (*RQS* 67 [1910]: 33).

blasting their opponents. The contemporary relevance of this alliance could easily be seen in the international popular success of Haeckel's *Riddle of the Universe*.[96] In the period of its greatest triumphs, Darwinism derived its chief support from the anti-clerical and anti-religious ranks in Germany.

The direct connection between a philosophy of science and politics was clear in the establishment of Giard's course in biological philosophy at the Sorbonne in 1888. The Municipal Council of Paris decided in 1886 to give 12,000 francs to the faculty of sciences for a "Cours de philosophie biologique (Fondation de la ville de Paris)."[97] Councillor Donnat's justification for the creation of such a course began by referring to the wisdom of the council in creating the Sorbonne professorship of the history of the French Revolution, which had been given to the staunchly Republican anti-clerical historian Aulard. It was unfortunate that the faculty of letters had not reserved a special place in its program of courses for the serious study of the most glorious period of French history. An equally serious gap existed in the faculty of sciences. The French Revolution had been a political and social revolution because of intellectual changes that had occurred since the seventeenth century. How could these progressive changes be explained except as the result of a series of various scientific discoveries that had changed the primitive views on the world, on life, and on society that had been rooted in minds by the teachings of theology and metaphysics? The origin of these ideas should also be taught at the Sorbonne.

Although astronomy had long been emancipated from the religious yoke and from subjectivity, sociology was still in the beginning stage. Donnat's *obiter dicta* on the history of science show the strong influence of the Comtian scheme. Biology was between the stages reached by astronomy and sociology; the surprising progress it had achieved had a fortunate connection with the French Revolution in Lamarck. Scientific ideas on the origin of species still faced opposition from the old and official dogmas on the fixity of species and the convenient hypothesis of successive creations, although the transformation of the species was a true scientific theory, proven by discoveries in paleontology and studies in embryology. Huxley and Fritz Müller were quoted as appropriate authorities. "The documents making up the transformist file are all drawn from observational and experimental sources, the true sources of scientific knowledge, outside which one looked in vain for the criterium of certainty."

A chair of natural philosophy would be a fitting complement of the histo-

96. *Die Welträthsel, gemeinverständliche Studien über monistische Philosophie* (Bonn, 1899), translated into French by Camille Bos, *Les énigmes de l'univers* (Paris, 1902). See "Une somme du monisme," *RCF* 30 (1902): 449–67, and "Les énigmes de l'univers," *RP*, 2e année, no. 4 (1902): 525–28.

97. "Proposition présentée par M. Léon Donnat, relativement à la création d'un cours de philosophie biologique à la Faculté des sciences de Paris," *Conseil Municipal de Paris, annexe au procès-verbal de la séance du 31 mars 1886, no. 39*. See also A. Dastre, "Une fondation de la ville de Paris à la Faculté des Sciences," *Revue internationale de l'enseignement* 16 (1888): 521–36. Many of the faculty were not happy with the ideological implications of the chair, but after eliminating the word "philosophy" from the title, they took the money.

ry of the French Revolution. Since biology was the science that best summed up man's intellectual evolution, the chair should be designated as one of philosophical biology. The chair would also be a new move by the City of Paris in higher education, an area that was its own and which it should not fail to uphold any less than its other claims to autonomy. "It is higher education that forms guiding ideas." The public mind had been misled long enough in the field of useless hypotheses; it was now time to lead it into the fertile path of positive science. A chair of biological philosophy was the best way of doing this. Eight separate justifications were carefully enumerated to explain the expenditure.

First, biological philosophy was a very French science created by Buffon, and especially by Lamarck and Etienne Geoffroy Saint-Hilaire, for whom the National Convention had created chairs at the museum. It was the Baron Cuvier with the support of Napoleon I who stopped the progress of this too-unorthodox science; Lamarck and Geoffroy died unknown and their doctrines were eliminated from the official teachings of the university. The second claim emphasized that in spite of the importance of evolutionary theory in science, Darwin and his emulators had not been dealt with at the Sorbonne except as dangerous innovators. This claim was denounced by Dastre as inaccurate and unfair. Third, in foreign universities, biological philosophy had an important place, reflecting the intrusion of evolutionary ideas into all branches of human knowledge. The implication was that linguistics, ethnology, medical science, which had been transformed by the application of these ideas, and sociology and ethics, which sought in these ideas a guide for the discovery of their laws, were all in a backward state in France. Fourth, since the scientific basis of the theory of evolution is the experimental study of living beings, in foreign universities biological philosophy was part of the sciences and was taught by such professors as Haeckel at Jena, Brühl at Vienna, Vogt at Geneva, and Cattaneo at Pavia. Fifth, in Germany there had been discussions, such as that between Haeckel and Virchow, about introducing the fundamental principles of philosophical biology into secondary education. The time was not far distant when the old philosophy taught in the German gymnasia would be replaced by ideas related to those taught in the universities. But, in the sixth place, in France the need of a complete reform of philosophical studies had hardly yet been understood. A hopeful sign was that the "école spiritualiste," attempting to rejuvenate itself with neo-Kantian injections, was opposed by a young experimental school, one of whose leaders, the sociologist Alfred Espinas, then at Bordeaux, had declared that the life sciences were sufficiently advanced to serve as the foundation of the sciences of man, which were then in a period of organization in the development of the modern mind. The seventh justification was ultrapragmatic. A clear idea of causality is rare, even among scientists, especially in the case of the complex and tangled phenomena in politics and ethics. Only experimentation could accustom the mind to appraise calmly the data of observation; philosophical biology was the most powerful generalization derived from observation. It was implied that there would be considerable value in emulating this method in dealing with political, ethical, and religious questions. Finally, a philosophical teaching established on scientific foundations could not be given in the Faculty of Letters. There were, moreover, five chairs of speculative and metaphysical philosophy at the Sorbonne. Surely it was not too much to ask that, alongside such superannuated teaching, a course of objective philosophy be established in the faculty of science, where it would be in the midst of the laboratories of the experimental sciences. In this course would be taught the master science envisaged by Francis Bacon, whose general outlines had been established in France by scientists like Buffon, Lamarck, and Geoffroy. There would be no difficulty over who would get the professorship, since the choice was already clearly indicated for the council as well as for the minister of education. The professor was proposed to the minister by the council after a commission had reported to it on the best candidate.

In 1888 Alfred Giard became *chargé de cours* ("Evolution des êtres organisés") and, in 1892, a holder of a *chaire magistrale*.[98] Giard had done his work in natural history at Roscoff, where Lacaze-Duthiers founded a zoological station. In 1873 he became the *suppléant* of Dareste in the chair of natural history at Lille and after several years the holder of the chair itself. He also taught zoology in the faculty of medicine and at the Institut industriel du Nord. He founded a laboratory in Lille and the zoological station at Wimereux (Pas-de-Calais). After being deputy mayor of Lille, he was elected to the Chamber of Deputies for the 1882–85 term. He established a serious school of zoology at Lille and trained a series of naturalists like Ch. Barrois, J. Barrois, P. Hallez, de Moniez, L. Dollo, and P. Pelseneer. In 1886–88 he was back at Lille; this was the period of the formation of zoologists like J. Bonnier and E. Canu. While the Sorbonne fought against or ignored the new ideas developed abroad in favor of evolutionary theories, Giard's teaching and work were especially influenced by Haeckel's *Generelle Morphologie*. Giard curiously put himself among the most enthusiastic disciples of Lamarck, although he liked the method of Darwin better. After his death in 1908 the journal he had founded in 1874, the *Bulletin scientifique de la France et de la Belgique*, described him as "Darwin, crossbred with Renan," although he did not like Renan. "The sad austerity of Darwin contrasted with Giard's smiling skepticism; he was essentially French, but the brilliant levity of our race did not detract from his profundity." But the impressive scientific qualifications of Giard and his service to the Republic through his forays into politics were not the only things making him an attractive candidate for the new chair created by the municipal government of Paris. Giard shared the anti-religious outlook fashionable among republicans in this period, and his position was public knowledge. The new Jerusalem would be built upon the foundations of science.[99]

98. See *Bulletin scientifique* . . . 42 (March 6, 1909), for the following information. The *Bulletin* was one of the publications of the Station zoologique de Wimereux. "Sans négliger aucune des parties des sciences biologiques, la direction s'attache surtout à publier des travaux ayant trait à l'évolution (ontogénie et phylogénie) des êtres vivants. Les recherches relatives à l'éthologie et à la distribution géographique dans leurs rapports avec la théorie de la descendance occupent aussi une large place dans le *Bulletin*."

99. "Parmi les manifestations les plus heureuses de l'esprit public en cette fin de siècle,

In addition to being a good scientist, Giard, like Berthelot and Delage, would proclaim the secular gospel to the young minds entrusted to his care, inspiring students to be good secular republican missionaries who would carry on the battle against the clerical forces of darkness. Not many of the Sorbonne's professors spiced up their science with anti-clerical *obiter dicta* that the politicians could use as scientistic components of the republican ideology.

Catholics generally thought that the faculties of sciences and of medicine as well as the Grandes Ecoles supported the position that the church is an enemy of intellectual progress because she rejects a scientific doctrine shown to be true. By 1888, according to Giard, this struggle between the church and science had entered a new phase. Faced with the fact of adoption of the evolutionary hypothesis by Catholics like Albert Gaudry, Giard declared that the church had passed from the first phase of fighting against evolution by word and fire to a second phase of showing that the doctrine was not really progress and that Scripture had always contained this so-called novelty.[100] In addition to expressing his astonishment that Giard, in the opening lecture of his course, should have proclaimed this nonsense from a chair at the Sorbonne, Sinéty noted that several works of popularization attacking religion and doing little honor to science had come out of Giard's circle. Giard himself condemned works of popularization, whether for or against evolution, on the grounds of their uselessness and incompetence. But, curiously, science provided a common ground for the meeting of the anti-religious and the religious: Giard, like Huxley, always welcomed those who came to work under him even if they were members of the clergy. "He forgot his anti-religious ideas and knew how to be the most sympathetic of friends and the most encouraging of teachers. Those who knew him well cannot forget him."[101] There were good scientific reasons, Sinéty recognized, for adopting evolution, but there were also reasons of a quite different order that would be ad-

il faut compter la tendance qu'a la science à prendre peu à peu la place et le rôle que tenait jusqu'ici la religion. Tel, qui naguère eut richement doté une église ou un monastère fonde un observatoire astronomique; tel qui eut entrepris un pèlerinage en Terre sainte ou une croisade, organise un voyage de recherches scientifiques dans les régions encore inexplorées": "Le laboratoire de Portal, les grandes et les petites stations maritimes," *Bulletin scientifique* 20 (1889): 298–314. For a Catholic complaint against the affluent and powerful Association française pour l'avancement des Sciences, see Abbé Hamard, "Le Congrès de Blois et l'homme tertiaire," *La Controverse et le contemporain,* n.s. 2 (November 1884): 483–87. After its merging with the Association scientifique founded by Le Verrier, it had a capital of about 700,000 francs and 5,000 members. The anti-clericals carried out several petty maneuvers against Catholics in the society.

100. *RQS* 67 (1910): 35. A. Hovelacque, "L'Eglise et le transformisme," *Revue internationale des sciences* 1 (1878): 385–87, predicted the acceptance of evolution by the church; this was an extrapolation from the concessions made by Fabre d'Envieu, Valroger, and Monsabré on the antiquity of man.

101. Sinéty knew Giard, who was one of the examiners at the defense of his thesis, *Recherches sur la biologie et l'anatomie des phasmes* (Lierre, 1901) published with the advice and encouragement of Giard himself: *RQS* 67 (1910); 36. Cf. the relations between le R. P. G. Hahn, S.J., and Huxley; see Hahn, "Thomas Henry Huxley," *RQS* 38 (1895): 467–521, and "Huxley et M. de Varigny," *RQS* 39 (1896): 572–75, criticizing de Varigny's oversimplifications on Huxley.

mitted by an honest person. Delage frankly admitted that he was absolutely convinced that one is an evolutionist *not* for reasons based on natural history but on the grounds of philosophical opinions.[102]

Unfortunately, Sinéty noted, no perceptible change in the anti-religious outlook occurred, at least in France, when Darwinism was substantially modified, if not nearly abandoned, in favor of a doctrine vaguely designated neo-Lamarckian.[103] Giard, who had created a Janus-like cult of both Lamarck and Darwin, was, in Sinéty's opinion, a ferocious anti-finalist. Sinéty also viewed Delage's system, a "theory of present causes," a mixture including Darwinian and Lamarckian ideas, as overtly mechanistic and anti-finalist. It seems that Sinéty was assuming that a mechanistic view necessarily involved an anti-teleological view as well. This was not true in the case of Giard, who was a mechanist in Bütschi's sense of the word but neutral on the teleological problem.[104] Sinéty found the Sorbonne biologist Le Dantec's theories so arbitrary as to vitiate whatever might have been scientifically useful in his system. Le Dantec was notoriously anti-finalist and anti-religious.[105] But the religious "cause" could profit considerably from the luxuriant confusion of theories dividing contemporary general biology, especially on the issue of evolution. Against the mechanistic Darwinists and anti-finalist neo-Lamarckians were aligned the vitalistic biologists, who were generally Lamarckian, and the finalist neo-Lamarckians. The neo-Lamarckians were, of course, divided over "the true causes of evolution." Arguing that outside finalism there was no possible explanation of evolution and that the theory of selection had become scientifically inadmissible, Gustav Wolff opposed both Darwinians and

102. Yves Delage, *La structure du protoplasma*, p. 184.

103. Conry, *Darwinisme*, pp. 39–40, points out the transformation of Lamarck from a precursor of Darwin to a rival of Darwin. The resurgence of Lamarckism between 1870 and 1873 is not without a connection to French nationalism, but the determinants were scientific: pathological anatomy and cell theory. Sinéty also deals with neo-Darwinism—a rather ambiguous term, he notes, including "le sélectionnisme germinal de Weismann et le mutationnisme de Vries": *RQS* 67 (1910): 490–96.

104. See Giard, "Néovitalisme et finalité en biologie," communication to the Second International Congress of Philosophy, Geneva, 1904, reprinted in part in *RP* (November 1, 1904), pp. 576–80, and reviewed in Paul Vignon, *Doctrines et opinions relatives à la philosophie biologique* (Montligeon, 1905), pp. 30–31, a work that had also appeared in *RP* in December 1904.

105. *RQS* 67 (1910): 105*n*1; Sinéty cites with relish the devastating judgment of Delage and Goldsmith, who concluded that Le Dantec's bold conceptions and novel vistas were really "mere intellectual gymnastics, academic juggling with difficult problems" (*The Theories of Evolution*, p. 270). Charles de Kirwan appreciated Le Dantec's politely stated arguments as compared with the insulting approach of Haeckel to his opponents. See his review of Le Dantec's *L'unité dans l'être vivant, essai d'une biologie chimique* (Paris, 1902), in *RQS* 52 (1902): 405–41. But de Kirwan dismissed Le Dantec's *Les lois naturelles, réflexions d'un biologiste sur les sciences* (Paris, 1904) as a sort of extended apology for Haeckel's monism, in *RQS* 56 (1904): 636–41. In a lecture to the general assembly of the Société scientifique de Bruxelles in 1905, V. Grégoire implied that in comparison with Hans Driesch, Gustav Wolff, and others, Le Dantec was an office biologist, not engaged in original research, and specifically designated him as belonging to the class of publicists who confuse a biological treatise with a "roman à thèse." See Grégoire, "Le mouvement antimécaniciste en biologie," *RQS* 58 (1905): 385–416. Joseph Grasset attacked Le Dantec and monism in his unfinished posthumous work *Le "Dogme" transformiste* (Paris, 1919).

anti-finalist Lamarckians.[106] Sinéty found the claims of the neovitalistic school of the psychobiologists like August Pauly, Raoul Francé, and Adolph Wagner, who admitted that *everything living* has a "soul" with psychic faculties, intelligence, and will, simply a wild exaggeration of a perfectly true doctrine. It did not seem wildly improbable that the old Darwinists themselves might evolve and join the ranks of the Pauly-Francé school. Catholics, who are finalistic theists, would then have to fight only the finalistic pantheists, who identified mind and matter. Following Wolff and others, Sinéty asked whether evolution, deprived of its chief support by the ruin of Darwinism, now lacked scientific proof. His reply was really the standard reply for most Catholic scientists since the scientific utility of evolution had become clear over a generation earlier. Universal evolution, asserting the unlimited variability of matter and an uninterrupted evolution from a monocellular being up to man, had arrived at an impasse. But a more limited evolutionary theory was acceptable: "independently of the theory of natural selection, the truth of a certain evolution of organic forms can be established," although the proofs of this evolution needed revision because they still rested on the ruins of Darwinism.[107] The new revisionism would not only eliminate all the elements of evolutionary theory clashing with religion but would probably make it a complementary doctrine, at least in its philosophical dimensions.

It could hardly be expected that Catholic intellectuals like Meignan would be in the vanguard of those switching scientific paradigms, especially when the old paradigms synchronized so well with conventional interpretations of the Mosaic hypothesis. It is significant that as the evolutionary hypothesis gained more support in the scientific community, the opposition to it by clerical intellectuals dropped off.[108] Indeed, by the first decade of the twentieth century, the avant-garde had developed such an affinity for using evolutionary derivatives in their historical and theological writings that the more traditionally minded custodians of orthodoxy took fright and, by the use of

106. Much used by Sinéty, Wolff's studies appeared in the *Biologisches Zentralblatt* in 1890. See *Der gegenwärtige Stand des Darwinismus* (Leipzig, 1896), *Beiträge zur Kritik der Darwin'schen Lehre* (Leipzig, 1898), and *Die Begründung der Abstammungslehre* (Munich, 1907).

107. Sinéty, *RQS* 67 (1910): 513. M. le docteur H. Lebrun, "Quelques faits de transformisme expérimental," *RQS* 72 (1912): 5-33, points out that one should really speak of a crisis of materialistic Darwinism—natural selection, the struggle for life, the survival of the fittest—rather than the crisis of evolution talked about especially in materialist circles. But it was a popular topic in Catholic circles as well, although a cause for rejoicing rather than regret. See Sinéty, "Les preuves et les limites du transformisme," *RCF* 72 (1912): 445-68; and R. P. L. Mélizan, O.P., "La crise du transformisme," *RT* 21 (1913), no. 1, pp. 64-71; no. 2, pp. 189-202; no. 6, pp. 641-54; *RT* 22 (1914), no. 5, pp. 636-51; *RT* 23-25 (1918-20), no. 6, pp. 39-61, 180-91, 251-70. Mélizan's articles, in spite of a notorious anti-evolutionary bias, are quite useful for a treatment of the intellectual and religious implications of evolution.

108. Of course, from the 1860s on, Darwinism was solidly established in a significant segment of the scientific community. Some of the leading European pioneer defenders of Darwinism, even applied to man, were Karl Vogt, Ludwig Büchner, Friedrich Rolle, Ernst Haeckel, G. Canestrini, and G. Pouchet, a selection that shows the European nature of support for Darwinism. In France, from the 1870s on, the new generation of biologists, like Alfred Giard and Yves Delage, were enthusiastic though not uncritical disciples of Darwin.

the power apparatus they controlled, tried to curb the enthusiasm of the neophytes for the current scientific theories. Certainly, the correlation of the eternal verities with the latest scientific theory had its disadvantages as well as its advantages. It was the misfortune of Meignan's generation that it could not see the problem because they, like most scientists, conceived of science as a set of eternal truths, comparable to Holy Writ in the religious sphere, rather than as a set of paradigms that could be jettisoned or substantially modified once their usefulness had been outlived. It was the misfortune of the generation succeeding Meignan's that the guardians of orthodoxy in the church insisted on the interaction of theology and a science firmly anchored in pre-Darwinian paradigms of natural history.

To the clerical community of Meignan's generation, Darwinism seemed philosophically absurd. In deriving the more perfect from the less perfect, Darwinism was in effect deriving being from nothing, an abomination in the eyes of many Catholic philosophers. Like atheism, Darwinism assumed an effect without a cause, or so Meignan interpreted the role of chance in producing the "magnificent series of living beings." Because of his unique ability to take cognizance of himself, man possesses the intellectual powers that make him the master of nature and lead him to knowledge of God, to the distinction between good and evil, to hope for immortality, and to belief in punishments and rewards. Between animal intelligence and that of man there is an unbridgeable gulf.[109] Man occupies a special place in nature because he alone is a free moral being and he alone knows God rather than because he is separated from the higher animals by a species barrier. Meignan could enthusiastically endorse de Quatrefages' concept of a human kingdom in nature along with the mineral, vegetable, and animal kingdoms. "Let us congratulate ourselves on thus seeing the progress of science more and more confirming biblical anthropology. Science leads to truth; revelation emanates from truth. Hopefully, in the near future these two sisters will no longer fight one another but will know . . . how to recognize, respect, and love one another."[110] Here Meignan was echoing the Catholic dream of Maistre and Gratry, a dream that would also be that of Teilhard de Chardin, on a future symbiosis of science and religion: "The tension [of science and religion] is prolonged, the conflict visibly seems to need to be resolved in terms of an entirely different form of equilibrium—not in elimination, nor duality, but in synthesis. After close on two centuries of passionate struggles, neither science nor faith has succeeded in discrediting its adversary. On the contrary, it becomes obvious that neither can develop normally without the other. And the reason is simple: the same life animates both. Neither in its impetus nor its achievements can science go to its limits without becoming tinged with mysticism and charged with faith. . . . Religion and science are the two conjugated faces or

109. Lecomte, *Le darwinisme*, p. 246, put forward articulated language as one essential difference between man and monkey. He rejected Darwin's idea on the formation of language as well as E. Dally's suggestion, in *L'ordre des primates et le transformisme* (Paris, 1869), that the big monkeys have the faculty of language but they have not used it because they do not need it.

110. Meignan, *Le monde et l'homme primitif*, p. 194.

phases of one and the same act of complete knowledge—the only one which can embrace the past and future of evolution so as to contemplate, measure, and fulfill them. In the mutual reinforcement of these two still opposed powers, in the conjunction of reason and mysticism, the human spirit is destined, by the very nature of its development, to find the uttermost degree of its penetration with the maximum of its vital force."[111] But this symbiosis could only be achieved by accepting the current evolutionary paradigm of the scientific community. It would therefore be the achievement of a new generation of Catholic intellectuals. The question that remains to be answered is how did the Catholic intellectual community come to accept the evolutionary paradigm that would be the basis of the Teilhardian synthesis.

111. Teilhard de Chardin, *The Phenomenon of Man*, cited in James M. Connolly, *The Voices of France. A Survey of Contemporary Theology in France* (New York, 1961), p. 125.

3

Evolution: The Road to Acceptance

"Spéculativement, je suis de ceux qui ne voudraient abandonner ni Moïse ni Darwin."

Lachelier, cited in Conry, *Darwinisme*, p. 409.

In spite of Pius IX's delight with Constantin James' anti-Darwinian diatribe *Du darwinisme ou l'homme-singe* (1877), Catholicism cannot automatically be equated with hostility toward evolution or even Darwinism. There existed throughout the nineteenth century a strong degree of support in certain Catholic circles for evolutionary concepts in biology and even outside science. Teilhard de Chardin was not a total novelty on the French Catholic scene. He had many honorable ancestors in nineteenth-century France. As the Comte Bégouën pointed out, Catholic evolutionary thought was hard to detect because a good deal of it, especially the clerical segment, was clandestine, although this was not true after the 1880s for the clergy who accepted it as an exclusively scientific hypothesis.[1] The clandestine activity is explained by the exploitation of evolution by anti-clericals and the not unrelated hostility of most of the intransigent hierarchy in the church to evolutionary ideas. The hostility of the powerful integrists to evolution was still a factor in explaining the care with which many Catholic intellectuals dealt with evolution well into the twentieth century. Bégouën's father wrote a little work in 1879, *La création évolutive*, arguing that the principle of the creation and the theory of evolution are not mutually exclusive and can be reconciled. What made the work more significant than any single defense of evolution by an ostensibly apostate Catholic was the fact that Canon Duilhé de Saint-Projet, who

1. Comte Bégouën (Chargé de cours de préhistoire à l'université de Toulouse), *Quelques souvenirs sur le mouvement des idées transformistes dans les milieux catholiques, suivi de la mentalité spiritualiste des premiers hommes* (Paris, 1945). An important Catholic treatment of Catholicism and evolution is P.-M. Périer, *Le transformisme. L'origine de l'homme et le dogme catholique. Etude apologétique* (Paris, 1938).

became rector of the Catholic University of Toulouse, gave him advice on matters related to religion and Emile Cartailhac gave him advice on some scientific matters. The Bégouën household was an intellectual center in Toulouse where believers and nonbelievers, evolutionists and *fixistes* met on neutral territory to discuss the great issues of the day. Bégouën *père* had an extensive correspondence with French and foreign scientists. "A convinced and fervent Catholic, he even found in his faith reasons for not fearing new theories of which he was a public partisan."[2]

Bégouën *père* recognized that "the laws of the Darwinian school" are true within certain limits, although clear and logical only for whoever sees them as the instrument of divine will. The "law of progress" from inorganic matter to man is summed up in Genesis and could have been achieved through a God-directed evolution. After referring to the evidence for evolution in horticulture and in comparative anatomy, Bégouën concluded that God could have created each species by a modification just as well as by the creation of each in a fixed form.[3] The idea of evolution is incomplete without the idea of God. In formulating his laws, Darwin had attributed to matter an independence it does not have. Moses had laid the bases for the progressive system: "Like Darwin, Moses shows the progression of being and demonstrates the successive organization of matter." Bégouën recalled that Haeckel had made the same point in his history of the creation, but this was hardly likely to strengthen his argument for Catholics. Evolutionary doctrine could be accepted by Catholics, not as a blind autonomous force of matter alone but as the slow continuous action of the logical and rational divine will, simple in its means of action. Bégouën wielded Occam's razor freely in insisting on the necessity of the idea of God: it replaced so many other laborious hypotheses used to explain the numerous mysteries that appear when one tries to get rid of a single mystery by explaining man without a soul and the universe without God. Although Bégouën's arguments were an ingenious and advanced move within Catholic circles at the time, his ingenuity succeeded in joining together what others would have to rend asunder—the theological and scientific aspects of the issue—before evolution could be given a fair hearing by most Catholic intellectuals. Probably because of the retrograde nature of Bégouën's ideas, practically nothing was ever said by Catholic evolutionists about his work during the debates of the last quarter of the nineteenth century.

One of the best late-nineteenth-century works on the various scientific problems arising out of research on the nature and development of life was

2. Bégouën, *Quelques souvenirs*, pp. 17–18.
3. "La toute puissance de Dieu est aussi grande, sa volonté aussi nettement déterminée, si pour créer l'éléphant, il s'est borné à modifier une molécule du *protoplasme* du germe d'un proboscidien de nos régions, que s'il avait intercalé violemment le gigantesque animal avec sa femelle au milieu des forêts de l'Afrique ou de l'Asie": Le Cte. Bégouën, *La création évolutive* (Toulouse, 1879), p. 26. Bégouën appréciated Darwin's genius in natural history although he complained that Darwin was swept away by the very subtlety of his intelligence and his desire to have a philosophical thesis triumph. He also made some technical criticisms of Darwin's theory of the variability of species and the idea of sexual selection.

by Denys Cochin, a Catholic whose early scientific work took him into the laboratories of Schutzenberger and Pasteur but who veered off into a political career noted for its devotion to Catholic causes. In spite of his sympathy and scientific support for a good many features of Darwinism, Cochin argued that the hypothesis of universal evolution was a scientifically indefensible doctrine. An absurdity resulted when the doctrine was joined to agnosticism, not uncommon in England, France, and Germany, although few reached the elevated heights attained by the agnostic pontiffs, Huxley, Le Dantec, and Haeckel.[4]

In judging evolution according to the data of natural science, Cochin concluded that the doctrine either falsified the evidence or exaggerated it. What the evolutionist.was really arguing for was a universal mechanical system. This was an impossible task because chemistry had not been reduced to mechanics, and physiology could never be explained by chemistry—chemical synthesis had not derived an organized germ from inorganic matter. Although alcohol and urea had each been made by a synthetic process, higher organic matter had not. Cochin did not think that the transformation of the animal species had been demonstrated with scientific certainty. Yet universal evolution assumed this hypothesis along with the even weaker hypothesis of spontaneous generation. Cochin recognized that there were good arguments in favor of the evolution of species, that is, an evolution restricted to the living world, but he thought that these arguments were completely contrary to the theory of universal evolution. Thus it was nonsensical to explain in terms of mechanics and chemistry the prodigious phenomena resulting from the law of heredity, one of the chief arguments in favor of the evolution of the species. The more partial evolution, restricted to the living world, would be verified, the more universal evolution would be disproved. The evolutionists had to be fought with their own weapons. Cochin argued that their chief mistake was to ask too much of science and to falsify its laws. Their agnostic brothers made the great mistake of accepting only the conclusions of the observational sciences. But Cochin insisted that observation and experiment have a limited role even in the experimental sciences; imagination and reason play the most important role. Cochin preferred the sanity of Aristotelian psychology to the exaggerations of some of the moderns.[5]

In contrast to Meignan, who had based his opinion on contemporary scientists like de Quatrefages, Cochin applauded Darwin's speculation about the Creator's giving life to possibly one or more primitive beings, which then developed into a magnificent variety of forms.[6]

4. Denys Cochin, *L'évolution et la vie* (Paris, 1886). A third edition was brought out in 1888. In 1886, the philosopher Caro praised it highly in a report to the Académie des sciences morales et politiques: "Qu'est-ce que l'évolution? Une pure hypothèse ... sans preuves ... ne tendant à rien moins qu'à faire rentrer dans la même série continue tous les phénomènes soit vitaux, soit matériels, soit physiques ... tous ne seraient que des modes différents de la force transformée. Nous ignorons, d'après la doctrine agnostique, ce qu'est une force, et ce qu'est une sensation; mais nous devons croire, d'après la doctrine d'évolution, que la sensation n'est que la force transformée. L'inconnu est égal à l'inconnu.... Telle est l'absurde formule de ces deux doctrines associées" (Cochin, p. 11).

5. Ibid., pp. 1΄-14.

6. "Quelle belle pensée! D'un côté le Créateur commande à la matière morte. Une loi

Cochin thought that there had been simply too much of an intellectual storm over the restricted type of evolution in Darwinism. No doubt aware of the innumerable, tedious, and heated objections of religious inspiration, Cochin insisted that the chief questions involved were questions that could be answered only by scientists. Cochin was pleased by the optimistic belief in progress he found in Darwin. "He [Darwin] believes in a continual tendency towards perfection, without turning back. If it is claimed that he offers us monkeys for ancestors, at least he promises that we won't have them for children. He is an optimist like Spencer, like Haeckel, and . . . like Renan."[7] Cochin has moved a long distance from the uncompromising hostility of Meignan and Lecomte toward acceptance of any part of Darwinism.

Cochin insisted that Darwinism did not exclude the principle of final causes or the idea of a Creator. Indeed, it could be interpreted to confirm both. "The great fact of the struggle for existence followed by the triumph of the most beautiful and the strongest beings has its finality: it is the means by which life cloaks the general and indefinite perfection of forms. The intervention of a Creator is made certain by this intelligent step assigned to nature. Just as so many phenomena formerly attributed to the direct action of the divine will have been recognized as the effects of laws or of secondary causes, so now it is necessary to consider the appearance and progressive variations of a living species as the effect of natural laws." Darwin himself provided the basis of Cochin's argument: "Authors of the highest eminence seem to be fully satisfied with the view that each species has been independently created. To my mind [Darwin's] it accords better with what we know of the laws impressed on matter by the Creator, that the production and extinction of the past and present inhabitants of the world should have been due to secondary causes, like those determining the birth and death of the individual." To clinch his case, Cochin reminded his readers that Lamarck had made essentially the same argument.[8]

---

immuable s'établit, les mêmes mouvements se répètent invariablement à travers les siècles. Mais, d'autre part, il crée la vie: et la loi qu'il lui donne est d'un autre ordre. C'est une loi de progrès. Une puissance se développera bientôt en des êtres innombrables: elle attirera en eux la matière environnante, la contraignant à entrer en des combinaisons chimiques, jusqu'alors inconnues, à se prêter à des fonctions très complexes, à revêtir des formes infiniment variées. Saisis par la vie l'eau, l'air, le carbone, iront tantôt réparer des muscles et tantôt renouveler des feuillages. Ils deviendront muraille dans le tronc du chêne, ressort dans le jarret du cheval ou du cerf, cuirasse d'écailles chez les poissons. La vieille planète tourne toujours, et cependant son écorce tressaille, fleurit, s'anime. Les descendants du premier germe ont peuplé sa surface. Ils se sont pliés à toutes les conditions, armés contre toutes les difficultés, vêtus suivant tous les climats; ils sont devenus de plus en plus beaux, forts, aptes à l'existence; car, pour cette foule sans cesse grossissante et proliférante, la place était trop petite, et les moins beaux, les moins forts, les moins bien appropriés à leur destinée devaient succomber dans la lutte. Tout le monde vivant est sorti de ce premier germe, jeté tout seul sur la terre déserte, mais animé du souffle du Créateur" (ibid., pp. 204–5).

7. Ibid., pp. 269–70.

8. Ibid., pp. 270–71 (quote from Darwin, *Origin of Species*, p. 428). "Sans doute rien ne peut exister que par la volonté du sublime auteur de toutes choses. Mais pouvons-nous lui assigner des règles dans l'exécution de sa volonté et fixer le mode qu'il a suivi à cet égard? Sa puissance infinie n'a-t-elle pu créer un *ordre de choses* qui donnât successive-

Those who damned or glorified Darwin as an atheist and a materialist were all strangely deluded. He was not a German pedant proclaiming a new dogma of matter; nor was he a freethinker in the new French fashion, a deliberate atheist, a declared democrat inclined to consider evolutionary theory as the new principles of 1789 for the animal kingdom. The conservative Cochin admired Darwin the conservative country gentleman, who was also a "connaisseur émérite" rather than a simple classifier like Charles Martins. Cochin found that Darwinism could easily accommodate the doctrine of final causes. "The living world is ruled in a general way by final causes, in the sense that the triumph of the most beautiful, the strongest, of the best armed in the struggle for food and reproduction assures the improvement and embellishment of the species." The final cause does not exist for the particular advantage of an individual but is general and leads to the preservation and constant improvement of the species. In his analysis of Darwin, Cochin accepted without any difficulty the reasonableness of a struggle in nature, of natural selection, and of sexual selection, all ideas that had caused many other Catholic commentators such anguish. When Cochin did criticize features of Darwinism, he did it with polite moderation. The Darwinian picture of nature would have pleased him completely if Darwin did not sometimes defend a thesis and also if Darwin were not so attached to his favorite paradox of finding human feelings in the animal world. In Darwinian sexual selection, Cochin found the a priori idea that we must seek in this activity the origin and first manifestation of our idea of the beautiful. After referring to some of the standard objections to Darwinian sexual esthetics, Cochin observed that the activities of animals were far from showing a knowledge of the beautiful. "I believe that nature is, on the one hand, under the domination of law, and, on the other hand, capable of ruling the empire of beauty. I firmly believe that these two things, scientific law and beauty, are accessible only to the mind of man and that by means of these two equally noble languages he is the only living being who converses with his creator."[9] Cochin insisted that there is no intermediary between man and the animal world; the mind that is conscious of itself and possesses the idea of good has no connection with the mind lacking these two characteristics. But Cochin hastened to add that these ideas were the least important although the most sensational of Darwin's hypotheses.

Cochin went far beyond simply showing the accord of most of Darwin's scientific hypotheses with religion. Stock objections to much of Darwinism included the accusations that it was not based on enough facts, that it was impossible to come to such conclusions about the modifications of species on the basis of such a short time span, and that Darwinism contained nothing resembling a true scientific experiment. Most objections of a scientific nature could be overcome, Cochin argued, by having recourse to the world of bacteria; this would give to the Darwinian system the regulation of true experiments, and all the difficulties resulting from the unmanageable nature of the

ment l'existence à tout ce qui existe et que nous ne connaissons pas?" (Lamarck, *Zoologie philosophique*, cited in Cochin, p. 271).

9. Cochin, pp. 280, 292.

slow effect of environment, imperceptible heredity changes, and the need for vast amounts of time, as well as other problems, would disappear.[10] The scientific work done by Pasteur and others had already ridiculed the hypothesis of spontaneous generation; the gap between inorganic matter and the living cell could not be bridged. Cochin also argued that the proof of various doctrines mingled under the name Darwinism would add further evidence on the opposition existing between the laws of life and the laws of inorganic matter, and the argument could be turned against the theory of universal evolution. "This theory needs transformism. In good logic such a contradiction is sufficient to enable us to say that the theory of universal evolution is not true."[11]

Cochin's general complaint was against positivist philosophy. It had exaggerated and falsified the data of experiment, and, in boasting that it was carrying science to its highest degree of generality, undertook to explain all phenomena by the same cause. Cochin did not think that there was any scientific basis for representing the inorganic universe as if it were living and thinking, a sort of great being animated by one force, producing crystals, plants, men, and societies by the same procedures and according to the same laws. There is no continuity in the sense the positivists thought. "We cannot understand the evolution of the inorganic world without the creation of ponderable matter, or the evolution of the living world without the creation of a first germ." Nor could the evolution of the moral world be understood without assuming the creation of a thinking and feeling soul. Ponderable matter, the living germ, and the intelligent soul had been the objects of three separate creations by God, for they could not be derived from each other. Each had its own special laws which man could understand through experiment and observation, as in the case of the Darwinian and Lamarckian explanations of life. To see a radical difference between the doctrine of special creation and that of evolution would be to fall into anthropomorphism, subjecting the eternal God to the laws of time. But did experimental science allow a belief in three special creations, each restricted to one world? Cochin said that he saw few reasons for not assuming three creations, and it seemed possible to deduce in each of the three worlds the series of phenomena making up its particular evolution. This interpretation of nature seemed to conform best to the data of science. In a piece of delightful perversity, Cochin advised combing the works of Spencer, *bête noire* of Catholics, for evidence of the three-creations hypothesis in spite of Spencer's adherence to the dogma of universal evolution. "We must recognize and admire Spencer's wealth of information and keenness of observation lavishly supporting such theses."[12] Such are the contradictions and surprises of the nineteenth-century Catholic intellectual world: many of the clerical intellectuals were heaping anathema on Darwinism and Spencerism while a scientist and an intellectual who was emerging as a leading Catholic layman and politician was recommending in

10. For the development of this ingenious proposal, see ibid., pp. 302–15.
11. Ibid., p. 315.
12. Ibid., pp. 335, 338–39. Spencer's works were recommended by the ministry of education for inclusion in school libraries and as prizes. Conry, *Darwinisme*, pp. 17–18*n*17.

one of the most important books of the decade of the 1880s the reading of Darwin and Spencer for scientific confirmation of the glories of the creation and the wisdom of the Creator.

One favorable reaction to Cochin's book came from the bastion of materialistic Darwinism, the Société d'anthropologie, in its journal. D. R. Collignon did a comparative review of Cochin's book and Blanchard's *La vie des êtres animés,* which had been serialized in the *Revue des Deux Mondes.*[13] Blanchard argued against evolution, viewing it as a chimerical conception, simply a novel. Collignon characterized Blanchard's arguments as those of an office naturalist, dependent more on feeling than on the scientific rigor characteristic of Cochin's work. All of Blanchard's arguments in favor of the admirable adaptation of each species to its present mode of life by the Creator showed better a progressive, natural adaptation of organs to functions, which was a simpler and more rational view in Collignon's opinion. And Fontenelle had an answer to Blanchard's famous challenge for anyone to show him an example of the evolution of a species. "Hélas! de mémoire de rose on n'a jamais vu mourir un jardinier." Cochin's acceptance of even a partial evolution limited to living beings was enthusiastically greeted by Collignon, even though Cochin did not go far enough. A great gulf really separated the two scientists on the issue of universal evolution. Collignon did not think that the synthesis of really organic products, albumins and sugar, was beyond the capability of chemistry, especially in light of the work already done by Löwig.[14] But Collignon admitted that except for Löwig's synthesis of glucose, Cochin's conclusions were correct, "in the present state of science." Collignon's disagreement was therefore essentially based on an optimistic belief that the great scientific hurdles to belief in universal evolution—the impossibility or difficulty of organic synthesis and the internal dissymmetry of organic substances— would eventually be scientific conquests like those that had occurred during the preceding fifty years in the chemistry of carbon. There was no compromise possible between Cochin's belief that the first particle of life was the result of a creation and Collignon's belief that it was the result of a "natural formation." Although Collignon rejected the idea of spontaneous generation as scientifically inadmissible, he rejected the deist hypothesis because it was mysterious. Following Spencer on the impossibility of scientifically observing the incognoscible and resigning himself to lack of knowledge about first causes, Collignon argued that since he had to be content with a hypothesis he would choose the simplest, a unit of energy, a unit of matter whose origin would simply be accepted as having been natural; to introduce a first cause would only introduce another mystery needing explanation. But these disagreements were not scientific. The striking fact was that Cochin and Collignon were largely in agreement on strictly scientific grounds. A Catholic and

13. D. R. Collignon, *Revue d'anthropologie,* 3d ser. 4 (1889): 78–83.

14. "Du procédé décrit par Löwig [*Journal für prakt. Chemie* 83:133] . . . . dans lequel l'oxalate d'éthyle, qui, lui, peut se fabriquer directement, mis en contact à une température élevée avec l'amalgame de sodium, abandonne, après traitement par l'éther et précipitation par l'eau, une masse grise qui est un mélange d'oxalate de soude et de glucose parfaitement fermentescibles. Voilà, ou je me trompe fort, une synthèse remplissant les conditions demandées" (ibid., p. 79).

an agnostic or atheist could come to a remarkably similar set of scientific conclusions. The disagreement with Blanchard was interesting because he represented the opposition of the fading old guard. This contrast between the views of Cochin and Blanchard is even more significant because the latter had no Catholic ulterior motives for his opposition to Darwinism. On strictly scientific grounds, the anti-religious segment of the scientific community easily found itself in essential agreement with the Catholic segment once both groups put aside philosophical and theological questions. But this agreement proved exceedingly difficult to expand because of complicating ideological and political reasons.

In the 1880s it was somewhat avant-garde for any of the clergy to support evolution, even when hedged with proclamations of total religious orthodoxy. Thus the Dominican Dalmas Leroy's pro-evolutionary work in 1887 was a sensation in the French Catholic world, although it carried some official approval. Leroy thought that the idea of evolution would follow the same path as the Galileo case: "after having first enraged the orthodox, truth, free of extremist exaggerations, would triumph when tempers cooled."[15] Looking at the issue from the religious viewpoint, Leroy did not believe that there was anything in Scripture or Catholic teaching contrary to evolution. Hyacinthe de Valroger, whose anti-evolutionary ideas Leroy did not share, had established the liberty of discussion for science. Drawing upon St. Basil and St. Augustine, Valroger showed that there was nothing in Scripture about *how* God produced species.[16] Leroy added that St. Thomas Aquinas and the scholastics believed in the fixity of species only from a metaphysical and logical viewpoint. Their definitions of species and genus were remote from those of the modern physiologist. To show the danger of using the ideas of the scholastics in a modern context, Leroy recalled their belief in spontaneous generation and the derivation of living forms from matter.[17] Any argument against evolution based on the authority of the fathers and doctors of the church was of extremely dubious value. The debate had to be placed firmly in its modern context. The method used by the Supreme Architect to create the universe was a matter of conjecture, completely open to scientific investigation.

Leroy emphasized that the chief credit for the evolutionary hypothesis went to Darwin, who was not exempt from all blame for the idea that the creation of the organic world and natural laws and forces could be explained without reference to God. Leroy was quite conventional and orthodox in accepting the idea of a universe planned, created, and ordered by a divine intelligence. The birth of the organic world through the working of natural agents required infinitely more genius than its direct creation. Acceptance of the

15. Le P. M.-D. Leroy, des frères prêcheurs, *L'évolution des espèces organiques* (Paris, 1887), p. 10; Approbation du T. R. P. Beaudouin; *Imprimatur*: F. Thomas Faucillon, Prior. Prov. FF. Praed.

16. Le Père Hyacinthe de Valroger, *La genèse des espèces, études philosophiques et religieuses sur l'histoire naturelle et les naturalistes contemporains* (Paris, 1873).

17. In art. 3 of quest. 76, first part of the *Summa*, Aquinas confuses man and animal in the same genus; to interpret genus in the modern sense would thus make Aquinas a materialist, *Reductio ad absurdum*. Leroy, *L'évolution*, pp. 19-25.

evolutionary hypothesis would therefore redound to the greater glory of God. This was a fairly typical argument of the Christian evolutionist. Having disposed of the anti-evolutionary arguments based on religion, Leroy then proceeded to give a competent summary of all the current scientific arguments in its favor, but not without pointing out the paleontological and physiological difficulties the theory still faced.[18]

There can be no doubt that many potential critics were disarmed by the prudence of Leroy in introducing his book with two letters of approval, one from a leading Catholic scientist and another from a well-known Dominican preacher. The professor of geology at the Institut catholique de Paris, Albert de Lapparent, certified the solidity of Leroy's geological arguments and confessed that Leroy's whole thesis corresponded to the views suggested to him by the organization of his own paleontological collection. Lapparent thought that Catholics had been wrong in taking an aggressive anti-evolutionary attitude. He therefore rejoiced in the publication of a work by a religious taking the opposite position. "There are ideas one gets used to because it seems that the future belongs to them." To take a position in favor of evolution in the name of an impeccably orthodox group was, Lapparent concluded, a useful act as well as a move showing foresight.[19] The letter of approval by Lapparent clearly had a considerable influence on readers. In an attempt to limit its impact after Leroy brought out the second edition, Dierckx emphasized that Lapparent, like Quatrefages, did not usually abandon an exclusively scientific ground. In the letter Lapparent was not speaking of the origin of man. All that could be concluded from the letter was that the geologist was not systematically hostile to all ideas of general evolution. And Dierckx noted that in the 1893 edition of the *Traité de géologie*, Lapparent showed his reserve about the hypothesis of the evolution of the species in the geological periods.[20]

The letter of Father Monsabré also emphasized the usefulness of Leroy's work, especially since certain minds were horrified by the theory of evolution either because of the shock administered to their scientific position or because of the erroneous conclusion that evolution leads inevitably to materialism. There were more than scientific advantages to the theory. It did no damage to Scripture; there are even biblical passages to justify Leroy's arguments, which although debatable were not questionable from the viewpoint of orthodoxy. Then a paean to the religious advantages of evolution: "Far from compromising orthodox belief in the creative action of God, it reduces this action to a small number of transcendent acts, which conform better to the unity of the divine plan and to the infinite wisdom of the all powerful being, who knows how to make orderly use of secondary causes to achieve

18. Leroy, pp. 55–56, 115–54.
19. Ibid., pp. 1–2.
20. Le R.P.Fr. Dierckx, "L'homme-singe et les précurseurs d'Adam en face de la théologie," *RQS* 36 (1894): 114. See also Conry, *Darwinisme*, p. 197. Dierckx also doubted that Monsabré would agree with Leroy's interpolations to the second edition on the evolution of the human body.

his aims."[21] Any argument about evolution should therefore be on strictly scientific grounds.

Within four years Leroy brought out a second, revised edition of his work that was at once more prudent and more daring: he limited evolution to the organic species below man and sharpened his previous arguments in favor of evolution, including a sharp reply to several of the clerical intellectuals who had opposed him.[22] His sharpest criticism was of the misinterpretations by clergy like Vigouroux and Brucker, who had attacked through the important Jesuit periodical *Etudes*, and Albert Farges. Brucker and Farges were Jesuits. Most of his critics condemned en bloc all opinions related to evolution and thus produced a confusion harmful to "the defense of the good cause."[23] The controversy swirled around four points: universal and atheistic evolution, which was also materialistic and fatalistic;[24] evolution restricted to the organic species;[25] evolution including man; and the different methods used to explain evolution. Leroy's chief problem was to make a convincing case for an evolution that generally excluded man from the process but still retained him as part of the natural world, a feat demanding the ultimate in subtle reasoning!

Before giving his solution to this problem, Leroy dealt with the relations between restricted evolution and faith. He struggled valiantly to establish the essential conservatism of his religious position and the large area of agreement between him and the supporters of the stability of the species. "I agree with the ideas and principles of the supporters of the fixity of species on the most important points: the primordial creation *ex nihilo* by divine power of cosmic matter as well as the physical forces with admirable laws regulating it . . . I attribute the introduction of the earth's vital principle to a special intervention of the first cause . . . I recognize . . . in the universe the constant action of divine Providence executing its work according to a great design that shows an infallible intelligence."[26] In addition to these typical Christian beliefs about God and the universe, couched in familiar catechistic language, Leroy declared his acceptance of the existence of specific types capable of perpetuating themselves by generation. But he recognized only relative stability, for the types are the result of evolution from earlier types—with the

21. Lettre du T. R. P. M.-J. Monsabré des frères-prêcheurs, maître en théologie, conférencier de Notre-Dame de Paris, Leroy, *L'évolution*, pp. 3-4.

22. Le P. M.-D. Leroy, *L'évolution restreinte aux espèces organiques* (Lyon, 1891). He reproduced the letters of Lapparent and Monsabré with an explanatory note: "Ces deux lettres ne visent à la vérité que mon premier opuscule . . . mais, comme mon nouveau travail ne fait que reproduire le premier, avec quelques développements en plus, elles s'y rapportent tout à fait" (p. 1). The work had appropriate official approval for publication.

23. Leroy cited Abbé Lavaud de Lestrade, *Transformisme et darwinisme, réfutation méthodique* (Poissy, 1885) as a well-intentioned confusion of the evolutionary and atheistic causes.

24. "La matière est éternelle: c'est le premier article de leur Credo." A heinous example of atheistic, materialistic evolution, according to Leroy, was Camille Flammarion, *Le monde avant la création de l'homme* (Paris, 1886).

25. I.e., "restreinte aux seuls types organiques inférieurs à l'homme," Leroy, *L'évolution restreinte*, pp. 1-4.

26. Ibid., p. 31.

exception of the *first* type! If this argument did not convert any fixists, it had the virtue of leaving them confused.

His argument was equally Daedalian on the dangerous and delicate topic of the origin of the human species. Catholic theology, as stated by the church fathers, by the scholastic philosophers, and by the Council of Cologne, formally condemned the opinion that the human body descended from an animal type. Divine power produced the body directly through the infusion of the rational soul. Since the rational soul is the substantial form of the body, it is impossible that our body substance derived from the animal. But this does not mean that man is totally distinct from the natural world and exempt from the evolutionary process. The *substratum* that had been destined to receive the human soul could have been prepared through the action of natural agents in the course of their evolution. This hypothesis provided a plausible explanation for the existence of rudimentary human organs and agreed with the biblical account of the preparation of the "dust" before it received the breath of life that made it man. In spite of his tortuous attempt to keep as many traditional beliefs as possible unchanged, Leroy had clearly accepted evolution and boldly interpreted some of these beliefs in evolutionary terms. For a late-nineteenth-century French clerical intellectual, this was a radical action in which he had few companions. In thirty years it had become possible to discuss evolution freely; the rest could come in due time. It would not be too soon to see the disappearance of "certain anti-scientific prejudices" in Catholic circles, even among the most renowned professors, which exposed the whole of Catholicism to the ironic scorn of its enemies.[27] Leroy's work put on the Index in 1895. Rome was not converted.

As the subtle reasoning of Leroy showed, the place of man in the evolutionary scheme, if indeed he had a place, was a very troublesome topic for Catholics. Disputes raging in the scientific world about the significance or the interpretation of anthropological findings made it easier for many to maintain a position of skepticism on making man the last link in the evolutionary chain. But the existence of pre-Adamites did not, even in the opinion of anti-evolutionists, represent a threat to Scripture or to dogma. Hyacinthe de Valroger saw nothing heterodox in the idea of pre-Adamites, precursors of the human race.[28] Inspired by Fabre d'Envieu, Monsabré viewed the existence of precursors of man as a way to explain the existence of instruments dating back to the Tertiary period. This also "solved" the chronological problem. Both Valroger and Monsabré departed from Mortillet, professor at the Ecole d'anthropologie de Paris, in denying any connection based on relationship between the pre-Adamites and the human race.[29] Fabre d'Envieu's Faustian speculation was that reasonable animals or races of men could have existed in the first three geological periods but that perhaps the perversion of the pre-Adamites led God to destroy them and begin again as recorded in

27. Ibid., pp. 260, 273, 281–83.
28. Le père H. de Valroger, "L'ancienneté de l'homme," *Revue des questions historiques* 16 (1874): 482–514, and "L'archéologie préhistorique," ibid. 19 (1876): 414–48.
29. Dierckx, *RQS* 36 (1894): 86–88. Monsabré made his remarks in his "Conférence de Notre-Dame," Easter 1875.

Genesis.[30] This view did not influence Catholic writers as much as Valroger's more limited speculation. Many apologists rallied to the idea of an intermediary anthropoid between the primates and true man because it preserved the truth of the Mosaic account and did not threaten the integrity of the faith. Within flexible biblical chronology, others interpreted Tertiary "man" as an Adamite. All declared, like Dierckx, that the simian origin of man through natural descendance and successive perfection was a pleasant dream invented by materialists.[31] But the related and delicate problem of determining the precise role of the Creator in the creation of the *body* of Adam remained a debatable topic.

The ideas of the English Catholic biologist Saint George Mivart were important in raising this debate to fever pitch. Although one of the chief opponents of the idea of natural selection, he argued that the animal body of man must have an origin different from the spiritual soul in it because of the distinction between the two orders. The body had evolved from secondary causes but the soul was the result of the direct action of God. The first man had emerged as an *adult* from the hands of the Creator. Mivart's ideas were condemned by some theologians but defended by others. Presumably to reward his efforts to reconcile science and religion, Mivart was made a doctor of philosophy by the pope in 1876. Cardinal Manning gave him the ring and hat in the ensuing ceremony. But Mivart's subsequent forays into theologico-philosophical questions resulted in his excommunication.

It was really the Mivart thesis that Leroy developed in the book giving him so much notoriety among French Catholics. In spite of the safeguards for dogma and Scripture clearly established by Leroy—the orthodoxy of evolution, the barrier between man and monkey, the transcendence of the human soul—he was attacked by Catholic writers, especially by Joseph Brucker in *Etudes.*[32] Hostile to evolution, Brucker asked Leroy for his opinion on the creation of the first woman. Leroy did not hesitate to exempt Eve from the laws of evolution; whereas a substratum of man was a natural product of secondary causes, Eve was the immediate and exclusive work of God. Dierckx called Leroy's idea a useless hypothesis not based on serious data. It did not eliminate the need of miracle even for the body of Adam; and it was unscientific because it contradicted the fundamental principles of Darwinism, on which it was supposedly founded.[33] Leroy had pushed his favorite idea too

30. Jules-Fabre d'Envieu, *Les origines de la terre et de l'homme, ou l'Hexaméron génésiaque considéré dans ses rapports avec les enseignements de la philosophie, de la géologie, de la paléontologie et de l'archéologie préhistorique* (Toulouse, 1873), obviously influenced by Alcide d'Orbigny's views.

31. Dierckx, *RQS* 36 (1894): 91.

32. Brucker, "Bulletin scripturaire," *E* 55 (November 1891): 488–97. The Brucker-Leroy exchange had overtones of a Jesuit-Dominican clash. For Mivart's difficulties, see J. W. Gruber, *A Conscience in Conflict: The Life of St. George Jackson Mivart* (New York, 1960).

33. Leroy, letter in *La science catholique* 6 (February 1892): 241–47, answering Brucker; Dierckx, *RQS* 36 (1894): 103 ff. Dierckx also drew on Cardinal González, *La Biblia y la ciencia*, 2d ed. (Seville, 1892), to argue against Leroy. He neatly summed up Leroy's thesis on man: "Il est probable que Dieu, en créant Adam, n'a pas travaillé sur des matières terreuses, mais que, par la seule infusion de l'âme raisonnable, il a transformé en

far. He was too far in advance of contemporary science on the origin of man, for paleontological and ethnographical discoveries were increasingly unfavorable to anthropological Darwinism. Most materialistic scientists echoed the notorious *ignorabimus* answer of du Bois-Reymond to the question of how force and matter had given rise to thought. Virchow's declaration at the International Congress in Moscow (1892) also confirmed the check suffered by anthropology in trying to discover the origins of man. Even Vogt emphasized the need for detailed research rather than the current type of generalization. Rejoicing in the confessed powerlessness of the enemies of religion, Dierckx nevertheless concluded that Catholics would be wrong in trying to place limits on the scientific movement. And in the question of the origins of man, less than in any other question, revealed doctrine had nothing to fear from future discoveries.[34]

Nothing significant had happened to change the negative conclusion arrived at by Jean d'Estienne about five years earlier concerning the efforts of the materialists to prove that only a difference of degree, not of essence, exists between man and animal.[35] But d'Estienne had emphasized that philosophically the theory of evolution as extended to the whole man must be rejected a priori, and that this was a fortiori the case in light of Christian tradition and belief in the Scripture. Broca's aphorism, echoed later by Duval, that he would rather be a perfected monkey than a degenerate Adam, was proof that the materialist position on man was more emotion than science.[36] D'Estienne ultimately fell back on the excessively clear triptych of the universe postulated by Denys Cochin as proof of the impossibility of the unified materialist view of life and matter: "We cannot understand the world without three interventions by the first cause, without three special creations, and we cannot conceive of a single and universal evolution." Once these eternal principles are admitted by scientists and philosophers, they are free to construct evolutionary theories to explain separate developments in each of the three worlds—that of inorganic matter, that of vegetable and animal life, and that of free and rational humanity in its physiological, historical, and social developments.[37]

In a long study in the *Revue des questions scientifiques* in 1898, the venerable Marquis de Nadaillac, quasi-official spokesman on anthropological ques-

---

Homme un animal anthropomorphe amené par l'évolution et sous la conduite de la Providence au point le plus rapproché possible de l'humanité" (Dierckx, pp. 110-11). On evolution in Spain, see Thomas F. Glick, "Spain," in Glick, ed., *Comparative Reception,* pp. 307-45.

34. Vogt, "Dogmes dans la science," *RS* 10 (1891): 79, cited in Dierckx, *RQS* 35 (1894): 117; Dierckx, *RQS* 36 (1894): 120.

35. Jean d'Estienne, "La transformation et la discussion libre," *RQS* 25 (1889): 76-141, 373-420; see esp. pp. 373 ff.

36. "Je trouve plus de gloire à monter qu'à descendre; et si j'admettais l'intervention des impressions sentimentales dans les sciences, je dirais, comme M. Claparède, que j'aimerais mieux être un singe perfectionné qu'un Adam dégénéré": Paul Broca, *Mémoires d'anthropologie,* 3:146 ("Sur le transformisme"), cited in Mathias Duval, *Le darwinisme, Leçons professées à l'Ecole d'anthropologie* (Paris, 1886), p. 425, and in d'Estienne, *RQS* 25 (1889): 381. Quotation is from Broca, *not* d'Estienne's citation of Duval.

37. Cochin, *L'évolution et la vie,* p. 302, cited in d'Estienne, *RQS* 25 (1889): 420.

tions in Catholic scientific and intellectual circles, defended the thesis that no human remains, whatever the date attributed to them, or whatever the region of their origin, belonged to a humanity different from ours. "Between animal and man, physically as well as morally, we see no possible comparison, no possible intermediary."[38]

The acceptance of a limited type of evolution by the Catholic Albert Gaudry, professor at the Museum of Natural History, provoked a minor crisis in Catholic circles and produced a long series of articles by Father A. Haté in *Etudes.* The title especially gave the clear but erroneous impression that Gaudry was a Darwinist. Haté argued that, in spite of his talent and his science, Gaudry had not made the hypothesis of organic evolution into a scientific truth. The Darwinian hypothesis contained too much imagination to be enshrined in the pantheon of proven truths. Applying logical criteria to Darwinism, a favorite procedure of the rationalistic French Catholic intellectual, Haté concluded that the entire complex Darwinian system was a paralogism; it was based on the fallacy of *post hoc, ergo propter hoc.* Haté echoed the Abbé Moigno: the species is divine.[39]

Obsession with the concept of species also pervaded the long philosophical essay on evolution by J. de Bonniot in 1889. Clarification could only come from philosophy, whose eviction from science was the cause of the confusion over species. Bonniot admitted that God is not the immediate creator of each of His works but rather that His idea is realized by the immediate agents operating under His direction. The idea of the Creator, insofar as it is imprinted in each creature and expressed by it, is the species of each creature. The best way of getting to know the species would be to know the ideas of which they are the types. Since we know immediately only our own ideas, this is impossible, and we get to know the ideas through the species. Because of the limitation of our intelligence this knowledge is always inadequate. But since the rational agent always acts with an end in view the work must be conceived in those terms. Behind the *telos* of the work is the final cause of which the intelligent causes are only the instruments. A zoological species is the total of natural aptitudes by which the animal achieves his destiny—including his organization, food, protection, and propagation. Acceptance of this Aristotelian-Platonic-Judaic-Christian mixture of intrinsic and extrinsic teleology would eliminate the chief weakness of evolution, chance, which had replaced God the Creator.[40]

38. Mis de Nadaillac, "L'homme et le singe." *RQS* 44 (1898): 182-220, 414-59; quote on p. 458. See also his "Unité de l'espèce humaine prouvée par la similarité des conceptions et des créations de l'homme," *RQS* 41 (1897): 415-48.

39. Albert Gaudry, *Les enchaînements du monde animal dans les temps géologiques. Mammifères tertiaires* (Paris, 1878); A. Haté, "Darwinisme. Un nouveau champion de l'hypothèse de la formation des espèces animales et végétales par voie de transformation organique," *E*, 6th ser. 2 (1878): 239-55, 321-45, 598-620. Six more articles appeared in 1879! The citation is from Moigno, *Les splendeurs de la foi*, 2:312.

40. Joseph Bonniot, "Essai philosophique sur le transformisme," *E* 46 (1889): 337-68. "Le monde doit être organisé par le jeu des causes secondes, tel est le principe fondamental de la nouvelle philosophie. Disons le mot, il est organisé par le hasard; le hasard est devenu le Démiurge, le grand facteur de l'ordre du monde": Bonniot, "L'instinct et le transformisme," *E* 44 (1888): 549.

Like many opponents of evolution, Bonniot seemed to have a secret fear that it might win acceptance by the scientific community. As insurance against this possibility, he echoed the widely accepted view that even if evolution were true, it would be evidence of greater power on the part of the Creator than that shown by other theories, for it required more wisdom and more power to create a creature with the faculty of self-propagation and self-perfection than to produce an already perfected work. Even though there was no point of contact between the dogmas of religion and evolution, it was also comforting to know that the guardian of scientific wisdom in the French Academy of Sciences had rejected Darwin as a possible corresponding member in 1873. The scientific solidity of the inventor of Darwinism was then no more sure than the hypothesis itself![41]

The hard-line defense of the fixity of the species remained an obsession of a substantial part of the Catholic community. In 1892 Lodiel, reviewing a group of works dealing with evolution, merely reaffirmed the fixity of the species, asserted the unscientific nature of evolution, and, after a consideration of the works in question, passed on to what had become the important issue, the development of atheistic evolution. Evolution had been turned into a war machine against religion. Lodiel did not forget the ritual of citing authorities. Gaudry was cited on the weakness of the struggle for life as an explanation. Godron's studies on vegetable variations showed the fixity of botanical species. And, as a clincher, a citation from the doubting Thomas of the French Academy of Sciences, Blanchard: "Show me one example of the transformation of a single species."[42]

But Catholic scientists did accept evolution and Father Leroy had become its champion. Catholics opposed to evolution had therefore to face the fact that most of the scientific community and an increasing number of other intellectuals were accepting evolution, in spite of the so-called irrefutable case against it. It was at this point that the opponents of evolution changed tactics, unconsciously perhaps, to emphasize that a great number of evolutionists, including some of the most famous, rejected *atheistic* evolution. If science were to force evolution on the theologians it would have to be evolution directed by God. Gaudry, Kelvin, Stokes, Siemens, Tait, Stewart, and Owen were among those mustered to support the first cause. This stage was preliminary to acceptance of a non-mechanistic and teleological variety of evolution. By the time the *Revue des questions scientifiques* published Sinéty's articles in 1910–11 and those of Teilhard de Chardin from 1921 on, the second stage was reached. It proved impossible for Catholics to maintain a position

41. Bonniot, "Le transformisme et l'athéisme," *E*, 5th ser. (1873): 428–40. Bonniot found consolation in two recent works: H. de Villeneuve-Flayose (ancien Ingénieur en Chef des Mines), *L'unité dans la création et les limites actuelles dans la variabilité des espèces* (Marseille, 1872), and H. de Valroger, *La genèse des espèces* (Paris, 1873). Darwin was admitted to the Société d'anthropologie in 1871, although Quatrefages was opposed; he was elected to the Academy in 1878 as a foreign corresponding member of the botany section. See Conry, *Darwinisme*, pp. 31–32.

42. Père D. Lodiel, "Quelques appréciations récentes des arguments transformistes," *E* 57 (1892): 573–96. The works considered included Blanchard, *La vie des êtres animés* (1888); Jousset, *Evolution et transformisme* (1889); Leroy, *L'évolution restreinte aux espèces organiques* (1891); and works of Gaudry, Quatrefages, and Vogt.

on evolution which did not conform to that of the scientific community. After the 1880s it became impossible to base total opposition to evolution on any respectable scientific opinion. The process of readjustment to a new position took several decades. The delay was probably due in part to the revisions made in evolutionary arguments by scientists themselves. Eventually the Catholic position was simply acceptance of the general evolutionary position upon which nearly the entire scientific community agreed.

The same change in attitude toward evolution we find in the *Revue des questions scientifiques* can be found in the *Annales de philosophie chrétienne*. Under Bonnetty's editorship the *Annales* published in 1878 an anti-evolutionary and anti-materialistic article by Antoine Béchamp, then dean of the medical faculty of the Catholic University of Lille. Apart from quite interesting twists to the argumentation which came out of Béchamp's profound knowledge of the chemistry of life, the article was a typical hard-line defense of Genesis and an attack on "le système *évolutionniste allemand*" and "le transformisme darwinien."[43] In 1882, when Xavier Roux was editor, the *Annales* reprinted from the *Revue scientifique* Huxley's summary of the facts that provided the basis of evolution. Roux found that nothing in Huxley's presentation of the theory was in conflict with Catholic orthodoxy. The first cause was retained and the creator God was not rejected. Roux noted that the deductions of science rest on the purely metaphysical principle that "the same effects imply the same causes." It was then ridiculous for some scientists to attempt to eliminate metaphysics from human knowledge when it was one of the foundations of the new scientific certainty. Roux also complained about the lack of rigor and precision in the paleontological arguments supporting evolution.[44] Lack of rigor in argument and lack of agreement with groups of facts were standard items in French criticism of Darwinism. The argument based on the scientific reputation of Darwin's opponents in France was also used in the *Annales.*[45]

The *Annales* showed considerable interest in the arguments of Saint George Mivart, "our illustrious collaborator," in favor of evolution and in Catholic counterattacks on Mivart like that by Father Murphy in the *Irish Ecclesiastical Record.* Mivart's reply to Murphy in the *Tablet* was of special interest to the *Annales* because Mivart asserted the liberty of science in purely scientific questions and invoked the example of Galileo to show the catastrophic consequences possible when the church intervenes in scientific questions. The article of Mivart in the *Nineteenth Century Review* warned that science had created a new theodicy, which would supplant the old in the

43. "Cosmogonie catholique et scientifique. De l'état présent des rapports de la science avec la religion au sujet de l'origine des êtres organisés," *APC*, 6th ser. 15 (1878): 54–77, 130–43. See Conry, *Darwinisme*, pp. 241–42.

44. Introduction to Huxley, "L'origine et les progrès de la paléontologie," *APC*, n.s. 6 (1882): 333–47. For emphasis on the facts against Darwinism, see the Marquis de Virieu, "Les théories transformistes et la pratique agricole," ibid., pp. 452–75.

45. See André Suchetet, "Coup d'œil rétrospectif sur la théorie transformiste," *APC*, n.s. 7 (1882): 97–126; Dr. A. Lhéris, "Darwin," ibid., pp. 549–73; de Quatrefages, "Note sur Charles Darwin ... à l'Académie des sciences dans la séance du 1er mai," ibid. 6 (1882): 262–68.

eyes of the masses if the clergy continued to ignore science. It was given a sympathetic hearing by the *Annales*.[46]

Maisonneuve also emphasized the right of science to liberty of discussion and ridiculed the blind opposition of some Catholics to evolution. The *Annales* carried his paper at the International Scientific Congress of Catholics in 1889.[47] An attack on the stupidity of much of the reaction against Darwin is found in a dialogue by Marcel Hébert in 1893 between Darwin and Plato. Darwin complains about the ridiculous travesty of his doctrine "I am treated as an atheist, although I inscribed the name of the Creator in the first lines of my work." Plato reminds Darwin that one must work for a small number; the masses will join up sooner or later. But Plato wonders about the anxieties Darwin has stirred up in so many pious souls. Darwin replies that the pious had erroneously taken literally the metaphors and symbols of the sacred books. The oriental style of Scripture led astray certain minds concerned above all with scientific rigor or used to logical formalism. "They confused parable with history; they claimed to find lessons of astronomy and geology in pages intended to develop the religious and moral life of the soul." Darwin also recognized that his worst enemies were some overzealous disciples who distorted his doctrine into a secularistic *Weltanschauung*.[48] This bold and clever defense of a limited Darwinism was typical of Hébert's intellectual courage, which eventually made him, along with the *Annales*, one of the victims of the modernist purge.

Beginning publication in 1894, the *Revue du clergé français* had the advantage of not having shared in the initial general French opposition to Darwinism. It had solely to concern itself with any threats to the faith arising out of the new theory. It also had the advantage of beginning at a time when Catholic acceptance of much of Darwinism was no longer a dangerous novelty. In the first issue, enthusiastic support was given to the motion of the natural sciences section of the Third International Scientific Congress of Catholics calling for research into the role that evolution could have played in the total of secondary causes that produced the present state of the physical world. The *Revue* did not like the word *transformisme* because of its ambiguity and its common meaning that the present-day lower species evolved into present-day higher species. No present-day species represent exactly any common ancestor. It was the theory of common ancestors, under the name of *évolutionnisme*, that had been defended at the Brussels conference. This "théorie des ancêtres communs" was a religious and Christian doctrine.[49] By this semantic maneuver, materialistic and atheistic associations were removed from the doctrine, making it more palatable to Catholics.

The chief concern of the *Revue* was the significance of evolutionary the-

46. "Foi et évolution," *APC*, n.s. 13 (1885-86): 204-8.

47. "Doctrines philosophiques et théories physiologiques contemporaines sur la vie," *APC*, n.s. 20 (1889): 297-306. See also Fr. M.-D. Leroy, "L'homme-singe et la doctrine évolutionniste. Réponse au Dr. P. Jousset," *APC*, n.s. 44 (1901): 516-35, for Leroy's defense of his own views against the attacks of Jousset in his book of the same title.

48. "Plato et Darwin," *APC*, n.s. 28 (1893): 157-74.

49. Guillemet, "Chronique scientifique. Le clergé et les sciences de la nature," *RCF* 1 (1894): 81-87.

ory for man. Guibert pointed out in 1896 that the exegetes had declared
that the Bible does not impose on Catholics any specific chronology. An important liberty had thus been gained. In the past, Catholics had been caught
in a dilemma: on one side were those delighted to assign a fabulous antiquity
to man in order to show the Bible wrong; on the other were Catholics who
wanted to keep the old interpretation and therefore insisted on too young an
age for man. (Guibert considered the figures 80,000 to 200,000 years to be
fantasy and 18,000 to be a reasonable one.) In two articles in 1896 on the
origin of man, Guibert concluded that no matter how far back in time one
went, the evidence did not show an animal origin of man. Science inclined in
favor of the thesis of the separate creation of man by God.[50] Catholicism was
once again regaining the comfortable position where it could delude itself on
achieving a scientific basis for its theodicy, the dream of Christian intellectuals since Aquinas.

Criticisms of evolution, especially its atheistic and materialistic interpretations and its scientific deficiencies, were common in the *Revue.* But it was
unusual when Abbé Elie Blanc, a philosopher-theologian of the Catholic faculties in Lyon, opposed evolution on metaphysical grounds. The general assertion of the right of metaphysics to define the parameters of science was
part of the Thomistic revival and would later be asserted forcefully by Maritain. Blanc happened to make a particularly bad application of this intoxicat-
ing principle. He classified as metaphysical the common belief of all evolutionists that the higher species of the animal kingdom issued from the same
protoplasm or from several vague types and differentiated themselves later.
It is a metaphysical argument dealing with the nature of living beings, with
their first principle of operation, and with the law of causality to which all
effects are rigorously subject. Since there are higher and lower organisms,
there are higher and lower natures or essences of these organisms. Assuming
that the generators are the chief cause of the engendered, the law of causality
makes it impossible to derive higher from lower species through generation.
The naturalists had no right to accept this hypothesis a priori. At this point,
Blanc's prejudice against evolution got the better of him, and he raved against
this disgusting chimera, which, applied to man, resulted in atheism.[51]

Blanc's easy metaphysical victory over evolution did not go unchallenged.
Mano questioned whether evolution really clashed with the law of causality.
The crux of the issue is to know if the complexity of antecedent causes, principal or secondary, could not justify the appearance of a new being, dissimilar
and perhaps superior. The complexity of the causes would explain the appa-

50. J. Guibert, "Antiquité de l'espèce humaine," *RFC* 6 (1896): 146–59. He noted the
anti-religious bias of the *Dictionnaire des sciences anthropologiques*, but he exonorated
the Darwinians, including Haeckel, from the charge that they argued that man descended
from monkeys: "l'enseignement transformiste est que l'homme et les singes descendent
d'un ancêtre commun": "Origine de l'homme," *RCF* 5 (1896): 314–31, 438–49. Guibert
considered some relevant works of Farges, d'Estienne, Mivart, de Nadaillac, Blanchard,
Huxley, Romanes, Richet, Flourens, de Bonniot, de Quatrefages, Jousset, Lavaud de Lestrade, James, Darwin, Haeckel, Perrier, and Duval.
51. "Le transformisme est-il une question purement scientifique?" *RCF* 21 (1902):50–
55.

rent superiority of the effect. Anticipating the argument that this reasoning could explain accidental modifications but not justify a specific evolution, that it could apply within species but not to passage from one species to another, Mano pointed out that one could deny the evolution of the lowly wild rose into a high-class rose on the authority of the ontological laws of causality just as one could deny the complete evolution of the animal kingdom. It was also difficult to define the notion of superiority in species, especially when reduced to Blanc's idea of a vital force. "It would be a question of knowing if the vital force of a mammal is *irreducibly* superior to the vital force of a zoophyte." It is not clear that each higher organism corresponds to a special, determined, invariable force. On the contrary, the same physiological laws explain the vital phenomena of all life. The animal scale shows more the complexity than the absolute transcendence of species. Mano argued that ontological principles are simply too general to supply through deduction formulas that satisfy reality. "The flexibility and complexity of reality hardly permit one to make the a priori coincide exactly with the exact investigations of science." The best way of proceeding in the debate over evolution, Mano concluded, is to study and criticize scientifically the positive proofs available. "If science should not exclude regulation by metaphysics, metaphysics certainly should not isolate itself from the scientific and earnest observation of facts." As at the international scientific congresses, this attempt to defeat evolution on philosophical rather than scientific grounds failed. Because the scientific reasons for accepting a variety of evolution had by now convinced a substantial segment of the Catholic intellectual community, the failure of the remaining opponents of evolution to shift the quarrel to philosophical grounds, especially in the period of the Thomistic revival, was an important victory for Catholic pro-evolutionary forces.[52]

An excellent touchstone for change in Catholic attitudes on evolution can be found in the five international scientific congresses of Catholics held be-

52. C. Mano, "Métaphysique et transformisme," *RCF* 21 (1902): 207-10. Dr. Surbled, "Chronique scientifique," *RCF* 22 (1902): 86-87, agreed with Mano: Darwinian evolution would die on its own; besides, *évolutionnisme* could be given a perfectly reasonable interpretation, like that given by Maisonneuve, which agreed perfectly with orthodoxy. Blanc was also vanquished in the *Revue thomiste* by Charles de Kirwan, who declared that no one has the right to reject evolutionary theory in the name of metaphysics and above all in the name of religious and Christian beliefs. For the Blanc-Kirwan encounter, see *RT* 9 (1902): 716-25. See the article of Chanoine A. Bouyssonie, "Fixisme et transformisme," *RCF* 62 (1910): 384-407, rejecting fixism and cautiously accepting an evolutionary hypothesis. With his brother, Abbé J. Bouyssonie, and Abbé Bardon, the author had discovered the Mousterian skeleton at La Chapelle-aux-Saints. See also L. Wintrebert (Professor at the Grand Séminaire d'Issy-les-Moulineaux), "L'état actuel du transformisme," *RCF* 60 (1909): 75-86; 64 (1910): 316-35, who accepts evolution as a principle but thinks Darwinism bankrupt as a general theory and looks forward to the triumph of a form of Lamarckism because it is finalistic. A. Bouyssonie, "A propos des conditions philosophiques de l'évolution," *RCF* 69 (1912): 230-42, agrees with Le Guichaoua's claim in the *Revue néo-scolastique de philosophie* (Louvain) in 1911 that *évolutionnisme* can be interpreted to fit the principles of traditional philosophy. The *RCF* held to an antievolutionary position on man: see L. Wintrebert, "Le problème de l'origine de l'homme," *RCF* 59 (1909): 112-17, reprinted from "feuilleton de l'Univers," du 24 mars 1909. Perhaps to comfort fixists, it reprinted from the *Ami du Clergé* an article on Fabre: "Un savant spiritualiste: J.-H. Fabre," *RCF* 70 (1912): 94-111.

tween 1888 and 1900, when the most controversial topic was undoubtedly evolution. The congress of 1888 gave rise not only to internal disputes but caused heated exchanges long after. One of the members of the anthropology section declared that it was a duty for Catholics to fight against evolutionary theory because it is clearly contrary to the faith and Holy Scripture. The proposal was not greeted enthusiastically by Catholic anthropologists and was not endorsed by the section. In the natural sciences section, Paul Maisonneuve, professor at the Faculté catholique des sciences d'Angers, spoke at considerable length on the proposal. He began by noting the number of competent people who supported evolution, which indicated a division in the scientific community on the issue. In the face of this polarization, one could ask how far a devout Catholic scientist could go in adopting evolutionary ideas. Maisonneuve did not want a collective opinion but rather the personal opinions of members of the congress. Although Catholics had at first nearly unanimously opposed evolution because it appeared to be an anti-religious weapon, some Catholics had, he noted, recently begun to look at the theory in a different light. Some scientists with no anti-religious bias and even some scientists who were Catholic unhesitatingly adopted evolutionary ideas. Maisonneuve gave short shrift to one argument still preventing many people from recognizing evolutionary theory, namely, that it denies divine intervention in the creation of life. This argument had been denied by Valroger, Leroy, and Monsabré, whose names carried great authority in doctrinal matters. Indeed, if one considered that certain church fathers saw no problem in admitting the idea of the spontaneous generation of life, one could just as easily admit the idea of an evolution of species; both ideas presupposed, of course, the guiding intelligence of a creator. For Maisonneuve, then, the issue was a purely scientific one, since the idea that evolution contradicts Scripture had been shown utterly erroneous. He did not argue in favor of evolution; he merely wanted to emphasize that it is possible: "I remain in a philosophical doubt that I find wise and convenient." He ended by asking the congress whether Catholics should not permit completely free discussion on the issue of evolution, thus letting experimental science alone establish the truth: "Science has its rights, which must be respected. As Catholics, we must show the concern we have for scientific questions, the importance we attach to them, and the respect we have for the opinions of other scientists."[53]

Clerical concern with evolution was well illustrated by the case of Abbé Smets, who had a doctorate in the natural sciences and taught in an ecclesiastical collège. Smets' ecclesiastical superior had given him the task of writing a work on evolution. After three years of preparation and research, the abbé became a believer in the theory without sacrificing his beliefs in the immediate creation of the soul of each man and in the necessary intervention of God in evolution itself. The abbé's reasons for converting to belief in evolution were nearly all purely scientific. The idea that evolution gave God a greater role in the universe was a further enticement to conversion.[54]

53. *Compte rendu du Congrès scientifique des catholiques* (1888), pp. 606–8.
54. "Les évolutionnistes chrétiens prétendent, non seulement ne pas supprimer l'action divine, mais encore lui faire la part plus large et plus éclatante" (ibid., pp. 608–9).

Others disagreed with Smets. Father Lacouture opposed him by citing anti-evolutionary scientists like Quatrefages and Blanchard. Others emphasized philosophical difficulties. Duilhé de St. Projet recalled his own previous remarks on the stability of instinct, only to be opposed by the pro-evolutionary Abbé Guillemet, who argued that "it is necessity that develops instinct." Father Bordes argued that science discovered daily new facts in favor of evolution, an opinion quite the reverse of the constant objection of many anti-evolutionists, especially Blanchard, that not one solitary fact could be cited in favor of the hypothesis. Bordes also echoed Cochin's idea that further light could be thrown on the topic by studying the world of tiny organisms rather than the higher species. In the face of these disagreements, Msgr. d'Hulst closed the discussion by pointing out that the question raised by Maisonneuve was not one that the congress could answer by a general opinion. The rules governing the congress wisely precluded a collective decision on the orthodoxy of any doctrine. All that could be done was to get individual opinions. This meant a clash of different opinions which were based on grounds each had to judge for himself.[55]

Although no collective opinion was approved regarding evolution, a motion was passed in the anthropology section approving the organization of a Catholic fight against atheistic anthropology.[56] The propaganda campaign of atheistic anthropology among school youth and the public promoted atheism and hatred of the church. Anthropology should therefore be taught in the Catholic universities and in the higher seminaries. Public lectures should be organized to counteract public enemy propaganda. A third part of the motion proposed establishing a scientific journal to deal competently with anthropological questions, but it was withdrawn when Father Van den Gheyn and Kirwan pointed out that this was already done admirably by Adrien Arcelin in the *Revue des questions scientifiques.* After some embarrassing moments, both for Arcelin and the authors of the motion, the section decided that Catholic scientists should propagate and support scientific journals, especially the *Revue des questions scientifiques.* The possibilities envisaged in the motion were well illustrated by the great success of a series of lectures by the Abbé Ducrost in Lyon.[57]

55. Ibid., p. 609.
56. There was a short-lived *Revue d'anthropologie catholique, étude de l'homme physique et moral* started in 1847. It was inspired by the impious nature of contemporary physiology, medicine, and natural history. All could be set right by replacing "the Baconian method" with "the Catholic method," which would eliminate the caprice of individual reason by imposing on it an intelligent obedience to superior authority.
57. "Vœu . . . déposé par MM. Dupuich et Davoust," *Compte rendu du Congrès,* pp. 785–86; Abbé A. Ducrost, *De l'évolution* (Lyon, 1884), extrait de *La controverse et le contemporain.* The following papers were read in the sixth section of the Congress (sciences anthropologiques): Abbé Hamard, de l'oratoire de Rennes, "Deux objections contre le monogénisme"; Chanoine Duilhé de Saint-Projet, professeur d'apologétique à l'Institut catholique de Toulouse, "Le problème anthropologique et les théories évolutionnistes"; Abbé de Broglie, professeur d'apologétique chrétienne à l'Institut catholique de Paris, "Le transformisme et la sociabilité de l'homme"; Adrien Arcelin, "L'homme tertiaire"; E. d'Acy, "Les crânes de Cronstadt, de Néanderthal et de l'Olmo"; Abbé Ducrost, professeur aux facultés catholiques de Lyon, "La station de Solutré"; M. le Comte Henri de Beaufort, "La Grotte de Spy"; M. le Comte Maricourt, "Les sépultures de l'Oise"; Le R. P. Van den Gheyn, S.J., "L'origine européenne des Aryas"; M. le Marquis de Nadaillac, "Les découvertes préhistoriques et les croyances chrétiennes" (ibid., pp. 613–771).

The discussions on evolution by a congress bringing together so many Catholic intellectuals had considerable impact outside the congress. *Le Correspondant* gave a fairly innocuous report, noting that there had not been any systematic opposition to evolution although, no doubt, most of the members were not fully convinced by the arguments in its favor. Of considerable interest to *Le Correspondant* was the defense of the "rights of science" made eloquently by Nadaillac, Lapparent, and Maisonneuve. Equally significant was the assertion by Msgr. d'Hulst, M. le Chanoine Duilhé de Saint-Projet, M. l'Abbé Guillemet and le R. P. Van den Gheyn that, leaving aside the immediate creation of the human soul, evolution was a theory that could be freely discussed by Catholics. *Le Correspondant* happily endorsed the conclusion of Nadaillac's "brilliant synthesis" on the unity of the human race: "Man has always resembled present man, resembled him by his bone structure and still more by his inventive genius."[58] How delightful it was to find one's religious beliefs confirmed by respectable science!

Not all the Catholic world was so smugly content as *Le Correspondant* with the turn taken by the discussions on evolution in the congress. Writing in *Etudes*, the Jesuit Raoul de Scorraille expressed his alarm over the discussions and their results.[59] He regretted that discussion did not always arise out of the desire of the participants to refute evolutionary theory. Scorraille described evolutionary theories as repulsive fictions. In his recapitulation of the evolutionary hypothesis embracing man, Scorraille rejected with horror the idea that "a female animal could have given birth to, nourished, and raised a true man, our ancestor and that of Jesus Christ!" The authority of the congress could unfortunately be used not only to cover such wild ideas but even to encourage them. Scorraille also complained, on weak grounds, about the doctrinal deviations of some members of the congress, which worried him because of the danger that the reputation of the congress for orthodoxy would be threatened if it became notorious for a few excessively bold opinions. What this fantasy meant became clear when Scorraille argued that if pontifical instructions had been followed in the discussion on evolution, questions would have been asked about the agreement of the evolutionary hypotheses with Scripture and Catholic tradition, as well as about the rights of theology and of the church to decide if the evolutionary hypothesis harmonized with the facts revealed in Scripture. It is hard to avoid calling these comments perverse and, in the light of Scorraille's own complaint that pontifical instructions had been followed too closely, simply inconsistent. The questions Scorraille wanted answered were precisely the ones having no place in the strictly scientific sections of anthropology and the natural sciences and, as the best minds of the congress emphasized, were questions excluded by a reasonable interpretation of papal wishes.

Scorraille's fear that the congress had opened Pandora's box was confirmed when an abbé turned a public lecture on the congress into an ardent defense of evolution. Not without considerable justification, the abbé argued that

58. "L'anthropologie au congrès international scientifique des catholiques," *Le correspondant* 151 (May 10, 1888): 575–79.
59. "Deux congrès de savants catholiques," *E* 44 (May 1888): 94–114.

one owed to the congress the power to treat the subject freely without being regarded as too cavalier toward church doctrine. Had not the congress done away with such scruples? Were not Catholic scientists given their liberty in the matter of evolution, once the issues of the creation of matter and of the soul were eliminated from discussion? After allowance is made for the exaggeration inevitable in the rhetoric necessary for the success of a public lecture, there was a good deal of truth in the abbé's arguments. It had been admirably summed up in the last session of the section of the natural sciences by a member who dubiously argued that a majority of members favored evolution. He argued that after the congress one would be ill advised to condemn evolution. No really serious objections emerged from the discussions. The member therefore concluded that the transformist doctrine, even applied to man, is not heterodox and is perfectly admissible.

In order to counteract the impression that the congress had been pro-evolutionary, Scorraille cited d'Hulst's careful denial and reproduced a long letter of a member who had spoken in the congress to deny the contention of the speaker just cited. This heated but trenchant denial left the theological question aside to proclaim evolution inadmissible because it was an unscientific hypothesis, a contention that astonished most members of the natural sciences section. "A hypothesis is anti-scientific when *it is useless*, when it is opposed to the best proven facts, when finally it is generally a pure affair of feeling and imagination: such is the transformist theory."[60] The hypothesis was useless because it did not explain any fact that had not already received its natural interpretation. All arguments based on morphological continuity and survival of rudimentary organs could be explained by the unity and harmony of the plan of the author of nature. *Natura non facit saltus*. Natural selection, the great source of evolution, did not exist in nature. Evolutionary theory was really in opposition to the most universal laws of nature. Drawing upon *Les Plantes potagères*, published by the firm Vilmorin-Andrieux in 1883, the speaker argued that more than five hundred thousand facts contradicted the idea of variability of species, "the fundamental basis of the evolutionary hypothesis." Ferrière's admission of the impossibility of hybrid races and his statement that Darwinism was above all an a priori conception were turned against Darwin, although Darwin had written a letter of approval to Ferrière. Adolphe Brongniart—"the illustrious founder of the science of fossil plants"—provided a good quote: "the transformists leave the ground of positive science and get lost in fairy tales."[61] Nadaillac's pronouncements on prehistory were inevitably cited against the idea of the evolution of man. How could one explain the success of evolution among serious scientists? The speaker used an explanation conventional in but not limited to anti-evolutionary Catholic circles: it was a matter of preference, an "affaire de sentiment." The feeling that actuated the preference was an instinctive hor-

60. Ibid., pp. 109–10. Entire letter by Ch*** is cited on pp. 109–14.
61. Ibid., p. 112. See Emile Ferrière, *Le darwinisme* (Paris, 1872). For this typical factual approach, see Godron, *De l'espèce*, 1:13. In order not to go astray, Godron said he completely abandoned the field of hypothesis, advanced step by step in constantly supporting himself on authentic facts, and then drew the conclusions that naturally followed.

ror, more or less conscious, of the supernatural. As the *Revue scientifique* had pointed out in November 1879, Giard, professor at Lille, usually given credit for being the first zoologist to teach Darwinism in a French faculty, did not have many followers in France. In ten years, the speaker prophesied, there would not be a single evolutionist among the professors of promise in the faculties. Like science, prophesy is best done by professionals! A sarcastic quote from Virchow's attack at the anthropological congress at Frankfurt in 1882 crowned the speaker's anti-evolutionary case with authority and wit.

Scorraille's alarm over the results that could stem from the idea that a congress of Catholic scientists had been favorable to evolution was somewhat lessened by an explanatory lecture on the subject by Msgr. d'Hulst, one of the chief organizers of the congress.[62] Msgr. d'Hulst took great pains to establish the orthodoxy of the positions taken at the congress and especially to emphasize that a majority of the participants had been opposed to Darwinism. Only two or three members expressed their personal opinion in favor of evolution considered from a purely scientific point of view. They also expressly qualified this opinion by stipulating their belief in the immediate creation of the human soul by God and in the necessity of a Creator and Supreme Organizer of the world in order to explain evolution itself, which would otherwise be an effect without a cause. In the philosophy section, a majority opposed the evolutionary hypothesis because of metaphysical difficulties not readily apparent to scientists. The section of anthropology, marshalled under the Marquis de Nadaillac as president, also contained a majority opposed to evolution. But in the natural sciences there were two currents of opinion. The scientists who studied living beings argued that there was no experimental fact in support of evolution, which was therefore an unjustified hypothesis. The paleontologists, on the other hand, agreed to challenging the idea that the fixity of species was always what experience had shown it to be in the nineteenth century. Several members of religious orders, who were also scientists opposed to Darwinism, did not want any barrier erected against scientific discussion of issues of this sort, where liberty could be allowed to reign without threatening religion. D'Hulst was probably correct in arguing that a majority of the members of the congress was opposed to evolutionary ideas. But it is equally significant for the changing attitude of Catholics toward evolution that a small if vocal and persuasive minority of voices was raised in defense of a restricted type of evolution, including some scientific aspects of Darwinism.

The attack in *Etudes* did not go unchallenged. In the course of a long study in the *Revue des questions scientifiques*, Jean d'Estienne effectively showed the emotional and puerile nature of Scorraille's attacks.[63] In a polite and brief dismissal of the good father's vigorous polemic, he classified it as an example of a total a priori opposition to all evolutionary ideas that was really based on personal feelings. D'Estienne gave more attention to the anonymous letter purporting to demolish the evolutionary hypothesis on scientific grounds.

62. *Le congrès scientifique international des catholiques–communication présentée à l'assemblée générale des catholiques le 17 mai 1888* (Paris, 1888).
63. "Le transformisme et la discussion libre," *RQS* 25 (1889): 76–141, 373–420.

The writer had unfortunately invoked Geoffroy Saint-Hilaire and Linnaeus in support of the creationist hypothesis, whereas the former had been explicitly evolutionary and the latter had been inclined at the end of his life to accept the principle of changeability of species. D'Estienne noted that the letter did not mention that Abbé Smets had effectively replied to the speaker at the congress. (Smets had been ferociously anti-evolutionary before his studies in comparative anatomy had converted him into a fervent believer in evolution.) The argument that the evolutionary hypothesis was accepted purely on the basis of feeling and of imagination applied more to materialist interpolations than to the hypothesis as a scientific tool. Only on one issue did d'Estienne agree with the authors in *Etudes*: evolution had been turned into a fearful war machine against philosophical and religious truth. But to oppose all of evolutionary theory was to fail to discriminate between an extremist and unacceptable interpretation and the simple evolutionary theory adopted by Wallace, Saint George Mivart, d'Omalius d'Halloy, Charles Naudin, Gaston de Saporta, and Gaudry.

It was the charge that evolution was a useless hypothesis that provoked the most interesting commentary by d'Estienne. He pointed out that in the "observational sciences," the utility of a theory is not the same as its certainty. This argument, developed in many varieties and with great sophistication, would become commonplace in science a few years later as a result of the writings of Duhem and Poincaré, although the way was prepared in the philosophy of science by Lachelier and Boutroux. D'Estienne used the classic example of the universal use, for so long, of the corpuscular theory in physics to explain heat and light phenomena. Although the theory was abandoned and replaced by the wave theory, which seemed to conform more to the "truth," it could not be argued that the older theory had been useless. Serving to coordinate and synthesize a great number of facts, it had favored scientific progress and inspired scientific discoveries leading to the establishment of the more ingenious wave theory. D'Estienne himself was not so free from conventional views that he could refrain from observing that the later theory was "truer and probably definitive." "Useless" evolutionary theory, however incomplete and dubious, had inspired some of the best works in contemporary science. If the evolutionary hypothesis provided the basis of the work of scientists like Gaudry and Saporta, the charge of uselessness was absurd. Besides, it was impossible to accommodate all contemporary scientific knowledge concerning the variety and closeness of species within the creationist theory as understood by Cuvier and Agassiz.[64] Excellent pragmatic justification existed, then, according to d'Estienne, for the adoption of evolutionary ideas in scientific areas where their utilization produced fruitful results. The distance from this idea to a type of Poincaré's conventionalism

64. A. Proost, "Les naturalistes philosophes," *RQS* 3 (1878): 140-57, 466-85; 6 (1879): 157-74, emphasized the advantages of *transformisme* over Darwinism in modern science. "Elle interprète en effet les destructions et les progressions singulières de l'histoire ancienne de la vie, l'existence actuelle des organes rudimentaires ou avortés, la nécessité du croisement chez un grand nombre d'espèces hermaphrodites, l'adaptation spontanée d'organes à des fonctions nouvelles, et l'unité fonctionnelle dans les deux règnes." Evolution gave a raison d'être to a host of otherwise inexplicable facts.

was not far, although d'Estienne did not take the step. But it would be in the same journal a few years later that Duhem's articles would alarm many Catholics, including scientists, who still adhered to a view of scientific theory that rejected, in the name of the eternal dichotomy of truth and falsehood, any hint of pragmatism in scientific theory.

The debate over evolution was equally passionate at the congress of 1891, also held in Paris. Nadaillac argued that the most important anthropologists confirmed that the great progress made in recent anthropology was not in favor of the evolutionary hypothesis. Nadaillac's paper was read to the session by Maisonneuve, who replied to it and tried to show the value of the arguments in favor of evolution.[65] But the chief debate followed Dr. Pierre Jousset's statement regretting that the congress, assembled to agree on scientific theories and, consequently, to present a strong front to the enemy, was divided on the serious problem of evolution. Jousset had a procrustean plan to end the division by using philosophy to get a definition of a species: "Philosophy teaches us the laws that regulate the harmony and hierarchy of beings." These laws were not vitiated by opposed facts in embryology and paleontology. Evolution could be reconciled with the idea of a God-Creator, but that was not enough for Jousset. One must admit that God created each according to his species. What is a species? Here the higher science of philosophy must enlighten the lower natural sciences and define species in such terms as what is immutable in time and space.[66] After an intervention by the pro-evolutionary Abbé Guillemet to defend Haeckel against the standard accusation that he had "falsified" the plates of His and Semper,[67] Msgr. d'Hulst made plain his doubts concerning Jousset's assertions. It was not the aim of the congress to get the agreement of Catholic scientists on freely debatable questions, still less to vote on a common doctrine. The only unifying bond of the congress was orthodoxy, which placed on the evolutionary hypothesis only the restriction that each individual human soul had been directly created by God. D'Hulst further emphasized that the biblical phrase "after his kind" in Genesis must not be interpreted so as to exclude the possibility of an evolution of species.[68]

Maisonneuve, who argued on scientific grounds with Nadaillac, refused to follow Jousset into the treacherous metaphysical bog; the question had to be decided on the dual basis of the study of facts and the use of logical reasoning. A somewhat technical discussion on crossbreeding dogs of different

65. Le Mis de Nadaillac, correspondant de l'Institut, "Les progrès de l'anthropologie," *Compte rendu du congrès scientifique des catholiques tenu à Paris du 1er au 6 avril 1891* (Paris, 1891), pp. 5–35; Le Dr. Maisonneuve, "Création et évolution," ibid., pp. 36–61. See also M. le Chanoine Duilhé de Saint-Projet, "La méthode et la certitude en anthropologie," ibid., pp. 62–69.

66. Jousset stated the four philosophical axioms relevant in this case: "In rebus bene ordinatus, natura non facit saltus;—Supremum infimi attingit infimum supremi;—Perfectum continet imperfectum; quae sunt dispersa in inferioribus unita sunt in superioribus" (ibid., p. 212).

67. The attacks of Arnold Brass on Haeckel's work in embryology were popular also among Catholics. See G.-G. Lapeyre, "Correspondance d'Allemagne," *Revue pratique d'apologétique* 9 (November 15, 1909).

68. *Compte rendu . . . 1891*, p. 213.

sizes followed. Father Poulain reminded the session of the need to distinguish several evolutionary systems, as Leroy did in his controversial book. Guillemet agreed, calling for a distinction between *évolutionnisme matérialiste* and *évolutionnisme spiritualiste et chrétien.* But the possibility of a non-materialist evolutionary doctrine was greeted skeptically by anti-evolutionists. Discussion ended with a debate over whether the existence of parasites, presupposing the existence of the higher host animals, did not contradict evolution. The president of the section, Nadaillac, asked Freppel, the Bishop of Angers, to end the session. It was not usual for the president to give his personal opinion, but Freppel, who had earlier spoken eloquently on male mammary glands, did not hesitate to proclaim his opposition to all "evolutionary and transformist hypotheses," even if restricted to the lower animals, because they were contrary to "the ideas of a healthy philosophy" and lacked a scientific base. He hastened to add that science enjoys complete liberty, as long as it says nothing contrary to divine revelation and the teaching of the church. Freppel thought that the partisans of the doctrine of the fixity of the species were in a stronger position than the evolutionists because there were more facts to support the anti-evolutionary side. If the supporters of evolution wanted to gain ground, they should group a greater number of facts for verification and discussion. On this platitudinous note, which did not differ much from the general outlook of the anti-evolutionary scientists, ended the discussion of evolution at the 1891 congress.

At the 1894 Congress in Brussels the most controversial figure in the anthropological section was Abbé C. L. Guillemet. Declaring himself a partisan of evolution in his paper "Pour la théorie des ancêtres communs," he vigorously attacked the basic postulate of the *fixistes,* the absolute stability of the species. He skillfully undermined the position of opponents who fell back on the authority of anti-evolutionary scientists by using in his argument the concessions made by Quatrefages in *Les émules de Darwin* and by Nadaillac in paleontology. He again made his plea for Catholic acceptance of a religious and Christian conception of evolution against the atheistic, materialistic variety. For reasons Guillemet condemned as pre-emptory, the *Commission directrice* of the congress refused to print the part of his paper dealing with the ancestors of man.[69] Nadaillac attacked Guillemet's arguments, but Guillemet pointed out that these objections, already well known, were beside the point; it was undeniable that evolution had a great advantage over the "fixist theory" because it provided a law. True, it was only a hypothesis, but it was a great hypothesis. It was not without significance that in speaking of recent work in anthropology, Nadaillac changed his emphasis from the anti-evolutionary trend he noted three years earlier to a contemporary anti-materialistic trend. So the results of recent anthropological research would please Catholic scientists. The easy answers of materialism increasingly evaporated with the

69. *Compte rendu du troisième congrès scientifique international des catholiques tenu à Bruxelles du 3 au 8 septembre 1894* (Bruxelles, 1895), pp. 19–30; N. Boulay, "Les sciences naturelles et l'anthropologie au dernier congrès international des catholiques," *Revue de Lille* 12 (1895): 619–22.

increase in scientific research.[70] Nadaillac was pleased with his report. It was evident in this congress that the anti-evolutionists were on the defensive and that initiative had passed to the other side.

Father Giovannozzi, although not sharing completely the pro-evolutionary enthusiasm of Guillemet, recognized the basis of truth in the evolutionary principle which especially attracted students. In France by this time it became clear that the new generation was following the typical pattern of rejecting the exhausted scientific hypotheses of their predecessors to embrace with enthusiasm the promising varieties of evolutionary hypotheses. Giovannozzi did not want evolution to disturb the faith of believers, or unbelievers to play a trick on the church in claiming to be evolutionists. He therefore proposed that the congress pass a motion to encourage the study of the role played by evolution in the development of the physical world. "The anthropological section of the third scientific congress of Catholics (Brussels) praises and encourages the studies of those who, under the supreme magistrature of the teaching church, devote themselves to research the role that evolution can have had in the collection of secondary causes that have brought the physical world to its present state."[71] The section passed the motion with noisy enthusiasm. In spite of its guarded language, the proposition represented a startling change from the climate of opinion of the first congress in 1888.

It was rather anti-climactic, therefore, when Abbé Boulay, a botanist (bryologist) of the Catholic Faculty of Sciences at Lille, declared that from a Catholic point of view, évolutionnisme was not impossible or contrary to the Christian faith, although it was still only a respectable hypothesis. In his technical paper Boulay declared that in botany, the problem of species, always rather obscure, did not seem to receive a scientific solution from the theory of evolution. But the theory did make the intervention of God more rational than the theory of successive creations.[72] Boulay argued, as Giovannozzi had, that the theory of evolution was more an object for research than a proven principle. This lack of solidity explained the precarious and nearly always exaggerated position of evolutionary theories in the best botanical treatises. Boulay's alarm at the adoption of evolution by youth led him to a general condemnation of their enthusiasm for imaginative hypotheses at the expense of the scientific realities established by the older generation.[73] This was clear-

70. *Compte rendu du troisième congrès*, pp. 209–305, esp. p. 295.

71. Ibid., p. 298.

72. "La théorie de l'évolution en botanique," ibid., pp. 126–38; the paper was given in the section of mathematical and natural sciences.

73. "Il n'y a rien, en effet, de plus propre à fausser l'esprit de la jeunesse que l'emploi, dans l'enseignement, de ces hypothèses ouvrant de larges perspectives à l'imagination. Les jeunes gens, qui vont droit au but, les transforment aussitôt en axiomes et négligent de se rendre un compte exact de l'état réel de la question. De là un enthousiasme irréfléchi qui aboutit presque toujours à une triste fin, à brûler le lendemain les idoles de la veille. Ce spectacle, trop fréquent dans l'histoire de la science, laisse une impression fâcheuse dans l'esprit de beaucoup de personnes. Il est désirable que l'on évite, en traitant de l'origine des êtres vivants, une nouvelle occasion de justes défiances" (ibid., pp. 137–38). Some other related papers given at the congress were A. Suchetet, "Hybrides des oiseaux et des

ly an eloquent protest on the part of that group too anchored in its anti-evolutionary paradigm to change to the new one but, at the same time, forced to recognize its power.

In 1897 the fourth congress was held in Fribourg, Switzerland, site of a five-year-old Catholic university. At this congress, Abbé Boulay pleaded for a revision of the popular Catholic chronology of the human species as derived from indications in Genesis. Man had certainly existed for more than 8,000 years and possibly for 140,000 years. Boulay reached this maximum by taking the estimation of 240,000 years given by Gabriel de Mortillet and subtracting 100,000 years for Mortillet's incorrect assumptions. It was probably an indication of the degree of sophistication characteristic of Catholic scientific circles that the abbé made no mention of Mortillet's notorious anti-clericalism.[74] Of course, many other Catholic commentaries on Mortillet's anthropology made up for the abbé's deficiency!

Embarrassingly obsolescent views were not absent from the congress. Abbé de Casamajor, whose book would appear the next year, irritated some members by the accusation that users of the terms species had distorted it.[75] He argued that it must be more precise or better applied if used as the basis of discussions on the fixity or evolution of species. Casamajor attributed the division on the Bible between fixists and evolutionists to a defect in the idea at the basis of their discussions. Botanists and entomologists did not mean the same thing by species. Much of the strength of *transformisme* lay in the too-restricted idea fixists had of the term species. Five members immediately inundated Casamajor with criticism. But he was not intimidated. After Kirwan gave an analysis of Albert Gaudry's *Essai de paléontologie philosophique*, Casamajor attacked Gaudry because his conclusions were contingent on the acceptance of evolution.[76] In the discussion on the distinction between intelligence and instinct, Kirwan had to deny Casamajor's accusation that he had derived intelligence from instinct. During the discussion of Zahm's "Evolution et téléologie," Casamajor again objected to evolutionary theory. With quite a different emphasis, a number of speakers succeeded in getting Zahm to eliminate the term "supernatural creation" from his work because it had no relation to science. What a dwindling few like Casamajor were struggling

---

mammifères rencontrés à l'état sauvage," whose careful conclusion generally upheld the fixity of species; R. P. Leroy, "De l'instinct des oiseaux," which upheld the fixity of species; and de Kirwan, "L'instinct, la connaissance et la raison," a continuation of what he had said at the second congress, part of which was devoted to a refutation of de Quatrefages' contention that human and animal intelligence are of the same nature, differing only in degree. See also V. van Tricht, review of de Quatrefages' *L'espèce humaine* (Paris, 1877), *RQS* 2 (1877): 635-66, although he finally plays down the disagreement: "Nous réservons au mot intelligence une signification plus haute et bien plus rapprochée de ce que M. de Quatrefages appelle la religiosité et la moralité."

74. Abbé Boulay, "De l'antiquité de l'homme," *Compte rendu du quatrième congrès scientifique international des catholiques tenu à Fribourg (Suisse) du 16 au 20 août 1897* (Fribourg, 1898), pp. 52-67.

75. *Hétérogenie, transformisme et darwinisme. Problème de l'espèce* (Bar-le-Duc, 1898), given a harsh review by C. de Kirwan in *RQS* 44 (1898): 296-99.

76. Charles de Kirwan, "De l'évolution progressive de la connaissance depuis les organismes primaires jusqu'à l'homme," *Compte rendu du quatrième congrès*, pp. 79-99.

to keep together, a growing number of the most powerful and original Catholic minds had long decided to rend asunder. Over a century of rapid change in science had shown the danger of seeking verification of religious truths in science. Separate if not equal altars had to be erected to Yahweh and Isis. The absence of the old type of dispute from the fifth congress (1900) in Munich showed clearly what an enormous distance had been traveled in the twelve years since the first congress in 1888. In one of the rare direct references to Darwinism in the science sections, J. Boiteux simply stated his acceptance of the hypothesis that all zoological species descended from some prototypes whose origin lay in an act of the Creator. Boiteux did not hesitate to speculate on a possible evolutionary link between man and animal, although he upheld a perfectly orthodox dualism. "As for the human species, I believe that it resulted from a totally separate operation, both from the physical and spiritual points of view; but even if it seems to be connected to an animal origin, a fact of real creation could not fail to be produced between the simple animal type and the eminent type of Man, assuming all living nature has been so constructed, that is to say by the express and voluntary acts of the Author of life."[77] Scientific views that had seemed so heretical a few years before could be safely proclaimed in the most respectable forums of "Catholic science." But not one jot or tittle of the eternal religious verities had been sacrificed. That this was possible was by no means the least of the claims of Catholic intellectuals to ingenuity, persistence, and even originality.

The immense intellectual distance that at least part of the Catholic world had come in the fifty years after the publication of Darwin's *Origin* became clear in 1909, when Cambridge University celebrated the centenary of Darwin's birth and the fiftieth anniversary of the publication of the *Origin*. (The year 1909 was one of a double centenary, for in that year, one hundred years after the appearance of *La philosophie zoologique*, the French government inaugurated a statue of Lamarck at the Muséum in Paris.) On receiving an invitation, the rectoral council of the Catholic University of Louvain decided unanimously to accept and to send to Cambridge Canon Dorlodot, director of the university's geological institute and a foreign correspondent of the Geological Society of London. After conveying the admiration of Louvain for the "illustrious naturalist," Dorlodot referred regretfully to the influence of Cuvier in establishing the doctrine of the fixity of the species, thus aiding Alcide d'Orbigny to get his theory of successive destructions and creations established with hardly any opposition. Few followed d'Omalius d'Halloy, in thinking the theory unworthy of the Creator. Dorlodot later gave high praise to his fellow Belgian: "Our national pride as Belgians here prompts me to recall that at the time when the learned world, dazzled by the glory of Cuvier, did not hesitate to accept the twenty-seven successive creations of Alcide d'Orbigny, rather than renounce the Cuvian dogma of the fixity of species, a Belgian Catholic scientist arose and protested against this theory in the name of the attributes of the Creator, and defended the transformation of fossil

77. *Akten des fünften internationalen Kongresses Katholischer Gelehrten zu München vom 24. bis 28. September 1900* (Munich, 1901), pp. 442–43. Albert de Lapparent was president of the congress.

species."[78] It was d'Omalius' good sense as a Christian naturalist, not his theological or metaphysical skill, which led him to conclude that the doctrine of successive creations turned the Creator into a repairman for his own original products and that it did not agree with the idea of the perfection of God. The attacks on Darwinism by unenlightened naturalists and theologians were unjustified. Darwin had established the truth foreshadowed by the genius of St. Augustine. Dorlodot honored Darwin as the Newton of the organic world, praising especially his powers of analysis and synthesis, his close reasoning, and his high moral value.[79] A hearty welcome was given to Dorlodot when he presented this address to the Chancellor, Lord Rayleigh. The English Catholic elite was also pleased. But in Belgium there was some surprise and even criticism of the enthusiasm shown by the delegate to the celebration for Darwinism.

In order to clarify the issues and to show that Louvain had not dishonored itself, Dorlodot gave several lectures after returning to Belgium. These were then enlarged and published, thus ensuring quite a bit of publicity. The address of Dorlodot at Cambridge had been approved by the Dean of the Faculty of Sciences and by the Professor of Dogmatic Theology at Louvain. It was clearly much more than a matter of a personal opinion. Why the guardians of the faith were defending a "heretic" had therefore to be explained, especially in view of the numerous Catholic attacks on Darwinism over the past fifty years. It must have been puzzling to many Catholics to be told that Darwin was not heretical in his thesis of the evolutionary origin of man. But Dorlodot pointed out that the people who declared Darwin a heretic on this point were wrong. Three competent doctors of divinity on the rectoral council did not make this objection, although it was difficult to imagine Louvain's sending a representative to a celebration of the birth of Luther, even if he were considered solely as one of the creators of the German language. But first Dorlodot wanted to judge Darwinism, excepting the origin of man, from the viewpoint of Catholic orthodoxy, rather than that of pure science.

Dorlodot limited himself to "the fundamental teaching of Darwin": first, "the primary origin of living things is the result of a special influence on the part of the Creator, who infused life into one or a few organisms," and, second, "these organisms, by evolving in the course of ages, have given rise to all the organic species which exist at the present time, as well as those which have come down to us only in the fossil state." Darwinism was a fairly moderate system of natural evolution. By contrast, absolute evolution denied the special intervention of God and explained the origin of life in terms of a natural evolution from inorganic matter; creationism, or fixism, attributed to God the creation of each species. Numerous variations of these two rigid

78. H. de Dorlodot, *Darwinism and Catholic Thought,* trans. the Rev. Ernest Messenger (London, 1922), p. 101. The first French edition was printed in 1918 but dated 1913 in order to avoid German censorship in Belgium. The theory of successive creations was invented to cover the insufficiency evident in Cuvier's theory of migrations: Cuvier "explained the variation in fauna in the successive strata of the known regions of the world by the annihilation of certain species and the migration of other forms." Cuvier's theory did not explain all the facts! Ibid.

79. Ibid., appendix 5, pp. 176–77.

positions were possible. From the viewpoints of "positive theology," which studies chiefly the Bible and the fathers and doctors of the church, and of "speculative theology," which is really Catholic philosophy based on the truths of positive theology, including the use of the "data of natural knowledge," Dorlodot came to a number of conclusions. Many of them seemed excessively rash to Catholic anti-evolutionists, although the origin of man was excluded from consideration. Dorlodot put forward first the proposition making up the negative part of his thesis: Scripture contains no argument against the theory of natural evolution, even absolute evolution. He then advanced three propositions making up the positive part of his thesis. The church fathers were very favorable to the theory of absolute evolution, and the example of some great doctors justified acceptance of contemporary scientific teaching on evolution. Dorlodot argued that the application of the certain principles of Catholic theology and philosophy to the concrete data of the observational sciences turned a very radical system of transformism into an absolute certainty. This meant that Darwin's view that living beings derived from one or a few very simple organisms was highly probable.[80] Given the scientific difficulties of the theory of absolute evolution, Darwin's hypothesis of God's special intervention at the origin of life seemed at that time a legitimate one. In this argument, Dorlodot was doing what the opponents of Darwinism had done: finding support for a scientific theory in scriptural and theological sources, a procedure that gave some consolation to souls in distress but had the grave disadvantage of making possible subsequent modifications of that theory appear heretical to those who took orthodoxy seriously. Dorlodot's fourth proposition was even more alarming: "The Catholic theory concerning the natural activity of secondary causes is capable of explaining a natural transformist evolution as Darwin understood it, and entitles us to reject as entirely superfluous the additional special interventions postulated by those who hold the fixity of species or by the moderate creationists."[81] These arguments clearly put Dorlodot in a position opposed to or seriously differing from many Catholic apologists.

Dorlodot boldly argued that the concordists, like Pozzi, Msgr. Lamy, and Brucker, had made a fundamental mistake in setting out "to establish a positive agreement between the Mosaic cosmogony and that of science. For, although two truths cannot disagree with each other, it does not follow that two statements equally true but dealing with different subjects signify the same thing. Now the Mosaic cosmogony (or rather the cosmogony of the Priestly Code, since we are here dealing only with the first chapter of *Genesis*) and that of science deal with different subjects." The sacerdotal cosmogony simply affirms that the world is the work of God and does not bother with God's possible use of secondary causes in His work. The cosmogony of the sciences, by contrast, deals with the part played by secondary causes in producing the present state of the universe; it does "not deny the ultimate action of the First Cause." Dorlodot apologized for spending so much time on the inane concordist theory since it existed then in name only. Many of the

80. Ibid., pp. 97 ff.
81. Ibid., pp. 6, 105 ff. (translation slightly modified).

key points had been conceded by the concordists: the day periods did not correspond to the first appearance of plant or animal life assigned to each day; day periods may overlap; and the number six has no special significance in the history of the universe. His sole justification for considering it at all was that it was the theory taught by most Catholic professors of religion or of apologetics and was still found in the manuals given to the young. Dorlodot emphasized that "the infallible teaching of *Genesis* obliges us to attribute directly to God the origin of all the vegetable or plant forms . . . whether they are called species or varieties." This was not inconsistent with his main thesis of the compatibility of Darwinism and Catholicism, for he carefully specified that by Darwinism he meant scientific evolution as Darwin held it, not the "unphilosophical theories" of atheistic and materialistic evolution.[82]

From the viewpoint of internal church polemics, Dorlodot built up an overwhelming case by showing that opponents of Darwinism, especially Brucker, had put themselves in the anomalous position of being "insulting towards some of the great luminaries of the Church," including Origen, Athanasius, Augustine, and Aquinas. Dorlodot also showed their mistakes on some technical issues in biblical exegesis. "St. Augustine upholds as certain the theory of the absolute natural evolution of living beings, from inorganic matter right up to the body of man inclusively."[83] Once this had been shown, Catholics could support Darwinism on the basis of an a fortiori argument. (It also turned Haeckel into a quasi-Augustinian.) Dorlodot did not advocate adopting the radical views of the fathers of the church on absolute evolution, but rather the less radical position of Darwinism. This would follow the example of the later doctors of the church and would also be in agreement with contemporary scientific theory. For scientific reasons, "Aristotelian scholastics generally limited the theory of absolute natural evolution to a section of living beings . . . but all the Doctors remained faithful to the spirit of Christian Naturalism. Provided we remain faithful to this spirit, we are therefore free to accept, at least provisionally, a less radical solution than that of absolute natural evolution if the present state of science makes this advisable." Dorlodot was sure "that if the great Doctor had belonged to the Rectoral Council of this University in 1909, he would have decided, as did our Deans, that for the sake of the honour of religion the Catholic University could not abstain from joining in the celebration at Cambridge."[84]

Dorlodot was aware that no contemporary scholar would openly uphold the proposition that Scripture maintained that the appearance of species was due to a special intervention by God. The approach had changed: "People usually content themselves with pious wishes: 'Be careful: at the very least, do not affirm anything. Darwinism had done so much harm! It had been so much exploited against religion! And then there is the question of man!'" It was the harsh judgment of Dorlodot that Darwinism had been so successfully exploited against religion because there had been no lack of misguided

82. Ibid., pp. 27, 42.
83. Ibid., pp. 46 ff., 63; see pp. 65 ff. for further commentary on Augustine and on St. Gregory of Nyssa and St. Basil.
84. Ibid., pp. 63–64, 87.

Catholic authors who had compromised Christianity by falsely representing it as irreconcilable with scientific theories, especially Darwinism. This move by Catholics had the unfortunate result of turning scientists away from religion because they saw clearly the truth of Darwinism; naturally, they did not even consider studying the foundations of a religion represented to them as opposed to the scientific theories they believed to be true. A horrible mistake had been made by apologists who had misinterpreted Scripture and who had been ignorant of the teachings of the fathers and doctors of the church relevant to the issues.[85]

Of course a current of Catholic opposition to Darwinism based on contemporary biology continued into the twentieth century. For those who wanted to find scientific attacks on Darwinism, the work of many leading biologists in the 1890s provided a cornucopia of criticisms. Hans Driesch was a favorite but by no means exclusive source for the ringing proclamation that Darwinism belonged to history like that other curiosity of the nineteenth century, Hegelian philosophy. How Father Gratry would have loved a "scientific" condemnation of Hegel! Darwinism and Hegelianism were, in Driesch's opinion, variations on the same theme of how one can lead an entire generation by the nose.[86] Again in 1909, Driesch claimed that "the complete bankruptcy of Darwinism as a *general* theory of descendance is absolutely free from doubt."[87] In spite of similar judgments by biologists like Reinke, Fleischmann, Wolff, and Pauly, the brunt of the attack was on Darwinian selection, not the doctrine of evolution, which was subscribed to by most biologists. Ironically, the Jesuit scientist Erich Wasmann discreetly defended evolution against the attacks of Albert Fleischmann.[88] Although most of these quarrels were peculiar to the great German debate over Darwinism, the repercussions were clearly registered in France.

An article by Father Donau in the *Revue des questions scientifiques* in 1910 made clear the attraction of Driesch's views for Catholics. The revival of Thomism necessarily aroused a great interest in Aristotle. Driesch also advertised his admiration for the great genius of Aristotle by using the word *entelechy* as a mould to be filled with new contents. In living matter there is a characteristic internal finality, different from that of machines, which cannot be explained by physico-chemical forces alone. But Donau lamented that Driesch's idealist prejudice prevented him from seeing that this internal

85. Ibid., pp. 61–62.
86. Ibid., cited by Sinéty, *RQS* 67 (1910): 7, from the *Biologisches Zentralblatt* (1896), p. 355.
87. Sinéty, quoted from "Biologie scientifique et transformisme," *RP* (November 1909): 494, which was translated from *The Science and Philosophy of the Organism* (Aberdeen, 1908; 2 vols., London, 1908-9). In his review of Teilhard's "bag of tricks," *The Phenomenon of Man*, P. B. Medawar argues that "the real weakness of modern evolutionary theory" is "its lack of a complete theory of variation, of the candidature for evolution": *Mind* 70 (1961): 99-106, reprinted in Philip Appleman, ed., *Darwin* (New York, 1970), pp. 476-85.
88. J. M., S.J., "Ontogenèse et phylogenèse," *RQS* 61 (1907): 174-218, 423-48, esp. p. 445. The earlier debate between German biologists over Darwinism is superbly analyzed by William M. Montgomery, "Germany," in Glick, ed., *Comparative Reception*, pp. 81-116.

finality requires a vital substantial principle essentially different from crude matter. So the gulf of idealism separated the most clearly vitalist of the "neo-scholastics" from the scholastics themselves. This rapprochement with the scholastics that was so pleasing to Donau was equally alarming to others. Adolph Wagner viewed the concept of entelechy as a regression to dependence on a sort of Demiurge or other principles hostile to science.[89] Catholics were delighted at a turn of events going beyond the wildest wishes of the promoters of Thomism and establishing a scientific-philosophical symbiosis that had seemed so remote, if not impossible, a decade or so before.

When the first volume of Driesch's 1907 Gifford Lectures was translated into French, the writer of the preface for the French reading public, Jacques Maritain, was a professor of philosophy at the Institut catholique in Paris and the Coryphaeus of the Thomist revival, at least in the twentieth century.[90] During his studies at Heidelberg (1906–7), Maritain got to know Driesch, although by then the latter was regarded by "official science" as outside its pale. A former student of Haeckel, His, and Roux, Driesch became famous through his research in the physiology of embryonic development but gradually shifted from zoology to philosophy after 1902 "in order to devote himself, according to custom, to the elaboration of a system and an original *Weltanschauung*." Maritain was just as critical of Driesch's "Kantian agnosticism" and solipsist idealism as Donau had been. But Driesch's biological work was an event of great significance in the history of science: "After the reign of pure phenomena and brute fact, after three centuries of mathematicization," Driesch had really announced a restoration of natural philosophy in the Aristotelian and scholastic sense, especially in the sciences of life. Maritain was struck by the fact that Driesch, the complete modern, nearly ignorant of the *philosophia perennis*, without any preconceived ideas and even with a Kantian philosophical substructure and intellectual equipment, had arrived at the idea of entelechy. He developed his vitalist theory before knowing the works of Aristotle or of Hartmann.[91] This indicated to Maritain the inexhaustible fertility of Aristotelian and thirteenth-century scholastic thought as well as the possibilities open to neo-Thomist thought, alone capable of assimilating in a living and progressive synthesis the materials accumulated by science.[92] In breaking the hierarchy established by Aquinas and in isolating itself from

89. F. Donau, S.J., "Un vitaliste idéaliste: Hans Driesch," *RQS* 67 (1910): 426–53; Ad. Wagner, *Geschichte des Lamarkismus, als Einführung in die psychobiologische Bewegung der Gegenwart* (Stuttgart, 1909), p. 182, cited in Donau, p. 453.

90. *La philosophie de l'organisme* (Paris, 1921). Translation of *The Science and Philosophy of the Organism* by M. Kollmann (Bibliothèque de philosophie expérimentale—Marcel Rivière, éditeur). See also *L'homme et le monde*, trans. Gabriel Gobron (Paris, 1930) (Bibliothèque de philosophie spiritualiste moderne et des sciences psychiques—Les éditions Jean Meyer). Driesch wrote a short preface recommending Edmond Wiétrich, *La réincarnation* (Lille-Paris, 1932).

91. See Maritain, pp. vi–vii, for his distinction between Driesch's scientific vitalism (better called animism) and the scientifically discredited vitalism of other schools, including most of the neo-vitalist schools in Germany and the school of Montpellier. The last was upheld by the Catholic medical scientist Joseph Grasset.

92. For an attempt to reconcile evolution and Thomism on the common ground of psychology, see R. P. Gardeil, O.P., "L'évolutionnisme et les principes de saint Thomas d'Aquin," *RT* 1, no. 3 (1893): 316–27, 725–37; 3, no. 2 (1894): 29–42: 4, no. 1 (1895): 61–84; 5, no. 5 (1895): 607–33; 6, no. 1 (1896): 64–86; 7, no. 2 (1896): 215–47.

metaphysics and the philosophy of nature, the experimental disciplines had been led into material growth but also into intellectual poverty. From the methodological viewpoint the animist doctrine could be established in three ways: by the metaphysician through the application of his knowledge of hylomorphism to the living organism; by the philosopher of nature through showing the principles by which the living body differs from a machine; and by the experimental biologist through showing that the living body is absolutely irreducible to a physico-chemical machine. After Driesch showed this last impossibility scientifically, he could assert the existence of his "factor E," which the philosopher could call "a soul."[93] This development in biology led Maritain and others to conclude that basic metaphysical teachings on man found complementary support in at least one segment of contemporary science. It seems that even theologians and philosophers hankered after scientific proof, the panacea of the nineteenth century. This did not undo the painful work of the separation of science and religion achieved over the last half century, especially in biology. The theologian and the philosopher possessed their own methods and certainty of knowledge, indeed of a "higher" sort. But it was at least a pleasant surprise that science confirmed one's discovery—or recovery, in the case of Thomism—of philosophical truth.

By the early 1920s the anti-evolutionist line that had been typical of such journals as *Etudes* and the *Revue thomiste* had been replaced with a cautious willingness to accept the reasonable conclusions of sober scientific work, even when these conclusions were pro-evolutionary. The reception of Louis Vialleton's important treatise on osteology, *Membres et ceintures des vertébrés tétrapodes*, is an excellent illustration.[94] Whereas the moderate acceptance of evolution by Gaudry had generally been cause for alarm in the Catholic journals, the work of Vialleton was widely praised. Vialleton could be mistakenly included in the anti-evolutionary camp. He was, however, a convinced *évolutionniste* who opposed the idea of continuous and mechanistic *transformisme*. He certainly could not be included in the tiny group of diehards who still held to the dogma of the absolute fixity of species. It satisfied Catholics that Vialleton's criticisms could be used against the anti-finalistic evolution subscribed to by nearly all biologists of the period. It was also comforting that Vialleton reserved a special niche for man in the creation and thought that Boule had exaggerated the simian nature of the Nean-

93. ". . . 'facteur' de spécification, irréductible à toute constellation d'agents spatiaux, 'facteur E' ou 'psychoïde,' qu'un scrupule de prudence scientifique l'empêchera toutefois de dénommer 'âme' parce qu'il ne le saisit que du dehors et n'en discerne pas métaphysiquement la nature" (Maritain, p. x). Maritain gave a technical exposé of Driesch's theory in "Le néo-vitalisme en Allemagne et le darwinisme," *RP* 18 (September-October 1910): 417-41, esp. pp. 431-39.

94. Vialleton, *Membres et ceintures des vertébrés tétrapodes. Critique morphologique du transformisme* (Paris, 1923). Vialleton was professor in the Faculty of Medicine at Montpellier. In 1908 he had published *Un problème de l'évolution, la théorie de la récapitulation des formes ancestrales au cours du développement embryonnaire*, in which he followed Oscar Hertwig in criticizing Haeckel's biogenetic law. In 1911, his minor classic, *Eléments de morphologie des vertébrés*, gave what Dalbiez called "une révision minutieuse des assertions du transformisme." See R. Dalbiez, "Le transformisme et la morphologie," *RT* 30 (1925): 357-74; 31 (1926): 48-61, 130-53, 245-62; and "Classification et sériation en biologie," *RT* 31 (1926): 342-57.

derthal skeleton found at La Chapelle-aux-Saints in 1908.[95] After 1912 Teilhard de Chardin frequently reviewed works on evolution for *Etudes*, formerly a bastion of anti-evolutionary argument. In his review of Vialleton, Teilhard raised some technical questions about interpretations, questioning especially the idea that mutationism and classical evolution were necessarily opposed. In applying the idea of mutations to the appearance of species, modern biology was only correcting and completing Lamarck and Darwin. Thus Vialleton was interpreted by Teilhard as having demonstrated on each page "the true and essential transformist position," which consists of regarding living forms as deriving functionally one from the other, according to scientifically analyzable conditions. Vialleton's attack was on the type of transformism based on a gradual and continual passage from form to form under the exclusive influence of mechanical forces. Rejecting the theory of mutations, especially directed by psychic force, Vialleton argued that zoology should orient itself toward a discontinuous theory of living forms—species could be regarded as appearing in "quanta." The basic evolutionary gospel remained.[96]

The critical concern of Catholic philosophers and scientists with the role of evolution in biology continued throughout the 1920s. A 1927 issue of the *Cahiers de philosophie de la nature*, which published the works of the active members of the Société de philosophie de la nature, an institution of intellectual cooperation between philosophers and scientists, was devoted entirely to evolution.[97] Although the five authors were able to accept the idea of descent as an explanation of the historical succession of living forms, they found the word *transformisme* a source of confusion, sometimes referring to an evolution free of causal explanation, sometimes referring to a purely mechanist theory of evolution. The authors were dissatisfied with this "metaphysic of evolution" because it seemed partly irrational. Certain classic proofs of evolution were useless or defective; evolution could become rational only if it superimposed a finalist interpretation on the contemporary mechanist one.[98] But the paleontologist Gagnebin reminded his readers that paleontol-

95. R. de Sinéty, review of Vialleton in "Philosophie scientifique. Une critique du transformisme," *Archives de philosophie* 3 (1926): 44–49. "C'est un type très indépendant et très particulier appartenant par son organisation à la classe des mammifères. Il [*man*] n'est ni un ordre ni une famille, car si certains de ses caractères anatomiques, comme la station verticale, permettraient d'en faire un ordre aussi légitime que celui des Chiroptères, par exemple, d'autres comme son développement cérébral et ses caractères, constatés dès les premiers fossiles connus qui savaient faire du feu et choisir des armes, le séparent tellement du reste des mammifères que c'est faire œuvre grossièrement pédantesque d'employer pour le classer les règles appliquées à ces derniers" (Vialleton, cited ibid., pp. 48–49).

96. P. Teilhard de Chardin, review of Vialleton in *E* 179 (May 1, 1924): 381–82.

97. Lucien Cuénot, Roland Dalbiez, Elie Gagnebin, W.-R. Thompson, and Louis Vialleton, *Le transformisme* (Paris, 1927). For an ultra-critical approach, see J. Lefèvre (directeur du laboratoire de bioénergétique), *Manuel critique de Biologie* (Paris, 1938).

98. "La théorie de l'évolution, dans la mesure où elle peut être scientifiquement adoptée par chacun, en fonction de sa propre critique et de la valeur systématique qu'elle assigne aux faits bruts, ne devient rationnelle qu'à partir du moment où elle superpose une interprétation finaliste à l'explication mécaniste courante": Cuénot et al., *Le transformisme*, p. 8. On the need for the idea of finality, see especially R. Dalbiez, "Le transformisme et la philosophie," ibid., pp. 173–218.

ogy did not show the fixity of species. He also warned Catholics about the incomplete and limited nature of Aristotle's knowledge: "If our mind, in order to attain some degree of truth, must subject itself to reality, there is no other possible attitude for it but to prefer the theory of evolution to the fixist hypothesis."[99]

This acceptance of evolution was counterbalanced by the critical morphological remarks of Vialleton on mechanistic evolution. Vialleton subscribed to the evolutionary action of unknown forces which, seemingly pre-directed and pre-guided, strikingly resembled the idea of creation. Following Novikoff's work on the parallelism of forms in different animal types, Vialleton agreed that comparative anatomy based only on homology is incomplete and unilateral; evolution had turned it away from the study of the regularity of vital phenomena and their laws, which had been stimulated by Cuvier's study of the correlation and the subordination of organs and by Etienne Geoffroy St.-Hilaire's law of the balancing of organs. Vialleton hoped that his study would serve to bring minds back to the path that had been traced by Cuvier.[100]

But the most critical remarks on evolution came from the head of the American "European Parasite Laboratory," Thompson, who had doctorates in the natural sciences and in Thomistic philosophy. In his study *Le parasitisme et la symbiose* (1912), Maurice had used parasites as a clear case of antifinalist and mechanist evolution. This was rejected by Thompson on good biological grounds. But behind these scientific arguments was his Thomistic philosophy, which aims at a harmonious synthesis of the data of experience and those of reason. In the philosophies of Aristotle and Aquinas, Thompson found a happy synthesis of the fixism of Parmenides and the basic evolutionism of Heraclitus; this synthesis resolved all things into the ideas of being and necessity but recognized also the realities of becoming and of contingency. A limited type of evolution could be incorporated into traditional philosophy if it observed the same limits and was a demonstrated fact or an intelligible hypothesis.[101]

By the 1920s and especially by the 1930s Catholic thought had moved so far in the direction of evolutionary theory, which itself had moved far from its Darwinian paradigm, that a sort of intussusception had occurred. A significant force for change was the existence of scientists among the clergy. Men like Teilhard, Sinéty, and Breuil exerted tremendous influence because of their scientific work and their moderation. This influence was wielded through the journals, the Catholic faculties of science, and their actual scientific work. Abbé Maurice Manquat did his work in the natural sciences under

99. Elie Gagnebin (chargé du cours de paléontologie à l'université de Lausanne), "Le transformisme et la paléontologie," ibid., pp. 9–59.

100. L. Vialleton, "Morphologie et transformisme," ibid., pp. 61–122.

101. "Un certain transformisme, pour autant qu'il respecte les exigences du réel, et les limites infranchissables des essences dont les interrelations fondent l'ordre cosmique, y trouve son compte. Pour autant que le transformisme est un fait démontré, ou même une hypothèse intelligible, il rentre sans difficulté dans les cadres de la philosophie traditionnelle": W.-R. Thompson, "Le parasitisme et la doctrine transformiste," ibid., pp. 123–51; see also *RT* 29 (1924): 460–80.

the zoologist Cuénot at Nancy. In his work on tropisms in animal behavior, Manquat followed up the work of von Buddenbrock and de Blees and contributed to the ruin of the prestige of the deterministic theories of Jacques Loeb and his successors. Manquat believed that any theory of tropism makes a basic mistake in giving the determining role of animal behavior to external stimuli. He argued that the determinant is in the organism, in the center of its material substance, where matter is individualized. This debate continues in biology: "Organismic biologists have seen a deadly foe in the theory of tropisms or forced-movements associated with the name of Loeb." Both groups of biologists had their dreams shattered: "The early claims for the general applicability of tropism models have been restricted largely because of the inability of the models to be modified in ways appropriate for yielding quasi-explanations of relevant phenomena." Extreme opponents of Loeb ended up in a possibly worse position, for vitalism failed "to generate model-explanations."[102] But it is interesting to note that Catholic bio-philosophical opinions were increasingly based on scientific work done by Catholic scientists. The growth of a Catholic scientific structure had important consequences for Catholic thought.

Whatever the philosophical criticisms that could be made of biological mechanism, its value as a methodological hypothesis in biology had to be recognized. In the 1930s it was also possible to make a similar if lesser claim for a vitalistic hypothesis in biology. Ewald Oldekop admitted that even if one recognized the equivalence of the two biological methods, it was clear that the mechanistic method had acquired a formidable preponderance in biological research since the middle of the nineteenth century. But the holistic or synthetic method had also rendered appreciable services to modern science in a short time after its hesitant introduction.[103] Oldekop noted that this dualism of biological ideas was inconsistent with the mind's tendency to seek unity in its activities, a trait especially characteristic of Catholicism's rejection of any intimation of a doctrine of two "truths." But growing recognition of the hypothetical nature of scientific ideas made it possible for some to accept in biology a situation similar to that existing for some time in physics with its corpuscular-wave dualism concerning light and electrons. Most Catholics, like most scientists who were not Catholic or even Christian, could not accept or acquiesce for long in this challenge to traditional logic.

102. Manquat, *Sur la théorie des tropismes dans le comportement animal* (Thèse, Nancy, 1921), p. 232. See also his *Aristote naturaliste* (Paris, 1932), *Cahiers de philosophie de la nature*, vol. 5. Quotes are from Beckner, *The Biological Way of Thought*, pp. 51, 111.

103. Oldekop, *Le principe de hiérarchie dans la Nature et ses rapports avec le problème du vitalisme et du mécanisme* (Paris, 1933), pp. 66–67. *Cahiers de philosophie de la nature*, vol. 6. Users of the synthetic method cited by Oldekop were Tschermak, Ungerer, Dacqué, Buytendijk, André, Armin, and Müller. See also Remy Collin (professor of histology, Faculty of Medicine, Nancy), *Physique et métaphysique de la vie. Esquisse d'une interprétation synthétique des phénomènes vitaux* (Paris, 1925), and Bohdan Rutkiewicz, *L'individualisation, l'évolution et le finalisme biologique* (Paris, 1933). Rutkiewicz had taken his doctorate in natural sciences at Grenoble and was a professor at the Catholic University of Lublin, Poland. His work was a translation from the Polish "Publications of the Philosophical Society of Saint Thomas Aquinas," vol. 1.

For some minds, the fight against biological mechanism took on the aspect of a fight for the defense of certain qualities of civilization especially associated with France. Ironically, the French mechanists could claim the sublime patronage of two Catholics, Descartes and Lavoisier. It was in volume four of the *Cahiers de philosophie de la nature* that Buytendijk made his Dutch plea for a French defense of vitalistic biology.[104] Buytendijk believed that science shows the imprint of the human mind and therefore reflects in its structure the basic attitude of the personality that creates it. Assuming that there is a national style of thinking, he argued that each nation has its preferred science, problems that fascinate it, and methods that are appropriate to it. Language is an expression of deep emotions, often the most deeply hidden but nevertheless the most true. Like all means of expression, it hides its essential significance by its dynamic form. French is an expression of the wish to achieve perfect clarity and quivers with a love for reality. Because of the role played in the French tradition by the various aspects of human life, no other people was better suited to proclaim the gulf separating man from animal.[105] During World War I, Bergson had given this anti-mechanistic argument a specifically anti-German twist. Bernanos gave it an anti-scientific twist. It satisfied Catholic scientific and philosophical egos to associate the anti-mechanistic trend with a segment of the contemporary scientific community and its admiration of the essence of the French tradition.

In his brief personalized account of Catholic evolutionary thought in late-nineteenth- and twentieth-century France, Bégouën noted a cooling off in the controversy over evolution at the end of the nineteenth and the beginning of the twentieth centuries.[106] He did not mean that the debate had ended but rather that the old violence had disappeared. Part of the explanation lay in the emergence of a new intellectual climate more favorable to religion. With Boutroux, Poincaré, and Duhem, the nature of science itself had undergone a transformation that limited it to a severely circumscribed area. Although some scientists like Berthelot, Delage, and Le Dantec kept up the attack on religion, it was easy for the apologists to take the offensive with powerful ammunition from the sciences themselves. Of capital importance was the widespread acceptance of the evolutionary hypothesis in prehistory,

104. F.-J.-J. Buytendijk, "Les différences essentielles des fonctions psychiques de l'homme et des animaux," in *Vues sur la psychologie animale* par Hans André, F.-J.-J. Buytendijk, Georges Dwelshauvers, Maurice Manquat; avant-propos, discussion, notes par Remy Collin, Roland Dalbiez, Jacques Maritain. Buytendijk, professor of physiology at the University of Groningen, created and directed the unique Institute of Animal Psychology in Amsterdam. He was significantly influenced by Husserl and Scheler, as well as by Bergson and Claudel. See "La Valeur biologique de l'art poétique de Claudel," ibid., pp. 127–36.

105. "La tradition française ne veut rien de moins qu'annoncer à la culture européenne la splendeur seigneuriale de la vie humaine, son luxe, sa joie, sa liberté. Il n'est pas un autre peuple que le vôtre [*the French*] pour être si profondément enraciné dans la terre solide d'une vitalité saine et pour ressentir davantage par une révélation merveilleuse que l'homme s'élève glorieusement au-dessus de toute vie animale" (ibid., pp. 35 ff.). On national styles of thinking and their relation to science, see Harry W. Paul, *The Sorcerer's Apprentice: The French Scientist's Image of German Science, 1840–1919* (Gainesville, Fla., 1972).

106. Bégouën, *Quelques souvenirs*, p. 30.

anthropology, and biology, even by Catholic scientists. It had become perfectly clear that not only did evolutionary doctrines not pose any threat to religion, but they could be used as a weapon in its defense. And some apologists were ingenious in finding support for evolutionary theories in the profuse opinions of the church fathers. But it must not be forgotten that a certain caution was evident in the works of most Catholic writers on the subject because of the possibility of condemnation by Rome and because of the vigilance of the opponents of evolution in speedily signaling to Rome the potential heresies of their fellow Christians. Thus the quarrel continued well into the twentieth century, with both sides vying for the support of Rome against their opponents, a practice typical of the vicious infighting of modern French Catholics.

The task of Msgr. Benigni and the integrists in Rome was facilitated by the quasi-international integrist organization and the ostensible ignorance of the Vatican on contemporary scientific issues. This ignorance was not total, for the Société scientifique de Bruxelles with its *Revue des questions scientifiques* and the Cardinals Bourne, Mercier, and Maffi probably had some enlightening effect in Roman circles. Yet the integrists seem to have been powerful enough to keep Rome on the side hostile to evolution. Unable to find enough support from the hierarchy, French Catholic scientists organized themselves to fight the evil effects of the integrists on Vatican opinion in scientific matters. In 1925 an international group of scientists, both clerical and lay, met in what was called the Council of Altamira. This was a bold stroke of humorous genius in view of the association of the place with prehistory. After four days of discussion of the idea of evolution, they decided to send a memorandum to the pope. In the text sent through the nuncio in Paris, particular attention was paid to the word evolution, in particular its key role in science and its lack of threat to Christianity. "This word evolution must be taken in its widest sense, without going into the discussions of the theories of the schools (Darwinism, Lamarckism, transformism, etc.). To state our thought precisely: evolution is after all neither a theory nor a hypothesis. Its principle is the scientific method itself, since it consists of considering beings and things in their normal order of succession. This is done in a way recognizing that they are at least partially the product of beings and events that preceded them and prepared for them and the principle of what follows them. This does not affect at all the ontological cause or the principle of creation by God. The theory of evolution reaches only the exterior surface of what the permanent creative act of God successively materializes in *time* and *space*. . . . On the whole evolution is only a condition of knowledge."[107] These views did not differ, it was emphasized, from those of Augustine, Gregory, and other fathers of the church, who explained the work of God as the creation of the universe with the potential for development.

107. Ibid., pp. 38–39. On the anti-modernist machinations of the international *Sodalitium Pianum* (S.P.) of the integrists, see Emile Poulat, *Intégrisme et catholicisme intégral. Un réseau international antimoderniste: La "Sapinière," 1909–1921* (Tournai, 1969), and *Catholicisme, démocratie et socialisme. Le mouvement catholique et Mgr Benigni de la naissance du socialisme à la victoire du fascisme* (Tournai, 1977). Both volumes are in the series "Religion et sociétés."

Through Cardinal Mercier, it became known that Rome would not take any action hostile to the cause of the evolutionists if the study of relevant issues remained "prudent and objective." The integrists had been beaten at their own game. Whether it was the weight of the scientific objections to any anti-evolutionary declaration from Rome that prevented such a declaration is another question. No doubt the scholarly Pius XI was the type of pope most likely to be impressed by scientific arguments. But the integrists themselves were in a considerably weakened position as compared with their power in the days of Pius X, and their powerful intellectual ally, Action Française, was about to be condemned. The evolutionists could not have chosen a more opportune political moment in which to defeat the integrists on the issue of evolution.

In spite of certain difficulties of the Catholic mathematician-philosopher Edouard Le Roy with Catholic authorities over theological matters, in which he committed "errors" necessitating retraction, his collaboration with Teilhard de Chardin and Teilhard's own work went beyond making evolution a safe subject for Catholics to win a general Catholic public in its favor. The work of the Abbé Breuil in the area of prehistory and his famous interview with the pope in 1935 also did much to further the acceptance of evolution as a scientific hypothesis without dangers for religion. Probably not without a certain influence in the softening of the stand of the religious establishment was the development of God-oriented attitude by some intellectuals and biologists. Lecomte du Noüy's *L'avenir de l'esprit* (1941) was an obvious source of support for the religious cause. It was even more comforting to find the biologist Cuénot fighting absolute determinism and referring to the action of a transcendent power, a sort of will or intelligence that guides nature or acts under the cover of secondary causes.[108] Bégouën hastened to ask what this power or intelligence or will could be if it were not God. This was hardly a non sequitur. Lecomte du Noüy himself had declared as much: "Nous sommes donc, bon gré, mal gré, ramenés à admettre l'idée de Dieu."[109] A precarious aid for the religious cause could even be derived from the rationalist Jean Rostand, still the toast of a freethinkers' congress in 1970: "Jean Rostand . . . after having noted, in his great book, *La genèse de la vie*, the check suffered by physico-chemical theories, speaks of a 'mysterious spark.'"[110]

108. Cuénot, *Invention et finalité en biologie* (Paris, 1941), cited in Bégouën, *Quelques souvenirs*, p. 47. Cf. Cuénot's general opinion of the Catholic situation. "Les théologiens catholiques furent longtemps fixistes. Ils acceptent aujourd'hui l'évolutionnisme, mais en lui donnant une base spiritualiste: Dieu serait Cause première en créant le monde; à partir de cet instant, celui-ci évolue par ses seules forces (causes secondes) selon le plan conçu par la Sagesse divine; à un moment donné du temps la Vie sortit de l'inorganique, puis se développèrent les espèces en progression ascendante jusqu'à l'Homme, bourgeon terminal de l'évolution. Mais que l'on croie ou non à une causalité finale de l'Univers, à un Principe transcendant au monde qu'il aurait créé ou immanent à celui-ci, l'observation et l'interprétation *scientifiques* ne diffèrent point: les biologistes, quelle que soit leur opinion métaphysique, conviennent que tout ce qui se passe dans le monde relève des causes naturelles ou facteurs de l'évolution dont l'étude est l'objet de la Biologie": Cuénot, *La genèse des espèces animales*, 3d ed. (Paris, 1932), pp. 27-28.

109. *L'avenir de l'esprit*, cited in Bégouën, *Quelques souvenirs*, p. 20. See George N. Schuster and Ralph E. Thorson, eds. *Evolution in Perspective. Commentaries in Honor of Pierre Lecomte du Noüy* (Notre Dame, Ind., 1970).

110. Bégouën, *Quelques souvenirs*, p. 20. Rostand is completely agnostic in his atti-

Bégouën could not refrain from comparing these speculations with the dogmatic attacks characteristic of the late nineteenth and early twentieth centuries. As an example of the extreme views sometimes expressed by "materialistic scientists," he cited the work of Delage and Goldsmith. After an introduction linking the ideas of causality and evolution, they went on to declare that the idea of causality had eliminated from human thought all traces of the marvelous and the supernatural. Bégouën gave the standard reply to this hoary argument: materialist evolution discovers and explains the succession of secondary causes but not the absolute origin of all things, the first cause of life and of matter itself. For Bégouën there was only one explanation, God: "Briefly, materialist evolution went bankrupt. It must give way to spiritualist evolution, which begins with the idea of a first cause and then admits the fertile idea of causality . . . but everything unfolds according to fixed, logical rules pre-established by God."[111]

This is an eternal discussion. The debunkers still proclaim their mechanistic or electronic dogmas: "The human brain is just a computer that happens to be made of meat."[112] The thoughtful are assailed by doubts: Erwin Chargaff recognizes that biochemistry is the chemistry of the living cell but asks "do we know what life is?" "The intermediary metabolism of living cells can, for instance, be studied with great precision. . . . But does all this really bring us much closer to the core problem, the chemistry of life? . . . We still cannot describe to you the chemistry of the living cell, though we have a pretty good idea of the dead one." And in another passage, Chargaff echoes the thoughts about the limitations of science which Bégouën found so comforting: "There is a famous saying of Virchow about the continuity of life stating that every cell must come from a cell. But how about the first cell, how was it formed? Since the time when the principles of evolution became popularized this question has been asked repeatedly, and many studies on the 'origin of life' have been undertaken. To what extent these studies belong to biochemistry and whether they are not one of the more elegant forms of science fiction remains undecided. If I were given a choice between the Book of Genesis and the latest text on the origin of life I might conclude that Moses was by far the better writer."[113]

By 1944 Bégouën was defending evolution against an ingenious attack by two polytechnicians who seized upon some weaknesses indicated by paleontologists and biologists in evolutionary theory to argue in a rigid sorites that evolution had occurred but in the reverse of what was usually argued.[114]

---

tudes toward these philosophical questions: "Je ne sais pas ce que c'est que la vie ni la conscience ni la pensée; j'ignore l'origine et la nature de ce qui, prenant racine dans la boue cellulaire, s'est épanoui en notre cerveau": Jean Rostand, *Ce que je crois* (Paris, 1953; rev. ed., 1956), p. 22.

111. Delage and Goldsmith, *Les théories de l'évolution* (Paris, 1909); Bégouën, *Quelques souvenirs*, p. 21.

112. Marvin Minsky, M.I.T. professor of electrical engineering, quoted in *Time*, February 22, 1971, p. 77.

113. Chargaff, "The Paradox of Biochemistry," *Columbia Forum* 12, no. 2 (1969): 17.

114. Georges Salet and Louis Lafont, *L'évolution régressive* (Paris, 1943), attacked by Bégouën in *Débats* (April 18, 1944).

Fortunately for the Catholic evolutionary cause as well as for the delicate harmony that had been established between science and religion on certain thorny issues, the Abbé de Lapparent, a well-known paleontologist, brought out a work, published by the *Œuvre des catéchismes* of Paris and based on encyclicals from *Providentissimus Deus* (1893) to *Divino afflante Spiritu* (1943), which was widely accepted as a statement of the orthodox position.[115] This careful interpretation of Genesis, in the light of the latest paleontological and biological work, by a professor of geology at the Catholic Institute in Paris, had much more ultimate influence than the polytechnicians' work carefully veneered with orthodoxy. The long and patient work of Catholics favorable to evolution had established its orthodoxy too firmly to be shaken by a seductive sorites.

Bégouën was pleasantly surprised by his own work's success among the clergy and Catholics generally. A bishop asked for fifty copies to distribute to his clergy; all the students of a *grand* seminary wanted a copy; the limited edition was soon used up and the big Catholic publisher Bloud et Gay undertook to bring out a new edition. This was especially gratifying to Bégouën, since it happened after the Vichy regime, which, not generally favorable to the idea of evolution, had provided limited opportunities for some of the more benighted of the clergy to try to reverse a century of intellectual change. The clash between the church and the nineteenth century had occurred, Bégouën argued, because the church was ignorant of the demands of human thought. This misunderstanding came chiefly from a serious difference of views on the role of science in the behavior of the universe, especially on the key point of the origin of man. Once the ban on the discussion of this question disappeared, the artificial barrier separating the church and its enemies fell. The church could now make a fertile contribution to the new civilization that was developing, a mutation that was unparalleled since the fall of the Roman Empire. "Nothing can now prevent the church, which, according to . . . Lecomte du Noüy, 'can alone reach the heart of the masses,' from making its rich contribution to the development of the new world." The new birth would be painful, but Christians should not be deterred by the sacrifices required by the new mutation. "Is not the aim to be achieved now higher and nobler, since it is not only an issue of the individual salvation of each person but the salvation of all humanity?"[116]

115. Abbé Albert F. de Lapparent, *Nos origines* (Paris: Société auxiliaire des caté-chismes, 194-). The decree of the Biblical Commission on June 30, 1909, demanded a literal historical meaning for the biblical facts relevant to the foundations of the Christian religion, including the special creation of man. But it said "peculiaris creatio hominis," not "corporis hominis." The idea of the evolution of the body and the later infusion of the soul into the body by a special creative act was therefore an orthodox possibility. The creation of Eve remained a problem, for the decree demanded literal historical meaning for the "formatio primae mulieris ex primo homine." See G. Drioux, "Théologien et savant. À propos de l'origine du corps humain," *RCF* 81 (1915): 557-70. For the contemporary Catholic position, essentially the same, see Paul, "Religion and Darwinism: Varieties of Catholic Reaction," in Glick, ed., *Comparative Reception*, pp. 435-36, and chap. 1 of John C. Greene, *Darwin and the Modern World View* (New York, 1963).

116. Bégouën, *Quelques souvenirs*, preface, pp. 1-8.

4

Albert de Lapparent: Religion and
"The End of the Laplacian Illusion"

Or, s'il est une vérité indéniable, c'est que toute ordon-
nance implique un ordonnateur, dont l'habileté se mesure à
l'harmonie qu'il a su établir dans son œuvre. Puis donc que
la science, en dernière analyse, réduit tous les phénomènes
de l'univers à des mouvements qui s'accomplissent avec la
plus harmonieuse précision sous l'influence de forces con-
stantes, on peut dire que, par là même, elle nous fournit la
meilleure démonstration de cette suprême intelligence qui a
disposé toutes choses avec nombre, poids et mesure.

Albert de Lapparent, *Les enseignements philosophiques
de la science*, p. 9.

In 1905 the geologist Albert de Lapparent gave a series of lectures at the
Catholic Institute in Paris examining the "new science" and its implications
for religion. The rector of the institute, Msgr. Péchenard, had asked Lapparent to give the lectures in a course in apologetics that a recent generous gift
had made possible at the institute. For three years philosophers, historians,
and theologians had given lectures, but no representative of science had spoken. Lapparent was asked to give five or six lectures on scientific matters related to apologetics. At first perplexed by the request, Lapparent tried to
decline the honor, but the rector finally convinced him to accept the invitation. Afraid of being accused of timidity or even cowardice, Lapparent
agreed to give the lectures to show his gratitude to the establishment that
had granted him so many favors. Lapparent was soon happy he gave the lectures. Selling two thousand copies in eight months, the published lectures
turned out to be one of the best achievements of a very successful career and
were also very profitable.[1] Published in book form, the lectures proved so

1. "The End of the Laplacian Illusion" is the title of chap. 16 of Milič Čapek, *The Philosophical Impact of Contemporary Physics* (Princeton, 1961). Lapparent, "Autobiogra-

successful a tract for the times that by 1914 the work had gone through twelve editions.

The task of relating science to apologetics was not so foreign to Lapparent as he thought when asked to do so in 1904. He had dealt with many essential issues very briefly in a speech to the international bibliographical congress in Paris in 1878.[2] The origin of science was not to be found in man's attempt to satisfy his intellectual curiosity, however important that became in later scientific progress, but was a natural consequence of the law of work imposed on man since his fall. Providence had not left man completely defenseless; his sociability contained the possibility of a sort of indefinite material perfectibility. As a result of the division of labor, crafts were born. At first guided by practical rules, some superior minds succeeded in giving a philosophical form to some of these empirical rules. Once the consideration of natural or concrete objects had been replaced by a certain number of abstract ideas without any immediate practical application, science was founded. What science did was to substitute for the idea of natural objects the supreme abstractions to which the material world can be reduced—mass, time, space, and force. Finally, it was necessary to determine the laws followed by the movement of atoms. This science was a reward God reserved for man as the price of his daily labor. Providence rewarded society's following the law of work by permitting man to elevate his mind to the point where he could jettison all material interests and contemplate the creation philosophically. Thus man could acquire knowledge of the *order* that exists in the creation. The word order sums up science.

Although science furnishes man with the ideas of order, origin, and end in the universe, Lapparent emphasized that however elevated man might place science, as the product of intelligence, it would always take second place to conscience. It would be impious to believe that Providence requires only a formal profession of belief in scientific demonstration, for faith is necessary to all and science is accessible to only a small number of initiates. Only the abuse of science could lead to a scientifically inspired attack on religion.[3] In the preface to the lectures of 1905,[4] Lapparent declared that his personal contribution to the institute's apologetics program would be based on his long scientific experience and on his reading of the works of the recognized masters who had submitted the foundations of human knowledge to their

phie manuscrite" (1906), in the possession of the Abbé de Lapparent at the Institut catholique, Paris.

2. *Les enseignements philosophiques de la science* (Paris, 1879). Lapparent was then "vice-doyen" of the Faculty of Sciences at the institute.

3. "Ainsi, quand on vous dira que la science contredit partout la foi, que les dogmes ont fait leur temps, et doivent désormais céder la place aux pures méthodes scientifiques, ne craignez pas qu'il y ait quelque risque à courir pour les croyances qui nous sont chères. Contentez-vous de plaindre ceux qui ont des yeux pour ne pas voir et des oreilles pour ne pas entendre; ceux qui, après avoir contribué par leurs travaux à glorifier l'ordre et l'harmonie de la création, se refusent à reconnaître et à aimer le Créateur; ceux surtout qui, après avoir établi la nécessité d'une fin pour l'univers, ne savent ni ne veulent se préparer à la fin qui les attend eux-mêmes" (ibid., p. 13).

4. Lapparent, *Science et apologétique* (Paris, 1914, 12th ed.). It was in the series "Etudes de philosophie et de critique religieuse" published by Bloud et Gay.

penetrating analyses. A single intention gave the work its characteristic flavor: to give renewed comfort to minds of good will by strengthening them in their convictions and by preventing them from falling into the excess of discrediting science on the ground that some had often been tempted to make bad use of it. Resolutely opposed to uncertainty, Lapparent aimed at giving believers new reasons for confidence in their religion and a healthy appreciation of the work done by so many generations of scientists in establishing our knowledge of the order that reigns in the creation. One of the advantages of this approach was, Lapparent argued, that he would be fair to science by not inflicting upon it the responsibility for the destruction wrongly undertaken in its name.[5]

In the introduction Lapparent noted that of all the contemporary arguments used to weaken religious beliefs, there was none assured of a better reception by the general public than that whose claims were formulated in the name of science: "The pronunciation of this magic word suffices to arouse a respect nearly bordering on superstition, especially among those who have never personally entered the scientific domain; and this respect is limitless when to the word science is added the qualification mathematical." To say that a thing is "*mathematically* demonstrated" is to give the argument a "sacramental.form," effectively removing it from the area of discussion. These laws are so necessary that they apply to the creative Almighty as well as to the humblest of mortals. From this position to the conclusion that the Almighty is unnecessary is only a step, which many hardly hesitate to take. The infallible character and primordial necessity attributed to mathematical rules soon encompass the things they seem to govern, and gradually the idea of a Ruler separate from the created universe is in danger of being judged superfluous.

In the accelerating evolution of the sciences toward a mathematicized form was the implication that eventually it would be possible in all scientific areas to pass, by ever increasingly sophisticated analysis, from concrete objects to the abstractions to which the concepts of mass and movement were applicable. Thus the study of the transformations of matter would be "a pure question of mechanics," which involved only those ostensibly immutable rules governing the concepts of quantity, extension, and energy. It seemed vital to Lapparent to examine the claim of epistemological superiority advanced for mathematics. This investigation was of key importance, for it was not feasible to discuss all the objections against religion that took refuge under the "cloak of science." Since this quasi-idolatry had already been given a brilliant and critical analysis in Henri Poincaré's *La science et l'hypothèse*, Lapparent quoted the statement of the thesis of scientific certainty that Poincaré gave in his opening pages.[6] It was this thesis that Lapparent subjected to critical scrutiny in the light of the revisionism then rampant in nearly all areas of science. He also went beyond Poincaré in assessing the significance of these developments for religion.

Lapparent first dealt with geometry, a paragon of certainty for mankind since its canons had been given their hieratic form by Euclid. Although the

5. Ibid., Preface, pp. 1–3.
6. Ibid., Introduction, pp. 5–12.

principles of geometry are abstract, they could not, in his opinion, clash with any experimental truth. These principles must also respect the rules governing mental activity, the first of which is always the principle of contradiction. Here Lapparent showed that he was a victim of the same brand of Cartesianism that had led Poincaré to declare that "Later generations will regard [Cantor's] *Mengenlehre* as a disease from which one has recovered."[7] The didactic basis of Lapparent's judgment became obvious when he asserted that his second limitation on geometry was the consequence of his own nature's being intimately penetrated by the feeling of order that must reign in things and which must profoundly damage any proposition capable of implying the identity of opposites. Whitehead's observation that "In formal logic, a contradiction is the signal of a defeat: but in the evolution of real knowledge it marks the first step in progress towards a victory" would have seemed a great absurdity to the geologist.[8] Thus Lapparent's treatment of the non-Euclidean geometries of Lobachevski, Bolyai, and Riemann is inevitably ambivalent because of his attempt to save as much of Euclid as was consistent with scientific honesty. Not even the most distant astronomical observations had impaired the rules of Euclid. Although their empirical certainty is beyond doubt, Lapparent warned that this did not mean that they were logically necessary, even to the point that they applied to the creative Almighty. Indeed, even mortals could legitimately free themselves of their yoke. The spirit of this observation is different from the rest of his remarks, and it was probably motivated by the desire to avoid falling into the trap of a Laplacian universe while saving Euclid. Euclidean doctrine is what it is because material bodies are what they are and because our intelligence has been modeled on a particularly noble type. The One who had created bodies and minds had, then, given this geometry its raison d'être. But He was not restricted by Euclidean parameters as the only necessary ones: things could be regulated in such a fashion that a different geometry, no less logical, had to come out of the scientific interpretation of phenomena.[9]

An added attraction of more conventional geometry was that it possessed more than any other science the *disciplinary* virtue. An enemy of fantasy, respectful of tradition, geometry gave no support to the contemporary "revolt" against the ideas of discipline, which were then in a lamentable eclipse.

7. Cited in Morris Kline, *Mathematics in Western Culture* (Oxford, 1953), p. 397. A fascinating account of how Cantor and others thought that "Cantor's revolutionary and disconcerting transfinite set theory might be reconciled with Catholic understanding of the nature of infinity" is Joseph W. Dauben's "Georg Cantor and Pope Leo XIII: Mathematics, Theology, and the Infinite," *Journal of the History of Ideas* 38, no. 1 (1977): 85–108.

8. Whitehead, *Science and the Modern World*, pp. 231–32. The rest of this paragraph is an incisive analysis applicable to much of French thought, including science, in the nineteenth century.

9. Lapparent, *Science et apologétique*, pp. 23–58. He returned to "le *plan géometrique*" in arguing for a final plan in the universe (pp. 161–63). On p. 161, he gives a classic summing up of his case for Euclid: "Il paraît donc légitime d'en conclure que le monde réel autant qu'il puisse nous être connu, a été créé sur le type euclidien." Compare a similar nostalgia for classical physics and Euclidean geometry in Werner Heisenberg, *Philosophic Problems of Nuclear Science* (New York, 1952), chap. 3.

In commenting on the quarrel over the *postulatum* of Euclid, Lapparent noted that geometry had to be done for present humanity, not for a future super race. He wondered whether it was not dangerous to take before the public a too subtle dissection of the foundations of knowledge. Should the discussion not be reserved for the small group in which these matters can be discussed without the value of the terms being misunderstood? If too many get into this type of high speculation, there is the possibility of confusion, whose effects, surpassing the prudent limits scientists had agreed to observe, could throw an undeserved discredit on very sound ideas. Especially in science, then, did "shallow draughts intoxicate the brain," while quaffing at the Pierian spring "largely sobers us again." Even in accepting non-Euclidean geometry, Lapparent pointedly incorporated it into a familiar framework: "No doubt the simple enunciation of such non-Euclidean propositions . . . produces a disconcerting effect. When one reflects on them, however, one recognizes that they have nothing of the absurd in them. Indeed, they represent a sphere to us."[10]

Obviously, Lapparent, however competent his technical grasp of the subject, had far from a typically modern view of scientific theory; his view was much different from Duhem's, some of whose conclusions about science alarmed Lapparent. A contemporary writer provides a convenient, exaggerated statement of the frightening interpretation of non-Euclidean geometry Lapparent so desperately strove to avoid: "Before 1800 every age had believed in the existence of absolute truth; men differed only in their choice of sources. Aristotle, the fathers of the Church, the Bible, philosophy, and science all had their day as arbiters of objective, eternal truths. In the eighteenth century human reason alone was upheld, and this because of what it had produced in mathematics and in the mathematical domains of science. The hope of mathematical truths had been especially comforting because they held out hope of more to come. Alas, the hope was blasted. The end of the dominance of Euclidean geometry was the end of the dominance of all such absolute standards."[11] His mind boggling at the idea of a "distinction between a mathematical space and physical space" and at the concomitant idea that "*systems of thought based on statements about physical space are different from that physical space*,"[12] Lapparent argued in effect the eighteenth-century position that the new rules "Are Nature still, but Nature methodized."

In considering arithmetic, Lapparent argued that the concept of number, like that of extension, derives from daily experience. As in geometry, our innate sense of order applied to perceptions provides a general explanation of arithmetical operations. Since he disclaimed any attempt to deal with the

10. Lapparent, p. 42. Cf. "*Every theorem of Riemann's geometry can be interpreted on the sphere merely by thinking the straight lines in the theorem as great circles on the sphere*": Kline, *Mathematics in Western Culture*, p. 246.

11. Kline, p. 430.

12. Both quotes ibid., p. 428. Of course, "the obvious starting point for the physical interpretation of the mathematical scheme in general relativity is the fact that the geometry is very nearly Euclidean in small dimensions. . . . Still, one can speak about a non-Euclidean geometry in large dimensions": Werner Heisenberg, *Physics and Philosophy* (New York, 1958, 1962), p. 176.

metaphysics of mathematics, it is difficult to say that Lapparent rejected the Kantian idea of the a priori character of mathematics, but the tenor of his argument certainly emphasizes how it is derived from concepts furnished by experience.[13]

The fundamental principles of mechanics are also to be found in observation. In analyzing the relations between bodies and thus deriving general laws, the mind makes the same demands as in other scientific areas: first, the need for order, by which we perceive that identical causes always produce the same effects; second, the need for logic, which leads us to avoid all contradictions. There can be no effect without a cause. Although based originally on experience, mechanics became a rational and mathematical science, but Lapparent noted it still had its "imperfections." Drawing heavily on the work of Emile Picard,[14] Lapparent took note of the changes in mechanics since the eighteenth century. It was no longer possible to accept the dogma of Laplace and Lagrange that the universe is a self-regulating system. Picard blamed the discrepancies now evident in this once divinely precise science on the fatal dualism between force and matter, seemingly the basis of the old mechanics. The development of energetics and the revision of the ideas of classical dynamics did not elicit from Lapparent any cosmic pessimism based on the idea of the entropy of the universe in the second law of thermodynamics but rather brought forth delight that the old mechanistic schemes had been dealt a severe blow. How disconcerting the new development must be to the schools which, smug in the possession of an instrument they deemed infallible, had so long indulged in the dream of reducing all the phenomena of nature either to the old Cartesian mechanism made up solely of figures and movements or to the classical mechanism of inert masses and conventional forces.[15] The role of the contingent in mechanics was greater than it was in the sciences of numbers and of extension. It would be well to mute the claims of a universal *mechanism* until it was founded on a more solid basis. It is instructive to compare our geologist's attitude toward change in mechanics with his homage to Euclid. The validity of non-Euclidean geometry, with its negative implications for absolutes so vital to traditional Catholicism, was only grudgingly admitted by Lapparent. But the scientific change that undermined the eighteenth-century mechanistic universe, which had supposedly obviated the Newtonian divine hypothesis, was welcomed with alacrity by Lapparent. It is hard to resist the conclusion that he was choosing his science with an eye on its implications for the Catholic faith.

In contrast to Lapparent's gloating over the cracks widening in the structure of classical mechanics, another Catholic scientist, Joseph Boussinesq, was saddened by the threats to the proud edifice. Boussinesq regarded classical or

13. For a lucid exposition of Kant on mathematical knowledge, see Frederick Copleston, *A History of Modern Philosophy*, vol. 6, pt. 2, pp. 30–41. In his discussion, Lapparent refers to Hilbert, Cantor, and the Vicomte d'Adhémar, whose *Le triple procès* (1904) he often mentions.

14. Picard, *Quelques réflexions sur la mécanique* (Paris, 1902).

15. Lapparent, *Science et apologétique*, pp. 79–91. He draws upon Charles de Freycinet, *Sur les principes de la mécanique rationnelle* (Paris, 1902), as well as Picard, Poincaré, Helmholtz, and Hertz.

Newtonian mechanics as the best representation of natural phenomena. Each science achieves its most important progress when it clothes itself in mathematical and particularly geometrical form. The Cartesian Boussinesq viewed non-Euclidean geometries as logical exercises, an amusing but perhaps dangerous game in which man's natural intuitions are mutilated.[16] Like Descartes, Leibniz, and Cournot, Boussinesq worried about reconciling his acceptance of physical laws with liberty. But he gave an original solution, based on Poisson's paradox, to the "problem of liberty" within the framework of classical mechanics. Poisson had noted that "The movement in space of a body subject to the action of a given force and starting from a given position and speed must be absolutely determined. It is then a sort of paradox that the differential equations on which the movement depends can be satisfied by several equations." If one imagines, instead of a single material point, a system for which at certain moments similar indeterminations exist, one can say that at these related times the initial state does not completely determine the subsequent states. This indetermination leaves room for the intervention of a directing power separate from the mechanical forces, "the causes modifying the accelerations." Thus the way is open for the co-existence of physico-chemical determinism with life and moral liberty. The flaw in Boussinesq's ingenious argument was pointed out later by a friendly critic, Emile Picard. Boussinesq assumed that the differential equations giving accurately the movements of the different points of the system had been obtained. But in simplifying, one moves away from reality. In most cases approximations suffice, and a number of natural laws are practically exact. The conditions of determination, as the history of science shows, could be changed by modifications in the analytical representations. The determinist argument was by no means destroyed by Boussinesq's marauding attack. Picard was justified in declaring that however ingenious his colleague's mathematical and philosophical argument, it hardly advanced the solution of the problem of reconciling liberty with determinism.[17]

But Picard's judgment was rendered in 1933, four years after Boussinesq died. When Boussinesq advanced the argument originally, it was hailed as a genuine contribution to the solution of a real problem. De Saint-Venant presented the mathematical form of the argument to the Academy of Sciences, which thus had the unique experience of hearing a note read on the agreement of moral liberty with the laws of mechanics. The philosophical develop-

16. For similar comment on non-Euclidean geometry, see Abbé de Broglie, "La géométrie non-euclidienne," *APC*, n.s. 22 (1890): 5–25, 340–69. See the reply to the abbé by Georges Lechalas, "La géométrie générale et l'intuition," ibid. 23 (1891): 56–75. But Paul Mansion of the University of Gand was an enthusiastic non-Euclidean and argued with the abbé and Lapparent at the scientific congress of Catholics in Paris. Mansion put forward the late-seventeenth- and early-eighteenth-century Italian Jesuit Saccheri as a precursor of non-Euclidean geometry. In 1891, Mansion gave courses in non-Euclidean geometry at Louvain. See A. Poulain "La géométrie non-euclidienne," *E* 54 (1891): 120–33.

17. See Joseph Boussinesq, *Conciliation du véritable déterminisme mécanique avec l'existence de la vie et de la liberté morale* (Paris, 1878). Précédé d'un rapport à l'Académie des sciences morales et politiques par M. Paul Janet, membre de l'Institut. Picard's *La vie et l'œuvre de Joseph Boussinesq* (Paris, 1934) was read to the Academy of Sciences on December 11, 1933.

ment of Boussinesq's argument was presented to the Académie des sciences morales et politiques by Paul Janet. The philosophical significance of Boussinesq's work was, in Janet's opinion, that it supported the fundamental idea of Boutroux on the contingency of natural laws but made it more plausible by limiting its application and by giving it more precision. Janet thought that Boutroux's famous thesis, *De la contingence des lois de la nature* (1874), which had been expressed in a popular form in Voltaire's poem on the Lisbon earthquake, had certain dangers. One could escape from fatalism only to fall into positivism by overemphasizing the approximate nature of natural laws. And, as a result of the closeness of contingency to chance, in escaping from strict causality one could fall into the clutches of chance. Boussinesq saved the phenomena by dividing the phenomenal world into two categories. In one the laws of mechanics, expressed in differential equations, alone determine the succession of states through which the system passes, thus leaving no role for any cause other than physico-chemical causes. Although liberty may impose itself on our conscience as a fact, determinism is more than a simple construction of the mind. In the second class of phenomena—where Poisson's paradox applies, since several singular solution differential equations could satisfy the movement, thus indicating indeterminism—it is necessary for a non-physico-chemical force to operate in a sustained manner outside the mechanical action to direct the system in each bifurcation that presents itself. Thus classical mechanics was saved but moral liberty was not destroyed. The dream of Descartes, Leibniz, and Kant had been realized, and, happy paradox, salvation had come from mechanics itself.[18]

That there is order in the universe was as certain in Lapparent's opinion as any scientific law.[19] The order and the harmony that reign in the creation manifest themselves in the generally very simple laws to which phenomena show themselves subject. The first of the few laws Lapparent chose to cite from among a large number was the hypothesis of universal gravitation, whose action extends over the entire visible universe. Although Lapparent was aware of the difficulty of applying Newtonian physics to "the smallest particles of matter," he reaffirmed his faith that "at least in the sidereal world an admirable order reigns, and its formula is marvellously simple."[20]

Lapparent found a second example of order in terrestrial matter, a topic well within his justly famous area of expertise. Order in mineral bodies is not in movement but in the reciprocal arrangement of parts, the best illustration of which is found in crystals: "Nowhere could the affirmation of order, founded on equilibrium, be more striking." Could it not be said that in crystals, that is, mineral matter organized and brought to a nearly ideal perfec-

18. Boussinesq's book split the academic community along predictable lines: against the jibes of Bertrand were opposed the support of Saint-Venant, Fizeau, Mascart, and Gilbert, backed by the philosophers Caro, Janet, and Franck. Boussinesq's career was adversely affected for a short while (AN, F^{17} 22471). See Mary Jo Nye, "The Moral Freedom of Man and the Determinism of Nature," pp. 280–81.

19. Chapter 4 deals with "L'ordre dans la création" and "Le principe de la moindre action."

20. Lapparent is aware of other difficulties in Newtonian science. He mentions the hypothesis of Marx's *L'éther, principe universal des forces* (Paris, 1904).

tion, nature proclaims the excellence of Euclidean geometry? Happily the inorganic world is absolutely repugnant to the amorphous state. In the mineral world there is brilliant affirmation of the famous scriptural verse "Omnia in numero, pondere et mensura fecit Deus."[21] Lapparent continued the same hymn to harmony with a reference to the law of Mariotte, the seventeenth-century Frenchman who arrived at the conclusion that pv = b in a fashion as Cartesian as Boyle's was Baconian. It is possible to admire the same order in the combinations of bodies as is found in the arrangement of parts of homogeneous matter. All chemistry is governed by the two fundamental laws of definite proportions and of multiple proportions. Noting that the doctrine of invariable molecules had been recently attacked from all sides and that certain enthusiasms of the atomist schools should probably be restrained, Lapparent nevertheless thought that it would be a great pity to abandon the concept of isolated and indivisible molecules for that of continuous matter, against which experience protests. If we accept the dictum of Max Planck that "Modern physics recognized two main conceptual schemes, the physics of discrete particles and the physics of continuous media,"[22] then Lapparent "remains faithful to the molecular doctrine" because the simple laws of this doctrine provide "one of the most striking proofs of the order that reigns in the material world."[23]

It was in discussing order in the universe as manifested in the laws of chemistry that Lapparent had to come to grips with the opinions of a fellow Catholic, the physicist Pierre Duhem, on scientific theory. Duhem alarmed Lapparent because he claimed that the laws of chemistry, like all natural laws, are postulates, or even definitions, which could not be verified by any direct experiment. In a famous article in the *Revue de philosophie* in 1905 Duhem showed that the law of multiple proportions, among other laws, is a mathematical statement, devoid of all physical sense, which no chemical analysis, of necessity imprecise, could ever weaken. Lapparent criticized the exclusively rational and algebraic approach of Duhem, who never asked what the symbols represent. Lapparent wondered if a deficient philosophical training was the explanation of Duhem's brilliant dance on a tight rope. Lapparent had no objection to the idea that in this world it is impossible to attain absolutes rather than approximations: "All scientific laws represent to a certain degree an idealization of the corresponding matter."[24] The law represents the mean of the imperfect verifications coming from experiments, which, although a little crude, serve to establish the law. To qualify the statement of this mean as a postulate entails reducing if not completely obscuring the manifestation of order and harmony in the creation. Thus Duhem was risking leading people to universal skepticism, all for the satisfaction of a philosophical accuracy that makes sense only if we could claim to reach the absolute. Of course, Lapparent admitted, it was good not to let oneself be hypnotized

21. Lapparent, *Science et apologétique*, p. 124.
22. Essay in *James Clerk Maxwell, a Commemoration Volume, 1831-1931* (Cambridge, 1931), cited in C. C. Gillispie, *The Edge of Objectivity* (Princeton, 1960), p. 476.
23. Lapparent, *Science et apologétique*, p. 128.
24. Ibid., p. 132.

by theories and formulas, but it was going far beyond this to discredit them completely and to exploit the simplicity of natural laws in order to represent them as an illusion born of the tendency of the mind to prefer what is more convenient at the risk of giving more clarity of expression to things than they had in reality. In Lapparent's opinion, Duhem was certainly one of the chief scorners of this search for what Duhem called the incontestable but outmoded dogma of the simplicity of the laws of nature, a dogma showing the weakness of our minds, a relic of a period in which physicists assumed that "the intelligence of the Creator was afflicted with the same weakness."[25] Even worse, Duhem labeled all physical laws as provisional and relative, in addition to their being approximate, and, for the strict logician, neither true nor false. Fortunately for Lapparent, Duhem applied these stringent remarks only to laws that physics stated in a mathematical form, and he generously and willingly conceded that he would give the designation "true" to laws revealed by common sense. The geologist could not refrain from noting that this distinction did not flatter the mathematicians much. But Lapparent insisted that he remained adamant in his resolve not to desert the domain of common sense, the only area in which there could be any certainty, while at the same time indicating the dangers of Duhemian forays into the frontiers of the absolute. It could be left to the doctors of quintessence to quibble over the acoustical law that the number of vibrations of a string varies inversely with its length and cannot be precisely demonstrated because the length of the string giving an octave is sometimes $499/1000$ and sometimes $501/1000$ of that which gives the original sound.[26] Such overrefined minds were not fit to guide intelligences in the path of a healthy discipline, their best protection against this dubious kind of scientific thinking.[27]

But it was Duhem rather than Lapparent who heralded the opinion of future scientists on these issues. Jeans was not far from echoing the opinion of Duhem when he declared that in an experiment, which "amounts to asking a question of nature," the "question can never be—'Is hypothesis A true?' but 'Is hypothesis A tenable?' Nature may answer our question by showing us a phenomenon which is inconsistent with our hypothesis or . . . not inconsistent. . . . She can never show us a phenomenon which proves it; one phenomenon is enough to disprove a hypothesis, but a million million do not suffice to prove it. For this reason, the scientist can never claim to know anything for certain, except direct facts of observation."[28] A later writer is much more Duhemian in his view: "The notion that scientific knowledge is *certain* is an illusion. A scientist . . . assumes the existence of a universe external to himself that is the source of his sensations. He notices certain regularities in his sensations, and infers that there are regularities in the behavior of the universe. He calls these regularities . . . *laws of nature* and attempts to represent

25. Duhem, cited ibid., p. 134.
26. Ibid., pp. 129–36.
27. For a modern example showing doubt about "the convincing power of reproducibility," see Michael Polanyi, *Science, Faith and Society* (Chicago, 1964; first published in 1946), p. 96.
28. Sir James Jeans, *The New Background of Science* (Cambridge, 1933; Ann Arbor, 1959), p. 49.

them by mathematical models. . . . It is tempting to infer that the model is beginning to resemble the *thing-out-there*, but such an inference can never be verified. No prediction can be known to be certain—nature may deviate from the model without prior notice, and it is in this sense that scientific knowledge is never certain."[29]

Duhem's views fitted into the category of those Lapparent lamented as among several of the most important and the most admired contemporary theories of science, which seemed to have lost all contact with the world of the senses. Not only were the theoreticians resigned to this separation, they boldly claimed the right to practice it. So Duhem denounced the erroneous view demanding that all the operations of mathematicians in a series of deductions connecting postulates to conclusions have a *physical* sense, meaning that one should reason only about *feasible operations* and introduce only magnitudes *accessible to experience*. To ask that all the magnitudes introduced into calculations correspond to a measurable property and that every operation carried out on this symbol be amenable to translation into concrete language in expressing a real or possible fact is, Duhem argued, an excessive demand. Although the request is legitimate in the question of the final formulas at the conclusion of theories, there is no reason for applying it to the intermediate operations establishing the transition from postulates to conclusions. To insist on this physical sense for these operations would paralyze the mathematician. Some feared the use of differential calculus. Indeed, to satisfy the demand completely would prevent the development of any calculus, for theoretical deduction would be stopped in its first steps. These conclusions, although quite in line with the avant-garde scientific thinking of the time, got little sympathy from Lapparent.

He did not want to contest the right of the mathematical physicists to a liberty of which several of them, especially Duhem, had made such fertile use; besides it was comforting to know that the opportunity for experimental control continued to hold good for the final formulas. What Lapparent merely wanted to establish was that to keep a distance from reality was to accentuate the inability that even a very advanced science would have in giving us information on "the essence of things." It is, of course, quite legitimate mental curiosity to aim at an increasingly accurate knowledge of what may be hidden under the first impressions derived from the senses. The certainty of never attaining the absolute should not discourage our desire to get as close as possible to reality. When one wants to know what heat, light, electricity, chemical combination, etc., are, it is, Lapparent complained, small satisfaction to hear the reply—applicable to all cases—"Let us assume a system of six differential equations!" Of course, this method can be viewed as a salutary penitence imposed on those who would juggle rashly with representative images. One comforting thought was that the inability of the scientists to give a categorical reply to those who wanted to look a little more clearly into natural phenomena sufficiently emphasized the mistake of those who claimed to

29. Marshall Walker, *The Nature of Scientific Thought* (Englewood Cliffs, N.J., 1963), p. 6.

get from science alone the solution of problems of a quite different scope.[30]

To end his commentary on contemporary scientific theory, Lapparent made some critical and pragmatic remarks on Poincaré's idea that all terrestrial movement is relative and that the question whether the earth does or does not turn makes no sense, since no experiment could answer it. Poincaré made the two propositions "the earth turns" and "it is convenient to assume that the earth turns" functional equivalents, the one having no more meaning than the other. It was chiefly the conclusion that all opinions were equally legitimate, which some individuals, losing all perspective, drew from Poincaré's remarks, against which Lapparent protested.[31] After attacking another example given by Duhem to show how misleading simple laws of nature could be, Lapparent summed up his own position. There is no single formula capable of embracing simultaneously all the phenomena of nature. The mind, guided by the senses, divides a phenomenon into categories and researches for each category the elementary laws governing it. Each of these laws corresponds to a certain ideal state, which the real circumstances more or less approximate. In each particular case several of these elementary laws must be invoked together, at least to the degree necessary. Which is better, then, to discredit these laws because each has a strictly limited domain, or to apply them with discretion while continuing to admire their characteristic simplicity? Lapparent confessed that the answer might depend on one's temperament, but that even if he had to risk the Duhemian accusation of weakness of mind, he much preferred the second answer.[32]

In attempting to answer the question "what is the scientific investigation of nature?" Lapparent asserted that "experiment is the only source of scientific truth." Experiment alone can teach us something new, it alone can give us certainty; to desert it in order to construct a priori systems would be deplorable. Of course, Poincaré was right in saying that observation does not suffice; it is vital to generalize. Lapparent enthusiastically endorsed Poincaré's statement that the scientist must create order: science is constructed of facts as a house is made of stones, but a pile of facts is no more science than a heap of stones is a house: "The idea of order is truly at the base of scientific research."[33] But this order is one that exists as the basis of reality and which we feel innately. In noting that the scientist has to establish the relations between things, the geologist followed Poincaré in agreeing that method in the physical sciences is founded upon a type of induction that assumes the repetition of a phenomenon in circumstances similar to its first appearance. Since all the circumstances are never the same, probability has a large role in the physical sciences. Prediction is possible, Lapparent argued, because the innate feeling of order in the true man of science is reinforced by the beautiful ordering of natural phenomena that becomes clearer as the scientist continues his observations. Each science is then an attempt to grasp

30. Lapparent, *Science et apologétique*, pp. 239–40.
31. Poincaré, *La science et l'hypothèse*, p. 141, cited in Lapparent, p. 137.
32. Lapparent, pp. 139–40.
33. Ibid., pp. 93, 94. See chap. 3, "Les sciences d'observation."

the knowledge of order present in each determined category of phenomena. All the sciences of observation pass through the same stages: gathering of facts; derivation of certain abstract ideas from the facts; and the perception of certain relations between the ideas. These relations become experimental laws, which are explained by theories when they attain knowledge of reality. Theories remain hypotheses as long as they are limited to summarizing and classifying logically a group of laws, without being able to affirm that the constructed framework corresponds absolutely to the truth.[34] Duhem's article on acoustics in the *Revue de philosophie* in 1904 provided a convenient example of the process that Lapparent presented as how science works. The point is that explanation is perfect when theory, ceasing to be a hypothesis, reaches empirical certainty, a degree rarely reached by any physical theory. For the most part, one has to work with a hypothesis unamenable to decisive verification, and one cannot know with certainty the cause of one's perceptions but only indicate that they originate as if reality, temporarily inaccessible, corresponds to the representation that the hypothesis gives of it. Optical theories were in this state when Lapparent wrote. Hypotheses have a fertile role in science: they are the guide and torch of the experimenter, suggesting to him the experiment to perform in order to verify in some important respect the already conceived theory. If the proof succeeds, the hypothesis is decisive; if not, science is enriched by a new idea that a wiser theoretician will know how to group with other hypotheses in a less imperfect synthesis.[35]

It would appear that Lapparent was out of touch with or at least out of sympathy with developments in contemporary physics. It is now commonly accepted that "A particularly fruitful idea in the development of physics, especially in the last hundred years, has been the concept of abstract laws of physics. By this I mean that the laws can be expressed as an abstract logical system, essentially in mathematical terms, quite apart from the material content of the Universe. . . . the concept of laws exists in an entirely abstract form. One could conceive of other abstract systems, the consequences of which could be calculated, without it being necessary to provide a realization in actual material terms. We can conceive of other universes without those universes being compelled to exist. This indeed is the business of the pure mathematician."[36] This is far from the spirit of Lapparent's remarks on method in the physical sciences, and it clearly comes close to the observations of Duhem. As Heisenberg has pointed out, it took considerable time for scientists to get accustomed to the new concepts introduced into physics in the last century. It may be that, in Kuhn's words, "The transfer of allegiance from paradigm to paradigm is a conversion experience that cannot be forced." Walker has stated that since new scientific models are usually the creations of young scientists, the older scientists seldom do much work on the basis of these models.[37] These explanations do apply to some extent to Lapparent,

34. Cf. Jeans, *The New Background*, chap. 2, "The Methods of Science," and Walker, *Scientific Thought*, chap. 1, "The Scientific Method."
35. Lapparent, pp. 99–101.
36. Fred Hoyle, *Encounter with the Future* (New York, 1965), pp. 102–3.
37. Heisenberg, *Physics and Philosophy*, pp. 173–74; Thomas S. Kuhn, *The Structure of Scientific Revolutions* (Chicago, 1962, 1964), p. 150; Walker, *Scientific Thought*, p. 6.

whose reluctance to jettison the comfortable framework of the nineteenth-century science on which he had been brought up has already been sufficiently indicated. It does not seem to be a case of either one paradigm or the other, but a matter of accepting as much of the new paradigm as is consistent with maintaining the integrity of the old paradigm,[38] a course of action dictated by his conception of the nature of science and, ultimately, his conception of the universe, its origin, its governance, and its end. Lapparent was fortunate in living at a time when it made good scientific sense to indulge in comforting ambivalence. Shortly thereafter few scientists could afford to pamper the cravings of their souls so easily.

Method in the physical sciences required amplified discussion. Given the tentative character of most physical theories, it would seem prudent not to state these hypotheses with excessive rigor and thus reserve mathematics exclusively for the branches of knowledge already in a high stage of perfection. How was it, then, asked Lapparent, that the use of mathematics had become common in nearly all the domain of physics? Lapparent's technical treatment of this issue falls largely outside our present concern. But he emphasized that the rigorous precision of the formulas of mathematical physics should not delude us. What can be mathematically demonstrated in this area is that if the premises stated in the differential equations are exact, the consequence will surely be that integration will result. But the premises can always be discussed. It is all the better that in order to make calculation possible, one invariably begins with some hypothesis that perhaps simplifies the question more than the thing under investigation admits of.[39]

It was of considerable concern to Lapparent that superficial minds might acquire from the passing parade of ephemeral fashions in mathematical physics a scornful skepticism for science. Such a feeling would be ill justified, for all theories, even those definitely abandoned, had given great services. And frequently the obsolescent theory shows up under a different representation in better accord with the facts. Had not Coulomb's electrical fluids arisen phoenix-like under the name of electrons? But the great thing is that relations continue to be exact and always permit the prediction of phenomena. Lapparent was not without a certain ambivalence of his own toward Isis. He thought it certain that in the great majority of cases science could not hope to penetrate to the "essence of things." This did not mean that science should renounce the hope of getting closer to it, for science advances by successive approximations, each progress of a hypothesis being marked by a conquest giving a lasting benefit. But again in proportion to the specification of details, a growing complexity gives birth to new problems capable of removing further the goal that one had flattered oneself on attaining. Although it has no final end, science harvests many satisfactions en route, and how noble its role must appear to those who do not ask the impossible of it.[40]

Lapparent realized that agnostics would deny the possibility of science's

38. Cf. the attempt to contain Einstein's theory within Euclidean geometry, Kuhn, *Revolutions*, p. 148.
39. Lapparent, *Science et apologétique*, pp. 101-3.
40. Ibid., pp. 105-8.

casting any light on any issues other than the practical results obtained by scientific investigation. With characteristic tolerance, he admitted no objection to such a systematic disregard of whatever is not clearly intelligible if it were limited to the group of objects that can be grasped by the human mind. The real threat came not from the agnostics, ever eager to enlarge the circle of the unknowable, but from those who, in order to ruin the authority of belief, claimed to be basing themselves on science, representing it as the only area in which an affirmative statement is permitted. Lapparent's response to this type of attack was not in complete harmony with his earlier treatment of science, in which he emphasized the characteristics of certainty and absoluteness in science, qualities that fitted in well with his case for the validity of religious beliefs.[41] One has the right to ask those scientistically inclined to furnish the justification for their confidence by giving factual proof that science is really the area of certainties, that science provides the key to all mysteries, that it has the gift of penetrating to the very essence of things, and thus that science can be truly relied on to fulfill all the aspirations of human nature. To rid oneself of such an illusion, Lapparent urged, in a Pascalian mood contrasting sharply with his generally solid Cartesian emphasis, it would suffice to review the gradual evolution and the present state of the different branches of scientific knowledge. In spite of the multitudinous benefits for material civilization and the multifarious intellectual contributions of science, what revolutions had occurred in scientific theory! How powerless science had been to give definitive formulas or to attain a fleeting reality, which, perversely, increases in complexity as one gets closer to it. What contradictions had been inflicted on those who flattered themselves on having built impregnable structures! "In no period has this philosophic malaise been more evident than in our day. Never will the impartial examination of the state of science produce a more striking lesson: skepticism for one group, prudence or, better, modesty for the others."[42]

One of the clearest signs of this state of things was the crisis in the mathematical sciences, whose former certainty had vanished. The ideas of size, quantity, number, direction, and distance had changed so much that only a few first-rate minds remained capable of forming a clear idea of them. As he had already stated, mechanics was in need of a complete overhaul. Photography and spectroscopy had changed the world of astronomy. The serene fixity of a sidereal world congealed in an immutable framework had been replaced by a variety full of movement, life, and the unexpected. Of no significance now was the dream of the contemporaries of Laplace and Poisson of having defined for all time the characteristics of an invariable tableau. How odd Lagrange's plaintive remark now seemed: "Newton est bien heureux d'avoir trouvé un monde à expliquer. Malheureusement, il n'y a qu'un ciel!" In physics the whirligig of theories on the nature of light indicated that the "present"

41. This response—chap. 6, "L'évolution des doctrines scientifiques"—does not follow his treatment of similar matters in chap. 3, "Les sciences de l'observation," but I have decided that topically it fits better with the earlier chapter. Besides, it is interesting to compare the significantly different general emphases in the two treatments.
42. Ibid., p. 215.

would be a poorly chosen time to boast excessively about the right of science to make infallible pronouncements. Even within mineralogy Lapparent saw a split between the French, most of whom looked for cause and effect in crystallography, and the foreign schools, most of which looked upon symmetry as an interesting geometrical fact whose cause it was idle to attempt to discover. The situation was little better in biology. Skepticism was rife among scientists concerning the mechanistic dogma that life is only a physico-chemical problem.[43] Although the evidence generally continued in favor of evolution, there was, Lapparent noted, a move away from Darwinist doctrines toward notions similar to Lamarck's ideas and to the old doctrine of successive creations. Taking note of the ideas of Hugo de Vries on biological mutation, Lapparent pointed out that the sudden appearance of new types or forms that remained fixed contributed to the same state of flux in biology as existed in the other sciences. Not that this was undesirable—quite the contrary; but those who wished to construct anti-religious systems on the unshakable foundations of scientific theory would do well, it was implied, to examine the nature of the masonry used in the structure.

Realizing the possibility of a pessimistic interpretation of the evolution of scientific theories, Lapparent pointed out that he had guarded against this by previously presenting the other side of the picture. Certainly, he had done that with excessive zeal. To be sure of no misinterpretation of his aim, he took ten pages to emphasize the move toward unity in modern science. An impartial examination of the results obtained in each branch of knowledge would show the large and beautiful scientific conceptions grouped around the idea of order. It is true that all sorts of mysteries remain in our minds in spite of the development of science. It would be wrong to expect from science the solution of the big problems related to the mind, problems that cannot be expressed in equations because neither number nor extension apply and the energy liberated cannot be quantified. But one of the results of contemporary science that Lapparent presented as in harmony with the emphasis of the initial part of his work was the tendency toward unity, clearly accented in the continued progress of theoretical knowledge. Beneath the growing complexity of the increasing body of scientific facts, an acute mind could detect the basis for Poincaré's judgment: "La science marche vers l'unité et la simplicité."[44]

This unity was the most characteristic sign in which could be recognized the order and harmony so dear to Lapparent's heart. It was fairly easy for the well-informed geologist to provide a plethora of examples to prove his case. One of the first results of the use of the spectroscope had been to show that the same chemical elements are common to all the celestial bodies, thus establishing the unity of the composition of the universe. Later the same in-

43. Exposition de 1900. Picard, *Rapport sur les sciences.*
44. But "Einstein remarks somewhere that as the concepts of science are simplified and become ever more beautiful, the mathematics expressing them grows correspondingly more esoteric. Only the mathematical physicist can follow the lengthening chain of abstraction which connects to human experience, and only he can appreciate the beauty of the simplicity" (Gillispie, *The Edge of Objectivity*, pp. 352-53).

strument furnished the means of ascertaining that the same law of attraction governed all the worlds. A strong example could be extracted from the identity of magnetism and electricity and from the close connection between electromagnetism and light. The grandiose claim of thermodynamics to embrace all the phenomena of nature under its laws was a revolution for unity. The close relation between the different forms of energy having been established, it was necessary for Lapparent to refer only to the unity evident in one field, that of electrical phenomena, due to the real change of position of electrons, a change also applying to Becquerel rays and to radioactive substances. The calculation of the electric charge and the mass of the electron and the discovery that there was no difference between the properties of the atoms of different bodies completed the pattern of unity that Lapparent detected in the energy area. Unlike Duhem, Lapparent looked with benevolence on the "tempting hypothesis" of the atomic structure of matter because it offered an example of unity that he found very appealing. What simplicity, what harmony and order: one matter, the atom; one force, electricity.

That the nature of the atom continued to give rise to all sorts of hypotheses, which might cause the logicians to denounce them all as illusions, dreams of the imagination, or dangerous chimeras that followed one upon the other after a temporary vogue, did not disturb Lapparent. The accusation of the logician was possible, but it was unwise to ignore that the new discoveries, all oriented in the same direction, led to the same idea of unity. At the same time, mathematical formulas were being applied to categories of phenomena that formerly seemed bereft of any common bonds. The consideration of unity was becoming the best *criterium* by which to judge the value of hypotheses. "If the true essence of things continues to remain inaccessible to us, we can console ourselves that the veil covering it lets us at least understand the beautiful harmony that it must obey. Unity and simplicity are certainly high and noble conceptions! To recognize that the progress of science is bringing us to them is to proclaim at the same time the signs distinguishing the sovereign wisdom that set everything in order."[45]

Jeans began his survey of *The New Background of Science* (1933) by pointing out that "A century which has run less than a third of its course has already witnessed two great upheavals in physical science. These are associated with the words Relativity and Quanta, and have forced the physicist of to-day to view nature against a background of ideas which is very different from that of his nineteenth-century predecessor."[46] Lapparent's attachments to the nineteenth century became clear in his treatment of "the principle of least action," which he saw working in striking fashion in all the phenomena of nature in conformity with his idea of a "Suprême Sagesse ordonnatrice." The principle of economy had been applied to light in the seventeenth century by Fermat and had been extended in the eighteenth century by Maupertuis into the principle that "objects invariably move in such a way as to make the total expenditure of action a minimum."[47] Lapparent drew on the

45. Lapparent, *Science et apologétique*, p. 270.
46. Jeans, *The New Background of Science*, p. 1.
47. Ibid., p. 128.

nineteenth-century version in mechanics, which stated that a material particle freely moving from one point to another on a determined surface always
follows a geodesic line, that is, the shortest distance between two points. Rejecting Poincaré's skepticism about a theory that assumed a "thinking" particle, Lapparent put forward his own venerable hypothesis to explain the
ostensible intelligence of the particle: the principle of least action is evidence
of the infallible wisdom with which all things were put together.[48] That this
principle, which integrated matter and radiation in a temporary synthesis,
should become so complicated that "it broke loose from the facts altogether,"
until corrected by the special theory of relativity,[49] would seem to cause
grave difficulties for Lapparent's inference of a supreme intelligence. It is
highly probable, however, that Lapparent would have soon harnessed the elements of the new theory, especially those related to the old principle, to his
unshakable belief in divine providence.

Connected with the principle of least action was the law of conservation
of energy. (The first law of thermodynamics: "the energy of the universe is
constant," in Clausius' words; "various forms of energy are qualitatively trans-
formable, quantitatively indestructible, imponderable objects," the statement
of Mayer's formulation of the law given by a leading historian of thermodynamics.)[50] Especially attractive to Lapparent was the idea that the law of the
conservation of energy was an expression of an experimental fact. Although
the number of experiments was insufficient and did not exclude certain di-
vergences, the unconquerable tendency of our minds that is reflected in the
need for order and harmony sees the means of grouping the experimental
results around this strikingly simple formula. What is apparent chaos thus
becomes arranged in a harmonious order. Lapparent did not think the fundamental law of conservation to be violated by the example of radioactive
bodies giving off energy continuously without an exterior source, although
some were attacking it on this ground. This turned out to be an essentially
correct position: "Except to a rider to the first law, which Einstein attached
in 1905 for mass-energy conversions, there are no clear-cut natural processes
known to violate the principle of conservation of energy."[51] Citing Poincaré's
judgment that the law of the conservation of energy could only be expressed
as "there is something that remains constant in all phenomena," Lapparent
added, not without a certain triteness, that this becomes a self-evident axiom
if one admits that the universe is governed by laws.[52]

The connection between the order of the world supposedly illustrated by
the laws of thermodynamics and a "sovereign architect" would seem to be just

48. Lapparent, pp. 140–41.
49. "For any true picture of nature, or principle to explain the workings of nature,
must permit of representation in the undivided four-dimensional continuum. The principle of least action . . . did not permit of representation in this framework until it had
been divided up into space and time" (Jeans, *The New Background of Science*, pp. 129–
30).
50. Erwin N. Hiebert, "The Uses and Abuses of Thermodynamics in Religion," *Daedalus* 95 (Fall 1966): 1050.
51. Ibid.
52. Lapparent, pp. 235–36.

as big a jump from science to metaphysics as Cardinal Mercier accused Helmholtz of doing when Helmholtz stated that "the quantity of all forces which can be put into action in the whole of nature is unchangeable and can be neither increased nor decreased."[53] But it was a common nineteenth-century practice. "The first and second laws of thermodynamics have been used, affirmed, rejected, manipulated, exploited, and criticized in order both to further and to censure religion."[54] Only in the arguments arising out of the prolific theories of biological evolution was there concocted, perhaps, a more fanciful and elaborate series of sorites concerning God and the universe. Hiebert has provided a masterly summary, into which Lapparent may easily be fitted: "During the nineteenth century, the meaning of the law of conservation of energy was examined within the context of theological issues dealing primarily with the mode of God's presence and action in the world. The law was commonly invoked to bolster the argument for the existence of a Deity who had ordered the world with perfect foresight, wisdom, and economy of action. Thus, matter (the stuff of the world) and energy (the action and process within the nature of things) were accepted as conserved quantities. They were built into a system of nature operating without over-all matter or energy losses. The argument for a world of law, order, and timeless permanence served theology very well as long as the laws of science were not seen to be so thoroughly successful in their account of the nature of things as to make God a mere benevolent, absentee landlord."[55]

Lapparent found the principle of least action operative in the marvelous structures of crystals, whose masterly combinations could only give evidence of the Legislator who assures to each species the conditions of most resistance, in virtue of the principle of least action, and even permits them to acquire, through skilful arrangements, more stability than the crystal's own nature would appear to allow it. It was not without some satisfaction that Lapparent noted that if the crystal combinations were found in the organic sphere, rather than in the mineral world, some disciple of Darwin would find the explanation in the law of the survival of the fittest, transmitting by heredity the qualities giving it victory. But who could speak of instinct, of survival, of heredity in the case of crystals? Only the great Law-giver could have done the job. More harmony and order.[56]

The Sovereign Architect had fitted together all the individual components of the universe with their variations so that the excesses of the one compensated for the deficiencies of the other, thus ensuring a perfect construction, just as if all the components were individually perfect. And the universe could still be understood in terms of Euclidean geometry. Not one of the created objects could have originated the idea of non-Euclidean geometry, Lapparent argued, and even peering into the visible universe as far as the telescope would allow did not suggest abandoning three-dimensional Euclidean space. The

53. H. von Helmholtz, *Vorträge und Reden* (1884), 1:152, cited and translated by Hiebert, "Uses and Abuses," pp. 1063–64.
54. Hiebert, p. 1049.
55. Ibid., pp. 1062–63.
56. Lapparent, pp. 153–56.

Euclidean model on which the world had been created was the common and only solution from which emanated all the varieties of metageometries. Who would be unwilling to recognize the simplicity of the Euclidean triangle compared with the convex triangle of Riemann or the curvilinear figure of Lobachevski? Since Euclid had never been deficient in accommodating our knowledge of the universe, did not this show that the greatest admissible simplicity presided over the organization of the surrounding world? This result was the effect of a long process of adaptation, and that the tired world, after being tossed by chance from one hyperspace to another, sought rest in the serenity of plane space was a hypothesis that Lapparent rejected because it was so bold as to be improbable. In this well-ordered simplicity of the structure of the world, Lapparent saw evidence of a final design or end, which was too natural on the part of a Sovereign Intelligence to suspect it of an inclination for useless complications or a fruitless expenditure of superfluous efforts.[57]

The ideas of origin and of end and the issue of finality in the world were quasi-metaphysical themes that rose from their eighteenth-century ashes to become matters of serious concern in the nineteenth and twentieth centuries. Thus for Lapparent it was important to answer the question "Does scientific analysis of phenomena lead to the idea of a beginning and to that of an end?" Or must the succession of phenomena be interpreted as an unlimited repetition of the same circumstances oscillating around an invariable mean? The question had been often debated by scientists, who, according to their temperaments, had given different answers. Even among those who accepted the idea of a definite beginning state of the universe, there were some who tried to show that the structure of the world is perfectly stable, without any indication of an end.[58] "So far had Cartesian rationality prevailed over Newtonian caution during the Enlightenment, that the physical universe had come to seem a problem in mechanics. An idealized solar system served as a gross model for a world of inertial billiard balls moving and impacting through an infinite void."[59] The Comte de Pontécoulant summed up the case when he spoke at the unveiling of a statue to Poisson in Orléans in 1851: "The physical world was founded in the beginning, then, on unshakable foundations, and God, in order to safeguard the human race, is not obliged, as Newton thought, to touch up his work."[60] In view of his usual adherence to the fetishes of order and harmony, it is surprising to find Lapparent quoting, with obvious relish, Poincaré's judgment that Laplace had failed to demonstrate the stability of the solar system; a satisfactory solution to the problem was, in Poincaré's erroneous opinion, a long way off. Lapparent thought that the idea of the universe's having a beginning without an end was a little contradictory. Thus the better informed science of the nineteenth century had corrected that of the eighteenth, and philosophy had ratified its correction. But even Laplace had an idea that could be used within the Christian cosmogony. This was the idea of origin, which, Lapparent noted, had been given a new

57. Ibid., pp. 156–63.
58. Ibid., p. 164.
59. Gillispie, *The Edge of Objectivity*, p. 354.
60. Cited in Lapparent, pp. 169–70.

force by the recent hypothesis that the primeval nebula was the origin of the solar system, whose heat was a transformation of the electric charge carried by individual atoms when they came together. Did these ideas apply to the universe at large as well as to the earth and the solar system? Yes: "The idea of origin and end applied to the entire creation seems to find a remarkable confirmation in the fundamental law of this energetics in which all the sciences of matter tend more and more to meet."[61] And "energetics became the opposite pole to mechanics in nineteenth-century physics."[62] But it was another question whether apologetic capital could be made out of the deficiency of the Newtonian concepts of extension, mass, and motion in understanding such phenomena as heat, magnetism, and electricity.

Lapparent, like many scientists, considered the religious implications of the laws of thermodynamics. In their statements of the first law, Mayer, Joule, and Colding were not reluctant to make theological observations. Joule could declare in 1843 that he was "satisfied that the grand agents of nature are by the Creator's fiat *indestructible*."[63] The second law of thermodynamics—"The entropy of the universe tends toward a maximum" was Clausius' terse definition—in asserting that "the availability of energy in a real process decreases" implied that "the world is living on its capital."[64] Lapparent saw that this conclusion was dependent upon the principle of the conservation of energy, which had a precise meaning only in a closed system. Of course, one could claim that it applied to the case of a finite universe; then only those who conceived of the universe as infinite could not admit that the laws of thermodynamics applied. Whatever the case may be, Lapparent commented, it is interesting to see the idea of an *évolution finaliste* presented . . . as the consequence of a universal principle including all laws of knowable phenomena.[65] Lapparent's lack of enthusiasm over the possible apologetic implications of Time's Arrow (Eddington's pithy description of the second law) in contrast to his joy over the lessons implicit in the first, did not necessarily involve him in a flagrant inconsistency. The geologist sensed, even if he did not state it explicitly, that Time's Arrow is, in Gillispie's words, too arbitrary and unreasonable a concept for entropy to be the ontological equivalent of energy and that there are "difficulties in the logical relations of the first and second laws," although the growing importance of entropy since the nineteenth century would seem, temporarily at least, to justify Eddington's assertion that it is "the most fundamental among the laws of nature."[66]

Although "evolution and entropy were the leading novelties which nineteenth-century science offered to the pundit,"[67] the conclusion that could be

61. Ibid., p. 180. In commenting on the introduction of energetics into chemistry and on the development of physical chemistry, Lapparent argued that the mystery of the constitution of bodies remained (p. 237).

62. Gillispie, *The Edge of Objectivity*, p. 360. See also p. 356 for comment on the polarization of "the two great aspects of nineteenth-century physics—thermodynamics and mechanics."

63. Cited ibid., p. 371.

64. Ibid., p. 402.

65. Lapparent, *Science et apologétique*, p. 182. See also his brief discussion of these issues in *Les enseignements philosophiques de la science*, pp. 9–12.

66. Gillispie, *The Edge of Objectivity*, pp. 400–403.

67. Ibid., p. 404.

drawn from the one was nearly the opposite of the other: an "Evolutionary creed was equated with hope, with the law of progress, the lay creed of men of science; entropy considerations prophesied a pessimism of despair, a future of disillusionment."[68] Not that the pessimism of the time should be attributed to entropy: the dance of death during the waning of the Middle Ages and the pessimism of the eighteenth century were not inspired by any comparable scientific law; rather "the idea of entropy had already been generalized in the vaguer, the more cosmic pessimism of the late nineteenth-century prophets of despair, for whom the idea of progress had turned to clinkers, and who sat among the ashes contemplating the heat death of the universe."[69] But the second law of thermodynamics did raise what seemed at the time important theological issues.

> If the principle of the increase of entropy of any operating system was extended to the world or the universe as a system, then the universe was moving toward . . . a condition of minimum availability of energy. This irreversible process, this unidirectional movement toward disorganization in history (time's arrow), led to a degradation of the energy sources and ultimately to that pessimistic state of affairs, that boredom or Nirvana, that was called the "heat-death" of the universe. Thermodynamics accordingly predicted an end to everything as a function of time.
>
> Such a theory, which injected into the minds of men a majestic dysteleology that would eventuate in the consummation of the world, was bound to unleash polemics from religion. Ends and beginnings—creation's end and origin—were matters that theologians could hardly sidestep. What would come to an end? And what constituted a beginning or a creation?[70]

It is probably evidence of Lapparent's solid grasp of science that he did not indulge in this type of cosmic pessimism. No doubt, as in the case of Pierre Duhem, Lapparent's firm belief in the fundamentals of Catholicism was also a strong factor against his becoming a Miniver Cheevy on the future of the universe.

Lapparent was firmly Aristotelian in his devotion to the sacred doctrine that every phenomenon has a final cause, which, like efficient cause, is essentially the same as form; the adaptation of natural phenomena and of life seemed a convincing argument for a moderate teleology. It was, he noted with regret, a dangerous exercise to talk about final causes, since many, finding the theme outmoded, disdainfully asked what sources are used to unveil the intentions of the Author of all things. But for the geologist the same inclination that had led him to seek order in the creation also let him show the value of examples in which the principle of finality emerges. The argument had a familiar ring; only the profusion of examples and the depth of the comments make it tolerable and worthy of consideration. The formation of crystals, whose symmetry enables them to resist the outside forces of destruction,

68. Hiebert, "Uses and Abuses," p. 1073.
69. Gillispie, *The Edge of Objectivity*, p. 404. Thus Henry Adams is a good example of "the intellectual who . . . found in entropy the excuse to indulge his mal du siècle."
70. Hiebert, "Uses and Abuses," pp. 1066–67.

presents a teleological phenomenon of the first order since it occurs in objects to which one cannot apply the explanations of instinct, heredity, etc. From rock to water. Was it not providential how water, especially the ocean, stayed the right temperature to maintain its liquidity in the cold zones? The organic world was also prolific in examples of finality. Lapparent drew on Paul Vignon's studies, in the 1904 *Revue de philosophie*,[71] on scientific materialism to demonstrate the case for finality. The work of the prolific and brilliant zoologist Yves Delage on the rhynchocephalic crustacean parasite *Sacculina*, its beginning and evolution, also provided a lode for exploitation.[72] Not to be overlooked was the example of mimesis in butterflies, a phenomenon that Vignon had dealt with and whose work Lapparent drew on again. Some argued that mimesis indicated a premeditated plan of the species itself, thus admitting that the animal could acquire by heredity a specific resemblance to an object that its ancestors had contrived to imitate intentionally. Lapparent agreed readily that a will had intervened, but in the case of butterfly, for example, not the insect's will, but the will of the Power that had formed the insect. Vignon's studies had shown, in Lapparent's opinion, that no anti-teleological mechanism could ever explain how birds differentiated themselves from a reptilian origin or how insects originally wingless acquired wings. Confronted with such transformations, the conscientious materialists found themselves obliged to profess a complete agnosticism. Without claiming to be better informed on the immediate causes that produced these evolutions, Lapparent declared that at least he would like to put them under a higher directing cause, namely the active harmony that governs nature.

Geology, the area that he knew best, gave Lapparent the best evidence for teleology. Finality is nowhere more evident than in coal reserves. The choice of the epoch in which the principal part of the reserves was formed, the process under which they accumulated, and the way in which they were preserved from destruction all bore witness to a marvelously executed plan, which man would be ungrateful to deny. The operation of the master hand could not be denied. Why the planning of coal resources? It was the plan of He who wished the earth one day to become the habitation of man.[73] All

71. See *Introduction à de nouvelles recherches de morphologie comparée sur l'aile des insectes* (Paris, 1929) and *Introduction à la biologie expérimentale. Les êtres organisés, activités, instincts, structures* (Paris, 1930). In 1902, Vignon, who was attached to the zoology laboratory of the Sorbonne and had the results of his research presented to the Academy of Sciences by Delage, published *Le linceul du Christ; étude scientifique* (Paris, 1902; translation, London, 1902). See also *Le Saint Suaire de Turin devant la science, l'iconographie, la logique* (Paris, 1938). He became a professor of philosophy at the Catholic Institute in Paris.

72. *Evolution de la sacculine* (Paris, 1884). Delage's thesis, *Contribution à l'étude de l'appareil circulatoire des crustacés édriophthalmes marins* (Paris, 1881), won the Grand prix des sciences physiques of the Academy of Sciences. In 1886, he replaced Milne-Edwards at the Sorbonne. Delage, an enthusiastic Darwinist, rejected teleological systems and hailed evolution not only as a great scientific advance but as a powerful weapon against the idols of religion. See *Les théories de l'évolution* (Paris, 1909; translation, New York, 1912).

73. It is unfortunate that the poetic quality of some of Lapparent's prose is lost in this analysis of his thought. Cf. "Cependant, si fière que soit une chaîne de montagnes, le temps impitoyable finit toujours par en avoir raison" (*Science et apologétique*, pp. 199–200).

of the complex operations of the formation of the coal reserves formed too well woven a plot to be the result of blind chance. Not only Europe had been the recipient of divine favors: when the resources of Europe reached exhaustion, the New World, i.e., America, would become the axis of "la civilisation matérielle." In finishing his consideration of the special arrangements of Providence for man, Lapparent, the practitioner of an empirical science par excellence, emphasized that he had presented no evidence that did not conform to observation. It remained, then, if one were to explain these remarkable chains of events, to choose between chance and the divine will. For those who are the privileged heirs of these arrangements and want to express their gratitude to One who would welcome it, it is undoubtedly natural that chance is a totally inadequate explanation.

Realizing that there would possibly be some who would be disappointed in not finding in his presentation more devastating arguments against objections being made against the faith, Lapparent admitted in all honesty that if religious truth were susceptible of being given a purely rational demonstration, agreement would have been reached among civilized men on these matters long ago, as it had been—although not completely—on the theorems of algebra and of geometry. But then faith would have ceased being a merit attainable by souls of good will and would have become an indisputable obligation, imposing itself on all minds free from the vice of conformity. It is not the function of apologetics to make faith useless but to furnish the motives of the *rationabile obsequium* on which the virtue of faith must be founded. This had been the aim of Lapparent's lectures: to try to establish the spirit of true science; to show it impregnated with the ideas of order, perfection, the ideal, and the infinite. Science is valuable because it furnishes weapons enabling man to put the powers of nature at his service; it is even nobler when it strives to make man comprehend the order and harmony of the creation; and it is very salutary when it harnesses man for intellectual discipline, although it always fails to penetrate to the very essence of things.

Of course, the inability of science to solve the problems of the mind was even clearer than the limitations of science within its own area. The claim of some of its interpreters that these problems be expressed in equations or even that science shed some light on them was sufficiently condemned, at least in the opinion of those who, like Lapparent, knew how to judge the results obtained. Besides, these methods were far from those of true science. More depressing was the fact that instead of leading intelligence gradually to the high abstractions whose relations reveal the laws by which the world is governed, the scientistically inclined intelligentsia was leading man down an opposite slope away from the wide horizons on which man had lovingly fixed his sights in times gone by. Lapparent thought this development an aberration resulting from intellectualism run wild. Intelligence is not the only human faculty. The heart has its place; it is not sentimental to want to maintain it. "Affection, devotion, honor, and sacrifice cannot be demonstrated or taught by formulas; we have, however, the innate sense that these are finer and nobler things than all the results of higher knowledge."[74] Oddly enough, Lapparent thought that there was one way of treating these concepts scien-

74. Ibid., p. 300.

tifically: to apply to them the general concepts that the sciences have eluci-
dated, i.e., to seek in them the ideas of order, of harmony, of the ideal, of
discipline, which are better suited to this domain than to that of matter. In a
different way, then, science, or Lapparent's interpretation of it, was having
an impact on his nonscientific ideas just as it was transforming the ideas of
the opponents of Catholicism. Both exploitations were, perhaps, equally futile.

There was no doubt in Lapparent's mind of what the result would be when
this method of treating the ethical concepts he had enumerated became the
source of inspiration for man. He knew in advance that behavior would be
based on these superb concepts when, in a systematic effort to raise human
nature above itself, man succeeded in silencing both pride and concupiscence,
which are, basically, the only enemies of all faith. And then from paradise
lost to paradise regained: the way to this victory lay only in boldly entering
the temple on whose pediment was inscribed the fundamental precept "Love
one another" and where, not content with giving only verbal teaching, man
excelled in furnishing at the same time the practical means of continual re-
invigoration in the spirit of sacrifice and struggle against the self. All this
could be done within the framework of the admirable institutions sanctified
by the ages. These were the motives of Lapparent's *rational obedience.* With
some rhetorical elasticity but not without some justification, he insisted that
these ideas had inspired the great men of science—Kepler, Pascal, Newton,
Ampère, Cauchy, Hermite, and Pasteur—who had honored them and had
never thought that out of their discoveries could come any weakening of the
deep convictions animating them. The more their knowledge widened, the
more they felt themselves seized by a double feeling: on the one hand a grateful admiration for the beauty of the work whose details revealed themselves
to them; on the other hand, a growing modesty, motivated by the too evident disproportion between the present state of their knowledge and the immensity of the problems that each new discovery inevitably brought forth.
The anecdote about Newton's comment to his nephew puts this in its classic
form: "I do not know what I may appear to the world; but to myself I seem
to have been only like a boy, playing on the sea shore, and diverting myself,
in now and then finding a smoother pebble or a prettier shell than ordinary,
whilst the great ocean of truth lay all undiscovered before me."[75]

In 1906 the editor of the *Revue pratique d'apologétique* asked Lapparent
to answer the question "Has your Catholic faith been a hindrance to you in
your scientific research?" His initial reaction to this request was to continue
his practice of not inflicting on the public the *moi haïssable* that he believed
best left out of view. But since his appearance in the *Revue de l'Institut catholique* had already created a precedent, he decided to give a reply, even
though the reading public of this publication was smaller than that of the
Revue pratique d'apologétique.[76]

75. Cited in Frank E. Manuel, *A Portrait of Isaac Newton* (Cambridge, Mass., 1968),
pp. 388–89.
76. "Questions et réponses. La recherche scientifique et la foi," *Revue pratique d'apologétique*, 15 juin 1906, pp. 266–72. In May 1906, Lapparent gave a lecture on creative

Lapparent's reply added no significantly new argument to those presented in his lectures at the Catholic Institute in 1905 and published as *Science et apologétique*, but it did offer a number of personal and no less important insights into the question asked. From a practical viewpoint, Lapparent observed, the question had already been answered by facts: thirty-one years of teaching with publications in general use among specialists, who found in these words an expression of scientific "orthodoxy" in the matters treated.[77] At the same time he was welcomed by the heads of the Catholic Institute and in constant agreement with the best qualified defenders of the church. The phrase "best qualified" had a special significance for Lapparent, who had been attacked by some of the more traditionally minded of the clergy. His heroes were more Duchesne and d'Hulst than Barbier and the anti-modernists. Having come out of the Polytechnique and the Ecole des Mines, he was directed to the interpretation of that part of the "book of nature" dealing with the constitution of the terra firma. It was not the aspiration of Lapparent to enter into this work as a theoretician but merely as a cataloger of detailed facts interested in their application. Both by temperament and education a deep enemy of disorder and obscurity, he could not conceive of a society not basically impregnated with the feeling of duty. Nor could he admit that this duty is defined by the individual; received by him from above in a clear and definite form, it is based on higher principles, which are not amenable to discussion without endangering the basis of society itself. This was the quasi-Bonaldian sociology underlying Lapparent's philosophy of science.

It was quite natural, then, that his scientific research was based on the idea of *order*. Quite early in his career he concluded that each branch of knowledge is a worthy effort to achieve knowledge of the order governing a determined category of phenomena. For Lapparent this was a paradigmatic assumption of science, the guiding thread that made research productive. Thus the convictions of a Christian, convinced a priori that all had been ordered with number, weight, and measure, certainly could not trouble the reflections of a man of science. Natural history has a unique privilege: when one wishes to envisage the terrestrial globe as a whole, not in the small details of its component elements, it has to be done in the great outdoors, far from the tumult of towns and the human influence that shrink and falsify everything. Then one can feel oneself nearer to the infinite power that all nature—except man, alas!—obeys without resistance, not in the sense of an imposed discipline one would like to shake off but a discipline accepted as the only way of produc-

Providence to the Œuvre des Eglises et Chapelles pauvres of Paris; Bloud published an extended version as *La providence créatrice* in 1907 in its series on science and religion. It developed certain ideas of *Science et apologétique* on the divine plan for the world, on harmony and unity, and on a geological theodicy, as well as the teleology revealed in coal deposits. Lapparent's fantastic symphony on the harmony and majesty of the creation is not far from the vision in Flaubert's *Bouvard and Pécuchet*, pp. 92–95.

77. Among Lapparent's numerous scientific publications were *Traité de géologie* (Paris, 1883; 5th ed., 1906); *Cours de minéralogie* (Paris, 1884); *La géologie en chemin de fer. Description géologique du bassin parisien et des régions adjacentes* (Paris, 1888); *Leçons de géographie physique* (Paris, 1896; 3d ed., 1907); and *Le globe terrestre*, 3 vols. (Paris, 1889).

ing, with order, this marvelously healthy harmony that life outdoors naturally gives to intelligences not perverted by a bad education. But this Rousseauistic experience cannot be enjoyed vicariously; one has to go to some quiet village, where the silence of the evening is broken only by the bell of the Angelus, in order to enjoy not only the poetry of nature but an intimate communication between the soul, uplifted by encouraging impressions, and the higher principle inherent in the order which one can just glimpse in one of its manifestations.

Lapparent showed that he was keenly aware of the issues discussed today in connection with the notion of the paradigm in scientific thought: "without deluding myself on the necessarily provisional character of the formulas obtained in an area of research where each day could not fail to bring something new, I applied myself completely in bringing out the merit of these disciplines. I strove to awaken in students, I would not dare say faith in the things taught, since no-one could claim infallibility, but belief in the reality of this order, of which all theory gives the least imperfect representation for the moment."[78] It was Lapparent's belief that such an approach could find support in Christian beliefs, and particularly in Catholic beliefs, where the idea of discipline, combined with the idea of the *rationabile obsequium*, was at the basis of all things. No doubt the ideologues of the Third Republic would have scoffed at such an idea, believing that the dynamo had conquered the Virgin. But the modern historian of science is less likely to adopt so cavalier and dogmatic an attitude. Lynn White, Jr., has argued that "the century in which the cult of the Virgin Mary achieved its most marvelous expression" was that "which likewise first envisaged the concept of a labor-saving, power technology." The Virgin and the dynamo are not opposing principles permeating the universe; they are allies. "The Middle Ages, believing that the Heavenly Jerusalem contains no temple, began to explore the practical implications of this profoundly Christian paradox."[79] Lapparent's argument is a nineteenth-century version of the venerable idea that *laborare est orare*.

Lapparent did not find his beliefs a hindrance but a source of valuable support in his work. Although his own scientific domain was, from a religious viewpoint, somewhat delicate, Lapparent saw nothing that had been clearly defined by the church as an area of conflict with what he gave the purely relative name of "scientific orthodoxy." Of course, he had been attacked on several occasions by self-appointed custodians of orthodoxy. But the only result had been to convince Lapparent of the great wisdom of the authorities to whom the snipers of apologetics had appealed but who had seen nothing in Lapparent's theories to get excited about. No professor had felt so free as he in writing and speaking. Having received the most explicit and constant encouragement from the church authorities, Lapparent interpreted this as proof of the wisdom of the church as well as the regard it had for sincere

78. See Thomas S. Kuhn, "The Function of Dogma in Scientific Research," in *Scientific Change*, ed. A. C. Crombie (New York, 1963), and Kuhn, *The Structure of Scientific Revolutions*.

79. White, "Dynamo and Virgin Reconsidered," *The American Scholar* 17 (1958): 192-94. See also ibid., "What Accelerated Technological Progress in the Western Middle Ages?" in *Scientific Change*, pp. 272-91.

opinions, if one submitted in advance to her jurisdiction. Nonscientific intellectuals would hardly have the same opinion in 1907, when *Lamentabili Sane Exitu* and *Pascendi Dominici Gregis* would create among the Catholic intelligentsia the opposite of the conditions Lapparent had found so congenial for his activities. But in the year before the fulminations from Rome, Lapparent publicly declared the joy he experienced at being able to work in the environment provided by Catholic institutions. His superiors and colleagues were men of virtue, zeal, and disinterestedness. No intrigues, no petty ambitions, no vulgar competitions—the heavenly city of the French educational world, it seemed. This was a completely unreal picture, of course, as the intellectual Donnybrook Fair of modernism showed. But Lapparent declared in 1906 that no other institution could provide an atmosphere so favorable to the peace demanded by the pursuit of works of an intellectual nature. Without contesting the validity of the second dubious part of this observation, one can say that at the Catholic Institute the world of the two cultures must have been hermetically divided. For Lapparent the institute provided an encouraging environment that powerfully helped him to fulfill his task as a man of science.[80]

One of the more subtle changes in the Catholic scientific community toward the end of the nineteenth century was that a distinction developed between the presentation of one's scientific work for the scientific community and one's support of the providential view of nature. This was necessary in order to get work accepted by a scientific community that had imposed on itself the rule of rigid religious and ostensible philosophical neutrality in the presentation of scientific results in the accepted scientific organs of the day. In order to get its science accepted by the entire scientific community, the Catholic group had to conform to this requirement. The change is evident in comparing scientists like Barrande and the Abbé Moigno to Lapparent and Duhem. The Thomist philosopher Domet de Vorges complained about the religious neutrality of the Catholic scientific community. When Lapparent's famous *Traité de géologie* appeared in 1883, Moigno personally reviewed it in his journal *Cosmos* to register the criticism that Lapparent had systematically eliminated the biblical vision from his cosmogonic hypotheses, had not even mentioned the flood once, and had left revelation and the Bible completely outside science. Moigno admitted that Lapparent belonged to a large school of apologists who had systematically broken all connections between revelation and science. These principles were in direct opposition to two important assumptions of Moigno's most important work, *Les splendeurs de la foi* (1879): that a considerable number of biblical texts concern the theories and truths of pure science and that the relevant biblical teachings are identical with those of the most advanced science. Moigno could not understand why a distinguished Catholic scientist would not want to proclaim these ideas in his work. He could not accept the clear separation of science per se from scientific-religious interactions that had become the accepted method of procedure for the Catholic scientific community and was becoming that of apologists as well.

80. Lapparent, *Revue pratique d'apologétique* (1906), p. 272.

An exchange of letters between Moigno and d'Hulst, rector of the Catholic Institute in Paris, established the irreconcilability of the two positions. For d'Hulst only a negative correlation between science and faith was possible, a limitation to showing that no antagonism is possible. Faith does not change; science progresses because it is always a partial truth. As science changes its data and its theories, the apologist takes it at a certain point and compares it to revealed doctrine to assure himself of the continued lack of opposition between the two. All that is needed for this negative agreement is that the scientist not exploit science in turning it against faith; the more the scientist limits himself to science, the more sure will be his testimony. Of course it is possible that biblical elements could enter into a hypothesis inspiring the research of a scientist, and this would be a positive correlation between faith and science, but d'Hulst admitted this only as a possibility. This hardly satisfied Moigno, who replied that the association of the Catholic Institute with the views of Lapparent compromised that institution and that the founding bishops should have been consulted before a reply was given. Moigno cleverly cited a part of a letter Leo XIII had written to congratulate him on his splendid use of science to defend the faith. Moigno was probably enjoying a bit of personal revenge in this quarrel, for he had not been asked to join the faculty of the institute when it was established in 1875. In spite of his labors, Moigno was not taken seriously by many of the other scientists and intellectuals of the institute and was effectively kept out. His paradigm of the interaction between science and religion was that of another generation, and it had no convenient place in the new institution.[81]

81. Letter of d'Hulst to Dupanloup, November 29, 1875, BN, NAF 24690. The d'Hulst-Moigno correspondence is reprinted in *APC*, n.s. 8 (1883): 164–95, 561–70. Pius IX conferred a doctorate in theology on Moigno in 1871.

5

Pierre Duhem: The Scientific Philosophy
of a Modern Believer

> "Il semble que la révolution des idées soit ici entière, ra-
> dicale: par delà trois siècles de mécanisme cartésien, par dela
> la Renaissance, on s'aperçoit avec stupeur que ce physicien
> catholique [Duhem] nous ramène jusqu'à la doctrine scolas-
> tique des formes substantielles, jusqu'à la physique d'Aris-
> tote et de Saint Thomas."
>
> D. Parodi, *La philosophie contemporaine en France. Essai de
> classification des doctrines* (Paris, 1919), p. 242.

There is a certain perversity in even considering the relations between
Pierre Duhem's scientific philosophy and religion. He persistently maintained that his scientific theories were autonomous, having no foundation in
either religion or metaphysics. But in a famous and penetrating article in the
Revue de métaphysique et de morale in 1904, Abel Rey aroused Duhem's
alarm by concluding that "In order to find and formulate precisely the expression of this scientific philosophy . . . it seems that we may propose the
following formula: In its tendencies towards a qualitative conception of the
material universe, in its challenging distrust with regard to a complete explanation of this universe by itself, of the sort mechanism imagines it has, and in
its animadversions, more pronounced than genuine, with respect to an integral scientific skepticism, Duhem's scientific philosophy is that of a believer."[1]

1. Rey, "La philosophie scientifique de M. Duhem," *RMM* 12 (July 1904): 744, translation by Philip P. Wiener in Duhem, *Physical Theory*, p. 273. Abel Rey (1873-1940),
Docteur ès lettres, agrégé de philosophie, professeur de lycée (1898-1908), chargé d'un
cours de philosophie (Dijon, chaire de M. Gérard-Varet, député, 1907-10). Gérard re-
sumed his duties as professor in 1910 and Rey became maître de conférences at the same
faculty, but he became Gérard-Varet's chargé de cours in 1910-11 when the professor
assumed other functions. In 1911, Rey was made a professor of philosophy in the faculty
of letters at Dijon. Among Rey's works in the history and philosophy of science are *La*

Since the conclusion that Duhem's scientific philosophy is "la philosophie scientifique d'un croyant" comes only in the last few lines of a generally flattering article, giving due praise to Duhem's originality, and since Rey excluded any judgment of Duhem's scientific work from his study, the detailed and painstaking reply of Duhem about a year later may seem a little odd to the contemporary reader. It is by no means evident from a reading of Rey's study today that his conclusion followed inexorably from the analysis he made of Duhem's scientific philosophy. One is also struck by the moderate tone of Duhem, who was noted for his ability to demolish intellectual opponents with more devasting logic and irony than Christian charity should perhaps have allowed.[2]

Even in the anti-clerical France of 1904, Duhem admitted with characteristic frankness and clarity that he was a believer in the teachings of the Catholic Church. "Of course, I believe with all my soul in the truths that God has revealed to us and that He has taught us through His Church; I have never concealed my faith, and that He in whom I hold it will keep me from ever being ashamed of it, I hope from the bottom of my heart: in this sense it is permissible to say that the physics I profess is the physics of a believer." This was not the sense in which Duhem interpreted Rey's formula, but rather in the sense of meaning that "the beliefs of the Christian had more or less consciously guided the criticism of the physicist, that they had inclined his reason to certain conclusions, and that these conclusions were hence to appear suspect to minds concerned with scientific rigor but alien to the spiritualist philosophy or Catholic dogma; in short, that one must be a believer . . . in order to adopt altogether the principles as well as the consequences of the doctrine that I have tried to formulate concerning physical theories."[3] Rey had not actually said that Duhem's theories were suspect because they were the scientific philosophy of a *croyant*; he pointed out several other possible objections to the theories. But obviously this was the part of the article that stung Duhem the most, and, perhaps, suggested the danger that his theories

---

science dans l'antiquité, 2 vols. (Paris, 1930–33); *Les mathématiques en Grèce au milieu du Ve siècle* (Paris, 1935); *La théorie de la physique chez les physiciens contemporains* (thesis, Faculty of Letters, Paris, 1907); and *Le retour éternel et la philosophie de la physique* (Paris, 1927). *La science dans l'antiquité* was in the series *L'évolution de l'humanité* (série complémentaire) and therefore has a preface by Henri Berr. Rey was one of the editors and collaborators of vol. 1 of the *Encyclopédie française* (*1: L'outillage mental*). Along with Berr, Lucien Febvre, and Paul Langevin, Rey also was one of the editors of the *Revue de synthèse* (1931–). Like most of the republican intellectuals, Rey was interested in ethics and in developing a nonreligious morality for the republican educational system. He also published *Leçons de morale fondées sur l'histoire des mœurs et des institutions: écoles normales . . . écoles primaires supérieures* (Paris, 1906) and *Logique et morale, suivies de notions sommaires de philosophie générale* (Paris, 4th ed., 1916): "Contenant les sujets de philosophie donnés le plus récemment aux examens des baccalauréats . . . et de la licence . . . aux concours de l'École normale supérieure, de Saint-Cyr, de l'enseignement secondaire des jeunes filles et de l'enseignement primaire." An excellent essay on Duhem's philosophy of science is Charles Evan Cardwell's "Representation and Uncertainty" (Ph.D. diss., University of Rochester, 1971).

2. See also Duhem's review of Rey's classic study, *La théorie de la physique chez les physiciens contemporains* (Paris, 1907) in the *Revue générale des sciences pures et appliquées* 19 (1908): 7–19, translated by Wiener, in Duhem, *Physical Theory*, pp. 312–35.

3. Wiener-Duhem, *Physical Theory*, pp. 273–74.

would henceforth be dismissed as Catholic science, instead of being considered on their own merits.

If the formula were accurate, Duhem lamented, he had been steering a wrong course and had missed his goal of showing "that physics proceeds by an autonomous method absolutely independent of any metaphysical opinion." Before admitting that he had produced a physics based upon the implicit axiom of religious faith or confessing his own ignorance about the direction in which his work was being consciously guided by the element he had most assiduously tried to exclude, Duhem decided to re-examine his work in its entirety. He fixed his "gaze particularly on the parts in which the seal of the Christian faith was believed noticeable" in order to find out "whether, against my intention, this seal is really impressed therein or else, on the contrary, whether an illusion, easy to dissipate, has not led to the taking of certain characteristics not belonging to the work as the mark of a believer."[4] If Rey had been the victim of an illusion, in spite of his careful reading of Duhem's works and his concern for accuracy, both of which Duhem admitted, it might have been due, Duhem urged, to certain "confusions and ambiguities." By clearing these up Duhem hoped to establish his innocence beyond doubt. "Whatever I have said of the method by which physics proceeds, or of the nature and scope that we must attribute to the theories it constructs, does not in any way prejudice either the metaphysical doctrines or the religious beliefs of anyone who accepts my words. The believer and the nonbeliever may both work in common accord for the progress of physical science such as I have tried to define it."[5] Although this generous aim would be accepted by the Third Republic in nearly all areas a few years after Duhem wrote, in 1904 it was an idea only a man of vision and hope could propose.

First Duhem analyzed the scientific influences to which he had been exposed: at the Collège Stanislas, Catholic but part of the university, from which he emerged as a convinced mechanist due to the influence of the physicist Jules Moutier; at the Normale, where his exposure to mathematics, especially under Jules Tannery, gave him a quite different idea of what theory should be; and at Lille in the Faculty of Sciences, where questioning by an "elite audience" led him to conclude "that physics could not be constructed on the plan we had undertaken to follow, that the inductive method as defined by Newton could not be practiced. . . ." It was only after concluding that methods used for the construction of a physical theory are important that Duhem had the intuition "that physical theory is neither a metaphysical explanation nor a set of general laws whose truth is explained by experiment and induction" but rather "that it is an artificial construction manufactured with the aid of mathematical magnitudes . . . that this theory constitutes a kind of synoptic painting or schematic sketch suited to summarize and classify the laws of observation."[6] He emphasized that his conception of physical theory had been forged in the furnace of teaching with its concomitant testing over a period of many years, as well as in the practice of scientific research.

4. Ibid., p. 274.
5. Ibid., pp. 274–75.
6. Ibid., pp. 275–77.

Duhem concluded, then, that even after a deep examination of his intellectual conscience, it was impossible for him to recognize any religious influence on his scientific ideas. Indeed, he found it unthinkable that the Catholic faith could be interested in the evolution of his ideas as a physicist. Did it not support his case that he had known sincere and enlightened Christians who resolutely upheld mechanical explanations of the universe? Some were ardent supporters of the inductive method of Newton. To any man of common sense, then, the aim and nature of physical theory has nothing to do with religious doctrines. As a clinching argument, Duhem pointed out that the most numerous and most vigorous attacks on his scientific ideas had come from fellow Catholics, who, unlike Rey, could not see the putative religious foundation of his scientific philosophy.

Duhem's reply to Rey evoked a brief clarifying letter from Rey to the *Annales*. Rey's chief point was that in his article he did not refer to Duhem's physics in the proper and scientific sense of the word but used the expression "philosophie des sciences d'un croyant." Duhem himself went beyond Rey's formula when he entitled his article "Physique de croyant" and attributed to Rey the idea that Duhem's metaphysics was absolutely necessary to acceptance of his physics. Rey argued that one must separate, on strictly scientific grounds, pure science as it exists in the period in which one examines it from the *ideal* conception one makes of science in its finished form, or at least insofar as it can be represented in this ideal form. But this ideal conception is a philosophical one, no more scientific than the facts it goes beyond. Always accompanied by value judgments (philosophical), these ideal conceptions, of which there exists a manifold variety, nevertheless have a strictly scientific appearance.[7] It was this Duhemian philosophy of physics, an ideal conception, that Rey classified in a broad group of conceptions under the label "philosophie des sciences de croyants," which could include diverse thinkers, like Kant, Schopenhauer, Secrétan, and Le Roy. Rey argued that this classification did not imply any belittling of their strictly scientific works. One must be judged by scientific criteria and the other by philosophical criteria.

This ingenious bifurcation neatly solved a problem that plagued secular, rationalist republicans: how to explain away the embarrassing fact that a large segment of the French scientific community held philosophical and religious beliefs subversive of the rationalist-secularist republican *Weltanschauung*. In his eulogy of Berthelot, Painlevé made use of a much less sophisticated version of Rey's elegant argument, using as his example the absence of correlation between Pasteur's anti-materialistic ideas and his bacteriological work.[8] The chemistry of life had been more fertile than physics in spawning secular ideologies.

All of these Duhemian philosophical ideas, generally based on a qualitative view of nature, upheld the non-explanatory nature of science (*"la science ne*

7. Abel Rey, "La physique de M. Duhem," *APC*, 4th ser. (1905–6): 535–37. "L'historien est forcé de constater la multiplicité de ces conceptions idéales et de remarquer que *toutes* elles accusent celles qui leur sont opposées de métaphysique et se donnent chacune comme rigoureusement positive" (p. 536).
8. See chap. 1.

peut être explicative"). (Rey noted that Aristotelianism was not logically connected to a philosophy of belief and, from the viewpoint of historical reality, was quite different. In a period when a Thomistically interpreted Aristotle had been incorporated into Catholic apologetics, this was an important note. Apart from Thomism, there was a general revival of interest in Aristotle in the late nineteenth century.) The logical reason behind Rey's calling Duhem's *philosophical conception*, not his purely scientific works, the philosophy of science of a believer was that the hypothesis "science cannot be explanatory" analytically involves another hypothesis, that the explanation behind the physical world must be sought outside it. At this point Rey separated himself from the typical secular rationalist to declare that he would similarly designate as the philosophy of an unbeliever any philosophy maintaining that science is capable of explaining the physical world without reference to anything outside it. It would be the philosophy of an unbeliever because this view claimed that scientific and rational methods alone give a sufficient explanation of phenomena and replace what are traditionally called beliefs.

Rey divided Duhem's ideas into two categories: his strictly scientific ideas, which received universal approval and depended only upon a scientific discussion of experiments, and his ideas going beyond the contemporary area of convincing assertions and clashing with diametrically opposed ideas upheld by others with the same good faith as Duhem. The most that could be said for the second group of ideas was that they are probable. Rey held to the idea that there exists an objective body of science capable of rallying the universal consent of the scientific community. All differences of opinion in the community were in the area of the philosophy of science, relating to hypotheses on the value, nature, and scope of science. The phenomena could be saved. As a historian of the ideas of contemporary scientists on science, Rey had to consider the existing polarization of scientific opinion: one group argued that science has no explanatory power, the other that it does. In the first group were found, among others, those who believed that an explanation of things requires an act of faith, whatever it may be, and that this explanation lies outside the province of reason.[9]

Duhem's interpretation of physical theory was "essentially positivist in its origins. Nothing in the circumstances which suggested this interpretation can justify the distrust of anyone who does not share metaphysical convictions or religious beliefs."[10] The self-designation of Duhem's physics as positivistic in its conclusions needs a word of explanation, for the word positivist is one of the most notorious multivocals in both French and English and, in at least one of its meanings, is overtly anti-Catholic. As Armand Lowinger has emphasized, "Duhem's concept of an autonomous physics must not be confused with positivism . . . as understood, for example, by Comte." Duhem's was "a methodological positivism, which avoids all entanglements with problems which do not lie strictly within the province of scientific methodology."[11]

---

9. "Le vrai positivisme ne serait-il pas, ni l'*ignorabimus*, ni le *scimus*, mais l'*ignoramus*, sans préjuger rien autre" (Rey, "La physique de M. Duhem," p. 537).

10. Wiener-Duhem, *Physical Theory*, p. 279.

11. Lowinger, *The Methodology of Pierre Duhem* (New York, 1941), pp. 18, 19.

Indeed, Duhem explicitly stated his anti-positivism: "the human mind loathes the extreme demands of positivism." He argued that he had tried to separate sharply the known from the unknown, but not the knowable from the unknowable. The autonomy of physics did not mean its hegemony: "our inquiry concerning physics has not led us either to affirm or deny the existence and legitimacy of methods of investigations foreign to this science and appropriate for attaining truths beyond its means." So Duhem fought against mechanism, or physical theories making the study of the material world exclusively into an affair of mechanics, concluding that none of the systems of the mechanistic schools provided a sound physical theory because none of them represented to a "sufficient degree of approximation an extensive group of experimental laws." He thus claimed to escape basing his position on metaphysics: just as to assert "that all the phenomena of the inorganic world are reducible to matter and motion is to be metaphysical," to deny it is also metaphysical. In constructing his own physical theory, Duhem "had to make certain mathematical magnitudes correspond to certain qualities," some of which would not "decompose into simpler qualities," but had to be "treated as primary qualities," although he did not exclude the possibility of future reduction. For "physics will try in every way to reduce it [a new effect] to qualities already defined; only after recognizing the impossibility of making this reduction will it resign itself to put into its theories a new quality and introduce into its equations a new kind of variable." By designating qualities as primary, then, Duhem was not postulating a sort of *Ding an sich* for his physical theory, but merely admitting that he could not make the reduction, which, he emphasized, might be done "tomorrow." A foregone conclusion: he had used exclusively the procedures of the physicist, he had condemned theories not in agreement with the laws of observation, and he had proclaimed a theory giving a satisfactory representation of those laws—all in accordance with the "rules of positive science."[12]

Did Duhem's claim that his interpretation of the meaning and scope of scientific theories—an interpretation not influenced by metaphysical opinions or religious beliefs—could be wholly subscribed to by a nonbeliever lead to the conclusion that the believer could gain nothing from his critique? This would not have been a surprising conclusion for a Catholic in the Third Republic. A barrage of governmental propaganda had been inflicted on the citizenry for years, making it "fashionable . . . to oppose the great theories of physics to the fundamental doctrines on which spiritualistic philosophy and the Catholic faith rest." Although Duhem asserted that only those who knew faith less than science could expect that religion would be bludgeoned out of existence by repeated blows from scientific systems, he was also forced to admit that segments of the intelligentsia, "men whose intelligence and conscience are far above those of village pundits and tavern physicists," had been preoccupied and disturbed by the struggles between science and religion. The great advantage of Duhem's system was that it swept away alleged objections to Catholicism as misunderstandings.[13]

12. Wiener-Duhem, *Physical Theory*, pp. 280, 281, 282, 296 (translation slightly changed); details in Duhem, *L'évolution de la mécanique* (Paris, 1903).

13. Wiener-Duhem, pp. 282–83.

To determine whether a principle of theoretical physics can agree or disagree with a metaphysical or a theological proposition, it is important to define the terms involved. A metaphysical proposition or a religious dogma—"judgments like 'Man is free,' 'The soul is immortal,' 'The Pope is infallible in matters of faith'"—affirms, argued Duhem, that a certain real being or objective reality possesses a certain attribute. For a judgment in science to be in agreement or disagreement with a proposition of metaphysics or theology, the judgment needs an objective reality as its subject and has to affirm or deny certain of their attributes. If two judgments do not have the same terms and do not have the same subjects, there can be neither agreement nor disagreement between them.[14] Since the facts of experience, i.e., not the experimental laws of physics but the laws of ordinary experience formulated by common sense without recourse to scientific theory, are affirmations about objective realities, it is possible to be within the bounds of reason in speaking of agreement or disagreement between a metaphysical or theological proposition and a fact or law of experience. Typical of Duhem was the apt and timely example he gave: if a Pope placed in the condition foreseen by the dogma of infallibility were to give an instruction contrary to faith, this would be a fact contradicting a religious dogma. The key question was, then, is a principle of theoretical physics a judgment about objective reality.

A contemporary answer might depend on acceptance or rejection of the notion of paradigm, implying that "science's history may be likened more to a series of Gestalt switches than to any linear progress toward, and ultimate attainment of truth" about reality.[15] Duhem's answer was based on his own view of the nature of scientific explanation. All those who make theoretical physics dependent on metaphysics, meaning especially Cartesians and atomists, also make a principle of theoretical physics a judgment about objective

14. "En effet, entre deux jugements qui n'ont pas les mêmes termes, qui ne portent pas sur les mêmes objets, il ne saurait y avoir ni accord ni désaccord": Duhem, *La théorie physique, son objet—sa structure*, 2d ed., "revue et augmentée" (Paris, 1914).

15. Cardwell, "Representation and Uncertainty," pp. 199–201, notes "some remarkable parallels" between Duhem and Kuhn, especially "the role of the scientific community in the development of the opinions of a scientist" and "the role of history in justification of scientific opinion." William A. Wallace, *Causality and Scientific Explanation* (Ann Arbor, 1972), p. vi. The Kuhnian idea of paradigm is a term relating closely to that of "normal science," which means "research firmly based upon one or more past scientific achievements." A paradigm is an achievement that has two major characteristics: the "achievement was sufficiently unprecedented to attract an enduring group of adherents away from competing modes of scientific activity. Simultaneously, it was sufficiently open-ended to leave all sorts of problems for the redefined group of practitioners to resolve." Thus, "some accepted examples of actual scientific practice—examples which include law, theory, application, and instrumentation together—provide models from which spring particular coherent traditions of scientific research," such as Ptolemaic or Copernican astronomy, Aristotelian or Newtonian dynamics, and wave optics. Thomas S. Kuhn, *The Structure of Scientific Revolutions* (Chicago, 1962), p. 10. Due to some misinterpretations, Kuhn has warned that paradigms are not to be entirely equated with theories. See Kuhn, "Commentary," *Comparative Studies in Society and History* 2 (1969): 403–12, and the postscript to the second edition of his book (1970). Less widespread than the idea of paradigm but also fruitful for the understanding of the development of scientific thought is Holton's idea of themata. See Gerald Holton, *Thematic Origins of Scientific Thought* (Cambridge, Mass., 1973), especially pp. 1–161.

reality. Since Cartesians and atomists believe that matter is objectively just what they say, it is not unreasonable to wonder whether certain principles of their physics agree or disagree with certain metaphysical or dogmatic principles. So Duhem could seriously assert that "it may reasonably be doubted that the law imposed by atomism on the motion of atoms is compatible with the action of the soul on the body; it may be maintained that the essence of Cartesian matter is irreconcilable with the dogma of the real presence of the body of Jesus Christ in the Eucharist." Newtonians were also relegated to damnation or at least recognized as being able to live with the Pelagian heresy. The Newtonian, believing a principle of theoretical physics to be "an experimental law generalized by induction" and a judgment involving objective reality, can view the fundamental equations of dynamics as embodying a universal rule, established by experiment, governing all motions of objectively existing bodies. It would be quite logical for Newtonians, then, to delve into the subject of a conflict between their theories and those of metaphysics or of religion. As we saw, the "Newtonian" Joseph Boussinesq spent a great deal of time trying to reconcile free will with the determinism of nineteenth-century mechanics and found the salvation of deterministic science and of man's freedom in Poisson's paradox. According to Duhem, the only way to avoid possible conflict was to accept the idea that "the principles of physical theory are propositions relative to certain mathematical signs stripped of all objective existence"[16] and can, therefore, have no conflict with metaphysical and religious doctrines, which are judgments about objective reality and can neither agree nor disagree with a scientific judgment that has no common term with it.

It was too tempting for him to resist commenting on the facility with which it was possible for a Cartesian, a Newtonian, or an atomist to deviate into metaphysical and religious opinions, solidly based on their science, which easily turn heretical, something impossible for subscribers to Duhem's scientific views. Duhem was no doubt correct in declaring that his scientific views had not been consciously influenced by metaphysics or religion. His view of science made it possible to have metaphysical and religious views unamenable to the critique of science, which had been the avenging angel of metaphysics and religion since the eighteenth century. Duhem himself was aware that his views fitted in with revival of Scholastic philosophy then flourishing in the Catholic world under the patronage of Rome. Regardless of the logical difficulties Rey had in proving his case, there were certainly strong a priori grounds for suspecting the sociocultural factors behind Duhem's science to be not entirely unconnected with his religion and with the contemporary intellectual revival of Catholicism. On strictly intellectual grounds the Rey-Duhem exchange seems a tie. Only by drawing upon psychology and sociology could any further progress have been made in the argument. Both would probably have been rejected by the austerely intellectual Duhem as a *lucus a non lucendo* argument, incapable of illuminating the Olympian heights of theoretical physics.

Duhem's argument is not that there can be no contact between science

16. Wiener-Duhem, *Physical Theory*, pp. 284, 285.

and religion. His argument, not without a certain Daedalian aspect, comes out clearly well into his reply to Rey. A principle of theoretical physics, being a mathematical form for the summary and classification of experimental laws, cannot be true or false but can give only a picture of the laws it claims to represent. Since the laws themselves are about objective reality, they can agree or disagree with metaphysical or theological propositions. But the theoretical principle in itself can neither add to nor subtract from any aspect of the laws. *"In itself and by its very nature, any principle of theoretical physics is of no use in metaphysical and theological discussions."*[17]

Duhem chose to test his conclusion in one of the areas in which there was thought to be a strong interaction between science and religion in the nineteenth century: "Is the principle of the conservation of energy compatible with free will?" Could the question have any meaning for those who knew the precise meaning of the technical terminology involved? The question did have meaning for those who used the principle as an axiom rigorously applicable to the real universe. The axiom could be derived from a philosophy of nature or obtained from experimental data by means of a bold and powerful induction. Duhem rejected both possibilities because he did not regard the principle as a statement about objects that really existed but as an arbitrary mathematical formula that came under all the limitations he placed on principles of theoretical physics. If the question could have had any meaning for Duhem, it would have to be put in a different form: "Is the objective impossibility of free acts a result of the principle of the conservation of energy?" Since Duhem argued that the principle has no objective result, the question is meaningless. How could the statement "free will is impossible" be derived from a principle equivalent to a system of differential equations governing changes of state in bodies under it? It is true that the state and motion of the bodies once being determined for an instant are then determined for the duration, thus making free movement impossible since a free movement would by its very nature be undetermined by the previous states and motions. The important thing, Duhem pointed out, is not to forget that the equations, or the principle they represent, are selected on the assumption that they are subject to a rigorous determinism. So a phenomenon whose smallest characteristic does not emanate from the initial data would be unamenable to any representation by such a system. It was known in advance that no place existed for free actions in the scheme. How naïve and absurd to conclude then that thermodynamic principles show free will a chimera. Duhem illustrated his technical argument by a characteristically brilliant analogy:

> Imagine a collector who wishes to arrange sea shells. He takes seven drawers that he marks with seven colors of the spectrum, and you see him putting the red shells in the red drawer, the yellow shells in the yellow drawer, etc. But if a white shell appears, he will not know what to do with it, for he has no white drawer. You would, of course, feel very sorry for his reason if you heard him conclude in his embarrassment that no white shells exist in the world.

17. Ibid., p. 285 (translation slightly changed; Duhem's italics).

The physicist who thinks he can deduce from his theoretical principles the impossibility of free will deserves the same feeling. In manufacturing a classification for all phenomena produced in this world, he forgets the drawer for free actions![18]

Duhem's refusal to grant any validity to objections to religion that were derived from physical theory was, he complained, no reason to classify his physics as that of a believer. Indeed, he danced on the razor's edge, for his physics also refused to recognize the worth of any arguments derived from physical theory in favor of religion. Just as well to label his theory the physics of a nonbeliever. Efforts like Albert de Lapparent's *Science et apologétique* were essays in futility. The realization of this implication for his work perhaps accounts for the strictures of Lapparent on Duhem's scientific theories. It is, Duhem emphasized, a mistake to cite a principle of theoretical physics in support of a metaphysical doctrine or a religious dogma. Thermodynamics again provided an apt illustration of this type of error.[19]

From Clausius' famous statement of the second law of thermodynamics, that the entropy of the universe tends toward a maximum, some philosophers had claimed to conclude that it is impossible that there be a world in which physical and chemical changes would be produced throughout eternity; these changes had begun, they would end; if matter had not been created in time, at least its capacity for change had; and the remote future result, as predicted by thermodynamics, was a state of absolute rest and universal death for the universe. Duhem argued that this argument was vitiated by a number of fallacies. First, it assumed that the universe is comparable to a finite group of bodies isolated in a space absolutely devoid of matter, a dubious proposition. Even if the comparison were valid, entailing an endless increase in the entropy of the universe, the principle imposed no upper or lower limit on the entropy, the magnitude of which could vary from $-\infty$ to $+\infty$, and the time could also have the same variation, thus making an eternal universe a theoretical possibility. Unlike Lapparent, Duhem was not satisfied with this kind of refutation; indeed, he recognized that the criticisms were ultimately defective because they did not show the impossibility of constructing a similar theory, which, immune from these criticisms, could provide the basis for the same predictions by the philosophers. A more fundamental critique was needed.

A return to the question of the nature of theory in physics could show the way to a satisfactory and devastating critique. In several remarkable pages, Duhem dealt with paradigm choice. Since a physical theory is a collection of mathematical propositions representing experimental data, and its validity is determined by the number of experimental laws it represents and by their accuracy, the methodology of physics cannot dictate a choice between two different theories representing the same facts with the same degree of accuracy. Any choice by a physicist would be based on such factors as elegance,

18. Ibid., p. 287.
19. On this topic and for a presentation of Duhem's argument, see Hiebert, "The Uses and Abuses of Thermodynamics in Religion."

simplicity, and convenience, for a forced choice on "scientific" grounds could only result if one theory represented a fact that the other theory could not accommodate. Kuhn has pointed out that in the choice of a paradigm, "the importance of aesthetic considerations can sometimes be decisive. . . . Even today Einstein's general theory attracts men principally on aesthetic grounds."[20] But, like Duhem, he recognizes that the most important factor in the victory of one paradigm over another is its ability to solve the problem that led to the crisis of the old paradigm, especially if the new paradigm is more quantitatively precise than its older competitor, as was the case with Newton's theory, Planck's radiation law, and the Bohr atom. Duhem cited Newton's law of planetary attraction $F \propto 1/D^2$ as representing with admirable precision all observable celestial motions, but he pointed out that some other function of distance could be substituted for the inverse square of the distance to construct another system of celestial mechanics giving the same accurate representation of astronomical observations. Of course, astronomers would keep on using the Newtonian law because its great mathematical properties lent simplicity and elegance to their calculations. If a phenomenon were discovered that could not be represented by the Newtonian law of attraction but could be represented by a new celestial mechanics, astronomers would be obliged to choose a new theory. This had been done, according to Duhem, when the introduction of the term "molecular attraction" had complicated Newtonian attraction in the hope of representing the laws of capillarity.[21] It is possible, then, to have two systems of celestial mechanics that are logically equivalent and whose calculations of the motions of heavenly bodies predict approximately the same positions for the heavenly bodies ten years hence. But it would be mathematically unwise to conclude by extrapolation that the two systems will agree eternally. One theory might predict the continuity of the present pattern of the solar system; the other system might predict the merging of all the bodies of the solar system into one mass or their separation in space at great distances from each other. Which prophecy should one believe, the one asserting the stability of the universe or the equally scientific one asserting its instability? Since the logic of the physical sciences cannot supply any criterion by which to choose, the decision has to be made on the basis of non-scientific concerns and biases. "So it goes with any long-term prediction."[22]

So it was with thermodynamics in Duhem's time. Alongside thermodynamics (representing a host of experimental laws), which declares that the entropy of an isolated system increases forever, it is possible, Duhem argued, to construct easily a new thermodynamics whose predictions would be in agreement with the old for ten thousand years but which could predict that the entropy of the universe after increasing for a hundred million years would

20. Cf. Kuhn, *The Structure of Scientific Revolutions*, pp. 155, 157.
21. "The law of gravitation is thus found to fail when material particles are separated from each other by too little distance, and it has to be modified by the introduction of a new symbol—capillarity—which renders the equations more complicated, but at the same time better able to reflect the richness and complexity of phenomena" (Lowinger, *The Methodology of Pierre Duhem*, p. 126).
22. Wiener-Duhem, *Physical Theory*, p. 290.

decrease over a new period of a hundred million years, after which it would increase again in a new cycle in a Sisyphean thermodynamics. "By its very nature experimental science is incapable of predicting the end of the world just as it is incapable of affirming its continual action. Only a gross misconception of its scope could have claimed for it the proof of a dogma affirmed by our faith."[23] This was a direct denial of the teleological claims being made by some Catholics and which were given a classic statement by Lapparent's lectures at the Catholic Institute in 1905.

Although Duhem claimed that he aimed at establishing the autonomy of physics rather than its hegemony, this did not mean that the metaphysician could ignore physical theories. Physics may be autonomous but metaphysics is not. At this point the distinction between autonomy and hegemony may appear a trifle blurred to minds unaccustomed to the empyrean realm of theoretical physics. But let us look at the admonition of Duhem to the metaphysician. Since it is clear that the philosophy of nature must take account of experimental facts and laws, which, unlike theories, have an objective importance and may agree or disagree with the metaphysician's cosmological systems, Duhem limited himself to considering the relevance of the theories of physics for the metaphysician's construction of cosmological systems. It is the mixed nature of a scientific fact or a scientific law that makes the task of the metaphysician difficult in seeing what is significant for his system. The metaphysician has to separate the part of the fact or law that is experimental observation and of objective importance from the part that is only a symbol, the theoretical interpretation, without any objective importance. It is only in the observational part that there can be any agreement or disagreement with the metaphysical system. Thus in an experiment on optical interference, any assertions are "intimately bound up with the hypotheses bearing on optical theory." The metaphysician "must know physical theory in order to be able to distinguish in an experimental report what proceeds from theory and has only the value of a means of representation or sign from what constitutes the real content or objective matter or the experimental fact."[24] Duhem considered it improbable that "the geometric mind with its clear and rigorous procedures, too simple and inflexible to be penetrating," would be able to recognize when physical theory crossed the boundaries of its own domain into cosmology. Only the "esprit de finesse" is endowed with the subtle methods needed to separate "real and objective matter" from "the merely theoretical and symbolic form," both of which make up the symbiosis called physical theory.[25] This is a vital operation because the genuinely empirical part has great significance for the philosopher, whereas the theoretical comes under the limitations Duhem established concerning the separation of physical theory from metaphysics and religion.

More serious for the metaphysician is the fact that no scientific method can justify itself without reference to principles other than its own. It is im-

23. Ibid. (translation slightly changed).
24. Ibid., p. 292.
25. On the distinction between the "esprit de finesse" and the "esprit géométrique," see ibid., Wiener's note, p. 60, and Paul, *The Sorcerer's Apprentice*, chap. 3.

possible within the confines of pure logic to justify the axiom of theoretical physics that states that "Physical theory must try to represent the whole group of natural laws by a single system in which all the parts are logically compatible with one another."[26] A physicist is justified, then, in using logically incompatible theories to represent sets of experimental laws or even a single group of laws.[27] But the conclusion that the physicist should have the right to develop a logically incoherent theory, a conclusion arrived at by those who limited themselves to an analysis of the principles of physics alone, was shocking to "a good number of those striving for the progress of physics," some of whom regarded this outrageous idea as a Catholic Trojan horse cunningly contrived to subvert the independence of science. Others saw "in this scorn for theoretic unity the prejudice of a believer desiring to exalt dogma at the expense of science." With some exaggeration, Duhem declared that this opinion was being proved by "the brilliant galaxy of Christian philosophers grouped around Edouard Le Roy" who "readily hold physical theories to be merely recipes." As Duhem quickly pointed out, there was nothing especially Catholic about such a theory. Was it not rather convenient to ignore that Henri Poincaré had been "the first to proclaim and teach in a formal manner that the physicist could make use, in succession, of as many theories, incompatible among themselves, as he deemed best." With heavy irony, Duhem added: "I am not aware that Henri Poincaré shares the religious beliefs of Edouard Le Roy."[28] No, Poincaré and Le Roy had arrived at their conclusions through a logical analysis of physical method. Those shocked by the skeptical overtones of their theories had very little basis for singling out Catholics as having ulterior motives for theories that were current among some leading scientists not of Catholic persuasion.

Duhem emphasized he did not believe that physics was "a junk heap of irreconcilable theories." From the study of the history of science, in particular the retracing of the evolution of physical doctrines, it was possible to conclude—and here Duhem and Rey agreed—that "Physical theory by no means presents us with a set of divergent or contradictory hypotheses. On the contrary it offers us . . . a *continuous* development and *genuine evolution.* The theory which seems sufficient at a given time in science does not collapse as a whole when the field of science is enlarged. Adequate to explain a certain number of facts, it continues valid for those facts. Only it is not adequate any longer for the new facts; it is not ruined; it has become insufficient. . . .

26. Wiener-Duhem, *Physical Theory*, p. 293 (translation slightly changed; italicized in the original). For treatment of this logic that "allows us to determine the object and structure of physical theory," see ibid., pp. 99–104.

27. The reader may be reminded of Bohr's concept of complementarity in interpreting quantum theory by using the two mutually exclusive pictures of wave and particle, although "we know from the mathematical formulation of the theory that contradictions cannot arise." See Werner Heisenberg, *Physics and Philosophy* (New York, 1958), especially chap. 3. But Duhem stipulated that the physicist must avoid mixing up two incompatible theories, "that is, not to combine a major premise obtained from one of these theories with a minor premise supplied by the other" (Wiener-Duhem, *Physical Theory*, p. 294).

28. Wiener-Duhem, *Physical Theory*, p. 294 (translation of last quotation slightly changed).

Scientific discovery . . . only gradually enlarges this field, gradually lifts certain restrictions, and reintegrates considerations judged negligible at first." After this long and conservative quote from Rey, Duhem summarized the whole history of physical doctrines as "Diversity fusing into a constantly more comprehensive and more perfect unity."[29] Duhem did not have a "passion for downgrading all of physics into a likely story."[30] Neither Duhem nor Rey went nearly so far as Kuhn's radical notion of paradigm change.

Duhem believed that physics should pursue the Holy Grail symbolized in the age-old "irresistible aspiration toward a physical theory which would represent all experimental laws by means of a system with perfect logical unity,"[31] a possibility becoming more and more a reality with successive physical systems. But the development of physical theory is not explicable on the basis of its own methodology; this was the limit of positivistic explanation, and the physicist, if he wants to find the origin of the tendency governing his own research, has to be metaphysical. Beneath the observable data are the hidden realities whose nature cannot be grasped by the positivist methods of study of the physicist. These realities have an order inaccessible to physical science, although the advance of physical theory "tends to arrange experimental laws in an order more and more analogous to the transcendent order according to which the realities are classified." Thus "physical theory advances gradually toward its limiting form, namely a *natural classification*," an order that cannot be reached if the theory lacks logical unity. So the physicist ends up justifying the "tendency of theory toward logical unity" with the metaphysical statement that "the ideal form of physical theory is a natural classification of experimental laws."[32] This explains, Duhem argued, why the physicist could "assert that experiment will discover a certain law . . . in the physicist's theory there is something like a transparent reflection of an ontological order."[33] But if the conchologist referred to earlier were to conclude from the presence of an empty cabinet drawer that there were blue shells in the ocean, he would be ridiculous because his system is purely arbitrary and does not take into account "the real affinities among the various groups of mollusks."[34] So the ideal and end of physical theory for Duhem was a natural classification, and its progress could be measured by the extent to which it approached this classification. This alone made the development of physics comprehensible for Duhem, but it was a title of legitimacy bestowed by metaphysics.[35]

29. Ibid., pp. 295–96. Cf. Werner Heisenberg, *Philosophic Problems of Nuclear Science* (New York, 1966), chaps. 1, 2, 3, 6.

30. Gillispie, *The Edge of Objectivity*, p. 498.

31. Wiener-Duhem, *Physical Theory*, p. 296. Einstein, who defined physics as "an attempt conceptually to grasp reality as it is thought independently of its being observed," sought unity, according to Gillispie, "in the proper domain of the intellect: in the laws of nature rather than in an imaginary entity out in nature" (Gillispie, *The Edge of Objectivity*, p. 519).

32. Wiener-Duhem, *Physical Theory*, p. 297.

33. Cf. "To reach the general theory of relativity, Einstein went beyond Mach into an ontology of his own creation, rising into higher regions where the real merged with the ideal in the bracing atmosphere of (non-Euclidean) geometry" (Gillispie, p. 495).

34. Wiener-Duhem, *Physical Theory*, p. 298.

35. Gillispie, *The Edge of Objectivity*, p. 500, points out that Duhem's idea that

Duhem's views on the nature of physical theory received their due share of interest in the philosophical world, even outside Catholic circles. In 1909, G. Lechalas, after arguing against Duhem that acoustical theory is truly explanatory, went on to argue, from a philosophical point of view, that the pragmatism of Duhem did not agree with certain of his affirmations. Although Duhem stated that physical theories could never truly be explanations of experimental laws, these theories did not seem to be an artificial system but rather a true natural classification. If theories are a means "to save the phenomena," they also seem to reflect a truly real transcendental order. "Belief in a [natural] order transcending physics is the only raison d'être of physical theory." Although Lechalas admired the frankness of Duhem in upholding these two theses, he wondered how they could be reconciled.[36]

Unlike Lapparent, Duhem did not make a fetish out of the concept of order. But the concept was nonetheless pivotal to his understanding of the fundamental meaning of physics and was obviously a yardstick by which he measured the soundness and sophistication of all science. No doubt Duhem believed that this order was ultimately the work of the Creator, but, unlike Lapparent, he did not think that it could be shown that science demonstrated this idea. This was not the area of theoretical physics. Like Faraday and Pasteur, he believed that knowledge about God is just as certain as scientific knowledge, but he did not think that much could be gained for either science or religion by arguing "that science was a Te Deum, a laudation, a demonstration of the wonders of God." For Duhem, science was not "a mighty bludgeon against atheism." He repeatedly denied what Newton had admitted: "When I wrote my treatise about our Systeme I had an eye upon such Principles as might work with considering men for the beliefe of a Deity & nothing can rejoice me more than to find it usefull for that purpose."[37] The foundation of Duhem's physical theory was its autonomy with respect to metaphysics and religion. A "physica sacra" would be a contradiction in terms. To write a nineteenth- or twentieth-century version of *Theologiae*

"physical theory has as its limiting form a natural classification" as seen in the "capacity of theory to guide experiment in the prediction of phenomena not yet observed and in the formulation of laws not yet expressed" turns out to be "simply the difficulty with which the fact of discovery and the aim of innovation always confronts a phenomenalistic logic. It was no new problem, and the resort to classification was no new answer." Gillispie does *not* point out that Duhem emphasized that "physical method is powerless to prove this assertion is warranted," i.e., "to the extent that physical theory makes progress, it becomes more and more similar to a natural classification which is its ideal end," which is entirely a matter of metaphysics. Gillispie's view is by no means a norm of any sort. Cf. Michael Polanyi, *Personal Knowledge* (Chicago, 1958; New York, 1964), p. 6: "I wish to suggest then that twentieth century physics, and Einstein's discovery of relativity in particular, which are usually regarded as the fruits and illustrations of this positivistic conception of science, demonstrate on the contrary the power of science to make contact with reality in nature by recognizing what is rational in nature." Of course, Polanyi's argument that *"Scientific knowing consists in discerning Gestalten that are aspects of reality"* differs significantly from Duhem's view: *Science, Faith, and Society* (Oxford, 1946; Chicago, 1964), p. 10.

36. Lechalas, "M. Duhem et la théorie physique," *L'année philosophique* (1909), and the "Recension des revues," *Revue de philosophie* 11 (November 1910): 546–47.

37. Manuel, *Newton*, p. 125.

Christianae Principia Mathematica would be a travesty of both science and religion.

One of the arguments used to support the idea that Duhem's physics was the physics of a believer was that Duhem made an explicit analogy between his physics and the cosmology of Aristotle and Scholasticism. No worthwhile cosmological system can be constructed without a knowledge of physics. But is physical theory of any use for the cosmologist? The answer, Duhem reasoned, would be negative "if physical theory were only a system of symbols arbitrarily created in order to arrange our knowledge according to a quite artificial order, and if the classification it establishes among experimental laws had nothing in common with the affinities unifying the realities of the inanimate world." But Duhem thought that physical theory has as its ideal form a natural classification of experimental laws. Thus there would be an exact correspondence between this natural classification or physical theory in its highest state of perfection and a cosmological order of the realities of the material world. Duhem emphasized that this is an analogy connecting cosmology and theoretical physics; it is not a genuine logical demonstration. Differences exist as well as similarities, and one man's analogy might be another man's opposition. The analogical argument is also weakened by man's inability to develop a perfect physical theory, which has attained the state of natural classification, corresponding to the ideal physical theory which must be compared with cosmology to furnish the analogical argument. The cosmologist must not be confused by the babel of physicists in this area; he is dependent on "unanalyzable instinctive judgment" suggested by the "esprit de finesse" but left unjustified by the geometric mind. In order to achieve this sublime uncertainty the cosmologist has to be learned not only in the "most secret arcana" of theoretical physics but also in the history of past doctrines of the subject. Only when he knows the past can he be sure of predicting the future path of the subject. "So the history of physics lets us suspect a few traits of the ideal theory to which scientific progress tends, that is, the natural classification which will be a sort of reflection of cosmology." Duhem's own prediction that contemporary "unreasoned exaggerations of the present time" about the role of molecules, atoms, and electrons in the contemporary world, through the study of past doctrines, would be seen as misleading turned out to be a piece of delicious irony: "the physics of atomism,... does not tend by continued progress to the ideal form of physical theory."[38] It might be argued that Duhem did not follow his own rule, for a variety of "atomism, the subsistence of reality in ultimate particles whose motions the laws describe, had provided classical physics with its ontology ever since the seventeenth century."[39] But Duhem had opted for the paradigm of general thermodynamics as the physical theory carrying the "germs of the ideal theory."

The extremely tenuous nature of the link between the ideal state of physical theory, itself a somewhat evanescent intuition, and natural philosophy by means of analogy is repeatedly emphasized by Duhem. Although the anal-

38. Wiener-Duhem, *Physical Theory*, pp. 301, 303, 304.
39. Gillispie, *The Edge of Objectivity*, p. 499.

ogy cannot be made without deep knowledge of theory and its history, the cosmologist "would be very foolish to take them as certain scientific demonstration."[40] So much for theoretical considerations. What was the contemporary form of physical theory Duhem thought to be progressing toward the ideal form, and what was the cosmology Duhem thought had the strongest analogy with this theory? Such an answer could not be given by Duhem in his capacity as physicist, for it took him outside the certainties and procedures of the positive method. Some scientists, as Duhem recognized, would refuse to emulate him in this transformation from Superman to Clark Kent. That was their prerogative, but Duhem doffed his positivist cape quite readily, just as his great predecessors had done and many of his contemporaries were doing.

In his foreword to the Wiener translation of Duhem's *La théorie physique*, Louis de Broglie points out that Duhem did brilliant scientific work, especially in thermodynamics, which remained his first love throughout his life. In theory, he was concerned with "the construction of a kind of general energetics (including classical analytical mechanics as a special case) and abstract thermodynamics."[41] Duhem thought that general thermodynamics offered "through the order in which it arranges experimental laws something like a sketch of a natural classification."[42] Duhem's choice of thermodynamics was based upon a number of factors, but the chief one was probably the amenability of thermodynamics to an abstract axiomatic system and to giving purely mathematical definitions to its fundamental ideas, as Duhem himself did for the quantity of heat. The harmonious whole of general thermodynamics was a secularization of what the image of the Pythagorean lyre had been for Newton.[43] The history of physics also showed Duhem that thermodynamics would be the wave of the future. His argument here is a demonstration of the role of paradigms in science as well as an explanation of how science manages to advance in spite of its adherence to the dogmatic position inherent in the paradigm position. The evolution of physics contains two movements: one is the succession of theories, of which one dominates science for a short period and is succeeded by another theory; the other is the progress represented by "a constantly more ample and more precise mathematical representation of the inanimate world disclosed to us by experiment." To the first movement belonged mechanistic systems like Newtonian, Cartesian, and atomic physics: "ephemeral triumphs followed by sudden collapses." But general thermodynamics, the result of the continual progress of the second movement, embodied "all the legitimate and fruitful tendencies of previous theories." It was the starting point "for the forward march which will

40. Wiener-Duhem, *Physical Theory*, p. 305.

41. Ibid., p. vi. See also Donald G. Miller, "Pierre Duhem, un oublié," *RQS* 138 (October 1967): 445–70; also in *Physics Today* (December 1966). *Scientia* 15 (1914): 267–72 has a review by Werner Mecklenburg of books on thermodynamics, including Planck's and Duhem's; he criticized Duhem for ignoring Nernst's theorem and for some prejudice in favor of French authors. Duhem's work was within the framework of classical thermodynamics rather than the modern thermodynamics of Planck and Nernst.

42. Wiener-Duhem, *Physical Theory*, p. 306.

43. Manuel, *Newton*, p. 391.

lead theory toward its ideal goal."[44] This may seem surprising to the modern reader, but he should remember that his surprise is probably the result of the limitation placed on his outlook by contemporary triumphs in atomic theory. As late as 1933 Jeans pointed out that "The province of atomic physics is to discuss the nature of particular events. . . . Yet this can give us but very little information as to what is happening to the universe as a whole." This problem falls within the province of thermodynamics, which, studying "events in crowds, statistically," discusses "the general trend of events, with a view to predicting how the universe as a whole changes with the passage of time."[45] Choosing thermodynamics as the scientific theory best suited for making an analogy with a cosmology was not in the early twentieth century, then, so arbitrary as it may seem today. Whether Duhem opted for thermodynamics as his *maîtresse en titre* because it was best suited to analogy with a cosmology is another question. His answer would be resoundingly negative, for the connection between thermodynamics and cosmology was metaphysical, whereas Duhem nearly made a fetish out of the positive and nonmetaphysical nature of his science per se. The austere, axiomatic, rigorously deductive nature of such works as the *Traité d'énergétique générale* certainly supports Duhem's own uncompromising judgment on the nature of his science.

What is the cosmology analogous to the ideal in sight at the point where general thermodynamics joins physical theory? Oddly enough, it is, Duhem argued, peripatetic physics, which was an unexpected answer because the creators of thermodynamics were mostly unacquainted with Aristotelian philosophy. Duhem hastened to emphasize that general thermodynamics was connected only "with the essential doctrines of Aristotelian physics." Obviously, one had to dig beneath the "superficial crust in which are conserved the dead and fossilized doctrines of former ages" to discover "the profound thoughts which are at the very heart of the Aristotelian cosmology." As an example he took the theory of the natural place of the elements, ostensibly the "babblings of an infant cosmology," removed the details of its external form in order to penetrate to the metaphysical ideas he considered the soul of the doctrine. Then it was possible to compare the ideal state of stable equilibrium of the universe assumed possible in the Aristotelian cosmology with the state of maximum entropy, which would be a state of stable equilibrium, imagined in a physical theory dealing with a set of inanimate bodies free from external influences. The analogy between metaphysics and physical theory thus showed that once Aristotle's physics and Scholasticism were shorn

44. Wiener-Duhem, *Physical Theory*, p. 306. "Ainsi, *disait Duhem*, la tentation sera moindre de ramener l'étude de tous les phénomènes physiques à l'étude du mouvement . . . on fuira dès lors plus volontiers ce qui a été jusqu'ici le plus dangereux écueil de la physique théorique, la recherche d'une explication mécanique de l'univers." Picard comments que "On ne pouvait formuler une profession de foi scientifique plus opposée à l'idéal poursuivi par les diverses physiques mécanistes depuis la physique cartésienne et la physique atomistique jusqu'à la physique newtonienne" (Picard, *Pierre Duhem*, pp. 11-12).

45. Sir James Jeans, *The New Background of Science* (Cambridge, 1933; Ann Arbor, 1959), p. 266.

of their outmoded scientific covering, the remaining cosmology resembled modern physical theory; "we recognize in these two doctrines two pictures of the same ontological order."[46]

The implications of reviving the cosmology of Aristotle and of Scholasticism were clear in Duhem's mind, as they would be for anyone who had spent twenty years in the university of the Third Republic. Both were associated with the Middle Ages and intimately tied in most minds with the church, then the mortal enemy of the Republic. The prevalent conclusion was that Duhem's physics, having an analogy with the subversive cosmology of the enemy, could only be the physics of a believer. It could hardly be expected that the terrible simplifiers would sacrifice a good piece of propaganda to a consideration of Duhem's complex arguments, especially if these arguments would expose the propaganda as fraudulent. As Duhem argued, there is nothing in this cosmology implying a necessary adherence to Catholic dogma. Since pagans, Muslims, Jews, and heretics had subscribed to and had taught it, could not nonbelievers as well as believers accept the doctrine? If not, why was the cosmology essentially Catholic? Because some of the greatest doctors of the church had supported it? Because a pope had recently proclaimed the services that the philosophy of Aquinas had given and could still give science? Duhem stubbornly argued with his usual relentless logic that it did not follow from these facts that the nonbeliever could not, without subscribing to Catholicism, "recognize the agreement of Scholastic cosmology with modern physics." And then, to add insult to injury, from the Republican viewpoint, Duhem ended by declaring that "The only conclusion that these facts impose is that the Catholic Church has on many occasions helped powerfully and that it still helps energetically to maintain human reason on the right road, even when this reason strives for the discovery of truths of a natural order. Now, what impartial and enlightened mind would dare to testify falsely against this affirmation?"[47]

When the Third Republic, during its weak embryonic period, tolerantly granted the church freedom in higher education in 1875, the newly established Catholic universities eventually became centers of diffusion for the rejuvenated Thomist gospel. Given this ramification of the connection of scientific theory with Aristotelianism-Scholasticism, it is not hard to see why

46. Wiener-Duhem, *Physical Theory*, pp. 307, 310, gives the bases of the analogy. First, among the attributes of substance, the category of quality was given equal importance with quantity in Aristotelian physics; this could be compared with the representation, in numerical symbols, of the various intensities of qualities, in addition to the various magnitudes of quantities, in general thermodynamics. Second, the Aristotelian subsuming of local motion under general motion—an idea denied by the three other cosmologies (Cartesian, Newtonian, and atomic), which agreed that the only motion possible is change of motion in space—found its counterpart in the dealings of thermodynamics with variations in temperature and electrical and magnetic states without reduction to local motion). Third, the Aristotelian notions of generation and corruption, which penetrated to the substance itself in the simultaneous process of creation and annihilation of substances, found an analogue in thermochemistry's representation of "different bodies by masses which a chemical reaction may create or annihilate; within the mass of a compound body the masses of the components subsist only potentially" (p. 307).

47. Ibid., p. 311.

the Republic in the early twentieth century, then in the midst of a battle against clericalism on all fronts, would greet Duhem's ideas with derision and hostility. The ideology of the Republic, derived to a large extent from the cluster of ideas issuing from the Enlightenment, had a definite anti-medieval syndrome. If the destruction of Aristotelian physics in the time of Galileo and Descartes had ruined Thomism, would not the resurrection of parts of that physics entail giving to Thomism a quasi-scientific basis? The absence of such a basis was one of the most powerful arguments in the republican arsenal impugning the intellectual nature of the Catholic revival. It was inconceivable at this time that Duhem's philosophy of science not be designated by republicans as the expected aberration of the physics of a believer.[48] Duhem's brilliant work in the history of science could easily be interpreted as further evidence for the republican side.

The intellectual and political implications of Duhem's work in the history of science were emphasized by Mentré in 1914, when he reviewed the second volume of Duhem's *Système du monde*. An examination of the contemporary state of public teaching in the history of philosophy made clear the philosophical importance of the *Système du monde*. Although the Greek philosophers and the moderns since Descartes received due attention in the official curriculum, medieval thinkers were ignored. Duhem restored the historical continuity that Fustel de Coulanges regarded as the very meaning of history. The implications for Christianity and Scholastic philosophy were hard to ignore. "He gives to Christianity the incomparable place that it is regaining in the development of mankind; he gives to scholastic philosophy a dignity and a value in the intellectual tradition forming an uninterrupted chain from the old Hellenic thinkers to contemporary philosophers." Candidates for the *agrégation de philosophie* could use Duhem's studies without fear. Indeed, Mentré thought it a great advantage that this philosophical work had been done by a scientist because "the great philosophers have generally been great scientists or at least amateurs of science, and in any case their systems carry the profound mark of the science of their time. To understand the evolution of philosophy, it is indispensable to know the evolution of science." Duhem was continuing the work of Paul Tannery and Gaston Milhaud in enlightening philosophy through science and in showing the philosophical influence of scientists. Equally important was the light thrown on modern philosophy by the *Système du monde*. The similarity of the ideas of Saint Augustine and of Bergson on time provided a convenient example for Mentré, since Duhem analyzed the Augustinian concept of time found in the *Confessions* and its probable later transmission and influence. The scientific significance of Christianity was thus an important conclusion developed in Duhem's work.[49]

48. Picard, *Pierre Duhem*, p. 9, argues that "La doctrine de Descartes est à l'opposé de celle des Scholastiques. Avec lui la notion de qualité est bannie du domaine de la Science qui devient la *Mathématique universelle*." One of the republican mandarins, an inspecteur de l'Académie de Paris, D. Parodi (*La Philosophie contemporaine en France. Essai de classification des doctrines* [Paris, 1919], p. 242), was dumbfounded because "ce physicien catholique nous ramène jusqu'à la doctrine scolastique des formes substantielles, jusqu'à la physique d'Aristote et de saint Thomas."

49. F. Mentré, review of *Le système du monde. Histoire des doctrines cosmologiques*

It would be hard to imagine a conclusion more repugnant to the scientistic ideologues of the Third Republic, although by 1914 the politics of the Republic had radically changed from the virulent anti-clericalism characteristic of the pre-separation era. One of the effects of Christianity had been to bring man to a contemplation of "things of the soul"; it gave him a sense of intimacy with God. Mentré saw this change as greater than the Socratic philosophical revolution and of more consequence. "Unlike Aristotle, who made movement the measurement of time, Saint Augustine shifts to within ourselves the appreciation of duration" (*durée*). In noting the probable influence of the Augustinian concept of time on Damascius, Jean de Bassols, and Bergson, Mentré concluded that the influence of Christianity could be seen even on doctrines claiming to rid themselves of such influence. Another great influence of Christianity on the take-off of modern science could be seen in its ruining of astrology. "So modern science was born when it was proclaimed that the same mechanics, the same laws regulated celestial and terrestrial movements, the circulation of the sun, and the tides. Before such a thought was possible the stars had to lose the divine status antiquity had given them; a theological revolution was necessary. This revolution was the work of Christian theology. The clash between the theologies of Hellenic paganism and of Christianity thus gave birth to modern science." In emphasizing the significance of the role of the theological revolution brought by Christianity, neither Duhem nor Mentré denied the great role of antiquity in the development of modern science, but they did challenge an interpretation current in popular republican circles that the Middle Ages represented a regression in the scientific march of mankind. The simplistic thesis of opposition between the church and science rested on a series of misunderstandings. "The truth is that the coming of Christianity remains in all respects the greatest date in history of humanity."[50]

Duhem was one of a dwindling minority of scientists in the nineteenth and twentieth centuries who thought seriously about the relations between science and religion. Duhem's piety was well known; it manifested itself in frequent prayer and communion, devotion to the Virgin, and constant reading of the gospel. Having different objects and operating in different areas, science and religion could not conflict because their ostensible disagreements rested upon misunderstandings. Science tends to harmonize with religion but it does not necessarily lead to it. But, as Mentré saw, this doctrine of a sort of double truth was only a practical and partial or superficial solution of a difficult problem that Duhem, so preoccupied with unity and coherence,

---

de Platon à Copernic, vol. 2 in *RP* 25 (1914): 205-8. R. N. D. Martin, "The Genesis of a Mediaeval Historian: Pierre Duhem and the Origins of Statics," *Annals of Science* 33 (1976): 119-29, shows that "Duhem's interest in medieval science was the result of his surprise encounter with Jordanus de Nemore while working on *Les Origines de la statique* in . . . 1903," rather than the result of "a religious or other motivation." The implications for the fertility of medieval science in France were not the less welcome for being a complete surprise. For a more traditional view of Duhem as a historian of science, guilty of not doing justice to the anti-clerical writers on natural philosophy in the Quattrocento, see J. H. Randall, Jr., *The Career of Philosophy from the Middle Ages to the Enlightenment* (New York, 1962), pp. 267-74.

50. Cited in Mentré, *RP* 25 (1914): 207-8.

could not avoid. Mentré cited a letter by Duhem to a childhood friend in which he dealt with the issue of the logical relations between scientific and religious truth. "I believed it my duty as a scientist and as a Christian to be the unremitting apostle of common sense, which is the only basis of all scientific, philosophical, and religious knowledge. My book on physical theory had no other aim than showing the scientific truth of this thesis."[51] To avoid ambiguity and possible contradiction of the arguments employed in the rebuttal of Rey's accusation that Duhem's physics was that of a believer, we should note that Duhem limited himself in his book to dealing with scientific certainty.

A common objection to some philosophical and religious beliefs was that they were based on worthless reasoning using indefinable ideas that were really meaningless words. Duhem refuted this objection by pointing out that since common sense is the foundation of all types of knowledge there is no reason to claim that one type of knowledge is more certain than another. "In thinking about these difficulties I perceived that we could say the same about all the sciences, including those regarded as the most rigorous—physics, mechanics, and even geometry. The foundations of each of these structures are formed of ideas we claim to understand, although we cannot define them, of principles we hold for certain, although we cannot demonstrate them. These ideas and principles are formed by common sense (*bon sens*). Without this basis of common sense, which is in no way scientific, no science could exist as such; the solidity of science comes from this basis. What is surprising, then, if it is the same for the basic ideas and first principles of philosophy and of faith? Suppose that I cannot define these ideas that nevertheless seem clear to me: body, soul, God, death, life, good, evil, liberty, duty. Suppose that I cannot demonstrate these judgments that seem nevertheless certain: the body cannot think; the world does not contain within itself a reason for its existence; I must do good and avoid evil. . . . The most certain of our sciences do not rest on different foundations."[52] Whether this argument showed the cer-

51. Mentré has an interesting note on Duhem's moral ideal: "Son ideál moral transperce dans une lettre au sujet de sa fille, citée par M. Garzend ["In Memoriam P. Duhem," *Cahiers catholiques*, February 10, 1922] il souhaitait qu'on lui confectionnât 'un vêtement moral assez aisé pour lui laisser toute la franchise de son tempérament, assez étroit cependant pour les excès de sa fougue, assez souple pour la laisser juger avec indulgence les écarts d'autrui, assez rigide pour la maintenir ferme et droite dans la voie du devoir.' La piété de Duhem devait avoir les caractères de la piété *personnelle* recommandée par l'abbé Henri de Tourville": *RP* 29 (1922): 457n1. Duhem's letter cited ibid., p. 458. Mentré points out that although in this passage "sens commun" is synonymous with "bon sens," this is not always the case. "En effet, Duhem montre que le capital du sens commun s'accroît par le progrès même de la science [*Théorie physique*, pp. 429–30]. Au contraire, le bon sens ou faculté de saisir le réel quoiqu'inégalement réparti, est immuable en chacun de nous [ibid., p. 357]."

52. *RP* 29 (1922): 458. Compare the argument of the philosophy of action: the unity of science and religion is human action; "Science and religion . . . necessarily meet on a common ground—that of the forms and concepts which correspond to natural facts." See Emile Boutroux, *Science and Religion in Contemporary Philosophy* (London, 1911), pp. 277–98. Reardon, "Science and Religious Modernism," pp. 48–63, sees Boutroux as the godfather of the formulation of a new relationship between science and religion, replacing both the theories of conflict and concord. But the new relationship is dualism. See *infra*, p. 194.

tainty of religious knowledge or relegated scientific knowledge to the limbo
of epistemological doubt is a question answered differently by various protagonists in the debate; both positions were argued intelligently by Catholic
scientists, theologians, and philosophers.

There are certain areas of human knowledge where only Delphic pronouncements are possible.

Mentré was very unhappy because of the obviously Pascalian inspiration
of Duhem, in spite of the influence of the Scholastic philosophers he had revived and pondered. Pascal's position was dangerous because it made reason
subservient to all forms of fideism; the position of Pascal did not give the
relations of pre-scientific ideas to metaphysical or religious ideas, or of scientific arguments to theological arguments, and it scorned the *rationabile obsequium*. By implication, Mentré's statement made Duhem's position appear
tainted with the "heresies" of one of his favorite authors, Pascal. More important was Mentré's argument that Duhem, in spite of his encyclopedic knowledge, did not have a sufficiently large view of reality to deal with the deep
and true relations between science and religion. More than the philosophy
of the mathematically based physical sciences, the philosophies of biology
and of psychology offer data of an incomparably superior scope to whoever
wishes to found his faith on as rational a basis as possible. Thus the philosophy of Aristotle, beginning with the study of individual beings and assuming
the competence of a naturalist, is preferable to a Platonic philosophy built
on the foundation of geometry. In addition to biology, Mentré thought that
psychology, including moral and social psychology, is necessary to view the
problem of the relations of science and religion because it provides an analysis of the personal being in itself and in its relations with other persons. Mentré pointed out that the solution to the problems associated with relations
between science and religion are found in Aquinas, although it could be completed and perfected. This criticism would not have been possible without
the revival of Thomism that reached a crescendo in the two decades before
the First World War. It also reflected the new vitalistic developments in biology, which were associated with a new interest in the biology of Aristotle, as
can be seen in the work of Hans Driesch, who was given considerable publicity in France by Jacques Maritain.[53] In a period of revolution in the physical
sciences, biology and psychology seemed more solid scientific foundations on
which to build the new harmony of science and religion that would hopefully
emerge from the revival of Thomism. So for Mentré, by 1922, the Duhemian
solution was disappointing and equivocal. He felt a certain uneasiness in reading some pages of *La théorie physique*, not because Duhem was wrong, as
some who knew Aquinas wrongly accused him, in asserting the autonomy
of science and of reason in their own spheres, but because Duhem's insuffi-
ciently developed analysis ended in certain badly disguised contradictions.
Although Duhem had furnished the apologist with excellent weapons, his
religious philosophy was defensive. Thomism provided the aggressive philosophy needed for modern Catholicism. It is unnecessary to labor the point
that this sort of commentary on Duhem was grossly unfair because Duhem

53. See *infra*, pp. 98–99.

never aimed at harmonizing science and religion, although his work incidentally provided some solid foundations for that harmony both in his philosophy of science and in his historical work on medieval science. (It may be
that Mentré was somewhat influenced by the fact that the *Annales de philosophie chrétienne*, with which Duhem was associated and in which his "Physique de croyant" appeared in 1905, was put on the Index in 1913. The years
1905 to 1913 were included in condemnation.)

Yet the wisdom of· Duhem's position became clear when Mentré considered the discussion that had arisen out of Duhem's analogy between peripatetic cosmology and the theory of general thermodynamics, the form of
physical theory then tending toward the ideal form, according to Duhem. "If
we strip the physics of Aristotle and Scholasticism of the scientific and anti-
quated clothing hiding it, if we reveal the living flesh of this cosmology in its
vigorous and harmonious nudity, we shall be struck by the similarity it has
with our modern physical theory." Given the cautious nature of Duhem's
analogy, Mentré expressed alarm over the unwise exploitation of this analogy
by some apologists. Given the tentative nature of the analogy, Mentré did not
find it surprising that Picard had found it a little strained and that the neo-
Thomist Msgr. Laminne had denied it. Noting the contemporary triumph of
atomism in optics, electricity, and chemistry, Mentré wondered if the situation indicated by Duhem would only be of brief duration. No reliance should
be placed upon such an agreement. "It is dangerous to tie the fate of a philosophical theory to the avatars of science, in spite of the continuity of its
progress; and we willingly add that it is not less dangerous to tie the fate of a
religion to the destiny of a cosmological doctrine."[54] But some well-meaning
if naïve Catholics had harmed the religious cause by giving to Duhem's subtle
and probable statement an absolute meaning he never intended. As Maritain
pointed out later, it was not a question of seeking a detailed agreement or
harmony between the Aristotelian-Thomist philosophy and the sciences but
rather "a general agreement, a good understanding, a natural friendship, of
which the very freedom of science is the best index."[55]

It may be more a comment on the ideology of a generation of students
of French history than a fair judgment on Duhem when Professor Gillispie
echoes Rey's view. Dulling the edge of objectivity, he disarmingly informs us
that "Not all *ad hominem* arguments are to be avoided, not at least when historical judgment is in play rather than logical analysis, and in the perspective
of the history of science it will appear more evident than it could to the protagonists—all men of good will—that energetics confronts us with a phenomenon by now familiar: a dissatisfaction with science ever latent among scientists themselves who would serve some grateful purpose. Thus, Duhem plays
the pundit as well as the philosopher in his preachments on abstracting in
theory and ordering by natural classifications. . . . It was natural and worthy

54. *RP* 29 (1922): 620.
55. Jacques Maritain, *Distinguer pour unir ou les degrés du savoir*, 4th ed. (Paris,
1946), p. 131. Originally published in the *Bibliothèque française de philosophie* in 1932.
A version of the chapter "Philosophie et science expérimentale" appeared in *RP* 35 (1928).
See chap. 3, note 82.

in Duhem to wish to rehabilitate the scientific merit of those medieval centuries which were the great ones for his church. But his reader may feel reservations about his enthusiasms for reducing physics to the status of a useful fiction, in the reflection that a religious metaphysics might then monopolize the realm of truth." It has already been argued that Gillispie exaggerates in referring to "Duhem's passion for downgrading all physics into a likely story." It must be reiterated that Duhem's views are characteristic of the period, a point that Duhem himself repeatedly emphasized. Faced with the need to explain similarities in the views of believers and nonbelievers, Gillispie jettisons the law of noncontradiction with Hegelian abandon to inform us that "Extremes of fidelity and agnosticism could touch in positivism. The religion which fired Ostwald's fervor was Comte's godless sociology revived. Ostwald thought to serve humanity by refounding all of physics in energetics."[56] One may wonder what is so Catholic about Duhem's metaphysical position. In its deliberative vagueness, it seems designed to avoid any specific attachment to any one creed. The leap from the metaphysical argument to Catholicism has to be made by the reader; Duhem carefully avoids any such inference. Without a prior knowledge of Duhem's religion, it would be impossible to make the leap. Unlike the medieval philosophers, he makes no use of Aristotelian thought as religious apologetic, "a colossal irony" that Duhem's erudition led him to eschew. Nowadays it is eminently respectable to indulge in comparative games that show the analogy of modern concepts with Aristotelian and Scholastic thought. Duhem played a large role in making this possible. The absence of an anti-clerical animus makes the procedure quite innocuous and fruitful. Who sees the shadow of the *Unam Sanctam* lurking behind Heisenburg's statement that the concept of the probability wave in quantum theory "was a quantitative version of the old concept of 'potentia' in Aristotelian philosophy"?[57] Yet such an analogy in early-twentieth-century France, especially if made by a Catholic, might produce a charge that such a statement could only issue from the physics of a believer. Of course, part of the difficulty was that frequently neither believers nor nonbelievers separated Aristotle from his Scholastic interpreters and commentators. Even if Duhem had attached "religious feeling to the ultimate postulate of his cosmological theory, to his ultimate principle of explanation for the world of processes," he would have been following a hallowed tradition stretching from the early Platonistic Aristotle to Einstein. Might we not echo the statement of Randall on Aristotle? "We need hardly wonder that he did so, since we have seen more recent physicists falling over themselves to do the same incomprehensible thing. If Aristotle be blasphemous, so are the long line from Newton down to Millikan, Whitehead, and Montague." Duhem's metaphysical position per se seems, like Aristotle's Unmoved Movers, to have no moral or religious significance: "It is a purely intellectual ideal."[58]

56. Gillispie, *The Edge of Objectivity*, pp. 501-2.
57. Heisenberg, *Physics and Philosophy*, p. 41.
58. John Herman Randall, Jr., *Aristotle* (New York, 1960), p. 137. But "the mature Aristotle . . . apparently had no interest in investigating . . . religion."

One of the grounds on which energetics was suspect to secular-minded thinkers was that of the ostensible connection between it and mysticism, or, in the case of Duhem, neo-Thomism. In his book on the wave of mysticism engulfing Europe, a book written before but published after World War I, Jules Sageret argued that the chief reason for Ostwald's opting for energetics was Ostwald's belief that the mechanist saw between physical phenomena, considered mechanical, and psychic phenomena an unbridgeable gulf. A long quote from Ostwald's *Die Energie*, published in French in 1910, two years after it appeared in German, clinched Sageret's argument: "psychological phenomena, as well as all other phenomena, can be understood and interpreted as energetic phenomena"; and "As soon as one gives up holding that the non-mental world is exclusively mechanical it becomes possible again to discover a continuous and regular connection to rejoin the theory of mental phenomena to that of other facts."[59] But Sageret lamented that the habit of thinking in terms of pure energy must lead to mysticism. Once the universe is reduced to only energy, there is no difficulty in imagining personality, life, and conscience separated from all material support and existing outside space and time. Nothing stood in the way of designating Energy as God and psychological energies as souls. The special meeting of energies producing matter and space could take the name of the creation of matter, and the energeticist philosophy could become a spiritualism. The weakness of this ingenious argument is best seen in the positivistic outlooks of the leading proponents of nineteenth-century energetics: Ostwald, Mach, and, in a special way, Duhem.

To prove that such a system was possible, Sageret cited the theories of the biologist Paul Vignon, also well known for his work on the Holy Shroud of Turin. But Vignon assumed that force, not energy, was the primordial entity: "Force is the eternal principle." And the universe had a beginning: "The history of the universe, such as science tends to write it today, does not enumerate an infinite series of equivalent transformations; this history forms a book that force writes with matter and which really has a first page." Thus creation; force existed before matter; in the beginning there was only force.[60] Vignon's combination of dynamism and energetics brought Vignon, according to Sageret, to Aristotelianism, to Scholasticism, and to Thomism, or neo-Thomism, as the rejuvenated doctrine of Aquinas was called. All of this was designated by Sageret as the orthodox metaphysics of Catholic theology.

Sageret argued that Duhem ended up in the same position. The argument showed what conclusions a sophisticated layman was likely to draw about the implications of Duhem's science. With Procrustean abandon, Sageret classified Duhem's scientific ideas as identical with Ostwald's but hastened to add that, quite unlike Ostwald, Duhem thought that energetics gave the best support to Aristotelian philosophy and therefore to Catholicism.[61] So ener-

59. Sageret, *La vague mystique* (Paris, 1920) (both Durkheim and Henri Berr were already on record against the late-nineteenth-century *devotio moderna*); Wilhelm Ostwald, *L'énergie* (Paris, 1910), pp. 144, 200, cited in Sageret, *La vague mystique*, pp. 98–99.

60. Vignon, "La notion de force, le principe de l'énergie et la biologie générale," *Causeries de la société zoologique de France* (1900), p. 269, cited in Sageret, *La vague mystique*, p. 99.

61. Sageret, p. 102, also points out that "Comme métaphysique . . . on voit donc que

getics accentuated rather than effaced the difference between psychic and other natural phenomena. As if to make amends for this oversimplification and, perhaps, distortion of Duhem's complex arguments, Sageret praised the perfect correctness of Duhem's scientific attitude in declaring that his conception of physical theory favored neither the believer nor the unbeliever and had no metaphysical meaning. But the claim of Duhem was unacceptable to Sageret because of the physicist's ostensible total disregard for "this fundemental key of the translation of experiment into mathematical language; he considers physical theory as a purely mathematical edifice."[62] This is not, of course, an accurate statement of Duhem's view of physical theory. For Sageret experimental laws still retained an absolute value and could be invoked to support a doctrine such as determinism without being nonsensical. Sageret could accept the view that the Republic should be based on scientific foundations, a view having no meaning in Duhem's science. Sageret's last chapter, "The moral value of scientism," represented the type of prostitution of science that Duhem had always deplored.

Abel Rey interpreted Duhem as returning to Scholasticism and thus, through the new course he gave to mechanics, toward the abandon of what had been the characteristic of the "scientific renaissance" in general and of the Cartesian revolution in particular. Ironically, the general acceptance of Duhem's history of medieval science makes Rey's distinction rather meaningless.[63] But Rey stuck to the general characteristics of Duhem's science, or rather his philosophy of science. What he disapproved of was Duhem's substitution of logical and conceptual relations for the relations of facts, for the relations that traditional scientific positivism claims to be imposed by sensible experience. The only difference that Rey saw between the tendencies of Duhem's mechanics and the tendencies of Scholasticism was that for Scholasticism, primary concepts were imposed by the nature of things, by an intuition of the absolute, whereas for Duhem these concepts were arbitrary; Duhem was perhaps a nominalist. It was equally disturbing that the "new physics" readmitted to the scientific fold a concept proscribed in "modern physics," quality, and gave to the idea of motion all the generality attributed to it by Aristotle. The creation of a mechanics founded on thermodynamics was for Duhem not only a rebuff to atomism and Cartesianism but *"a return"* —totally unforeseen by its creators—*"to the most profound of peripatetic*

la thermodynamique ou énergétique s'interprète, si l'on veut, en faveur du néo-thomisme ou spiritualisme catholique, et que, contrairement à la thèse de W. Ostwald, elle ne fait pas rentrer nécessairement les phénomènes psychologiques dans l'ordre général des phénomènes naturels."

62. Ibid., p. 101.

63. See, for example, chap. 4 of Kuhn, *The Copernican Revolution. Planetary Astronomy in the Development of Western Thought.* Rey could cite the *mécanisme* of Jean Perrin against the *énergétique* of Duhem to show that at least one segment of contemporary physics supported his argument. Rey argued that the mechanistic method is better for the construction of physical theory because it does not break with the traditional development of modern physics, agrees better with the fundamental law of the acquisition of knowledge (known to the unknown), and satisfies better our psychological needs of intelligibility and clarity: Rey, *L'énergétique et le mécanisme au point de vue des connaissances* (Paris, 1907).

doctrines."[64] Of course, vast differences existed between Aristotle and the medieval philosophers. In fact, Duhem summarized, it was only by the logical analysis that the Stagirite applied to various physical ideas that peripatetic physics and the physics of Duhem's day approximated one another. Peripatetic physics, Duhem admitted, was in contemporary terms really a branch of metaphysics. Rey saw Duhem's claim that quality could not be reduced to quantity as meaning that there was a need for a number of absolute beginnings in physical properties, for given principles, occult and unknowable in themselves.[65] Like mechanistic doctrines, then, Duhem's physics was metaphysical in spite of itself, or so Rey thought, for it was based on its own ontology and epistemology. In the light of comparable accusations against Newton's innovations in his day and, not to be forgotten, the attacks of Duhem on the atomists, one wonders whether the charge of occultism is not the tropistic reaction of the human mind to innovations that destroy or modify paradigms that have given mental comfort for so long and have seemed on the verge of succeeding in the Sisyphean task of banishing mystery from the universe. To a commentator afflicted with a set of metaphysical prejudices somewhat remote from both Duhem's and Rey's, it may seem that Rey's case against Duhem has little to recommend it. In general, Duhem's defense seems solid, although perhaps overly subtle in parts. Today, as it seemed to Duhem, Rey's conclusion seems strangely out of place.[66] Wiener made a fair and solid judgment on "Duhem's defense of his pragmatism against the mechanistic views of Abel Rey" and on Duhem's distinction of "positive science from metaphysics and theology: Without sharing Duhem's Catholicism, the translator [Wiener] submits that Duhem has offered a very strong case for the autonomy of physical science, shown by its internal logic and evolution."[67]

It is rarely recognized that Duhem's philosophy of science was severely criticized in Catholic scientific and philosophical circles, even in the Thomist camp with which he had strong ties as well as serious disagreements. The extent of this Catholic criticism of Duhem may be judged by considering the anti-Duhemian position within the Thomistically inclined Société scientifique de Bruxelles and among the Thomist philosophers themselves, including the leading Thomist, Jacques Maritain.

Duhem's famous article "Quelques réflexions au sujet des théories phy-

64. Rey, *RMM* 12 (1904): 734.

65. It is interesting that before the "precise mathematical formulation of quantum theory," it seemed that Bohr's theory "gave a qualitative but not a quantitative description of what happens inside the atom"—not an example that Duhem would have appreciated! Heisenberg, *Physics and Philosophy*, p. 38.

66. Rey's treatment of Duhem's philosophy of science as that of a believer may be compared to the treatment of Aristotle by a Platonist or by a medievalist. See Randall, "Foreword" to *Aristotle*, p. iv, who "tries to point out some of the ways in which Aristotle's thought is relevant and suggestive for two of the most important present-day philosophical concerns, that with the analysis of language and that with the analysis of natural process."

67. Wiener-Duhem, *Physical Theory*, p. xvi. It is significant that Jacques Maritain, *Philosophy of Nature* (New York, 1951), pp. 60–62, does not get much out of Duhem for the Thomistic philosophy of nature. For some trenchant criticism of Duhem's methodological ideas, see Lowinger, *The Methodology of Pierre Duhem*, chap. 10.

siques," in the *Revue des questions scientifiques* in 1892, alarmed a segment of the Société scientifique de Bruxelles. A long and heated reply to Duhem appeared in the same journal in 1893 by a fellow member of the society, Eugène Vicaire, who taught at the Ecole des Mines, the Collège de France, and the Catholic Institute in Paris, and was for many years "le plus haut fonctionnaire du corps français des Mines." In a reply to Vicaire, Duhem summed up Vicaire's argument quite simply and fairly: "It is not true that the aim of positive science in building theories is simply to classify experimental laws; its legitimate aim is the search for causes; to deny that is to maintain a doctrine suspected of being positivistic and capable of leading to skepticism. This doctrine, condemned by the tradition of the great physicists, is dangerous because it kills scientific activity."[68] The intellectual dangers of Duhem's view of physical theory were clear then: it destroyed scientific curiosity; it led logically to incoherence; and it ignored the true aim of science, the search for causes. Duhem's views fitted into a constellation of ideas Vicaire associated with Poincaré, Kirchoff, Axel Harnack, and ultimately David Hume: "In my opinion, these ideas destroy all science, and I believe it important to refute them, especially when they penetrate a journal whose relations and program would seem to make it more resistant to this invasion of skepticism. The evil being greater than one would have supposed, the more urgent the need to fight it."[69] In Catholic circles the implications of a science tainted with skepticism and positivism needed little amplification.

After the Vicaire-Duhem exchange, the Catholic philosopher Domet de Vorges expressed his alarm at Duhem's attempt to place his views under the protection of Thomism, thus saving himself from the charge of novelty, at least in the philosophy of science. The philosopher accused Duhem of changing the grounds of the quarrel in his ingenious reply to Vicaire that metaphysics alone has the right to have an opinion on the nature and origin of physical phenomena. As a clever man, Duhem had called on the tradition of the school, claiming to have based his opinion on that of Aquinas and trying to harness in his favor the entire Scholastic movement. Domet de Vorges remarked that Duhem must have had a "prompter" or that he had a great faculty of assimilation; how else could one explain such great skill in the use of Scholastic terminology by a professor in a faculty of sciences? The whole question had been shifted to the grounds of general method and higher phi-

68. Duhem, "Physique et métaphysique," *RQS*, 2d ser. 2 (1893): 55–56. See Duhem, "Quelques réflexions au sujet des théories physiques," *RQS*, 2d ser. 2 (1892): 139–77, and Eugène Vicaire, "De la valeur objective des hypothèses physiques à propos d'un article de M. P. Duhem," *RQS*, 2d ser. 3 (1893): 451–510. Duhem's article "Physique et métaphysique" and Vicaire's "De la valeur objective des hypothèses physiques" were reprinted in the *Annales de philosophie chrétienne* in April, May, and August-September 1893. Georges Lechalas, "Quelques réflexions soumises à M. Vicaire," ibid. 126 (June–July 1893): 278–82, disagrees with Vicaire on a point in mechanics but otherwise gives his complete support to Vicaire's "belle étude." See also Nye, "The Moral Freedom of Man and the Determinism of Nature."
69. Vicaire, *RQS* 3 (1893): 453. On Vicaire, polytechnicien, Inspecteur général des Mines, president of the Société mathématique de France (1892) and of the Société scientifique de Bruxelles (1895–96), see M. d'Ocagne, "Eugène Vicaire," *RQS* 49 (1901): 420–31.

losophy. But Domet de Vorges was not happy, for Duhem had compromised the metaphysics and philosophy of St. Thomas by connecting them with the new and dangerous intellectual tendency denounced by Domet the previous year in *La science catholique*.

The philosopher agreed that one could hardly better Duhem's definitions of metaphysics and physics. ("Metaphysics, in this part that the moderns often connect with cosmology, seeks to know the nature of matter considered as the cause of phenomena and the raison d'être of physical laws; physics is the study of phenomena whose basis is raw matter and of the laws regulating them.") Noting the equivocal nature of the word cause, Domet de Vorges argued that Duhem did not perceive that there is a physical cause and a metaphysical cause. Duhem had certainly gone too far for Domet in denying Vicaire's contention that the legitimate aim of positive science is the search for causes. Metaphysical cause is "the substance which, through an essential property, gives being, whether to a phenomena or to another substance. Thus my mind is the cause, in the right sense of the word, of my thoughts, and life is the characteristic cause of the general guidance of physiological phenomena. Why is this so? Because thought as well as living being are basic, irreducible facts. . . . These facts are based on substance and are the immediate product of its activity."[70] Metaphysical cause does not claim to explain facts in the modern sense of the word. Physicists use the word cause in a much broader sense to refer to the numerous and variable conditions contributing to the materialization of a phenomenon. The heat that causes the expansion of the thermometer is a physical cause and must be studied by physics. But there is a more profound type of physical causation, such as operates in apparently irregular planetary motion or in two sounds canceling one another. To arrive at an explanation of whatever escapes the simple operation of the senses in such cases is also a legitimate use of science.

In developing his thesis, Duhem had forgotten an essential thing: to show that the use of hypotheses to throw light on the essential nature of matter is illegitimate and must not be used in physics or in metaphysics. But Duhem had not shown this, and Domet de Vorges added that if this usage is legitimate it belongs to science, which alone could give it verification, the necessary completion of the hypothesis. "Is not a hypothesis the great instrument for conquering truth?" The philosopher found it really odd that there was a tendency in the new generation of physicists to deny all objective value to the big hypotheses that had been for several centuries the glory of science and the hope of all progress. Was not this doctrine taught at the Sorbonne as well as in Bordeaux? This was probably a reference to Poincaré's ideas and certain similarities which they had with Duhem's. The philosopher sternly reminded the physicists of the nature of true science: "The true scientific spirit does not have such narrow limits; above all, it seeks everywhere the truth about things." Duhem's first works seemed inspired by this horror of metaphysics. In answer to Duhem's protest, Domet de Vorges replied only that if Duhem was not himself a skeptic, he supported a thesis whose origin was un-

70. Comte Domet de Vorges, "Les hypothèses physiques sont-elles des explications métaphysiques?," *APC* 127 (November 1893): 138, 139.

deniably skeptical. This was more serious than an intellectual game because young Christians were thrown into an atmosphere of unbelief, and although they kept their faith, they acquired unintentionally a set of prejudices incompatible with that faith. One could have hardly concocted an accusation that would have wounded Duhem more.

The third part of Domet de Vorges' article on Duhem attacked the idea that Duhem's "new opinion" had a basis in "scientific tradition." The texts cited by Duhem were not conclusive. The text of Posidonius was given without the context, which would greatly alter its significance. Duhem did not have the right to cite in favor of his arguments all the texts in which doubts were expressed on the truth of different hypotheses. Aristotle was concerned with whether or not an explanation corresponded to reality, although he recognized the limitation on the certainty of certain explanations. Since the ancients did not have the chief means of verifying physical hypotheses—experiments on their consequences—their theories necessarily always had something risky about them. It was evidence of the profundity of Aristotle's scientific thought that he recognized this; the Scholastic doctors had not always been so wise. Domet de Vorges did not find the citations of Archimedes, Copernicus, Laplace, and Ampère to be solid evidence of the antiquity of Duhem's views. But he found the citation of Aquinas, presumably the key which put Duhem's philosophy of science solidly in the Thomistic tradition, to be completely misinterpreted by Duhem. Duhem interpreted Aquinas as saying that it is not necessary for one to believe that hypotheses are true in order to use them. But in the text cited by Duhem, Domet de Vorges argued, Aquinas said that Aristotle treated hypotheses as if they were true although it is not necessary to consider them true. Aquinas had not said that it is unimportant whether one introduces real or fictional hypotheses into science. The hypotheses may not be true; the reason is that it is not proven that one can explain appearances by another hypothesis of which one has no idea. This implies the contrary of Duhem's system: for Aquinas a hypothesis must be held to be true when it is the only one possible, the only one in agreement with the facts, as was the case with several hypotheses in modern physics. The contrary interpretation of Duhem's texts was therefore possible. Duhem had classified the texts as in agreement with his hypothesis because of his preconceived ideas on the subject.

An important argument against Duhem's thesis was that it was absolutely contrary to the essentially objective spirit of ancient philosophy. Above all, the Scholastics believed in truth and that the aim of science is to attain it. "If one had spoken to them about arbitrary hypotheses serving only to connect the facts, they would certainly have replied that such hypotheses must not appear in science, that science must search for the true bond uniting facts in nature, that it is not admissible to assume the truth of a thing which has no chance of being so simply to create a convenient order, and that a theory is good only insofar as it offers an appearance of conformity to the facts."[71]

71. Ibid., p. 151. Georges Lechalas (Ingénieur en chef des Ponts et Chaussées), "M. Duhem est-il positiviste?," *APC* 127 (December 1893): 312–14, supported Domet de Vorges' argument that Duhem was a positivist ("caractère positiviste des tendances intimes de M.

Domet de Vorges concluded that the antecedents of Duhem's doctrines were to be found among the neocriticists and the positivists, not in traditional philosophy.

Doubts in the scientific community about the objectivity of physical theory gave rise to anxieties in Catholic philosophical circles. Writing in *La science catholique* in 1892, and in the *Annales de philosophie chrétienne* in 1893, Domet de Vorges criticized both Duhem and the "new school." Although the new ideas found favor among the defenders of Scholasticism, who hoped thereby to revive certain ancient physical theories that had been destroyed by modern interpretations of nature, Domet de Vorges thought that the advantage of being able to re-establish certain unimportant parts of thirteenth-century philosophy was of minor significance in light of the dangers of the new school of physical theory. Unlike Mentré, he detected Duhem's disdain for metaphysical ideas in science. "He doesn't want this foreign plant on his personal estate. He thinks that physics must not accept the yoke of metaphysics or impose its own yoke on it." The philosopher interpreted Duhem's position as demanding that both disciplines operate independently, although philosophy would have to put itself in harmony with the sciences while science would refuse to give any support to philosophy. This was certainly a more accurate interpretation of Duhem's position than was Mentré's. Domet de Vorges doubted that a study renouncing the search for what "things are in themselves" and their causes is still a science. Of course he recognized the right of the physicist to modify physical theories as he sees fit. But what scandalized the philosopher was the idea that science must give up its claim to penetrate the true nature of phenomena and limit itself to constructing arbitrary methods for more convenient calculation. After lamenting the abandonment of the search for the *Ding an sich*, Domet de Vorges said that Duhem was in reality inspired by Kantian metaphysics! By the late nineteenth century, when neo-Kantianism was in full flower in French philosophy, Kantianism had replaced Hegelianism as a Catholic *Schimpfwort* indicating the most heinous of philosophical heresies.

Domet de Vorges noted that most of the young physicists had been taught to hold metaphysics in horror as a concoction of fantasies. "They concluded from this that it was necessary to reject all that cannot be seen or touched. This meant rejecting the very basis of science, for science wants above all to understand, and in order to understand, it is necessary to go beyond what

Duhem") by comparing Duhem's course in optics with that in acoustics. Duhem explicitly condemned a mechanical explanation of light, but he himself gave a mechanical explanation of sound. Duhem complained about Lechalas' mistakes in reporting on an unpublished course (optics), *APC* 128 (April 1894): 91–93. Lechalas apologized for the mistakes and asked for technical clarifications as well as pointing out that there was nothing insulting in being called a positivist ("en parlant de ses tendances positivistes je n'avais aucune pensée blessante, car les tendances ne sont nullement incompatibles avec des opinions de la sincérité desquelles il serait justement blessé qu'on pût douter"). See also Lechalas, "La théorie physique," *APC*, 4th ser. 4 (1907): 144–62, where he points out that the history of the wave theory of light differs from the history of other theories. Lechalas also gives an ingenious defense of the value of the metaphysical hypothesis in science by using Jean Perrin's justification of the molecular hypothesis (*Principes de la chimie physique*), as well as the hypothesis of the existence of microbes.

one sees." A second factor explaining the new views of physicists was "the excessive predominance of mathematics in the teaching of physics." No physicist could any longer imitate Jamin, who had supposedly employed a friend to do the calculations needed for his three-volume treatise in physics. But some physics courses were like courses in algebra. Domet protested that he was not attacking mathematicians; indeed, this would have been a curious thing for a Catholic philosopher to do, since, as Domet noted, there were more true Christians among mathematicians than in any other group. He simply condemned the excessive preoccupation of physicists with formulas. Unless considered as a tool, mathematical procedure prevailed over the search for truth. "If the new tendency succeeds in asserting itself, as several signs make me fear, this will be the beginning of scientific decadence. The desire for the discovery of the true will be extinguished by a preoccupation with formulas. Medieval metaphysics discredited itself by an abuse of logic; modern physics will vanish by an abuse of mathematics. We shall still have good practitioners, but we shall no longer have great scientists."[72] In the end the new approach would be fatal for both science and philosophy. This argument has a certain resemblance to the curious later view that French physics had a minor role in the late-nineteenth- and early-twentieth-century "revolution" in physics because of its excessively mathematical nature. No doubt Cassandras like Domet de Vorges, had they lived long enough, would have been quick to point out that a good Catholic respect for reality might have had more fruitful results for physics in France than the symbolist games the new physicists were accused of playing. "The great scientists of the early nineteenth century would certainly not have undertaken such fine work, such delicate experiments, such deep meditations, if it had been only a question of finding a convenient procedure of calculation. What sustained them was that they were looking for and hoped to find the true meaning of the creation. The new doctrines have persuaded scientists that reality is inaccessible; we laugh at the naïveté of those who still want to reach it. Thus philosophy will only be a mental game and science an algebraic exercise." Unfortunately a number of Catholic scientists, Domet de Vorges noted, found it prudent to follow the latest scientific orthodoxy because they saw only the convenient aspect of the new ideas and missed the "poison of skepticism hidden in their origin."[73]

The Vicaire-Duhem exchange had its repercussions in the religious periodicals of the clerical intelligentsia. Writing in the *Revue thomiste* in 1893–94, Fr. P.-B. Lacome, o.p., noted that Vicaire, a Catholic scientist, had taken fright at the Duhemian radicalism that had ostensibly reduced science to an intellectual game. The significance of Vicaire's fears for religion was reduced by Lacome's condescending remark that the knowledgeable Vicaire seemed to know everything except Catholic philosophy, while he dealt with little science and much philosophy in his polemic with Duhem. In any case, Duhem's

72. Domet de Vorges, "Les hypothèses physiques sont-elles des explications métaphysiques?," pp. 146–47.
73. Domet de Vorges, "Bulletin philosophique," *La science catholique* 6 (June 15, 1892): 655. On the decline of French mathematical physics after 1830, see T. S. Kuhn, "Mathematical versus Experimental Traditions in the Development of Physical Science," *Journal of Interdisciplinary History* 7 (1976): 30–31.

religious credentials were impeccable: "M. Duhem is as sincere a Catholic as [Vicaire], more Scholastic, less Cartesian and academic." Lacome argued that it was quite misleading to range Duhem, Poincaré, and Kirchhoff under the same banner, at least concerning the religious significance of their scientific positions.[74] The essential for Lacome was that Duhem was a believer in religion and a dogmatic in philosophy; Poincaré was a skeptic who smiled at all metaphysical ideas; and Kirchhoff always assumed the pose of the agnostic scientist.

After his defense of Duhem's position and its perfect orthodoxy within the Catholic *Weltanschauung*, Lacome gave a fairly technical treatment of a question raised by Duhem, the relation between the quality heat and the quantity temperature, a question that could be considerably illuminated by Scholastic philosophy and reason. Modern science put to philosophy thousands of analogous problems, which were debated by scientists among themselves because no philosopher had tried to enlighten them. Here was a great opportunity for Catholic philosophy. "[Catholic philosophy] was born with Aristotle from the analysis of the sciences known in his period. It attained maturity on being enlisted in the service of the divine sciences. It marvelously achieved this task, and it still fulfills this role. But today it has fallen in the opinion of the profane, if not of its friends. Why does it not think of regenerating itself, why not go sit at the sumptuous banquet of the modern sciences? There is an empty place which she can take, welcomed by all. The church invites her, science waits for her. Just think of the force truth would have against modern pride if Catholic philosophy snatched the flag of science this pride unjustly flies and uses to cover all its crimes and errors. There are Catholics and thinkers in the French university, and there are strong philosophical traditions and enough talent in the religious orders. Why is it that Catholic philosophy does not have a few vocations for this glorious work?"[75] These were the hopes and fears that inspired Catholics in the late nineteenth century to create a new set of higher educational institutions and to revamp several existing moribund institutions of ancient vintage. In France, in Belgium, in Italy, and in the United States, altars were erected to Isis in the hope that her veneration would ultimately redound to the greater glory of Jehovah and lead to the ignominious defeat of the scientistic enemies of religion. This paradoxical strategy was not without its considerable successes, although in the end it must be admitted that philosophical scientism, like all excesses, destroyed itself.

Most of Duhem's work *La théorie physique* had appeared in article form

74. Lacome quoted from the preface to Poincaré's *Théorie mathématique de la lumière* (1889) to show Poincaré's radical position and its closeness to Duhem's: "Les théories mathématiques n'ont pas pour objet de nous révéler la véritable nature des choses. . . . Leur but unique est de coordonner les lois physiques que l'expérience nous fait connaître, mais que sans le secours des mathématiques nous ne pourrions même énoncer. Peu nous importe que l'éther existe réellement, c'est l'affaire des métaphysiciens. L'essentiel pour nous, c'est que tout se passe comme s'il existait, et que cette hypothèse est commode pour l'explication des phénomènes. Après tout, avons-nous d'autre raison de croire à l'existence des objets matériels? Ce n'est là aussi qu'une hypothèse commode."

75. Fr. P.-B. Lacome, o.p., "Théories physiques. À propos d'une discussion entre savants," *RT* (1894): 104-5.

in the Thomist *Revue de philosophie* and in the *Revue des questions scienti-fiques*, organ of the Société scientifique de Bruxelles, which had given its ad-hesion to Thomism in 1890 on the request of Leo XIII. When it appeared as a book, F. Mentré, then professor at the Ecoles des Roches, hailed the work with the eulogy it deserved but also voiced certain criticisms not uncharac-teristic of many Catholic intellectuals unable to reconcile themselves to the destruction of familiar arguments and elimination of useless categories by the Duhemian razor. Within the Catholic intellectual establishment, a nearly idolatrous respect for reason was matched by a veneration of fact and proof by experimentation. The nineteenth-century triumphs of Aristotelianism-Thomism were made easier by these features of Catholicism; these move-ments in turn accentuated the traditional features of Catholicism. The bases of religion are susceptible of rational proof. Science is one of the magnifi-cent creations of the human mind. For centuries the triumphs of science had been correlated with a strengthening of the basis of Christianity, the most rational of religions. Certain post-eighteenth-century aberrations that had de-veloped into the scientistic horrors of the nineteenth century could be dis-missed as temporary excrescences, which would disappear when sound reason reasserted itself within the entire corpus of science. Just as in the Copernican period, so in the nineteenth century, at least for many Catholics, any radical revisions concerning the nature of scientific theory had serious implications for the bases of religion itself. Any argument, especially by a Catholic scien-tist, which denied such a cherished belief was bound to be greeted with a great deal of suspicion and hostility. Most of the criticisms of Duhem made by Catholics stemmed from the fundamental revision of the relation between religion and science required by his view of the nature of physical theory. The scientistic anti-clerical attacked religion by attempting to show that modern science relegated it at best to the realm of fable; the Duhemian philosophy of science seemed to destroy the tottering view that science supported religion. For a beleaguered Catholic in the Third Republic, it was hard to tell which was the worse enemy. Mentré's comments in 1906 and especially his further comments in 1914 and 1922 reflected the anxieties prevalent in the Catholic world.

In 1906 Mentré limited his criticism of Duhem's views of physical theory to saying that Duhem did not take experimental data seriously enough in the elaboration of his formulas unifying the field of physics. Mentré thought that the symbolism of the abstract laws of physics is "a translation of the true re-lations that exist between things": "The experimenter believes he seizes the links between phenomena, the articulations of reality. M. Duhem claims that a physical law is neither true nor false, but approximate; the experimentalist will reply to him that it is really an approximation of the true, of reality, and that consequently it is not purely artificial and possesses some objective value. The verifications of laws are not absolutely exact because one does not operate in sufficiently ideal conditions or with sufficiently precise instru-ments, but the verifications oscillate around a mean responding to natural conditions. M. Duhem wants to show that to the same practical fact can cor-respond an infinity of theoretical facts logically incompatible." But by taking

Duhem's example of the measurement of the increase in the voltage of a battery, Mentré was hardly consistent with his earlier observation that Duhem ignored the facts of laboratory workers. In the light of Duhem's experimental work at Bordeaux, this was of course a meaningless observation. Mentré therefore fell back on another standard accusation against Duhem, that his theories were excessively subtle. No doubt the apostle of the *esprit de finesse* regarded this as a compliment and proof of his success in shaking up the complacency of the terrible simplifiers inspired by the *esprit géométrique*. But Mentré emphasized that since 1892 Duhem had been one of the pioneers in raising important problems and in changing the prevalent conception of the nature of science itself. This was a healthy evolution. Mentré emphasized Duhem's important role in defining the idea of scientific explanation, in marking the limits of common sense and of science, and of science and philosophy. Not least of Duhem's contributions was his ridding philosophy of the fetishism of scientific principles. The independence of philosophy as a discipline, whose conclusions could stand without the aid of science, also a key point of Maritain's position, was a powerful weapon in the Catholic arsenal against scientism. But this was more an unintended consequence of *La théorie physique* than its explicit conclusion. Quite the reverse might be argued, as Duhem himself did for the metaphysician who deals with cosmology. Mentré's conclusion, however, can hardly be disputed: "In this Pleiad of scientific logicians gracing our epoch, [Duhem] occupies a special place because of his clarity of mind and his brilliant, limpid style."[76]

In a long study of Duhem in 1922, Mentré was also very critical of the aspects of Duhem's thought that had been bothering many Catholics for a long time. Like Lecome, however, Mentré carefully separated Duhem from other groups of thinkers who had some similar ideas. Following a note in *La théorie physique*, Mentré argued that the analysis of the experimental method made by Duhem had been taken up and distorted in the direction of rationalism by such people as Milhaud, Le Roy, and Wilbois.[77] Picard had detected an evolution in Duhem's ideas on the nature of physics: "His Physics, at first purely descriptive and symbolic, becomes asymptotic to a metaphysics."[78] Perhaps Duhem had considered some of the criticism that had been made of his earlier statements and had been somewhat influenced by the Thomists whose critical acceptance of his ideas he certainly did not ignore. It would have been difficult even for Domet de Vorges to complain about the explicit Duhemian concessions to the attempts of physics to reach reality. Mentré was especially pleased by Duhem's better-known statements. "In being perfected, [physical theory] takes on the characteristics of a natural classification, with the groups [of experimental laws] it establishes leading us to surmise the real relations of things." In spite of certain Duhemian statements,

76. Mentré, review of *La théorie physique* in *RP*, 6ᵉ année (January 1, 1906).
77. After referring to their recent works, chiefly articles in the *Revue de métaphysique et de morale* between 1886 and 1889, Duhem noted that the authors drew conclusions going beyond the boundaries of science, whereas he would stay within the limits of physical science (Wiener-Duhem, *Physical Theory*, p. 144n1).
78. Emile Picard, *La vie et l'œuvre de Pierre Duhem* (Paris, 1922), p. 21.

which should not be considered in isolation, he should not be grouped with the pragmatists and less still with the skeptics: "The more theory is perfected, the better idea we have that the logical order, in which theory arranges experimental laws, is the reflection of an ontological order." Although Duhem, like all theoreticians, looked for the simplest and most convenient representations, those shortening logical discourse the most, it could not be concluded that he subscribed to the *commodisme* of Poincaré.[79]

Duhem's argument that physics is autonomous and not in any way dependent on metaphysics, although any metaphysics has to take account of physical theory, was not a common argument among Catholics, especially in a period of the revival of Thomism. A more characteristic approach was taken by the Louvain geologist Canon Dorlodot, like Duhem a member of the Société scientifique de Bruxelles. In his work reconciling Darwinism and Catholicism, Dorlodot emphasized that when he used the term "sciences of observation" he meant "the sciences in the widest sense of the word—that is to say, including their philosophic foundation." Although a scientist who is not a professional metaphysician can do good science, "every rational branch of science derives its rational basis from metaphysics." It is true that Duhem's scientist of Cartesian common sense could qualify as a sort of Dorlodotian metaphysician on the basis of Dorlodot's admission that "true metaphysics is simply the science of sound common sense." But this should not be taken too seriously, for Dorlodot hastened to add that a scientist who does not know "scientific metaphysics" is likely to come to grief, at least when he ventures beyond the strict confines of his specialization. Thus specialization and professional pride, its frequent satanic companion, could lead a scientist to repudiate "the laws of common sense." This had happened with many modern mathematicians who had "arrived at conclusions the absurdity of which will astonish a future and more enlightened generation" because they had not taken into account the basic independence of the *genera* "figure" and "quantity," or the distinction between continuous and discontinuous quantity or number, and had also imagined that the idea of number arrived at independently of observation could alone give exact certainty. "The same thing has happened to many unbelieving naturalists, and especially to those who profess an atheistic and materialistic theory of evolution." A second reason explaining the frequent difficulties of a scientist ignorant of metaphysics, Dorlodot observed, is his inability to analyze scientifically the foundations of his beliefs or fully justify them or know their degree of certainty. This produced the paradoxical situation in which the scientist could pass from "an undue or even excessive trust in the value of theories, like that manifested in the nineteenth century, to a state of scientific skepticism like that presented by some otherwise eminent scientists today, and which is the greatest danger of all at the present time from the religious point of view." In 1906 Abbé Bourgine

79. Duhem, *La théorie physique*, cited in F. Mentré, "Pierre Duhem, le théoricien," *RP* 29 (1922): 449–73, 608–27. R. N. D. Martin argues that Duhem reacted to criticism by devising the theory of natural classification and by revising his notion of physical law in a way that destroyed the empirical certainty of things, thus knocking out the basis of Vicaire's naïve falsificationist methodology (Martin's letter to Paul, Oct. 28, 1977).

warned on different grounds that the new scientific philosophy was more dangerous than the old. Perhaps this was not far from the truth, at least from the viewpoint of strict doctrinal orthodoxy, when one considers the theological errors Edouard Le Roy had been forced to retract in the case of his startlingly pragmatic explanation of dogma in terms of rules of practical conduct. Henri Poincaré's lack of sympathy for Catholicism and his suspicions of its threat to intellectual freedom were a matter of public record.[80] A third disadvantage of the scientist's not knowing metaphysics, Dorlodot argued, is that he is sometimes stumped by the spurious objections put forward by sophists to his legitimate conclusions and he is thus forced to rely solely on his personal conviction of their truth. Only a grounding in scientific metaphysics could enable him to expose the flimsy basis of sophistic objections. Dorlodot concluded that it was only at considerable cost to science itself and especially to its plausible defense that the scientist could ignore metaphysics.[81] It would be hard to find a clearer example of a Catholic anti-Duhemian position.

In order to distinguish his position from that of Duhem, with which some people had confused it, Jacques Maritain detailed the points of Duhem's argument which he rejected. For Maritain, mathematical physics is a science of physical reality, but it knows this reality only in transposing it and not "as physical reality per se." Maritain thought that Meyerson's criticism of the positivist position also applied to Duhem: the ontological concern, the explanation of physical causes cannot remain foreign to science. "But the encounter between the law of causality, which is immanent in our reason, and the mathematical conception of nature has as its result the construction in theoretical physics of more and more remote and geometrized universes. In these universes, fictive causal entities based on . . . [reality], whose sole function is to serve as a support for mathematical deduction, come to include a very detailed account of empirically determined real . . . [causes] or conditions." Maritain thought that here mathematical physics was simply reviving the old hypotheses of mechanist metaphysics, which it completely transformed or changed by introducing into the hypotheses "vast zones of dislocation and of irrationality." "Mechanism is the only way of representing causality that can stand up . . . within a general reduction of physics to geometry."

Pierre Duhem . . . thought that "a physical theory is not an explanation; it is a system of mathematical propositions which have, for their purpose, to represent, as completely and simply as possible, a whole complexus of experimental laws." It does, indeed, actually happen that

80. Dorlodot, *Darwinism and Catholic Thought* (London, 1922), pp. 95, 96; Abbé Bourgine, *Foi catholique et science moderne* (La Chapelle-Montligeon, 1906); Poincaré, "Le libre examen en matière scientifique," *Revue de l'université de Bruxelles* (December 1909), pp. 285–95.

81. Dorlodot regarded the principle of sufficient reason as the foundation of Christian metaphysics; it is a first principle, from which the principle of causality is derived, and not simply a logical consequence of the principle of contradiction. For a demonstration of the canon's logical skill and use of metaphysical assumptions, see his "Refutation 'a posteriori' of the objection to evolution based on the principle of causality" (*Darwinism and Catholic Thought*, pp. 106 ff.).

in some of its parts (for example, energetics as Duhem conceived it, or in our own day, wave mechanics according to the interpretation that Heisenberg proposes and to which Louis de Broglie has rallied) physics makes use of pure mathematical symbols without therein attempting either *causal explanation* or the constructing of figurative hypotheses through which the mind may in some way take the mechanism of phenomena apart. But to tell the truth, when it does refrain from doing so, it makes a virtue of necessity because it cannot do otherwise. Where Duhem went wrong was in seeking the very model of physical theory in these rather exceptional cases, which he regarded as pure cases. Actually, these cases stand at the very limit of physical theory and in them the mathematical transposition of phenomena is momentarily sustained all alone in the mind without any supporting physical image. So little are they typical of physical theory that the mathematical symbols they use are just awaiting a chance to leave the realm of pure analytical forms and become explanatory entities. (This is what happened in the case of energy. For, "almost all scientists today admit that it is not merely an abstract conception," let us say a pure mathematical symbol. The somewhat crude case of atomic number could also be cited, for it has finally ended up by designating the charge of an atomic nucleus and the number of electrons gravitating about it, when at the outset it was simply a periodic number.) On the other hand, causal entities, and the structural patterns built by the physicists, derive their noematic consistency only from the mathematical symbolism they, so to speak, embody. The interpenetration of mathematics and entitative representations thus seem essential to physico-mathematical knowing. Whence it happens that . . . "These academic quarrels seem quite outmoded and the two points of view are curiously mingled in the work of scientists today." Let us say, rather, that they constitute but one point of view. Moreover, Duhem's over-rarefied conception would have destroyed the main incentives arising from the discovery of facts, without which physics would not exist at all.[82]

By contrast, "the essence of biology does not consist in a mathematization of the sensible. However great use biology may make of mathematics in progressing . . . towards the material analysis of life . . . [mathematics] remains for it a simple instrument. . . . It does not set itself up as a mathematics of the phenomena of life." Thus Duhem's theory, which identified "saving the phenomena" with the pure translation of physical data into a system of mathematical equations, was, by contrast, much too narrow, an abstraction of the search for causal explanation. It was natural that the philosopher who had publicized the developments in vitalistic biology in Germany and had written a preface to the French translation of Driesch's *The Science and Philosophy of the Organism* would find in the sciences of life the possibility of restoring natural philosophy in the Aristotelian and Scholastic sense. But the argu-

82. Maritain, *Distinguish to Unite; or, the Degrees of Knowledge* (New York, 1959), pp. 43–44 (newly translated from the fourth French edition under the supervision of Gerald B. Phelan). Quotes by Maritain are from Emile Picard's speech of December 16, 1929, to the Académie des Sciences.

ments against Duhem were based on a caricature of the physicist's position, for Duhem had come round to argue that, in perfecting itself, physical theory takes on the traits of a natural classification, thus getting close to the reality of things. The logical order in which it puts experimental laws reflects an ontological order. But Maritain assumed for Thomism a guiding role not accepted by Duhem, whose view of the autonomy of physics did not require it to have the metaphysical framework demanded by Maritain.[83] In order to overcome the dangers of paradox and begging the question, ever present in physics because it is based on common sense knowledge and mathematical deduction, Duhem used the correction of the *history* of physical principles. The importance of the historical method in physics is that it shows "that physical theory is not merely an artificial system . . . but that it is an increasingly more natural classification and an increasingly clearer reflection of realties which experimental method cannot contemplate directly."[84]

The apologetic significance of the *history* of scientific doctrines is clearly stated by Duhem in the conclusion of the second volume of *Les origines de la statique*:

> However, while all these efforts contributed to the advancement of a science that we contemplate today as fully completed, none who exerted these efforts suspected the greatness or the form of the monument they were building. . . . Masons clever at cutting and laying stones, they worked on a monument whose plan was not revealed to them by the architect.
>
> How could all these efforts have contributed so precisely to the materialization of a plan unknown to the laborers, if a clearly perceived plan did not exist before in the imagination of an architect and if this architect did not have the power of directing and coordinating the labor of the masons? The development of statics shows us, as much and even more than the development of a living being, the influence of a guiding idea. In the complex facts making up this development we detect the continuous action of a Wisdom that foresees the ideal form the science must aim for and we detect a Power directing all the efforts of the thinkers towards this goal. To sum up, we recognize there the work of Providence.[85]

Considering that Maritain, in spite of his assertion of the independence of philosophy, also left to the sciences placed under the aegis of Thomist philosophy their own independence, it is hard to see that he and Duhem were far apart on the key point of an important role for Thomist philosophy in modern intellectual life. Both were key figures in the writing of articles for the *Revue de philosophie*, and the debate over Duhem's views was largely con-

83. Ibid., pp. 194–95. See also Maritain, *Philosophy of Nature* (New York, 1951), pp. 60–62, for a repetition of some of the criticism of Duhem. This volume contains "Maritain's Philosophy of the Sciences" by Yves R. Simon.

84. Wiener-Duhem, *Physical Theory*, p. 270.

85. *Les origines de la statique* (Paris, 1905–6), 2: 289–90. This passage is curiously close to Lapparent's opinion.

ducted in the same journal. Was it not a family quarrel among Thomists? Apart from their disagreements—and Thomism was not conceived of as an intellectual *Gleichschaltung* for Catholics—nearly all could agree on the general significance of Thomism for modern science. "The Aristotelian-Thomist view . . . by showing how contingency in the course of singular *events* is reconciled with the necessity of *laws* known to science, shows how it is possible to insert into nature the liberty proper to spirits which, as such, do not form part of sensible nature and of the corporeal universe but which do, however, act in that universe."[86] The general significance of the revival of Thomism was boldly put by Maritain in the conclusion of his chapter on philosophy and experimental science in the *Degrees of Knowledge*.

> One is right in holding that Thomistic philosophy is, more than any other philosophy, in a position to provide the sciences with metaphysical frameworks within which they may deploy their own necessities unhampered and suffer no violence. This is so not only because Thomistic philosophy is essentially realistic and gives a critical justification for the extramental reality of things and the value of our powers of knowing, which every science implicitly takes for granted, but also because it guarantees the autonomy and specific character of each and because its metaphysical explanations of the real have as their necessary consequence no systematic deformation tyrannically imposed on experience.
>
> And here the reproach levelled at Scholasticism by poorly informed minds recoils against modern systems. For it is indeed from these systems that necessarily and *per se* derive such systematic prejudices as mechanism, monism, psycho-physical parallelism, the Cartesian theory of consciousness, universal evolutionism, etc. These systems impose on science the most deplorable metaphysical shackles.
>
> It is not a question of seeking between the sciences and Aristotelian-Thomistic philosophy the concordance of detail that we rejected just a moment ago, but rather of noting a general over-all agreement, a good understanding, a natural friendship, of which the very freedom of science, the ease with which it develops, is the best indication. This statement is explicitly made by many representatives of the sciences of nature, while elsewhere, a striking renewal of themes proper to the moral philosophy of Thomas Aquinas is evinced in the moral and legal sciences of which we have not spoken in this essay.[87]

When the *Revue de philosophie* was founded in 1900 Duhem played a key role in its foundation and in supplying it with articles in the history of philosophy and science. In 1900 Abbé Elie Blanc came to Paris from Lyon to discuss with the fathers Bulliot and Peillaube the founding of the *Revue de philosophie*. Peillaube took the chief responsibility for the task of establishing and, later, of editing the new journal of Thomist philosophy. Peillaube, Canon Bernies, and Duhem discussed the foundation of the journal for several days on one of the peaks of the *Montagne noire*: "One day, fortified by

86. Maritain, *Degrees of Knowledge*, p. 30.
87. Ibid., p. 66.

a substantial *cassoulet* and made optimistic by the *blanquette de Limoux*, while two of us were stretched out on the moss and the third seated in a tree branch at a certain height, Pierre Duhem exclaimed, 'If we establish it . . . I have just finished a volume on *Le Mixte* and I'll give you my manuscript.' The foundation was settled."[88] By the volume, high quality, and revisionary nature of his contributions, Duhem helped to make the *Revue de philosophie* an important organ in the history and philosophy of science.[89] He thus made a considerable impact on the movement that would, perhaps more than any other, shape modern Catholic thought; its influence on him was no less important.

88. See "Rapport du R. P. Peillaube" in "Trentenaire de la 'Revue de philosophie,'" *RP*, n.s. 1 (1931): 12. For further recognition of Duhem's role see "Nécrologie. Pierre Duhem (1861-1916)," *RP* 26 (1919): 460.

89. Duhem's articles on "La notion du mixte" appeared in numbers 1-4 and 6 of the *Revue de philosophie*, beginning with the first number in December 1900. Two articles on "La théorie physique; son objet, sa structure" appeared in numbers 4 and 5 of 1908. In 1907-8, Duhem published in the *Revue* twelve articles of a series that picked up again in 1914 and formed part of his *Système du monde*. Other contributors were Albert de Lapparent and Paul Tannery. On Tannery, see Paul, "Scholarship and Ideology: The Chair of the General History of Science at the Collège de France, 1892-1913," *Isis* (1976): 376-97. R.N.D. Martin's paper on "Pierre Duhem and Neo-Thomism" (XVth International Congress of the History of Science, Edinburgh, 1977) makes a strong case for clearly separating Duhem from the Thomist movement. A very useful collection of papers on Duhem is in *Etudes philosophiques* 4 (1967): 395-438.

6

Thomism and Science: "Wonderful Harmony under the Shield and Authority of the Angelic Doctor"

> Saint Thomas is properly and before everything else *the apostle of the intelligence*: this is the first reason why we must regard him as *the apostle of modern times*.
>
> Jacques Maritain, *St. Thomas Aquinas* (New York, 1958), p. 98.

Although the roots of the Thomist revival go well back into the nineteenth century, relations between Thomism and modern science developed only after Leo XIII's promotion of Thomism as a panacea for modern intellectual ills, many of which were intimately related to scientific trends. It was probably as much intellectual as political developments that inspired the revival of Thomism as a quasi-official philosophy, for the experiences of Reformation and French Revolution had not led to an earlier restoration.[1] The encyclical *Aeterni Patris*, prescribing the Christian philosophy of Aquinas for Catholic schools as the antidote to the false philosophies pullulating in the nineteenth century, was published by Leo XIII on August 4, 1879. A year later an apostolic letter made the Angelic Doctor the common patron of all Catholic schools. That science was not exempt from the "force and light and aid the Scholastic philosophy, if judiciously taught, would bring" is explicit in the encyclical: "And here it is well to note that our philosophy can only by the grossest injustice be accused of being opposed to the advance and development of natural science. For, when the Scholastics, following the opinion of the holy Fathers, always held in anthropology that the human intel-

1. The phrase "wonderful harmony under the shield and authority of the angelic doctor" is from the papal encyclical *Aeterni Patris*. Pierre Thibault, *Savoir et pouvoir. Philosophie thomiste et politique cléricale au XIXᵉ siècle* (Québec, 1972), argues that Thomism was revived as an ideology by a few politicized Italian Jesuits and promoted by Leo XIII because of its potential for maximizing priestly power. See also Friedrich Heer, *The Intellectual History of Europe*, 2 vols. (Stuttgart, 1953; New York, 1966, 1968), 1:13, 216, 220.

ligence is only led to the knowledge of things without body and matter by things sensible, they well understood that nothing was of greater use to the philosopher than diligently to search into the mysteries of nature and to be earnest and constant in the study of physical things. And this they confirmed by their own example; for St. Thomas, Blessed Albertus Magnus, and other leaders of the Scholastics were never so wholly rapt in the study of philosophy as not to give large attention to the knowledge of natural things; and, indeed, the number of their sayings and writings on these subjects, which recent professors approve of and admit to harmonize with truth, is by no means small. Moreover, in this very age many illustrious professors of the physical sciences openly testify that between certain and accepted conclusions of modern physics and the philosophic principles of the schools there is no conflict worthy of the name."[2]

The principal roles in the restoration of Thomism were played by Italy, Germany, Belgium, and France. Leo himself paid for a new edition of the works of Aquinas. The Roman Gregorian University had an international contingent studying theology and philosophy by 1890: out of a total of 781 students, there were 237 Italians, 139 French, 130 Germans, 83 Americans, 49 English, 29 Swiss, and 29 Poles. Italian touting for Thomism abounded: *La Civiltà cattolica* in Rome, *Scienza italiana* in Bologna, and the *Divus Thomas* in Piacenza. A score or so authors were busy reconciling modern science and Thomism. Liverani tried to found modern physics on scholastic principles, Scarpati tried to create a syllogistic anthropology, and Gaudezzi studied atomism from a Scholastic viewpoint. The modern Italian Catholic intellectual revival contained a strong Thomistic component.[3]

Thomism had great success in Germany. In 1888 there were 23 Catholic student associations with 985 members. *Aeterni Patris* had an important influence in southern Germany and in the Rhineland. The constitutional and political power of German Catholics, in spite of their minority status, was matched by an attempt to re-establish an intellectual unity through a return to Thomism in philosophy and in theology. Thomist doctrines invaded many old Catholic journals and inspired several new ones. Among prominent periodicals were the *Theologische Quartalschrift* of Tübingen, *Natur und Offenbarung* of Münster, the *Historisch-politische Blätter für das katholische Deutschland* of Munich, the *Stimmen aus Maria-Laach* of Freiburg im Breisgau, the *Saint-Thomasblätter* of Regensberg, and the *Jahrbuch für Philosophie und spekulative Theologie* of Paderborn and Münster. The *Philosophisches Jarhbuch*, organ of the Görres-Gesellschaft, whose program was sketched by the Bishop of Mainz, began in 1888 under the guidance of Gutberlet and Pohle, professors at the schools of philosophy and theology in Fulda, and had the collaboration of professors and priests, including Jesuits,

2. *Aeterni Patris*, translated in Etienne Gilson, *The Church Speaks to the Modern World* (New York, 1954), pp. 49–50.

3. On the general Thomistic revival, see François Picavet, "Le mouvement néo-thomiste," *RP* 33 (1892): 281–308. For a sketch of the history of relationships between Thomism and science, see William A. Wallace, "Thomism and Modern Science: Relationships Past, Present, and Future," *The Thomist* 33 (1968): 67–83.

Dominicans, and Franciscans. Aiming to establish a Christian philosophy, it admitted that it was possible to improve on, to complete, and even to contradict St. Thomas when his principles were not in complete agreement with the truth: "In dubiis libertas, in necessariis unitas, in omnibus caritas." A great deal of energy went into attempts to reconcile science, especially new developments in biology, with Thomism. Not all Catholics agreed that the new wine could be safely poured into the old bottles without doctoring it considerably.

Only Belgium rivaled and perhaps surpassed Germany in its adoption of Thomism. In addition to their political muscle, Belgian Catholics had educational institutions that responded well to *Aeterni Patris*. A higher institute of philosophy existed at Louvain University for the effective dissemination of Thomism. Scientific courses in the physical and mathematical sciences enlightened the teaching of cosmology; social sciences leavened ethics and law; and the biological sciences were joined to psychology. Saint George Mivart lectured on natural philosophy as an introduction to cosmology, psychology, and "critériologie."[4] Dorlodot taught cosmology and general metaphysics to the law students. Courses in mathematics and the physical sciences were given by Gilbert, Mansion, Siebenaler, Henry, de la Vallée-Poussin, Pasquier, and Van Bieroliet. By the 1890s the Société scientifique de Bruxelles and its journal, the *Revue des questions scientifiques*, were also lending their support to the Thomist movement. But it is not possible to separate the society and its publications from French Catholicism.

Thomism had revived in France in circumstances essentially repugnant to the republican mentality. Louis Foucher gives 1851 as the date of the beginning of French Thomism as a significant collective movement, for then the Second Republic was ended by the triumph of authoritarian ideas in politics, and the superior of the Theatines, Ventura de Raulica, established himself in Paris with the protection of the government. Building on the authoritarian traditionalism of Bonald and Lamennais, Ventura completed the structure by putting in the coping stone of Thomism, the only Christian philosophy, whose lack, Ventura thought, had caused traditionalism to fail in its basic mission.[5] Thomism soon became the ideological spearhead of the clerical intelligentsia, especially when the newly created Roman periodical *La Civiltà cattolica* and the reconstituted Society of Jesus gave strong support to the movement.

France was the scene of considerable Thomist activity, especially in the new Catholic universities of Paris, Angers, and Lille. Journals like the *Annales de philosophie chrétienne* and *Etudes* played important diffusion and discussion roles. Weighty and learned tomes appeared analyzing all aspects of Scholasticism.[6] The works of Albertus Magnus were re-edited. The fight against a great deal of modern philosophy and of modern science, combined with an

4. See his *Introduction générale à l'étude de la nature* (Louvain, 1891).
5. See Louis Foucher, *La philosophie catholique en France au XIXᵉ siècle avant la renaissance thomiste et dans son rapport avec elle (1800–1880)* (Paris, 1955), chap. 9, "La montée du thomisme."
6. See Abbé Elie Blanc, *Traité de philosophie scolastique* (Lyon, 1889).

182   *The Edge of Contingency*

attempt to establish the superiority of Aristelo-Thomism in all areas, found a doughty leader in the Jesuit Albert Farges, whose voluminous studies examined Scholasticism in the light of the modern sciences, to establish its eternal truth.[7] In 1884 the movement was given intellectual leadership by the establishment of an Aquinas society.

The Société de Saint Thomas d'Aquin started in Paris with twenty members and provincial correspondents. It included the abbés Guieu, Lesserteur, de Broglie, Vallet, Bernard, Lelong, and de Foville, and Msgr. d'Hulst. Among the correspondents were a member of the Academy of Sciences, Barré de Saint-Venant—an excellent catch—Msgr. Bourquard, Abbé Blanc of the Catholic Institute in Lyon, and Abbé Couture of the Catholic Institute in Toulouse. In about a year the society had attracted forty-four members and was continuing to grow. A high intellectual level was maintained in the discussions and publications of the society with stars of the calibre of Gardair, de Broglie, Vicaire, and the clever Dr. Ferrand of the Séminaire d'Issy, who was expert in both theology and physiology.[8] D'Hulst was elected president, Domet de Vorges vice-president, and Abbé Pisani and Gardair secretaries for the first year. Only Catholics could be members, although non-Catholics could be correspondents. Works of either group were read at the annual session and followed by a discussion during which it was decided if the works should be sent to the *Annales de philosophie chrétienne*, the usual organ of the society. Specifically formed to take up the challenge of *Aeterni Patris*, the aim of the society was the study of Christian philosophy.

This aim was achieved through a two-pronged effort. The search for philosophic truths took place under the inspiration of the fathers and doctors of the church, especially Aquinas. Equally important, perhaps, was the attempt to expose and refute modern errors from the double viewpoint of Christian philosophy and the "natural and experimental sciences." This ambitious program was carried out not only by theologians and philosophers but by scientists and especially by medical doctors, whose collaboration was so useful in a period of close relationships between psychology and physiology. In organizing the best Catholic minds in France, the society hoped to show that religion keeps abreast of all progress and that the church has nothing to fear from science and science nothing to fear from the church.[9]

By the 1880s there was evidence of interest in Thomism outside Catholic circles. In 1885 Domet de Vorges read before the Académie des sciences morales et politiques a memoir on Thomist cosmology, still viable in the light of

7. *Etudes philosophiques pour vulgariser les théories d'Aristote et de saint Thomas et leur accord avec les sciences*, 8 vols. (Paris, 1888-). By 1902 several of the volumes were in their sixth edition.
8. "Séance annuelle de la Société de Saint Thomas d'Aquin et rapport sur les travaux de la Société pendant l'année 1884-5," *APC*, n.s. 12 (1885): 489–512. Thomist aims in Germany were quite similar. See Picavet, "Le mouvement néo-thomiste," esp. pp. 292-93.
9. "Notes et chroniques," *APC*, n.s. 11 (1884–85): 188–91. Ollé-Laprune presided over the fourth session in 1888. A hero of the society for carrying the Catholic standard at the Normale, this "disciple of Aristotle and Aquinas" was the author of the much admired *De la certitude morale*. Standard intellectual topics of the day included "la possibilité du vide," "la possibilité d'une quantité rigoureusement innombrable," and "le determinisme scientifique et la liberté."

modern science. This was probably the first time in two hundred years that the Scholastic theory of matter and form was defended before an important learned body in France.[10] In 1889 Gardair, as a result of the continued request of several members of the Sorbonne and the Protestant *Critique philosophique*, gave a series of lectures (*conférences libres*) at the Sorbonne.[11] By 1888 Gardair and Domet de Vorges had succeeded in getting a chair of Scholastic philosophy definitively established at the Catholic Institute in Paris. The Sorbonne lectures partially filled the gap of sixteen centuries in the history of philosophy taught there. The baccalauréat program jumped from the Stoics to Bacon and Descartes. This was probably regarded as ideal by the republicans who viewed the university as the republic's seminary of secularism. But one cannot blame the university for not teaching a subject which did not really exist before the second half of the nineteenth century. Once Thomism became recognized as intellectually significant, it soon found serious critics outside Catholic circles.

The obsession of Catholic thinkers with reconciling Thomism and modern science was closely linked with the attempt to create unity in the teaching of philosophy in Catholic institutions. Inevitably, the attempt at unity produced a great deal of disagreement. But intellectual unity has never been a strong characteristic of Catholicism. The Jesuit Henry Ramière found such an encouraging response to his attempt at reconciliation in an article in *Etudes* in December 1876 that he published a full-length study the next year.[12] Having the new Catholic universities in mind as likely spearheads of the movement, Ramière checked out his scientific comments with colleagues in the physical sciences. The problem of how to remain abreast of the latest novelty while returning to antiquity and the Middle Ages was neatly solved by proclaiming Aristotle one of the moderns. This turned out to be a happy paradox, for the relevance of Aristotle to certain areas of cosmology and even modern biology was soon upheld by scientists like Duhem and Driesch. Ramière's judgment was based on his own view of the nature of scientific activity, a view rather common among the more unimaginative Catholic intellectuals before the late-nineteenth-century revolution on the nature of scientific thought set off a fierce debate, centering on Duhem, within Catholicism itself. Aristotle was more modern than the neo-peripateticians because he based his work on observation, limiting speculation in physical questions to a subordinate role. His disciples were less observant and therefore more dogmatic. Although modern science could not be reconciled with the views of the neo-peripateticians, it could easily be reconciled with Aristotle and Aquinas. Since the materialistic bent of medicine was one of the chief anxieties for nineteenth-century Cath-

10. "Saint Thomas d'Aquin à l'Académie des sciences morales et politiques," *APC*, n.s. 12 (1885): 191.

11. "L'homme comparé aux autres êtres corporels d'après S. Thomas d'Aquin," reported in *APC*, n.s. 21 (1889-90): 611-13. See also *APC*, n.s. 23 (1891-92): 388-93. For the furor over Abbé Piat's thesis on Aquinas, see Msgr. d'Hulst, "S. Thomas et le spiritualisme à la Sorbonne," *APC*, n.s. (1890): 376 ff.

12. Ramière, *L'accord de la philosophie de Saint Thomas et de la science moderne au sujet de la composition des corps pour faire suite à l'unité dans l'enseignement de la philosophie* (Paris, 1877).

olics, Ramière was delighted that Félix Frédault of the Faculty of Medicine of Paris upheld the necessity of returning to the basic theories of Scholastic physiology. Of course it was inconvenient that although Frédault accepted Thomist doctrine on the general composition of bodies, he rejected it on the role of the elements in the formation of compounds—Aquinas had gone astray because of a lack of experimental data and an excessive confidence in Aristotle.[13] But, initially at least, the important thing was the general agreement on the need to return to the Angelic Doctor for the inspiration and the fundamentals with which Catholic science could face the modern Babel of atheistic science.

Ramière's nonchalant dismissal of the neo-Scholastics did not go unchallenged. Abbé Bourquard, a learned and formidable Thomist, professor at the Catholic University in Angers, took him to task for his low opinion of the neo-Scholastics and engaged in some polemics of his own. Ramière's doctrine was compared to that of Büchner and he was accused of fabricating texts of Aristotle.[14] In 1884 Bourquard, then a monsignor and a member of the Accademia romana di S. Tommaso d'Aquino, published a hard-line defense of integral Thomism, first in the *Bulletin ecclésiastique de Strasbourg* and later as a separate brochure.[15] As could be expected, Bourquard followed the herd of enthusiastic Thomists in proclaiming the virtues of Scholastic physics and the continuity of several of its theses by modern physics, which was tantamount to a recognition of their *truth*. A return to the fountainhead of truth in medieval science would avoid the evils issuing from the sophisms of Mill, Bain, and Spencer on causality as well as the negation of finality in Helmholtz and Dubois-Reymond. The principles of traditional philosophy would facilitate the drawing of conclusions present in embryo in the magnificent discoveries in modern science. To Thomism would fall the quixotic and Sisyphean task of restoring the First Cause to the center of scientific philosophy. Only then would science cease being the chief source of the anti-religious forces of modern times.

In contrast to the situation of the 1890s, when the reconcilers of Thomism struggled with evolution and Aristotelian cosmology, the most serious problem in the 1870s was the relationship between Thomism and modern chemistry, especially the composition of bodies. Frédault's *Forme et matière* (1876) had dealt a heavy blow against the peripatetic system's teachings on the composition of bodies. It was to rescue Aquinas from a potentially dangerous sit-

13. See Félix Frédault, *Forme et matière* (Paris, 1876), written as a result of a request to publish in book form the articles he wrote in *Univers* to reply to the articles of Father Liberatore on Frédault's *Traité d'anthropologie*. Chapter 21 proclaimed the "Confusions et dangers de la métaphysique péripatéticienne." See also his *De la scolastique à la science moderne* (Paris, 1867), extrait du *Monde catholique*.

14. Lettre du père H. Ramière . . . à M. l'abbé Bourquard (Toulouse, 1877). Bourquard's thesis was on the *Doctrine de la connaissance d'après saint Thomas d'Aquin* (Thèse présentée à la Faculté des lettres de Besançon, Angers, 1877).

15. See Joseph Gardair, "Analyses et critiques. L'encyclique *Aeterni patris* par Mgr. L.-C. Bourquard," *APC*, n.s. 10 (1884): 154–67. Emphasizing observation, facts, reasoning based on the facts, Bourquard's view of the facts did not differ greatly from Ramière's. He echoes Naville's view that one of the mistakes of modern philosophy was the elimination of causes and ends from science. See Naville, *La physique moderne* (Paris, 1883).

uation that Ramière distinguished between the neo-peripatetic and chemical schools and carefully disassociated Aristotle and Aquinas from the teachings of the neo-peripatetic school on the composition of bodies.[16] It was vital to show that a modern Catholic chemist could also be a Thomist without sacrificing any of the teaching of modern chemistry on the nature of organic and inorganic compounds. Frédault had argued that the question of being and the role of matter were the great philosophic issues of the day. The old struggle between matter and mind had been reborn and revitalized. In traditional hylomorphism natural bodies result from the union of the two principles of primary matter and substantial form. Aquinas followed Aristotle in saying that in the case of substantial change the body retains its primary matter but changes its old form for a new one.[17] Ramière found the doctrines of the "chemical school" perfectly consonant with important dogmatic teachings, such as that on the Eucharist, in contrast to the errors and confusions of the neo-peripatetics, especially the editor of *Scienza italiana*, Father Cornoldi.[18] He was able to retain the key idea that the soul is the principle of the substantial unity of man while accepting the new scientific teachings on the nature of matter, including the idea of the molecular structure of the human body. But the soul is the vital force dominating and unifying the mutual interaction of the body's chemical forces, thus giving the body human form, life, and feeling. The difficulty with this type of revisionism was that it made metaphysics dependent on physical theories, although perhaps as an unintended consequence. Later commentators would play it safe by making "Scholastic metaphysics independent of any *particular* theory of physics" and ground it "on principles so general that no changes in the theories of physics can affect them."[19]

16. Ramière, *L'accord de la philosophie de saint Thomas et de la science moderne*.

17. Garvin Ardley, *Aquinas and Kant. The Foundations of Modern Science* (London, 1950), pp. 210, 213. Copleston clarifies Aquinas' thought on this theory. "In every material thing or substance there are two distinguishable constitutive principles." These are substantial form and first matter. Matter and form here are not chemical elements or logical principles but rather "principles of being" (*principia entis*); "they are not themselves physical entities." The substantial form, Aristotle's "entelechy," is the determining principle making a thing what it is, "an immanent constitutive principle of activity." The substantial form of the thing is determined by its first matter, "a purely indeterminate potential element which has no definite form of its own and no definite characteristics." By contrast, "Visible matter, secondary matter, is already informed and possesses determinate characteristics; but if we think away all forms and all determinate characteristics we arrive at the notion of a purely indeterminate constitutive principle which is capable of existing successively in union with an indefinite multiplicity of forms." First matter has no independent existence and cannot be seen; "but its presence as a component metaphysical factor in corporeal substances is manifested by substantial change." This hylomorphic theory was for Aquinas "the result of metaphysical analysis, not of physical or chemical analysis. The language of the theory of form and matter belongs to the language of metaphysics." F. C. Copleston, *Aquinas* (London, 1955), pp. 85–88.

18. See Ramière, *L'accord de la philosophie de saint Thomas et de la science moderne*, appendix, "Exposé parallèle des deux systèmes soutenus dans les Ecoles catholiques, relativement à la composition des corps," pp. 101–3.

19. Ardley, *Aquinas and Kant*, p. 217. See also Pedro Descoqs, *Essai critique sur l'hylémorphisme* (Paris, 1924), p. 279n2. It was possible in the 1870s and later to get out of any inconsistency between atomic theory and Thomism by rejecting atomic theory—on good scientific authority, even if one did have to make a temporary pact with the devil in

Those who advanced the theories of hylosystemism in twentieth-century neo-Scholasticism to replace traditional hylomorphism in explaining "the essential constitution of inorganic bodies" would run into similar difficulties. Taking into account modern physics on the nature of matter and the structure of the atom, "hylosystemism . . . explains the constitution of the natural body as an *atomary energy system*, in the sense that the atom of an element and the molecule of a compound are composed of sub-atomic particles . . . united into a *dynamic system* working as a *functional unit*."[20] But soon wave mechanics threatened hylosystemism with a "return to a modified theory of the *continuity* of matter as distinct from a system of discrete particles on which hylosystemism is founded." The mistake of the revisionists was to "have ascribed a real ontological status to the picture of nature of the physical world advanced by the modern physicist." Since physics is always changing, the philosopher has no obligation to adjust his metaphysics to follow the physicist. *"The general conclusion, then, is that the traditional doctrine of hylomorphism of Aristotle and St. Thomas is unshaken."*[21] The universal and general nature of the observations on which hylomorphism was founded renders it impervious to an attack based on protean physics. Maritain would later seek a way out of the difficulty by arguing in favor of the dualist solution of a separation of the physical and the ontological orders. Why the two orders are independent, if they are, and what the relationships are between them remain eternal questions for the philosophers of science.

It was perhaps inevitable that philosophers and theologians would get round to declaring or implying the primacy of the ontological over the physical order, at least in the metaphysical quest for certainty that was so important a part of the Thomist revival. Of course Thomism shared in the general re-thinking of the nature of scientific and of religious thought that took place at the end of the nineteenth century. In 1897 the Dominican Father Schwalm gave a sophisticated if traditional Thomist analysis of the comparative basis of religious and of scientific thought.[22] He argued that the act of science and the act of belief have in common the fact that they are both acts of judgment. They both know formally the real existence of things in our thought. This existence is more than the phenomenon of thought itself, more than the logical relationship of ideas; it is the very being of things; according to the axiom of Aquinas: "objectum intellectus est ens." A quote, especially in Latin, from the Angelic Doctor always seemed to clear up an obscure point. Schwalm believed in the objectivity of both religious and scientific knowledge. Unlike Maritain, Schwalm did not benefit much from contemporary theories on the nature of science.

Schwalm found an even closer resemblance between science and faith than their objectivity; both are certain, although this certainty is founded on opposed principles. The certainty of science is necessary; the certainty of faith

---

relying on Henri Sainte-Claire Deville and Berthelot. See L. Picherit, *Le thomisme et la chimie moderne* (Paris, 1878).

20. C. N. Bittle, *From Ether to Cosmos*, cited in Ardley, *Aquinas and Kant*, p. 212.
21. Ardley, pp. 214–15.
22. M.-B. Schwalm, "La croyance naturelle et la science," *RT* 5 (1897): 627–45.

is voluntary. Science thus escapes from the strange skepticism that led some scientists to regard their own theories as intellectual games without any corresponding objective reality. However approximate or symbolic scientific theories are, they certainly reach the partially obscure reality of existence, the inevident and partially unknown necessity, which is the object of faith in science. This scientific faith is belief in a *necessity unknown in itself*, known only from the outside, through clear signs, from its action on the reality one sees.[23] Although Schwalm carefully refrained from any reference to a Kantian *Ding an sich* or to phenomena and noumena, he had not strayed far from certain Kantian beliefs in the philosophy of science. It was all properly Scholastic, of course.

Does belief have any role in science? Schwalm thought that it does, especially when science is in the process of discovering reality. Belief has a role in a mature science if the science is of a subordinate nature and the scientist remains a narrow specialist. Fortunately, it is possible to eliminate the role of blind faith in science by accepting metaphysics as the queen of the sciences. Metaphysics knows reality or being in its universal nature, its transcendent attributes—unity, truth, and goodness—and in act and potentiality. All sciences take their first data—the ideas of cause, substance, movement, and end—from this first science, which is directly enlightened by its knowledge of first principles and has no need for faith as a basis for proceeding. With metaphysics at the head of the sciences, intuition, not faith, becomes the basis of the sciences. Faith is only a condition of hierarchical inferiority or a provisional instrument of discovery. Schwalm hoped that Thomists, united on these solid neo-Scholastic principles, would triumph against subjectivism and idealism, so prevalent in contemporary circles.

We should keep in mind that Aquinas' general view of the role of the metaphysician in "interpreting and understanding the data of experience" was that "the metaphysician concerns himself primarily with things considered in their widest and most general aspect, namely as beings or things." In trying to understand the existence of things the metaphysician finally seeks knowledge of God. "At the same time, the metaphysician first considers the intelligible structure of things regarded precisely as such and the fundamental relationships between them . . . the categorical structure of empirical reality." Copleston gives an interesting moderate interpretation of Aquinas' position on the interaction of metaphysics and science, in contrast to the prevalent metaphysical imperialism of French Thomists: "Aquinas does indeed imply that metaphysics gives the general heuristic principles which the scientist employs. But he does not mean that the scientist need consciously accept heuristic principles from the metaphysician. It is rather that the scientist, like anyone

23. Schwalm sums up in slightly different terms. "Dans l'ordre de nos connaissances scientifiques naturelles, l'acte de science s'entend de notre adhésion nécessaire à un intelligible ramené à l'évidence des premiers principes; l'acte de foi, de notre adhésion volontaire à un intelligible demeuré inévident, mais dont l'utilité pour la science nous est extrinsèquement certifiée. Tous deux sont certains; mais l'acte de science l'est, avec évidence et par rapport à l'être intime de ce qui est su; et l'acte de foi l'est, sans évidence intrinsèque de ce qui est cru, mais par rapport à l'évidence extrinsèque de sa crédibilité" (ibid., p. 644).

else, grasps implicitly, for example, the distinction between a thing and its relations and thinks in these terms. What a metaphysician does is not to dictate to the scientist but to isolate and analyse abstractly the most general principles and categories which in Aquinas' opinion the scientist, as anyone else, necessarily uses in practice, not because the human mind is determined or conditioned by purely subjective forms or categories but because every mind apprehends them implicitly in experience. Metaphysical analysis, provided that its metaphysical character is preserved in its purity, can attain a certain state of finality; but scientific knowledge can go on increasing. And increasing scientific knowledge does not necessarily involve a revolution in metaphysics. For their functions are different."[24] This last point was a leitmotif of French neo-Thomism. Copleston does not think it correct to say that Aquinas' philosophy claimed to "deduce the state of the world from *a priori* principles." Obviously, in Aquinas' time there could have been no clear separation between metaphysics and the particular sciences. It should be kept in mind that although metaphysics was a science for Aquinas, "possessing its own self-evident principles," the word science simply meant "certain knowledge possessed in virtue of the application of principles which are either self-evident or known as true in the light of a higher science," such as dogmatic theology, "the primary science, in the sense of a branch of study with absolutely first principles, revealed by God and yielding certain knowledge." For Aquinas natural science was "the body of certain propositions about nature" and was "the part of philosophy which treats of things as capable of motion. He could discuss, therefore, the relation between physics and metaphysics. But the question what is the precise relation between physics and philosophy would not be a natural question for him to ask, since he regarded physics as a part of philosophy."

Perhaps the decision to return to the thirteenth century to solve modern problems puzzled even the defenders of Leo's action. Abbé Boulay noted that the return indicated a lacuna in tradition, although the sixteenth, seventeenth, and even eighteenth centuries had representatives of Scholastic philosophy. Whatever the pope's thought on these centuries, the new results in science and in philosophy in these centuries had produced some unfortunate diversions in philosophy and even in theology which had caused the Scholastics of the time to confuse good and evil and true and false in their work, and worse still, to cover all the new developments with anathema. It was a good thing to turn away from these confusions and renew the chain of tradition. Unfortunately, some of the new Scholastics remained in their Gothic rooms with their yellow folios; but the disciples true to the methods of Albert and Thomas were busy salvaging what is healthy in the past and leaving what is outmoded. Success depended on the profundity of their knowledge of ancient philosophy and of the contemporary sciences.[25] This constituted a mod-

24. Copleston, *Aquinas*, pp. 32–35, 70–71. For enlightenment and therapy, the reader may consult Bertrand Russell's famous essay "Mysticism and Logic," in *Mysticism and Logic and Other Essays* (London, 1918).

25. N. Boulay, "De l'enseignement scientifique dans les séminaires," *RL* 14 (1896): 124, 228.

erately enthusiastic endorsement of the Thomist movement with a clear statement of its limitations and dangers. But it was clear that among Catholics
"Thomism and philosophy of science would be the two principal factors of
future speculation."[26]

After a generation of intellectual labors, what were the results of the revival of Thomism? Obviously not the intellectual unity hoped for by the
Catholic establishment, for whom the rich quarrels of the nineteenth century
had been distasteful and, in the face of the secular threat, dangerous. Thomism had an important role in the late-nineteenth- and early-twentieth-century
delineation of the parameters of orthodoxy and in thus making possible or
at least aggravating during the modernist period the greatest intellectual crisis
in the church since the Reformation. Heterodoxy is the Siamese twin of
orthodoxy. From good intentions frequently come disagreeable unintended
consequences. Leo may have had pacifying intentions in taking Thomism as
the intellectual, political, and social guide for the church and in thereby going beyond and completing the conservative theologism of Pius IX and *La Civiltà cattolica*. As can be seen in comparing *Quanta cura* to *Rerum novarum*,
Leo passed from the defensive stance of Pio Nono to an offensive one. And
fair critics could admit that the return to Thomism was wise because Aristotelian metaphysics was capable of assimilating the results of modern science
and of being adapted to Catholicism.[27] Thomism was the only system capable
of preserving the essentials of Catholicism and of assimilating relevant modern scientific developments, the only way to attain Leo's aim of making an
impact on the vast horde of scientific unbelievers. Why was there not a triumph of Thomism within the church, at least not by the first decade of the
twentieth century?

The idea of the relative failure of Thomism was even accepted by the Abbé
Charles Denis, editor of the *Annales de philosophie chrétienne* between 1895
and 1905, in his review of François Picavet's book on medieval philosophy.[28]
Picavet noted the difficulties of reconstructing a viable Thomism because of
the knowledge explosion of the nineteenth century. But Picavet's most serious explanation of the failure of Thomism was, in Denis' opinion, his contention that a metaphysical, a priori, and dialectical philosophy cannot renew

26. Picavet, "Le mouvement néo-thomiste," p. 308.

27. Copleston, *Aquinas*, pp. 79–80, points out the difference between Aristotle's and
Aquinas' metaphysics: "Aquinas . . . while retaining the Aristotelian analyses of substance
and accident, form and matter, act and potency, placed the emphasis in his metaphysics,
not on 'essence,' on *what* a thing is, but on existence, considered as the act of existing."
While Aristotle analyzes substance against the background of an eternal and uncreated
world, Aquinas assumes the world to consist of finite substances, "each of which is totally
dependent on God." Emphasis is changed to "the act by which substances exist, an act of
existing received from an external cause." This concentration on existence (*esse*) "set in a
new light the world which Aristotle described in his metaphysics."

28. Charles Denis, "Pourquoi, d'après M. Picavet, le néo-thomisme n'a-t-il pas triom-
phé?," *APC*, 3d ser. 6 (1905): 73–83, reviewing Picavet, *Esquisse d'une histoire générale et
comparée des philosophies médiévales* (Paris, 1905). As was proper for a directeur-adjoint
à l'Ecole pratique des Hautes Etudes, Picavet wrote a letter to *APC* later pointing out that
he was not Thomist in sympathy and that he had not interpreted any documents in favor
of Thomism. He had simply been a historian. A republican professor, like a Catholic intellectual, could not be too careful in 1905! Denis died in 1905.

itself. By contrast, a philosophy founded on the laws of sensible and phenomenal knowledge endlessly renews itself and progresses in all senses of the word. Somewhat Procrustean, the explanation is interesting as a piece of evidence of the republican intellectual mentality and its images of the feeble intellectual basis of Catholicism and the solid intellectual foundations of republicanism. Denis boldly argued that proclaiming a ready-made philosophy, as Leo did in 1878, put Catholics in a false position. Leo wanted scientific and philosophical advances taken into account but did not realize that traditionalist Catholic groups regarded Thomism as the equivalent of a defined and official doctrine. No philosophy could claim such a privilege. All philosophy is human and to give it the status of dogma is to impose an assimilation that is the most false and biggest of ambiguities. Most guilty in Denis' opinion were the Roman Congregations and certain powerful and authoritarian religious orders, probably the Jesuits and the Dominicans. Some Catholics must have regarded these statements from the editor of a journal supposedly committed to Thomism as the most dangerous since the heyday of Bonnetty's polemics in the Second Empire.

But Denis went to the heart of the debate over the wisdom of renewing Thomism in arguing that a philosophy founded on a "purely metaphysical ontology" could not authenticate sciences founded since Descartes on sensible and experimental knowledge. Basing itself on the hypothesis that all science is a priori and absolute and maintaining that *truth* is objective and justified from inside in a somewhat substantial way, Thomism reduced science to a simple equation of the real and intelligence. "With such a system how would Galileo, Copernicus, and Newton have founded our modern astronomy?" Finally, if the theory of knowledge of St. Thomas is true, how was Lavoisier able to make a chemical analysis of water and prove that it is not a simple body, a body *"adequate to the essential idea of water*, that it is not one of the four substantial elements?"[29] For the Thomist the sciences founded on the mathematical and rational determination of "distinct" phenomena are a subjective phantasmagoria of the imagination, an idealism leading straight to skepticism. In Denis' opinion, the recent debates of the Thomists in philosophy showed that wherever the Thomist mentality survived, it entailed inevitably a broad philosophical-scientific conflict. A more fundamental indictment of Thomism as a philosophy of science could not be found in the enemy camp. In a certain sense, the whole enterprise of basing a philosophy of science on Thomism was a quixotic venture. "It is . . . useless to look to the writings of Aquinas for any explicit and thorough discussion of the relation between philosophy and sciences which were still in embryonic condition" in the thirteenth century. But of course Aquinas did "say enough to indicate his general line of thought,"[30] and the modern Thomist enterprise

29. Denis, "Pourquoi . . . le néo-thomisme," p. 81. The achievements of Kepler and Torricelli were also impossible on the basis of a Thomist philosophy of science. "Si la science est objective, les lois de Keppler [*sic*] sont impossibles à formuler et pourquoi? Parce que ces lois déterminent des phénomènes et non un être en soi. Comment Toricelli [*sic*] et Descartes auraient-ils créé la physique et l'optique si tous les accidents sont inhérents à la substance et s'ils n'exigent pas, pour être formulés en lois rationnelles et mathématiques une conception phénoméniste?" (ibid.).

30. Copleston, *Aquinas*, p. 70.

was not fatuous. Denis' views made more sense before the rethinking of fundamental scientific questions that took place at the end of the nineteenth
century, especially in physics and in biology, accompanied by the revision of
ideas on the nature of science itself. The nineteenth-century Aristotelian revival necessarily ensured a certain scientific relevance for the Angelic Doctor.

Denis also saw nonmetaphysical reasons militating against the adaptability
of Thomism to modern science. The terminology of the period from the
thirteenth to the sixteenth century coincided only vaguely with accepted
contemporary terminology. So after five years of study the young Thomist
was incapable of having a long useful discussion with contemporary intellectuals, including scientists. For Denis this was the saddest failure of Thomism.
The polemics resulting from the difficulties encountered when the best apologists—Ollé-Laprune, Brunetière, Blondel, Fonsegrive, and Laberthonnière—
dealt with Thomist questions led to the disaster of these thinkers being sad-
dled with ideas they did not hold and to a waste of time, or worse still to
official condemnation. The *Annales* would soon be a victim of official anathema. What Denis wanted to save in Thomism was its theodicy, built on a
metaphysic independent of scientific knowledge. Denis' method of saving
Thomism must have looked to some like a plan for its destruction. "Kant, in
rehabilitating the *a priori* of the categories against the sensualists and deists
of his time, taught us not to surrender to a philosophy of a purely phenomenal order. The *a priori* subsists in a substantial subject; in other words, *reason
exists in itself* and metaphysics remains a science and a reality."[31] Aquinas
was impregnable here. Unfortunately, many Thomists did not know how
to separate Aquinas' metaphysics from his philosophy of science. Thomism
could renew itself and live again only when the Thomists rallied to the un-
likely trinity of Descartes, Kant, and Maine de Biran.

In his popular lectures at the Catholic Institute (Paris) in 1905, Lapparent also warned against an idolatrous return to the thirteenth century. "The
greatest philosophical genius who had ever lived" had tried to master all the
science of his time and had built on this experimental basis a metaphysics
comprising all things beyond physics. The duty imposed on the theologian is
quite similar to the one imposed on the metaphysician by Duhem: although
it is not necessary for the scientist to know any metaphysics, for science is
not based on any metaphysics, the philosopher should know the theory of
physics to ensure that he does not exploit it wrongly in his own theories.
Lapparent argued that Aquinas had left a model to be followed. Significantly,
perhaps, he did not argue that the thought of Aquinas should be accepted as

31. Denis, "Pourquoi le néo-thomisme," p. 83. Denis' defense of Kant, the "founder of
modern cosmology," was unusual in Thomist circles. Denis found in Kant a marvelous theodicy, not the source of German rationalism, which he blamed on Hegel (ibid., pp. 79–
82). For a more typical view see Martial, "La théorie kantienne de la science," *RT* 30
(1925): 124–46, an article inspired by the celebration of the bicentenary of Kant's birth
by French intellectuals and the universities. For Kant's views on scientific knowledge, see
Frederick Copleston, *A History of Philosophy. Modern Philosophy, Part II—Kant* (New
York, 1964), chap. 12. For some critical comments on the idea "that whereas mediaeval
philosophy was concerned with the problem of being, modern philosophy has been concerned with the problem of knowledge," see ibid., pp. 225–29.

a *vade mecum* in all matters, which was in some quarters an unfortunate result of the papal promotion of Thomism as the quasi-official philosophy and theology. In Lapparent's opinion, to remain faithful to the Thomistic method, the point of departure of metaphysics must be advanced as the domain of physics grows, a position nearly identical with that of Duhem. It may be that Lapparent was discreetly criticizing intransigent Thomists when he emphasized that obstinately defending all Thomistic definitions against modifications was not doing much honor to the saint, who in all probability, would have made the changes himself if thirteenth-century science had been in possession of the conquests made in the centuries after his death. Would not his idea of a first matter and of form have been different if he had suspected that Lavoisier's balance would show the invariability of masses throughout chemical reactions and that the principle of the conservation of energy would give Lavoisier a more universal scope? The implication was clear: many of the Thomists lacked the genius and science of the seraphic doctor. At least they should have the good sense not to compromise the faith by defending as essential to religion certain erroneous elements of thirteenth-century science.[32]

It may be of some use to end this discussion of French clerical quarrels over the scientific relevance of Thomism with the commentary of Cartesian clarity made half a century later by the English Jesuit Father Copleston. The hylomorphic theory is a metaphysical theory independent of the results of empirical scientific research; so "no new empirically verifiable scientific propositions can be derived from it." From this viewpoint, the theory is useless in natural science. The theory has a general usefulness, however, in insisting on a world characterized by intelligibility. Some knowledge of the intelligible structure of things comes from thinking about their activity and behavior. "And it is arguable that this picture of the world as intelligible and of material substances as proportionate to the human mind and as relatively transparent in their formal structure acted as a preparatory condition for, and stimulus to, empirical scientific research."[33] It was vital then for the modern Thomists to emphasize this separation in order to prevent the entanglement of Thomism with scientific theories, whose obsolescence would impair the validity of Thomism itself. Yet the rehabilitation of Thomism as a viable modern philosophy necessitated the dangerous procedure of reconciling it "with an acceptance of the ascertained results of modern science and with the spirit which animated the scientists." In the opinion of some Thomists, an attempt to integrate the conclusions of science into Thomism endangered the claim of metaphysics to be independent of changing scientific hypotheses, and in the case of Cardinal Mercier of Louvain led to the tendency "to substitute for the distinction between the data of ordinary experience and philosophic reflection on these data the distinction between the established results of the sciences and philosophic reflection on these results."[34] Yet the vitality of

32. Duhem was also very critical of the superficiality of certain neo-Thomists, totally ignorant of Aristotle, Aquinas, and Scholasticism. See quotation of letter by Duhem in le R. P. Lecanuet, *La vie de l'Église sous Léon XIII* (Paris, 1930), pp. 478–79.

33. Copleston, *Aquinas*, pp. 88–90. Cf. Whitehead, *Science and the Modern World,* p. 48.

34. Copleston, *Aquinas*, pp. 239–42. For the attempt of neo-Thomists to develop a

Thomism as a perennial philosophy, in spite of its claim that there is an intelligible, permanent metaphysical pattern in the developing universe, depends on its openness and on its acceptance of "the concept of a developing insight rather than the concept of a static and once-for-all expression of insight."[35] Its problem is no different from that of other philosophies that try to determine the philosophical relevance of knowledge of the world resulting from the exponential growth of science.

It may be that the peculiar problem of attempting "the conjunction of *fides* and *ratio*" that is the burden of Christian philosophy is solved only by the mystical experience. Perhaps "Mysticism is . . . the only power which is capable of uniting in a synthesis the riches accumulated by other forms of activity."[36] Pieper agrees that "When we bring natural knowledge into the more comprehensive truth of revelation, we see for the first time the true illuminatory power of scientific and philosophic discoveries—assuming that we make this synthesis *legitimately*, that is to say, upon the basis of a good and accurate knowledge both of theological and of natural truth."[37] Christian intellectuals rarely enjoy the same good fortune as Aquinas, who finally had the experience that makes the ordinary intellectual attempt at the conjunction of *fides* and *ratio* seem "like so much straw." Hence they are condemned to the Sisyphean task of considering the implications of the relative revelations of Isis for the absolute revelations of Jehovah. It is because of this task that Thomism has achieved the paradoxical status of a recurring paradigm. " 'Christian philosophy' is not a more or less abstruse brand of philosophical activity corresponding to the special ('religious') interests of individuals. It is *the* only possible form of philosophy[38]—*if* it is true that the *Logos* of God became man in Christ, and *if* by 'philosophy' we understand what the great forefathers of European philosophizing (Pythagoras, Plato, Aristotle) meant by it. The thinkers of the Middle Ages perceived that a 'Christian philosophy' depended upon the conjunction of *fides* and *ratio*. This was the task they set themselves, and into this task they poured their full intellectual resources. This task is continuous and never-ending. Anyone who addresses himself today to this same task cannot afford to ignore the demanding and multiform paradigm of medieval philosophy. But in answer to the questions posed he cannot take the medieval view; he will have to find his own answer."[39]

Thomist epistemology, see ibid., pp. 243–46, and especially Van Riet, *L'épistémologie thomiste*. Although his work is in the history of philosophy, Van Riet is especially interested in making a contribution to the still controversial and somewhat nebulous area of Thomist epistemology.

35. Copleston, *Aquinas*, pp. 252–53.

36. Teilhard de Chardin, *Lettres de voyage 1923–1939* (Paris, 1956), cited in Joseph Pieper, *Scholasticism: Personalities and Problems of Medieval Philosophy* (New York, 1964), p. 161.

37. Ibid.

38. Note of Pieper referring to Joseph Pieper, *Gibt es eine nichtchristliche Philosophie? Weistum, Dichtung, Sakrament* (Munich, 1954), pp. 51 ff.

39. Pieper, *Scholasticism*, p. 162. For the continuing effort, see Joseph Gredt, *Die aristotelisch-thomistische Philosophie*, 2 vols. (Freiburg im Breisgau, 1935); Joseph de Tonquédec, *Les principes de la philosophie thomiste*, 2, *La philosophie de la nature* (Paris, 1956–59); Ardley, *Aquinas and Kant*; and, above all, *The Thomist*, "a speculative quarterly review edited by the Dominican Fathers," Washington, D.C.

For those unable to accept the Thomist *Tao* or unlucky enough to be immune from the mystical infection, there remains the more conventional view of the irreducible dualism of science and religion. This was admitted, however reluctantly, and cogently put by Emile Boutroux in his well-known study of science and religion in 1909.

> In spite of their relations, science and religion remain, and must remain, distinct. If there were no other way of establishing a rational order between things than that of reducing the many to the one, either by assimilation or by elimination, the destiny of religion would appear doubtful. But the struggles which contrasts engender admit of solutions other than those which science and logic offer. When two powers contend, both of them equally endowed with vitality and with fertility, they develop and grow by that very conflict. And, the value and the indestructibility of each becoming more and more evident, reason strives to bring them together through their conflicts, and to fashion, from their union, a being richer and more harmonious than either of them taken apart.
>
> Thus is it with religion and science. Strife tempers them both alike; and, if reason prevails, from their two distinct principles—become, at once, wider, stronger, and more flexible—will spring a form of life ever ampler, richer, deeper, freer, as well as more beautiful and more intelligible. But these two autonomous powers can only advance towards peace, harmony, and concord, without ever claiming to reach the goal; for such is the human condition.[40]

40. Boutroux, *Science and Religion in Contemporary Philosophy,* pp. 399-400.

Bibliography

1. *A limited selection of works on science and religion.* Unless otherwise indicated, the place of publication is Paris.

Adhémar, Vte. Robert d'. *La philosophie des sciences et le problème religieux* (1904).
——. *Le triple conflit. Science, philosophie, religion* (1905).
——. *Les variations des théories de la science* (1907). (These three volumes are in the Bloud series "Science et Religion.")
Aubin, Abbé Victor. *Actualités, ou réponses aux objections de la science antichrétienne* (1878; 5th ed., 1882).
Aubry, Jean-Baptiste. *Quelques idées sur la théorie catholique des sciences et sur la synthèse des connaissances humaines dans la théologie. Oeuvres complètes*, vol. 1 (1895).
Baille, Louis. *Qu'est-ce que la science?* (1906).
Baudrillart, Alfred. *L'apostolat intellectuel de Mgr. d'Hulst* (1901).
——. *Le catholicisme en France et les élites intellectuelles* (1930).
——. *Le renouvellement intellectuel du clergé de France au XIXe siècle* (1903).
Baunard, Louis. *Les deux frères. Cinquante années de l'action catholique à Lille. Philibert Vrau. Camille Féron-Vrau* (1910).
——. *Un siècle de l'Eglise de France, 1800–1900* (1902).
Béguinot, Mgr. *Des causes du dissentiment extérieur entre la science et la foi dans les temps actuels* (Nîmes, 1898).
Bettex, Frédéric. *La religion et les sciences de la nature* (1898).
Blainville, Henri-Marie Ducrotay de. *Histoire des sciences de l'organisation et de leurs progrès, comme base de la philosophie.* "Rédigée d'après ses notes et ses leçons faites à la Sorbonne de 1839 à 1841, avec les développements nécessaires et plusieurs additions par l'abbé Maupied."
Blanc, Abbé Elie. *Dictionnaire de la pensée. Essai sur la synthèse des sciences et l'encyclopédie chrétienne* (Montbéliard, 1874).
——. *Exposé de la synthèse des sciences* (1877).
Bonald, Vte. Victor de. *Observations adressées à M. Marcel de Serres, sur son ouvrage intitulé: "De la cosmogonie de Moïse comparée aux faits géologiques"* (Avignon, 1841).
Bonniot, Joseph, S.J. *Les malheurs de la philosophie. Etudes critiques de la philosophie contemporaine* (1878).
——. *Le miracle et les sciences médicales* (1879).
——. *Miracle et savants. L'objection scientifique contre le miracle* (1882).
Bougaud, Abbé Louis-Emile. *Le christianisme et les temps présents* (1886). Published originally in 1868. The edition of 1871 was withdrawn by the author; an eighth edition was published in 1901.

Boulay, Abbé Jean-Nicolas. *Le congrès scientifique international des catholiques tenu à Fribourg, 1897* (Arras, 1898).
——. *De l'enseignement scientifique dans les séminaires* (Arras, 1901).
——. *Que dire? Que faire?* (Arras, 1902).
——. *Où en est la question de l'enseignement scientifique dans les séminaires?* (Arras, 1899).
——. *Goethe et la science de la nature* (Strasbourg, 1869).
——. *Science et philosophie* (Arras, 1902).
Bourgine, Abbé E. *Foi catholique et science moderne* (La Chapelle-Montligeon, 1906).
Boutroux, Emile. *De la contingence dans les lois de la nature* (1874).
——. *De l'idée de loi naturelle dans la science et la philosophie contemporaines* (1895).
——. *Questions de morale et d'éducation* (1895).
——. *Science et religion dans la philosophie contemporaine* (1909). (Much of Boutroux is translated into English.)
Broglie, Abbé Paul de. *Le positivisme et la science expérimentale* (1880-81).
——. *La science et la religion* (1883).
Broglie, Louis de, et al. *L'avenir de la science* (1941).
Brucker, Joseph, S.J. *Questions actuelles d'Ecriture sainte* (1895).
Brunetière, Ferdinand. *L'action sociale du christianisme* (1904).
——. *Discours de combat* (1912-14).
——. *La renaissance de l'idéalisme* (1896).
——. *La science et la religion; réponse à quelques objections* (1895).
——. *Sur les chemins de la croyance. Première étape. L'utilisation du positivisme* (1912).
Buisson, Ferdinand. *La religion, la morale et la science, leur conflit dans l'éducation contemporaine* (1901).
Candolle, Alphonse de. *Histoire des sciences et des savants depuis deux siècles* (Geneva, 1873).
Carbonnelle, Ignace. *Les confins de la science et de la philosophie*, 2d ed. (1881).
Chaubard, Louis-Athanase. *L'univers expliqué par la révélation, ou essai de philosophie positive* (1841).
Chauchard, P., et al. *Science et foi* (1962).
Chaudé, Abbé Aquilas. *Botanique descriptive . . . Démonstration de l'existence de Dieu tirée du règne végétal* (1876).
Cléré, René de. *Nécessité mathématique de l'existence de Dieu* (1899).
Cochin, Augustin. *Le progrès des sciences et de l'industrie au point de vue chrétien* (1863).
Congrès scientifique des catholiques—comptes rendus (1889-1901).
Constant, Abbé M. *Science et révélation, ou la conception scientifique de l'univers et le dogme catholique* (1892).
——. *Le matérialisme et la nature de l'homme* (1900).
Courbet, Pierre. *Convenance scientifique de l'incarnation* (1898).
——. *La faillite du matérialisme* (1899).
——. *Nécessité scientifique de l'existence de Dieu*, 2d ed. (1898).
Cyon, Elie de. *Dieu et Science. Essai de psychologie des sciences* (1910).
——. *La guerre à Dieu et la morale laïque. Réponse à M. Paul Bert* (1881).
Desorges, Abbé. *Les erreurs modernes* (1878).
Devers, Dr. Alfred. *Accord de la science et de la religion* (1889). (An anthology of the opinions of leading scientists and intellectuals.)
Draper, John William. *Les conflits de la science et de la religion* (1875).
Duilhé de Saint-Projet, Mgr. François. *Apologie scientifique de la foi chrétienne* (1885). (See Senderens.)
Dürr, Charles. *La banqueroute de la science* (1896).
Eymieu, Antonin, S.J. *Le naturalisme devant la science* (1911).
——. *La part des croyants dans les progrès de la science au XIXe siècle* (1910).
Fabre d'Envieu, Abbé Jules. *Les origines de la terre et de l'homme, d'après la Bible et d'après la science* (Toulouse, 1873).
Favaro, Antonio. *Paolo Tannery* (Padova, 1905).
Faye, Hervé. *Sur l'origine du monde, théories cosmogoniques des anciens et des modernes* (1884; 3d ed., 1896).

Ferrière, Emile. *L'âme est la fonction du cerveau* (1883).

——. *Les apôtres. Essai d'histoire religieuse, d'après la méthode des sciences naturelles* (1879).

——. *La matière et l'énergie* (1887).

——. *La vie et l'âme* (1888).

——. *La cause première d'après les données expérimentales* (1897).

——. *Les erreurs scientifiques de la Bible* (1891).

——. *Les mythes de la Bible* (1893).

Fiessinger, Dr. Charles. *Science et spiritualisme: les valeurs de la science* (1907).

Fonsegrive, George. *L'attitude du catholique devant la science* (1900).

Fournier, Abbé A.-C.-E., and Thouvenin, Maurice. *Le matérialisme et la science* (1912).

Français, Jean. *L'Eglise et la science* (1908).

Frémont, Abbé Georges. *Démonstration scientifique de l'existence de Dieu* (Poitiers, 1897).

——. *Les origines de l'univers et de l'homme selon la Bible et les sciences* (1898).

——. *La religion catholique peut-elle être une science?* (1899).

George, André, et al. *Pensée scientifique et foi chrétienne* (1953).

——. *Qu'est-ce que la science?* (1926).

Giran, H. *Ce que l'avancement des sciences doit au protestantisme français* (Valence, 1932).

Girard, Abbé André. *Emile-Hilaire Amagat* (Sancerre, 1941).

Giraud, Léopold. *La science des athées* (1865).

Godard, André. *Le positivisme chrétien*, 4th ed. (1901).

Godefroy, N.-P. (Ernest de Bréda). *La cosmogonie de la révélation, ou les quatres premiers jours de la Genèse en présence de la science moderne* (1841; 2d ed., 1847).

——. *Date de la création et sa raison finale* (1859).

Goix, Dr. A. *Le surnaturel et la science. Le miracle* (n.d.).

Goux, Dr. L. *La science actuelle mène à Dieu; les anti-Christ* (1908).

Grandclaude, Mgr. Eugène. *La question biblique, d'après une nouvelle école d'apologistes chrétiens* (1893).

——. *La chronologie biblique* (1895).

——. *La chronologie des temps primitifs et la science contemporaine* (1895).

Grasset, Dr. Hector. *L'œuvre de Béchamp* (1911; 2d enlarged ed., 1913).

——. *Un savant méconnu. A. Béchamp* (1899).

Grasset, Joseph. *L'Evangile et la sociologie* (1910).

——. *L'idée médicale chez les romans de Paul Bourget* (1904).

——. *Introduction physiologique à l'étude de la philosophie* (1908).

——. *Les limites de la biologie* (1902; 4th ed., 1906). Preface by Paul Bourget.

——. *Morale scientifique et morale évangélique devant la sociologie* (1909).

——. *Le spiritisme devant la science* (Montpellier, 1904). Preface by Pierre Janet.

Guibert, Abbé Jean. *Le mouvement chrétien* (n.d.). Sermons preached in 1902.

Guthlin, Abbé. *Les doctrines positivistes en France* (Rev. and enlarged ed., 1873).

Hébert, Marcel. *Science et religion* (1895).

Hillereau, Abbé. *Foi et sciences expérimentales* (Vannes, 1899).

Houtin, Albert. *La crise du clergé*, 2d ed. (1908).

——. *La question biblique chez les catholiques de France au XIXe siècle* (2d rev. and enlarged ed., 1902).

——. *La question biblique au XXe siècle* (1906).

Hulst, Mgr. Maurice d'. *Le congrès scientifique international des catholiques* (1888).

——. *L'empoisonnement de la science* (1883).

——. *Mélanges oratoires* (1901).

——. *La mission chrétienne de la science* (Evreux, 1884).

——. *Philosophie ancienne et nouvelle. Le positivisme et la science expérimentale* (1881).

——. *Le rôle scientifique des Facultés catholiques* (1883).

——. *La science chrétienne et le devoir des croyants* (1884).

——. *La science de la nature et la philosophie chrétienne* (1885).

——. *Le vrai terrain de la lutte entre croyants et incroyants* (1884).

Huxley, Thomas Henry. *Science et religion* (1893).

Imbert-Gourbeyre, Dr. Antoine. *Discours sur les origines chrétiennes de la médecine* (Clermont-Ferrand, n.d.).

Isoard, Abbé Louis-Romain-Ernest. *Le clergé et la science moderne, à propos de quelques publications récentes* (1864).

Jouffroy-d'Abbans, Cte J. de. *Etudes expérimentales. Accord de l'expérience et de la science avec la foi* (Besançon, 1902).

Kirwan, Charles de. *Bible et science. Terre et ciel* (1911).

———. *Comment peut finir l'univers d'après la science et d'après la Bible* (1899).

———. *Comment s'est formé l'univers* (1877).

———. *Le déluge biblique et les races antédiluviennes* (Bruxelles, 1895).

———. *Le déluge de Noé et les races prédiluviennes*, 2 vols. (1899).

———. *La science et l'exégèse contemporaines* (1879).

———. *La vieille apologétique et l'"immanence"* (1905).

———. *Le congrès scientifique de Fribourg* (1897).

Lambert, Abbé Edmond. *Accord de la science et de la religion. Le déluge mosaïque, l'histoire et la géologie* (1870).

———. *Nouveaux éléments d'histoire naturelle à l'usage des séminaires, des pensionnats de demoiselles* (1864–65).

La Perrière, J. de. *Dieu et science* (Lyon, 1909).

Lapparent, Albert de. *La providence créatrice* (1907).

———. *Science et apologétique* (1905).

———. *Science et philosophie* (1913).

Leblais, Alphonse. *Matérialisme et spiritualisme. Etude de philosophie positive.* Précédé d'une préface par Littré (1865).

Leclère, Albert. *La morale de demain et la science* (1913).

Le Dantec, Félix. *L'athéisme* (1907).

———. *Le conflit. Entretiens philosophiques* (1901).

———. *Eléments de philosophie biologique* (1907).

———. *De l'homme à la science. Philosophie du XXᵉ siècle* (1907).

Leenhardt, Franz. *Foi et science* (Montauban, 1890).

———. *Quelques réflexions sur les rapports du christianisme et des sciences* (Montauban, 1884).

Lefèvre, André. *Le christianisme et la science* (1890).

Lefranc, Abbé E. *Les conflits de la science et de la Bible* (1906).

Lemoine, Georges. *L'enseignement agricole libre* (1917).

Lemonnyer, A., O.P. *La révélation primitive et les données actuelles de la science, d'après l'ouvrage allemand du R. P. W. Schmidt* (1914).

Letourneau, Dr. Charles. *Science et matérialisme* (1891).

Lévi, Lucien. *Science, philosophie et religion* (1911).

Lévi-Wogue, Fernand. *Pages scientifiques et morales* (1913). An anthology.

Lorenzini de Buttafoco, May. *Le problème spirituel devant les récentes données de la science et de la philosophie* (1952).

Loudun, Eugène (Balleyguier). *Les découvertes de la science sans Dieu* (1884).

———. *Les ignorances de la science moderne* (1878).

Luzzati, Luigi. *Science et foi* (1900).

Maindron, Ernest. *L'œuvre de J.-B. Dumas* (1886).

Malvert. *Science et religion*, 2d ed. (1895).

Mandet, Abbé J.-P. *La chute d'une idole ou la faillite du scientisme* (Moulins, 1931).

Mano, Abbé C. *Le problème apologétique* (1899).

Martin, Thomas-Henri. *Philosophie spiritualiste de la nature. Introduction à l'histoire des sciences physiques dans l'antiquité* (1849).

———. *Essai de critique philosophique et religieuse* (1869).

Maupied, Abbé F.-L.-M. *Du déluge au point de vue scientifique et théologique* (1846).

———. *Dieu, l'homme et le monde connus par les trois premiers chapitres de la Genèse, ou nouvelle esquisse d'une philosophie positive au point de vue des sciences dans leurs rapports avec la théologie* (1851). "Cours de physique sacrée et de cosmogonie mosaïque, professé à la Sorbonne" (1845–48).

Meignan, Mgr. Guillaume-René. *Le monde et l'homme primitif selon la Bible* (1869; 3d ed., 1879).

——. *Les Evangiles et la critique au XIXe siècle* (new corrected and enlarged ed., 1870).

Milhaud, Gaston. *Nouvelles études sur l'histoire de la pensée scientifique* (1911).

Moigno, Abbé François-Napoléon-Marie. *Actualités scientifiques* (première sér.). No. 24: *Religion et patrie vengées de la fausse science et de l'envie haineuse* (1872); No. 45: *La foi et la science, explosion de la libre pensée* (1875); No. 46: *L'univers sans Dieu* (1876); No. 51: *La foi offerte à tous: le retour à la foi par ses splendeurs* (1880).

——. *Impossibilité du nombre actuellement infini. La science dans ses rapports avec la foi* (1884).

——. *Les livres saints et la science. Leur accord parfait* (1884).

——. *Les splendeurs de la foi, accord parfait de la révélation et de la science, de la foi et de la raison.* I: *La foi* (1879); II–III: *La révélation et la science* (1877); IV: *La foi et la raison* (1879); V: *Le miracle au tribunal de la science* (1882). A fourth edition appeared in 1888.

Molinari, G. de. *Science et religion* (1894).

Molloy, R. Gerald. *Géologie et révélation* (1875). Traduction par M. l'abbé Hamard.

Moreux, Abbé Théophile. *Les autres mondes sont-ils habités?* (1912).

——. *Les confins de la science et de la foi* (1925).

——. *Les énigmes de la science* (1925).

——. *D'où venons-nous?* (1939).

Motais, Abbé Alexandre. *Le déluge biblique devant la foi, l'Ecriture et la science* (1885).

——. *Moïse, la science et l'exégèse. Examen critique du nouveau système d'interprétation proposé sur l'Hexaméron par Mgr. Clifford* (1882).

——. *Origine du monde d'après la tradition* (1888).

Munnynck, R. P. de. *La conservation de l'énergie et la liberté morale* (1897).

Murat, Louis and Paul. *L'argument classique de la finalité* (1911).

——. *La finalité en biologie* (1908).

——. *Les grands témoignages de Dieu dans la nature* (1940).

——. *L'idée de Dieu dans les sciences contemporaines.* I: *Le firmament* (1909); II: *Les merveilles du corps* (1912).

Nadaillac, J.-F.-A. du Pouget, Mis de. *Les découvertes préhistoriques et les croyances chrétiennes* (1889).

——. *Foi et science* (1895).

——. *L'homme* (1892).

——. *L'origine de la vie* (1880).

——. *L'origine et le développement de la vie sur le globe* (1888).

——. *Un cri d'alarme* (1894).

——. *L'homme et le singe. L'évolution est-elle la loi générale de la vie?* (1899).

——. *Unité de l'espèce humaine prouvée par la similarité des conceptions et des créations de l'homme* (1898).

Naville, Ernest. *La science et le matérialisme. Etude philosophique* (Geneva, 1891).

——. *La physique moderne* (1890).

——. *Le libre arbitre* (1890).

Netter, Dr. A. *La science et la religion* (Nancy, 1896).

Orin, J.-M.-H. *La foi vengée, ou explication populaire de la Genèse selon la science et selon Moïse* (1872).

——. *Le plan divin dévoilé aux libre-penseurs comme aux croyants* (1890).

Ortolan, Th., O.M.I. *Astronomie et théologie, ou l'erreur géocentrique, la pluralité des mondes habités et le dogme de l'incarnation* (1894).

——. *Etude sur la pluralité des mondes habités et le dogme de l'incarnation* (1897).

——. *La fausse science contemporaine et les mystères d'outre-tombe* (1898).

——. *Le levier d'Archimède, ou la mécanique céleste et le céleste mécanicien* (1899).

——. *Savants et chrétiens. Etude sur l'origine et la filiation des sciences* (1898).

——. *Vie et matière, ou matérialisme et spiritualisme en présence de la cristallogénie* (1898).

Parodi, D. *La philosophie contemporaine en France. Essai de classification des doctrines* (1919).

——. *Du positivisme à l'idéalisme. Etudes critiques.* I: *Philosophies d'hier.* II: *Philosophies d'hier et d'aujourd'hui* (1930).

Parodi, D., et al. *Morale et science* (1924). "Conférences faites à la Sorbonne (2e sér.)."

Pauly, Jean. *Accord de la science et de la foi* (Lyon, 1914).

Péchenard, Mgr. Pierre-Louis. *L'Institut Catholique de Paris, 1875–1901* (1902; 2d ed., 1907).

Périssé, Sylvain. *Sciences et religions à travers les siècles* (1908).

Pesnelle, Eugène (des prêtres de la miséricorde). *Le dogme de la création et la science contemporaine,* 2d ed. (Arras, 1891). The first edition, *La science contemporaine et le dogme de la création,* was published in 1879.

Pioger, Abbé L.-M. *Le dogme chrétien et la pluralité des mondes habités* (1874).

——. *L'œuvre des six jours en face de la science contemporaine. Question de l'ancienneté de l'espèce* (1880).

——. *Dieu dans ses œuvres: L'astronomie* (1887); *Les insectes, leurs métamorphoses* (1882); *Le monde des infiniments grands* (1876); *Le monde des infiniments petits* (1877); *Le monde des plantes et ses merveilles* (1895); *Les mystères du ciel* (Lille, 1892); *Les splendeurs de l'astronomie* (1883–84).

Poincaré, Henri. *Dernières pensées* (1913).

——. *La science et l'hypothèse* (1902).

——. *Science et méthode* (1908).

——. *La valeur de la science* (1906).

Poincaré, Henri, et al. *Questions du temps présent* (1911).

Pozzy, Benj. *La terre et le récit biblique de la création* (1874).

Retterer, Ed. *Religion, science et morale* (1927).

Richard, T., O.P. *Philosophie du raisonnement dans la science d'après saint Thomas* (1919).

Ribot, Paul. *Spiritualisme et matérialisme. Etude sur les limites de nos connaissances* (1873).

Ringoot, Marcel. *La Bible devant la science* (Dannemarie-les-Lys, 1936).

Robert, Jean-Dominique, O.P. *Approche contemporaine d'une affirmation de Dieu. Essai sur le fondement ultime de l'acte scientifique* (1962).

Rod, Edouard. *Les idées morales du temps présent,* 2d ed. (1892).

Roys de Saint-Michel, Marquis de. *Petit résumé de géologie. Accord de la science avec la révélation* (1863).

Sageret, Jules. *La révolution philosophique et la science* (1924).

——. *La vague mystique* (1920).

Saintyves, Pierre. *Le miracle et la critique scientifique* (1907).

Schmidt, Ed. Oscar. *Les sciences naturelles et la philosophie de l'inconscient* (1879). A translation by Jules Soury of *Die naturwissenschaftlichen Grundlagen der Philosophie des Unbewussten* (Leipzig, 1877).

——. *Science et foi, ou la méthode scientifique comparée avec le procédé de la foi* (Le Mans, 1886–87).

Séailles, Gabriel. *Les affirmations de la conscience moderne* (1903).

——. *Le dogme et la science* (1904).

Sée, Henri. *Science et philosophie d'après la doctrine de M. Emile Meyerson* (1932).

Senderens, Abbé J.-B. *Apologie scientifique de la foi chrétienne, d'après l'ouvrage de Mgr. Duilhé de Saint-Projet* (1903; 1908; Toulouse, 1921).

Serre, A. *Religion de Goethe et de l'abbé Moigno* (1881).

Smedt, Charles de, S.J. *L'Eglise et la science* (Louvain, 1877).

Sortais, Gaston, S.J. *Précis de philosophie scientifique et de philosophie morale* (1905).

——. *Pourquoi les dogmes ne meurent pas* (1905).

——. *Le procès de Galilée. Etude historique et doctrinale* (1905).

——. *La providence et le miracle devant la science moderne,* 2d ed. (1905).

Soulier, Edouard. *De la science et de la morale* (Montauban, 1896).

Tannery, Jules. *Science et philosophie* (1912).

Tiberghien, Abbé Pierre. *La science mène-t-elle à Dieu? Introduction scientifique à la question religieuse* (1933).

Touchet, M. le vicaire-général, Besançon. *Des rapports de l'Eglise et de la science* (Besançon, 1892).

Ubald d'Alençon. *Les idées de saint François d'Assise sur la science* (1910).

Vacherot, Etienne. *Le nouveau spiritualisme* (1884).

Vigouroux, Abbé F. *La Bible et la critique. Réponse aux "Souvenirs d'enfance et de jeunesse" de M. Renan* (1833).

——. *La Bible et les découvertes modernes en Palestine, en Egypte et en Assyrie* (1879; 6th ed., 1896).

——. *Les livres saints et la critique rationaliste. Histoire et réfutation des objections des incrédules contre les Saintes Ecritures*, 2d ed. (1886).

——. *Mélanges bibliques. La cosmogonie mosaïque, d'après les Pères de l'Eglise* (1882).

——. *Manuel biblique, ou cours d'écriture sainte à l'usage des séminaires. Ancien Testament* (12th ed., 1906).

——. *Le nouveau Testament et les découvertes archéologiques modernes* (1890).

Villard, A., O.P. *Dieu devant la science et la raison* (1894).

Vitteaut, Dr. J.-B. *La médecine dans ses rapports avec la religion, ou réfutation du matérialisme théorique et pratique* (1857).

——. *La question scientifico-religieuse* (Chalon-sur-Saône, 1900).

White, A. D. *Histoire de la lutte entre la science et la théologie* (1899). Translated and adapted by H. de Varigny and G. Adam.

Zahm, J. A. *Science catholique et savants catholiques* (1895). Translated by Abbé J. Flageolet.

2. *Evolution*. For a complete bibliography on evolution, see Yvette Conry, *L'introduction du darwinisme en France au XIXe siècle* (Paris, 1974).

Aubin, Abbé Victor. *Du transformisme* (1898; 2d ed., 1899).

Blanc, Abbé Elie. *Les nouvelles bases de la morale, d'après M. Herbert Spencer* (1881).

Bost, John D. *Création et évolution* (Montauban, 1881).

Boulay, Abbé N. *L'évolution et le dogme* (Arras, 1899).

Broglie, Abbé de. *La morale évolutionniste* (1885).

Cochin, Denys. *L'évolution et la vie* (1886; 3d ed., 1888).

Cuénot, Lucien. *L'évolution biologique; les faits, les incertitudes* (1951).

Darwin, Charles. *De l'origine des espèces, ou des lois du progrès chez les êtres organisés* (1862; 2d ed., 1866). "Traduit en français sur la troisième édition par Mlle Clémence-Auguste Royer, avec une préface et des notes du traducteur." Note: title in 1866 was *De l'Origine des espèces par sélection naturelle, ou des Lois de transformisme des êtres organisés.* A new translation based on the fifth and sixth editions was done by J.-J. Moulinié in 1873 with the title *L'origine des espèces au moyen de la sélection naturelle, ou la Lutte pour l'existence dans la nature.* The same title is used by Ed. Barbier for his translation in 1876 based on the sixth edition.

——. *La descendance de l'homme et la sélection sexuelle* (1872). Traduit de l'anglais par J.-J. Moulinié. Préface par Carl Vogt. The third French edition in 1881 was based on the second English edition and translated by Ed. Barbier.

Delage, Yves. *Les théories de l'évolution* (1909). Translated into English in 1912.

Depéret, Charles. *Les transformations du monde animal* (1906). Translated into English in 1909.

Dorlodot, Henry de. *Le darwinisme au point de vue de l'orthodoxie catholique* (Brussels, 1921). Translated into English in 1922.

Ducasse, F. *Etude historique et critique sur le transformisme, et les théories qui s'y rattachent* (1876).

Dumont, Léon A. *Haeckel et la théorie de l'évolution en Allemagne* (1873).

Ebersolt, P. *L'athéisme et l'évolution humaine* (1906).

Farges, Albert. *La vie et l'évolution des espèces avec une thèse sur l'évolution étendue au corps de l'homme* (1894). Vol. 3 of *Etudes philosophiques.*

Ferrière, Emile. *Le darwinisme* (1872).

Flourens, P.-M. *Examen du livre de M. Darwin sur l'origine des espèces* (1864; 2d ed., 1881).

Giard, Alfred. *Controverses transformistes* (1904).

Giraud, Léopold. *L'homme fossile: découvertes récentes faites dans le terrain diluvien* (1860).

Godron, D.-A. *De l'espèce et des races dans les êtres organisés et spécialement de l'unité de l'espèce humaine* (1859).

Hartmann, Eduard von. *Le darwinisme. Ce qu'il y a de vrai et de faux dans cette théorie*, 3d ed. (1880).

James, Constantin. *Du darwinisme; ou l'homme-singe* (1877).

———. *Moïse et Darwin. L'homme de la Genèse comparé à l'homme-singe; ou l'enseignement religieux opposé à l'enseignement athée* (1882).

Jousset, P. *Evolution et transformisme: des origines de l'état sauvage* (1889).

Lalande, André. *La dissolution opposée à l'évolution dans les sciences physiques et morales* (1899).

———. *Les illusions évolutionnistes* (1930).

Lambert, Abbé Edmond. *L'homme primitif et la Bible* (1869).

Lavaud de Lestrade, Abbé. *Accord de la science avec le premier chapitre de la Genèse* (1885).

———. *Transformisme et darwinisme, réfutation méthodique* (1885). An abridged version of this work was also published in 1885, intended chiefly for use in the *grands séminaires*.

Lecomte, Abbé Alphonse Joseph. *Le darwinisme et l'expression des émotions chez l'homme et chez les animaux* (Louvain, 1881).

———. *Le darwinisme et l'origine de l'homme* (Brussels, 1873).

Le Dantec, Félix. *La crise du transformisme* (1909).

———. *Lamarckiens et darwiniens, discussion de quelques théories sur la formation des espèces* (1899).

———. *L'unité dans l'être vivant, essai d'une biologie chimique* (1902).

Leenhardt, Franz. *L'évolution, doctrine de liberté* (Sainte Blaise, 1910).

Le Roy, Edouard. *L'exigence idéaliste et le fait de l'évolution* (1927).

Leroy, M.-D. *L'évolution des espèces organiques* (1887).

———. *L'évolution restreinte aux espèces organiques* (1891).

Letourneau, Charles. *L'évolution religieuse dans les diverses races humaines* (1892).

Nadaillac, Marquis de. *L'évolution, est-elle la loi générale de la vie?* (1899).

Omalius d'Halloy, J.-B.-J. d'. *Des races humaines, ou éléments d'ethnographie* (1845).

Paquier, J. *La création et l'évolution. La révélation et la science* (1931).

Paulesco, Nicolas. *Physiologie philosophique*, 2 vols. (1907).

Périer, P.-M. *Le transformisme. L'origine de l'homme et le dogme catholique. Etude apologétique* (1938).

Perrier, Edmond. *Le transformisme* (1888).

Pouchet, Georges. *De la pluralité des races humaines* (1864). Translated into English in 1864.

———. *Science et religion. Lettre à M. de Saint-Philibert* (1859).

Quatrefages de Bréau, Armand de. *Charles Darwin et ses précurseurs français; étude sur le transformisme* (1870).

———. *Les émules de Darwin* (1894).

Rabut, Olivier. *Le problème de Dieu inscrit dans l'évolution* (1963).

Reusch, Franz Heinrich. *Bibel und Natur* (Freiburg im Breisgau, 1867).

Trémaux, Pierre. *Origine et transformations de l'homme et des autres êtres* (1865).

———. *Origine des espèces et de l'homme*, 4th ed. (1878).

Wallace, Alfred Russel. *Le darwinisme. Exposé de la théorie de la sélection naturelle, avec quelques-unes de ses applications* (1891). Translated by H. de Varigny.

3. *Journals.* I shall list only the most important of the relevant journals of this period of optimum Catholic journalistic fertility. I have not listed well-known secular journals like the *Revue des deux mondes*, the *Revue de métaphysique et de morale*, the *Revue scientifique*, and the *Revue philosophique*. I have gone through the following important Catholic journals from their beginnings to the 1920s: the *Annales de philosophie chrétienne* (up to 1913), *Etudes*, the *Revue de Lille*, the *Revue de philosophie*, the *Revue du clergé français*, the *Revue des questions scientifiques*, and the *Revue thomiste*.

Annales de philosophie chrétienne, 1830–

Bulletin de l'Institut catholique de Toulouse (merged with *Bulletin de littérature ecclésiastique*), 1877–

Bulletin de l'université catholique de Lyon, 1877–

Bulletin des facultés catholiques de Lille, 1879–

La Civiltà cattolica (Rome), 1850–

Le Contemporain, 1866- (merged with *La Controverse* in 1884 and became *L'Université catholique* [Lyon] in 1889)
Le Correspondant, 1843-
Cosmos, 1852- (merged with *Les Mondes* in 1874 to become *Cosmos–Les Mondes*)
La Critique philosophique, 1872- (supplement: *La Critique religieuse*, "Protestant" publication of Renouvier)
L'Enseignement catholique, 1851-
Etudes, 1857-
La Quinzaine, 1894-
L'Observateur catholique, 1856- (put on Index in 1859)
Revue catholique de l'Alsace (later *d'Alsace*), 1859-
Revue catholique de Bordeaux (later *du Midi*), 1878-
Revue catholique de Normandie, 1891-
Revue catholique du Languedoc (later *Revue de Nîmes*), 1859-
Revue chrétienne, 1854-
Revue de Lille, 1889-
Revue de l'Institut catholique de Paris, 1896- (merged with the *Bulletin du denier de l'Institut catholique* to become the *Bulletin de l'Institut catholique de Paris*)
Revue de philosophie, 1900-
Revue du clergé français, 1895-
Revue du spiritualisme moderne, 1904- (*Le spiritualisme moderne* began in 1897)
Revue des questions historiques, 1866-
Revue des questions scientifiques (Brussels), 1877-
Revue de la science nouvelle, 1887-
Revue des sciences ecclésiastiques, 1860- (merged with *La Science catholique* to form *Revue des sciences catholiques et la science catholique*)
Revue du monde catholique, 1861-
Revue du monde invisible, 1898-
Revue néo-scolastique (Louvain), 1894-
Revue pratique d'apologétique, 1905-
Revue thomiste, 1893-
La Science catholique, 1886-
L'Université catholique (Lyon), 1889-

Index